Rituals of Spontaneity

Rituals of Spontaneity

Sentiment and Secularism from Free Prayer to Wordsworth

Lori Branch

Baylor University Press
Waco, Texas USA

Copyright © 2006 by Baylor University Press
Waco, Texas 76798

All Rights Reserved. No part of this publication may be reproduced, stored in a retrieval system, or transmitted, in any form or by any means, electronic, mechanical, photocopying, recording or otherwise, without the prior permission in writing of Baylor University Press.

Cover design by David Alcorn, Alcorn Publication Design
Cover image is a portrait of the Third Earl of Shaftesbury by John Closterman, ca. 1704–1705. Image by the National Portrait Gallery. Reproduced by permission of Lady Shaftesbury, Wimborne, St. Giles.
Book design by Diane Smith

The Library of Congress has cataloged the hardcover edition as follows:

Library of Congress Cataloging-in-Publication Data

Branch, Lori.
 Rituals of spontaneity : sentiment and secularism from free prayer to Wordsworth / Lori Branch.
   p. cm.
 Includes bibliographical references (p.) and index.
 ISBN-13: 978-1-932792-11-9 (acid-free paper)
 1. English literature--18th century--History and criticism. 2. Spontaneity (Philosophy) in literature. 3. English literature--Early modern, 1500-1700--History and criticism. 4. Christian literature, English--History and criticism. 5. Sentimentalism in literature. 6. Secularism in literature. 7. Christianity and literature--Great Britain--History. 8. Christianity and culture--Great Britain--History. 9. Prayer--History. I. Title.

PR448.S75B73 2006
820.9'384--dc22

                                  2006016972

The ISBN-13 for the paperback edition is 978-1-60258-342-9.

Printed in the United States of America on acid-free paper.

In memory of my mother,
Jan Branch

For there is nothing but it may be played upon in delight . . .
For GLASS is worked in the fire till it partakes of its nature . . .
For GOD is an extravagant BEING and generous unto loss.

—Christopher Smart, *Jubilate Agno*

Contents

List of Illustrations		ix
Acknowledgments		xi
Introduction		1
1	The Rejection of Liturgy, the Rise of Free Prayer, and Modern Religious Subjectivity	35
2	"As Blood Is Forced Out of Flesh": Spontaneity and the Wounds of Exchange in *Grace Abounding* and *The Pilgrim's Progress*	63
3	"True Enthusiasm": Moral Sense Philosophy and Fissures of the Secular Self in Shaftesbury' Private Writings	91
	Coda to Chapter 3: "Divide Youself, Be Two"—Images of the Modern Subject	123
4	At the Sign of the Bible and Sun: John Newbery, *The Vicar of Wakefield*, and the Ghost of Christopher Smart	135
5	Wordsworth's "Spontaneous Overflow" and the "High Service Within": From *Lyrical Ballads* to *Ecclesiastical Sonnets*	175
Conclusion: On the Religiousness of Criticism		211

Notes	227
Works Cited	293
Index	321

Illustrations

Figures

1. Opening from *A Directory for the Publique Worship of God* (1644). Courtesy Lilly Library, Indiana University, Bloomington, IN. 54

2. Title page and illustration of John Bunyan, *The Pilgrim's Progress*, first edition (1678). Reproduced by permission of The Huntington Library, San Marino, California. 86

3. Opening from Francis Hutcheson, *An Inquiry concerning Moral Good and Evil*, second edition (1726), 182–83, under the marginal heading "How we compute the Morality of Actions in our Sense of them." Photo courtesy of The Newberry Library, Chicago. 95

4. Anthony Ashley Cooper, Third Earl of Shaftesbury, Ασκηματα manuscript, pages 2:194–95. The National Archives (Public Record Office) PRO 30/24/27/10 pt 2. Photograph by Hugh Alexander. 110

5. Emblem designed by Shaftesbury and engraved by Simon Gribelin for *Soliloquy*, in the second edition of *Characteristicks* (1714). 124

List of Illustrations

6. Engraving of Shaftesbury by Simon Gribelin, prefixed to the second edition of *Characteristicks* (1714).   125

7. Portrait of Shaftesbury by John Closterman, 1704–1705[?]. Image by the National Portrait Gallery. Reproduced by permission of Lady Shaftesbury, Wimborne, St. Giles.   126

8. Portrait of Shaftesbury by John Closterman, detail of first figure.   129

9. Portrait of Shaftesbury by John Closterman, detail of second figure.   129

10. Portrait of Shaftesbury by John Closterman, detail of hand.   132

11. Shaftesbury's "Parchments," page 26, detail. The National Archives (Public Record Office) PRO 30/24/27/11. Photograph by Hugh Alexander.   132

Acknowledgments

At its earliest stages this project took shape as a doctoral dissertation at Indiana University under the direction of Mary Favret, who is all that one could hope for and certainly what I most needed in a mentor and committee chair. By turns critical and persuadable, always generous and frank, in some of the bleakest hiring years of our profession she warned against trying to follow critical trends that most likely would change by the time I entered the job market; she encouraged me rather to take the opportunity graduate school offered to write a book that I would care deeply about because of its integrity with my thinking and experience. I am more thankful for this than I can say. This is that book.

Eight years into this project and as it goes to press, I am often able to see only its shortcomings, which are many and my own, but I am gratefully distracted by the thought of the errors and infelicities from which it has been saved by many kind and thoughtful readers across that period. I owe a great debt of gratitude to professors and colleagues at Indiana, the University of Iowa, and elsewhere who have read chapter drafts, offered insights, and otherwise enriched this project: Misty Anderson, Sam Baker, Matt Brown, Linda Charnes, Anna-Lisa Cox, Huston Diehl, Diane Elam, Heather Frey, Sondra Smith Gates, Kathy Gehr, Eric Gidal, Everett Hamner, Martin Harris, David Jasper, the late Jim Jensen, Dorothy Johnson, Ken Johnston, Oscar Kenshur, Priya Kumar, Bill Kupersmith, Maria LaMonaca, Phyllis Mack, Teresa

Mangum, Peter Manning, Leanne Maunu, Chris Mounsey, Alan Nagel, Richard Nash, Judith Pascoe, Ioana Patuleanu, Michael Rosenblum, Fr. Lev Smith, Janet Sorensen, Maso Tomasini, Beth Weisenberger, Jon Wilcox, and Nick Williams. Graduate students in my three doctoral seminars at the University of Iowa have also expanded my thinking about these texts immeasurably. In May of 2005, the introduction benefited from the intense and fabulous intellectual community at the Fourth Annual Bloomington Eighteenth-Century Studies Workshop, where Deidre Lynch, Jonathan Elmer, and Jonathan Sheehan offered particularly provocative comments and queries. Finally, Dr. Carey Newman and the two anonymous readers for Baylor University Press offered rich, helpful suggestions together with encouragement for which I am extremely thankful. From our first hour–long phone conversation, which ranged from Karl Barth to Lacan, to his Hutchesonian equations for spontaneity and insanity, Carey has been more than I had hoped for in an editor. I cannot express enough my gratitude for his thoughtful interaction with every chapter; his support and encouragement have made the publication process a joy.

The research and writing of this book would not have been possible without several fellowships and grants. The Pew Charitable Trusts provided not only generous support for my doctoral work but the wonderful summer conferences and intellectual relationships that have shaped my hopes for what scholarship can be. A Dissertation Year Fellowship and International Travel Grants from the Indiana University College of Arts and Sciences made possible an extra year of writing as well as research trips to the Bodleian Library. I am also thankful for the committed research support of the University of Iowa and its Division of Sponsored Programs: for an Old Gold Summer Fellowship, for International Programs travel funds, and particularly for the Arts and Humanities Initiative Grant that allowed me to spend a month in London with the Shaftesbury Papers. My research has been greatly aided by kind and inquisitive library staffs at home and abroad, to whom I owe much: at the Bodleian and Duke Humfrey's Libraries, Oxford; the Indiana University and Lilly Rare Book and Manuscript Libraries, Bloomington; the British National Archives and Public Record Office, Kew, Surrey; and by Kathy Magarrell and David Schroeder at the University of Iowa Library. I also thank the Iowa Department of English for supporting my work with a series of brilliant, diligent research assistants with whom it has been a pleasure to work: Heidi LaVine, Jean Fernandez, Tracy Stuhr, and especially Young Hee Kwon, who not only turned up valuable new sources but checked every reference, and Erica Daigle, who in addition to lightning-speed detective work performed heroic feats with the notes and bibliography.

Acknowledgments

My warmest gratitude goes to the friends and family who have supported me in this project and far beyond its bounds by their love and friendship, and without whom much more than this book would have been impossible. These include families and choir members of the three parishes where I have worshiped in the last decade, All Saints in Bloomington, Indiana; St. George in Cedar Rapids, Iowa; and St. Raphael of Brooklyn in Iowa City, particularly the amazing women who continue to inspire and nurture me as mothers, intellectuals, and friends: Kristi Abuissa, Michelle Bayouth, Anna Sluz Cook, Elena Gavruseva, Olga Impey, Karen Kuntz, and Joanna Ploeger; Mother Gabriella and the nuns of Holy Dormition Monastery in Rives Junction, Michigan; Fr. Philip and Lilija Vreeland; Stephanos and Juliana Bibas; members of the Geneva Lecture Series advisory board; and my families by both birth and marriage, especially my remarkable sister Amber Branch. Robert Peterson, my husband, is the love of my life and in a category all his own. He has the heart and patience of a saint, and daily life with him is the sweetest ritual I know. Together with the appreciation I can never express enough to him, my deepest gratitude is expressed in the dedication and epigraph of this book.

A shorter form of chapter 1 was published as "The Rejection of Liturgy, the Rise of Free Prayer, and Modern Religious Subjectivity," *Restoration* 29 (2005): 1–28, and a version of chapter 2, "'As Blood Is Forced out of Flesh': Spontaneity and the Wounds of Exchange in *Grace Abounding* and *The Pilgrim's Progress*," will appear in the pages of *English Literary History* around the time this book is published. I thank the editors of both journals for their feedback on these chapters and for permission to include them here.

Iowa City, Iowa
5 September 2005
SS. Zachariah and Elizabeth

Introduction

> As the occasion of this Poem was real, not fictitious; so the method pursued in it was rather imposed by what spontaneously arose in the Author's mind on that occasion, than mediated or designed. Which will appear very probable from the nature of it. For it differs from the common mode of poetry, which is, from long narrations to draw short morals. Here, on the contrary, the narrative is short, and the morality arising from it makes the bulk of the Poem. The reason of it is, that the facts mentioned did naturally pour these moral reflections on the thought of the Writer.
>
> —Edward Young, "Preface" to
> *The Complaint: or, Night Thoughts* (1742)[1]

Anticipating *Lyrical Ballads* by a half century, Edward Young's "Preface" to his popular *Night Thoughts* sketches both the familiar and the more surprising contours of the story of spontaneity that this study tells. Having arisen spontaneously in its author's breast, this poem, Young tells us, stands apart from the common mode of poetry which, full of artifice and witty narrative, is implicitly fictitious, fallacious even. This poem, on the other hand, is natural: it springs from authentic emotional responses to the "facts" of a "real occasion"—a claim to virtuous originality that Young later expounded into a full-blown theory of poetic inspiration in *Conjectures on Original Composition* (1759). What this imposing reality impresses on the writer are, crucially, natural *moral* reflections; these empirically collected moral responses, he tells his readers, are the very stuff of the poem. And, as the opening pages of *Night Thoughts* make it hard to miss, these effusions flowed from the pen of a lawyer turned clergyman, who was perhaps prouder of the mantle of poet than of either public office. Adored by his readers, Young was an Anglican priest who in a quasi-religious, quasi-secular career as a poet earned thousands of pounds from poetry that inspired at least one eighteenth-century couple to wonder why he had not been made the Archbishop of Canterbury.[2]

As commonplace as Young's account of poetic inspiration seems today, the magnitude of the cultural shift it represents can hardly be overestimated. Rituals—the pageantry and ceremonies of the life cycle, the church year, and the seasons—were for centuries the primary means by which premodern peoples imagined and embodied their communities. As the first chapter of this study recounts, for a variety of cultural and intellectual reasons, in the early modern period ritual increasingly became the object of Reformers' critiques and of their efforts to purify the church of superstition and to revise the content of its liturgy, but not of any attempt to do away with ritual or liturgy altogether. Following the dramatic Restoration of Charles II to England's throne and the episcopacy to its church, in 1662 the Act of Uniformity fanned the free-prayer controversy into a firestorm. In its wake, a small but increasing number of English Protestants became convinced that liturgy was sinful and that the only true prayer was spontaneous. Unwilling to conform to the Book of Common Prayer and, increasingly, to forms of prayer in general, on an ominous August Sunday that Samuel Pepys recorded in his diary, over 2,000 ministers left the pulpits of the Church of England over precisely this issue, never to return, sowing seeds of nonconformity and dissent which would grow and cross-pollinate in a variety of related denominations and emotionally charged worship styles over the next three hundred years. By the late eighteenth century, when Britain witnessed the rise of what we now call literary Romanticism, Wordsworth, the poet generally conceived of as its helmsman, could confidently define poetry as "the spontaneous overflow of powerful feelings . . . recollected in tranquility." In the interim, and as early as Young's preface, a broad-based cultural sense had coalesced that located spontaneity—an unpremeditated emotional freshness coveted in phenomena as disparate as poetic effusion, enthusiastic worship, romantic attraction, and consumer desire—at the heart of meaningful human experience. Considered together with their potent afterlives in modernity and postmodernity, these dramatic sea changes beg for broad-based interrogation as to how they took place.[3] How and why did the popular conception of poetry shift from ritual recitation and communal performance to the unstoppable pouring forth of the individual inspired heart? How was it that the history of Christian worship seemingly stopped on a dime—that an evolving millennium-and-a-half-long liturgical tradition suddenly witnessed a principled defense of the effusions of free prayer that lives on in today's televangelism and megachurches?

Pinpointing a single origin of such deeply rooted and far-reaching cultural transformation is of course impossible, and yet, from the critique of ritual, to the incarceration of Christopher Smart for spontaneous prayer, to Wordsworth's "Preface," the long eighteenth century was punctuated by crystallizing events and controversies that make it ideal for investigating modernity's tempestuous love affair with the spontaneous and for understanding the discourses and debates in which it took shape. And the paradoxes and contradictions that emerge from the love of spontaneity are provocative in themselves, not least because the abandonment of ritual even at the height of Enlightenment was never total or final: one has only to think, for instance, of the initiation rites and secretive ceremonies of the Freemasons. And then, the poem Smart wrote in his seven-year imprisonment for spontaneous prayer, the *Jubilate Agno*, was oddly enough the greatest monument to liturgy the century produced. Wordsworth, too, lived long enough to share the Tractarians' antiquarian passion for liturgy—at least until ritual seemed to equate with Rome, and John Henry Newman scandalized England by converting to Catholicism. One of the unavoidable side effects of a love for spontaneity, it seems, has been a vexed nostalgia for the ritual that was jilted in its favor.

By examining the literatures of the period, from free-prayer pamphlets, spiritual autobiography, and moral sense philosophy, to sentimental novels and poetry, this book excavates the historical process—and the affect-laden, intensely repetitive role of interpretive acts within it—by which modernity shifted from a pre- and early-modern belief in ritual to an ultimately moral and aesthetic valuing of spontaneity. It tells a story of strange twists and turns, by which religious enthusiasts proclaimed their legitimacy and remade their spirituality with a discourse of spontaneity that, within a generation, would be derided and disavowed yet refashioned and embraced by deists and secular philosophers as a part of what they called the "true enthusiasm." As Leon Guilhamet describes, "even before the term 'enthusiasm' had lost its connotation of opprobrium, an ideal of spontaneity was coming into being," the ideal of emotional sincerity that beat at the heart of the culture of sensibility and its esteem for politeness and moral sensitivity.[4] The culture of sensibility would attempt to forge a union of rationalized faith with this new philosophy of feeling, retaining and periodically reviving its explicitly religious overtones. "While Enlightenment did seek, often, to found itself on the ruins of enthusiasm," Anthony La Vopa and Lawrence Klein observe, "the defense of Enlightenment could equally rely on enthusiasm," and "the cultures of modernity are as generously laced with attempts to preserve or reinvent enchantment as they are with attempts to abolish it."[5]

In *Elations: The Poetics of Enthusiasm in Eighteenth-Century Britain*, Shaun Irlam characterizes Young's aesthetics of spontaneity as an effort to displace the precise scriptural typology of Milton and earlier poets into "a more dispersed and secularized emblematic practice, in which a newly divinized Nature substitutes for the overtly scriptural references of *Paradise Lost*."[6] Why a clergyman and his religiously inclined reading audiences should be such eager devotees of a self-secularizing enthusiasm is one of the great themes in the story of spontaneity's rise, and an enigma this study helps unravel. The period 1650–1750 has been identified as "the crucial transitional period" that witnessed the supposed "end of the theological cosmos and the beginning of the modern era of rational enlightenment, experimental science, historical awareness, and political understanding."[7] The story of spontaneity—and of ritual's decline—I have come to argue, is the story of the secularization of goodness, but one that is not so smooth or evenly paced as has been supposed. It is the story of seventeenth- and eighteenth-century English men and women coming to understand goodness less in the traditionally religious terms that had been rendered problematic by seventeenth-century enthusiasm and the wars of religion, and more within the logic and language of an increasingly empirical and economic rationality and in the forms of the expanding print marketplace, with which it was, to understate matters, by no means immediately compatible. Spontaneous emotional effusion—both the sort Young claims and the sort that had earlier found expression in enthusiasm—was taken as *evidence* of the condition of one's heart, I argue, when that heart came to be conceived of as an object of investigation, appraisal, and exchange like so many others in the given world. The literatures that expound this new value for spontaneous emotional feelings resonate with the languages of experimental discovery and with mercantile and emerging consumer discourses of being current and up-to-date. In these terms, ritual and repetition figure not just as superstitious, but as boring, authoritarian, and out-of-date, stultifying and obscuring the natural responses of the soul.[8] The fate of ritual in eighteenth-century Britain, so often figured as an idol which rational iconoclasts sought to cleanse from the temple of enlightened society, was inextricably bound up with a freshly modern valuation of spontaneity, novelty, and the technologies and market rationality of print. To understand the derision and disavowal of ritual in Enlightenment is, therefore, in part to account for the discourses and contexts in which spontaneous emotions and behaviors became increasingly, almost irresistibly, compelling.

Examining the contexts and logic of spontaneity, this study ultimately generates a new understanding of the concept of the secular and the ideology of secularism that took shape during the Restoration and Enlightenment. Revising sociology's secularization thesis—so much critiqued but still so critically dominant in the humanities and social sciences—it ultimately enables us to understand secularization as something other than a simple decline in religious belief and practice, part and parcel with modern economy and technological advances.[9] J. G. A. Pocock has rightly observed that Catholic historians as often as secular ones have made the mistake of telling a Whiggish history in which "the first step away from orthodoxy is irrevocable and the outcome in secularization inevitable."[10] As the French sociologist of religion Danièle Hervieu-Léger has pointed out, embarking on a sociological study of religion twenty-five years ago meant *a priori* accounting for the decline of religion. But today, the "cultural reversal" of the intervening decades —the rise of fundamentalism, and the perseverance and adaptation of traditional religions—has generated a new scholarship practically "prepared to jettison the whole conceptual achievement that the theorists of secularization have built up over the years." Even if we do not go that far, she claims that the current political and academic climate resolutely "favours theoretical forms of revision which are as agonizing as they are ambivalent."[11] "If the secularization thesis seems increasingly implausible to some of us," writes Talal Asad, the current global political situation calls us to go beyond recognition of the "obvious fact" of religion's perseverance to pursuing "questions that need to be systematically addressed": namely, "how, when, and by whom are the categories of religion and the secular defined?" and "what assumptions are presupposed in the acts that define them?"[12]

Across the long eighteenth century, spontaneous sentiment was a contested site for the implicit conceptualization of the religious and the secular, and this study's focus on language and discourse reveals many of the assumptions Asad asks us to uncover, enabling us to understand secularization in a wholly new dimension: as a *rhetorical process*, which takes place first of all *within religious discourse itself*, by which economic and empirical discourses make it harder and harder to speak of the value of *faith*—or of anything—except in terms of certainty and possession. Though they never do away with belief (and indeed, this kernel of impossibility perpetually unsettles rational and empirical epistemologies), discourses and practices that value the spontaneous are secularizing even in religious contexts, in both symbolic and practical ways. Symbolically, in the abstraction of knowledge from spontaneous experiences and natural evidences, truth is paradoxically separated further and further from its grounds in the world and in time, and the bifurcation between, on the one hand, the world of concrete, given things and experiences and, on the other hand, the realm of abstract value and meaning ostensibly drawn from them, grows wider and wider. Practically, the thinking that values spontaneity is secularizing in that it removes religious experience from what Hervieu-Léger characterizes as traditional or premodern religion: from conscious, performative forms of *believing* and from processes leading to *the formation of the self* in which tradition and rite, though not impervious to change, nonetheless serve to connect the individual to a lineage of belief across history and to a living community of believers in time.[13] But the spontaneous subject, that is, one who imagines subjective responses to be truly spontaneous and not (at least partially) constructed by performance and belief, is, as Slavoj Žižek points out, still profoundly implicated in belief, which is "radically exterior." In his turn of phrase, people may proclaim that they "no longer believe" in the modern ideologies associated with capitalism, for instance, *"but the things themselves believe for them"*—that is, the structures of subjectivity and desire generated in the marketplace nonetheless organize rituals of daily life, through behaviors like money exchange that seem inevitable and desires that seem spontaneous.[14] Ritual and belief do not vanish in the imagined secular space of spontaneous responses, but crucially are naturalized and made invisible, less and less subject to resistant behaviors and credible reimagining.

With secularization, other unforeseen consequences followed on succumbing to the siren call of the spontaneous, and each chapter of this study attends carefully to the costs and losses incurred by conflictedly religious, empirical, increasingly possessing and possessed modern subjects under what quickly became in the late seventeenth and early eighteenth centuries an imperative for spontaneity. The ideology of spontaneity that emerges in this period is marked, I argue, not just by the displacement of traditional rituals, but by the inventions of new ones necessary for maintaining a sense of freshness and felt certainty. Not recognized as ritualistic, these "rituals of spontaneity"—free prayer, Dissenting and philosophic forms of self-scrutiny in the quest for natural moral responses, and the behaviors associated with sensibility, including effusions of joy, weeping, or poetic inspiration—are the sacraments of an increasingly consumeristic culture and tend to bear three striking characteristics. They translate primarily into a limited set of market behaviors, namely buying and selling, authorial production, and readerly desire and consumption; they give rise to an array of painful anxieties about individual authenticity and the performance of spontaneity; and they render agency difficult to imagine, making the very moral improvement at which they aim highly problematic and ultimately undermining the quest for an empirically verifiable, universal morality. In fact, the peril of maintaining a sense of agency and responsibility in modernity is the key note resounding in the etymology of the word *spontaneous* and its shifting usage in the seventeenth and eighteenth centuries. From the Latin *sponte*, "of free will," by the period this book examines the word had come primarily to mean "without effort or premeditation."[15] Sentimentalizations of piety such as we see in Oliver Goldsmith's *The Vicar of Wakefield*, when laid alongside the incarceration of his coworker, Christopher Smart, reveal how supposedly spontaneous sentiment was in fact more passive than free, circumscribed by market forces and the peculiarly secular public sphere in which the invisible hand best operates. Similarly revealing, Smart's bizarre liturgical poetry, like Wordsworth's erstwhile Tractarianism, seems much less strange and waxes quite eloquent when heard as part of this far-reaching story of the vexed dialectics of ritual and spontaneity, sentiment and secularism, agency and passivity in modernity. In *Formations of the Secular: Christianity, Islam, Modernity*, Talal Asad has suggested understanding modernity less as a coherent or clearly bounded object and more as a set of ideals, a "project" underwritten by particular political ambitions, such that we can speak of modernity not in (highly contestable) ontological terms but rather in terms of epochs when people in certain places have aimed at institutionalizing modern ideals such as moral autonomy, democracy, freedom of the market, and secularism; it is in this way that modernity as a set of goals and ideals has a practical and political reality.[16] Spontaneity, like the nation and the secular, is clearly an undergirding concept of that modern ideal, and its story is full of particular, identifiable tensions, pulled as it is between an impossible ideality it never reaches and a premodern past and rituality that it defines itself against, yet can never quite leave behind. To critique our notions of spontaneity and secularism is not, however, to suggest a return to a premodern or theocratic past, any more than to critique capitalism is to recommend a barter economy.[17] It is rather to ask us to imagine how we might relate differently to systems of economy and knowledge. Moreover, it is, I believe, to live up to our critical moment, after the linguistic turn of twentieth-century philosophy and the way it calls to our attention the inevitability of interpretation and faith in the production of knowledge.

This introduction is relatively lengthy, and so a map is in order to allow readers to chart their own courses through it, or to sail around it altogether. The pages that follow summarize each of the five chapters and narrate them as one book-length argument. They are followed by a section that may be of interest mainly to specialists in eighteenth-century studies and to the theoretically inclined, on the critical contexts and methodologies of this book. The final three parts play out what I take to be the most important implications of this study: that is, the ways it prompts us to question our inherited narratives about the emergence of secularism; to consider secularization as a process of rationalization that takes place first of all within religious discourses and practices themselves; and to see the ideologies of both spontaneity and secularism as indispensable supports of what we have come to think of as modern subjectivity. Readers to whom these previews and ruminations seem like so much delay are invited to head straight for the deep waters of the chapters.

The first chapter of this study lays the historical, rhetorical groundwork for the chapters that follow, locating the backgrounds of modern spontaneity in the early modern crisis of representation and the critique of ritual to which it gave rise. Based on my study of nearly one hundred pamphlets and tracts in the holdings of the Bodleian, Duke Humfrey's, and Lilly libraries, I document in this chapter the terms in which spontaneity was first and most contentiously argued as important, in the seventeenth-century debate over liturgy and spontaneous prayer. Against the backdrop of Renaissance and Reformation crises of representation, vehement scriptural debate about ritual and heated political wrangling surrounding the imposition of the Book of Common Prayer, this chapter shows how the language of late-seventeenth-century English free-prayer tracts continually and anxiously appealed to discourses of evidence, exchange, and emotional experience to determine the validity of prayer and of the heart that prays. Defenses of free prayer dramatize the process by which rationalistic, empirical, and economic modes of reasoning—what we may call a secular rationality—produce the rationale of spontaneity and free prayer when they are mapped onto traditionally religious concerns and come to bear on a distinctly modern religious subject. When the matter at hand is eternal salvation or damnation, the "unsettled soul" looks for evidence of her spiritual condition as close to the knowing self as possible, in the most immediate thoughts and feelings, evinced by spontaneous, emotional prayer, which she takes both scientifically and economically as proofs and tokens of grace. In the consolidation of the discourse and practice of free prayer, I argue, we see the culmination of Renaissance crises of representation and the fruition of the dramatic Reformation attacks on ritual, when under increasing pressures toward certainty and ever more entrenched economic logics, spontaneity becomes policy: not an option for personal devotion, but for growing numbers of Protestants an obligation and the *sine qua non* of a saved subjectivity and of valid individual and corporate prayer. Even more strikingly, we witness the anxieties attendant on requiring spontaneity. Dissenting ministers eventually produced guidebooks to spontaneous prayer that coached believers to collect "scripture phrases" to arm themselves against the nervous silence that threatened to quash free prayer. While these documents open a window into the anxious inner lives of emotional pulse-taking to which an ideology of spontaneity led, they also hint at the way its evidentiary, economizing logic seems to be at odds with the very notion of personal relation with God or others, and perhaps with the very religiousness of religion.

The four subsequent chapters build on the first chapter's central insight into spontaneity as epistemological-economic proof of religious, moral value. They each constitute an intimate account of the labyrinthine workings of spontaneity in various cultural phenomena registered on the individual level, with an eye toward their shared contexts, ideological contours, and subjective symptoms. By examining works of John Bunyan, chapter 2 delves into the spirituality of spontaneity and anxious inner life borne of free prayer. Beginning with Bunyan's defense of spontaneous prayer, *I Will Pray with the Spirit* (1662), I show how his spiritual autobiography, *Grace Abounding to the Chief of Sinners* (1666), expresses the excruciating cost of Bunyan's ideology of spontaneity, constantly scrutinizing his inner experience for evidence and viewing himself as an object of exchange before God. After opening episodes recounting his inner search for the "true tokens of a truly godly man," the middle third of *Grace Abounding* recounts a single traumatic experience of a wholly different sort of ritual and spontaneity: a voice haunts Bunyan day in, day out, for over a year, urging him to "Sell him, sell him"—to sell Christ "for this or that." Where criticism has ignored the economic form of this episode, I argue that in it we see the psychological toll of an early or newly modern religious subjectivity coming to understand itself in related evidentiary and economic terms. This trauma bespeaks the incommensurability between economic logic and personal relation, as well as the partial recognition that Bunyan's spirituality has already "sold Christ" in its contract-oriented covenant theology. This analysis opens the pathway to a rich new reading of *The Pilgrim's Progress* (1678), with its fascinating central episode at Vanity Fair. More than the "creative reworking" of *Grace Abounding* that criticism has generally claimed, *The Pilgrim's Progress* has achieved its astounding popularity over the past 300 years, I argue, precisely because of the way it sutures the spiritual-epistemological gaps that emerge in *Grace Abounding*, assuring readers that salvation can be evidentially certified with Christian's contract-like roll and that they, like Christian and Hopeful, can "buy the truth."

Writers conventionally conceived of as religious were not the only ones, however, to find spontaneity a persuasive answer to questions of virtue. Spontaneity in the form of the "moral sense" was at the heart of Britain's nearly single-handed invention of modern moral philosophy in the eighteenth century. Against religious enthusiasm like Bunyan's, Hobbes's materialist account of human selfishness, and Locke's debunking of innate ideas, Anthony Ashley Cooper, eventually the third Earl of Shaftesbury, sought to articulate rational foundations for an objective, universal ethics. In *Characteristicks* (1711), Shaftesbury posited the "moral sense" as the basis for the secular morality he pointedly called the "true enthusiasm." Spontaneous and prereflexive, the moral sense as Shaftesbury imagined it allowed a rational person to determine right and wrong, in Terry Eagleton's words, "with all the swiftness of the senses," by observing his natural emotional responses.[18] Shaftesbury's private writings, however, tell another story. Brooding, rambling, bitter, and violent, the notebooks Shaftesbury labeled Ασκηματα or "Exercises" (1698–1707) are vastly different from the affable *Characteristicks*; but I contend that they are intimately related to them by a mappable logic. Chapter 3 therefore shows how Shaftesbury's quest for spontaneous, "natural affection" for his fellow man at the beginning of the notebooks leads to an angry paralysis at the roadblock of his intractable sexual desires and to a loathing of the "effeminate," vulnerable permeability of his body.

Faced with the lack of mastery that his bodily desires presented, Shaftesbury turned, in his quest for spontaneous benevolence, to a ritualistic "Regimen" of severe psychological *ascesis*. Alongside his disavowal of physical intimacy, the language of Shaftesbury's journals reveals his aggressive sexualization of philosophy, culminating in a metaphorical sexual assault on the "Deity" whom he had previously set out as the guarantor of universal moral order. The image of the violation of God in the Ασκηματα parallels a visceral disgust with Christ graphically manifest in Shaftesbury's final notebook. Together, these notebooks illustrate how ideologies of masculinity, national superiority, and class privilege are connected to a libidinally invested, frequently vengeful or violent secularism that echoes in the works of Hume, Richardson, and Sade, and how such ideologies share a sense of self defined by mastery. This mapping of the plate tectonics of the split Enlightenment subject rumbling in the Ασκηματα enables me to conclude the chapter with a coda that advances a new argument as to the identity of the 300-year-old mystery figure in Shaftesbury's great, puzzling portrait by John Closterman. One of the many allegorical works Shaftesbury designed and commissioned, this painting represents, I argue, the violent splitting of the self that Shaftesbury consciously engaged in and that the ideology of spontaneity entails. The replacement of this split image with the engraving of a single magisterial self as the frontispiece of the *Characteristicks* eloquently expresses the continuities between Shaftesbury's "true enthusiasm" and the enthusiasm that preceded it; the Shaftesbury who comes to us as the author of the *Characteristicks* is as much a fantasy of progress and spontaneous wholeness as Bunyan's allegory and its elision of the trauma represented in the "Sell him" episode—and in the course of Anglophone modernity, ultimately a more appealing and proselytizing one.

The first three chapters of this study, then, combine to highlight both the secularizing trajectory inherent in the ideology of spontaneity and the sense of anxious paralysis it bred.[19] Uneasy passivity and incipient, quasi-religious secularism were the defining features of spontaneity in its most widely accepted manifestation, the literature and culture of sensibility. The fourth chapter therefore investigates the problems of agency and religion in midcentury sentimental literature as seen by two of its most intimate critics, both of whom plied their trade at the London shop of bookseller and children's literature pioneer John Newbery. At the Sign of the Bible and Sun, Newbery built an empire under sensibility's flag of moral improvement, and employed two of the century's most gifted writers, Christopher Smart and Oliver Goldsmith, as its chief architects. While both men appreciated Newbery as less profit-hungry than other booksellers, each in his own way critiqued the world of the Bible and Sun, particularly its consumer excess, greed, and the print market that pandered to it, and for both, the tension between ritual and spontaneity figured into their critiques. In *The Vicar of Wakefield* (1760–1762; published 1766), Goldsmith consciously set out to reform what he saw as impotent sentimentality and moral philosophy into an active sensibility enlivened by religious ritual and practice. Goldsmith put private daily devotions and family reading from the Book of Common Prayer at the heart of the Vicar's perseverance and ability to impart sensibility to others, but these daily practices are never directly narrated in the text. For the novel to move forward, such repetitive actions must take place, as it were, offstage, and the piety Goldsmith recommends as the source of "true sensibility" is sentimentalized and subjected to the commercially acceptable rituals of the print-commodity form it is supposed to redeem. Critiquing the troublesome novel-reading of the Primrose women from within a novel itself, *The Vicar of Wakefield* carries with it the implicit knowledge that passive, consumerist reading practices provide only the slimmest chance of cultivating virtue based on sentimental impulses which, as the women of the novel illustrate, seem ever prey to other influences.

The particular shortcomings of Goldsmith's sentimental-religious reform, however, are thrown into relief by his coworker, the prize-winning Cambridge poet Christopher Smart. After a dramatic brush with death, Smart experienced a religious conversion, not only deciding to quit writing hack assignments for Newbery but becoming convinced that it was wrong to resist the urge to pray. Pulling friends like Samuel Johnson to their knees in St. James Park and praying in a loud voice, as he playfully put it, "till I routed all the company," Smart was incarcerated in various insane asylums for the better part of seven years. There, at the ritual pace of two to three lines each day, Smart wrote a stunningly bizarre and beautiful poem, *Jubilate Agno* (1759–1763). Setting this liturgical rhapsody, like Goldsmith's novel, in the context of Newbery's shop, I argue that the poem and its self-conscious recourse to ritual constitute an explicitly religious resistance to empirical epistemologies and market-fed desires, based in Smart's creative, performative sense of language and the self as made in the divine image. As Smart put it, "a man speaks HIMSELF from the crown of his head to the sole of his feet." The creative potential inherent in the indeterminacies of language enabled Smart to recover a sense of agency and performative self-fashioning—and a different ritual of spontaneity, the composition of the *Jubilate*—outside the sway of "the coffin and the cradle and the purse" of economic and scientifically imagined determinism. Goldsmith's novel, on the other hand, also written in the early years of Smart's imprisonment and in the context of Newbery's shop, is in my reading haunted by Smart, a rewriting of this odd little man as Goldsmith wished him to be, pious but polite, and praying in private. The pious but prayerless Vicar looks toward what Graham Ward calls the status of religion as "special effect" in commodity culture, as Smart's incarceration and the embarrassed silence of his friends stand as fitting emblems of what Asad sees as a coercive secularism, albeit within religious sensibilities. Even as the culture of sensibility insisted on recognizing itself to some degree as religious, its embrace of a carefully limited spontaneity as the basis of polite consumer culture entailed a secularism that placed the Vicar's prayers—and with it, a sense of agency and practice—off the page of the novel, and Smart's, behind the walls of an asylum.

Chapter 4 thus demonstrates the extent to which the naturalized spontaneous emotions that both religious and secular writers looked to for guidance were increasingly shaped and compromised by the market and the forms of print culture. The market-friendly culture of sensibility and politeness proved problematic for individual agency, in either representing or practicing behaviors that would resist greed and consumer excess, and religion repeatedly emerged as a potential but compromised site of agency and resistance to market culture. Moral agency at odds with the natural and spontaneous, and market rationality along with its implicit secularism and its discontents are, I argue, the coordinates of the moral philosophy and literary marketplace of late eighteenth-century Britain out of which, as much as from the French Revolution, Wordsworth's thought emerges. In the final chapter, then, I turn to his poems, arguing that his engagement with this constellation of issues simultaneously interested and unsettled a large readership and accounted, in part, for his growing appeal into the nineteenth century.

Wordsworth's popularity in his day was based not as much on the early works that interest scholarship in our day as on his later poetry, dismissed by not a few modern critics as a recanting of his youthful idealism and as an ossification into conservatism. I argue, rather, for the vital connection of these later poems to the concerns at the heart of *Lyrical Ballads* (1798); the picture of sharp disjunction between the young radical and the mature, conservative Wordsworth is made possible, I contend, only by ignoring the late religious poetry and enacting precisely the sort of cordoning, secularizing gesture that this study suggests we critique. The chapter on Wordsworth, therefore, traces the logic by which his early insistence that "all good poetry is the spontaneous overflow of powerful feelings" leads, not unlike Smart's spontaneous prayer, to an interest in liturgy and an attempted recuperation of agency together with ritual, which was already foreshadowed in *Lyrical Ballads'* concern with repetition, but which culminated in the sonnet sequence *Ecclesiastical Sketches* (1822; later renamed *Ecclesiastical Sonnets*) that along with the "Thanksgiving Ode" coincided with his rising public esteem. Against commercial culture's "lore / Of nicely calculated less or more" and the ambition that succumbs to "abject sympathies with power," Wordsworth in these sonnets proposes a self ascetically shaped, architecturally constructed in language, and liturgically performed as "high service" to God in the life of "the pious, humble, useful Secular." This evocative phrase bridges the gap between ritual and spontaneity, sacred and secular in a way nicely emblematic of Wordsworth's resacralization of the everyday and of his refusal of the split between immanence and transcendence. In his early quest for moral certainty, Wordsworth arrived at an un-Newtonian "fixed law" of human freedom, "from which all spiritual dignity" springs: the chance—continually represented by uncertainty and by the temptation either to submit to absolute authority or to legitimate one's own egomaniacal self-rule—to hope creatively and to love. In *Ecclesiastical Sonnets*, ritual and liturgy emerge, much as they do for Smart, as sites where a person may "weave a crown for hope" and recuperate a carefully measured—circumscribed, yet radically free—sense of personal agency. By ritual Wordsworth points simultaneously to the public, communal liturgy of the church but also to intentional rituals of spontaneity: to what he calls in *The Prelude* the "high service within," the consciously cultivated habits of mind by which one looks at the world. This insistence on inner agency accounts, to my mind, for Wordsworth's leeriness, despite his interest in ritual, of the Tractarians' making liturgy into a movement, drawn as they were toward Rome, so he felt, by their own sympathy with power. His later poetry thus creates a rhetorical space for what Hervieu-Léger sees as the religious in an earlier sense—for communal tradition and public praxis as potentially formative of a loving, irenic self—but with the perpetual insistence on leaving the agency of engaging in that praxis appropriately, if difficultly, interior to the person, who is always seeing, reading and interpreting, and shaping the "I" that sees.

One of the great surprises of this project, then, is not just that valuing spontaneity and denigrating ritual is so integral to the process of secularization, but that prayer and love emerge as the recurring sticking points in the ideology of spontaneity. The crises, ruptures, and turning points of these texts occur at the moment when the writers concern themselves explicitly with love: with trying to define it, possess it, or prove its existence. And prayer is a key category not just for a religious thinker like Bunyan, but for a Grub Street essayist like Goldsmith and a philosopher like Shaftesbury, in his own day most suspected of deism or atheism. It seems that imagining a spontaneous, natural self problematizes both the notion of love as anything besides instinct and the notion of praying altogether; if the world is completely determined, there is no point "Expostulat[ing] with Providence" (*A*, 93), as Shaftesbury puts it, however much he wishes (and he does) to do so. Prayer and agency, it seems, hang in the same balance. Prayer is recuperable, surprisingly enough, by someone like Smart or Wordsworth, who entertains something like a postmodern notion of the infinite dissemination of meaning in language; the uncertainty and room for play that language introduces seems for these writers, as Derrida puts it, the very thing that "makes the conscious freedom of man fathomable"—and with that freedom, the possibility of construction, resistance, and the hope (for oneself and in another) necessary for prayer.[20] And it is this indeterminacy that gives faith and agency their peculiarly performative, repetitive, ritual structure. As philosopher John Caputo puts it,

> Faith is always—and this is its condition—faith without faith, faith that needs to be sustained from moment to moment, from decision to decision, by the renewal, reinvention, and repetition of faith which is . . . continually exposed to discontinuity. Faith is always inhabited by unfaith, which is why the prayer in the New Testament makes such perfect sense, "Lord, I do believe, help my unbelief" (Mark 9:24). For my faith cannot be insulated from unbelief; it is co-constituted by unbelief, which is why faith is faith and not knowledge.[21]

It should not come as a surprise, as perhaps it does, that prayer should be a recurring site of tension across a century obsessed with questions of virtue: the place where, either in secularizing scientific, economic terms or under threat of religious uncertainty, culture revisits the question of the nature of the self and the possibility of shaping one's actions and desires—and the possibility, amidst all the uncertainties of language, of love.

Spontaneity, Sentiment, and Secularism—Critical Contexts and Methodology

An archaeology of modernity's love affair with spontaneity and the story of its imbrication in secularism, this study takes part in the last thirty years' rich fabric of scholarly conversation on the history of emotion in the eighteenth century, particularly concerning gender, economics, and epistemology, and speaks to its strange critical silence about the role of religion in sentiment. Early-twentieth-century studies had approached sentimentality saddled with the task of explaining the embarrassment (in terms of modernism) that was eighteenth-century sentimental literature, and early on the alibi offered was generally philosophical and religious. R. S. Crane's 1934 essay in *English Literary History*, "Suggestions toward a Genealogy of the 'Man of Feeling,'" identified late-seventeenth-century Cambridge Platonists and "anti-Puritan, anti-Stoic, and anti-Hobbesian" Latitudinarian divines as Harley's and Yorick's forefathers.[22] This theological, philosophy-heavy lineage was contested and by some accounts laid to rest by Donald Greene in his 1977 essay "Latitudinarianism and Sensibility: The Genealogy of the 'Man of Feeling' Reconsidered." But well before that time, a new political criticism and contextualization of sentimentality was already underway, one that, not unlike the phenomenon it tracked, meandered away from theology but never left morality far behind.[23]

In 1974 R. F. Brissenden's *Virtue in Distress: Studies in the Novel of Sentiment from Richardson to Sade* steered the conversation toward the perverse undertow of sentimental literature and in some ways anticipated the political critique of sensibility in terms of class and gender that began in the late 1980s. Janet Todd's *Sensibility: An Introduction* made sensibility as a literary movement and a multifaceted cultural phenomenon available to a new generation of students, and Robert Markley's "Sentimentality as Performance: Shaftesbury, Sterne, and the Theatrics of Virtue," Carol Kay's *Political Constructions: Defoe, Richardson, and Sterne in Relation to Hobbes, Hume, and Burke*, and John Mullan's *Sentiment and Sociability: The Language of Feeling in the Eighteenth Century* situated sensibility as a set of variously gendered and class-inflected counterresponses to Hobbes's insistence on man's antisociality and the subsequent necessity of an absolute sovereign, inaugurating a flowering of critical work on the history of emotion in the 1990s.[24] The most capacious of these, G. J. Barker-Benfield's *The Culture of Sensibility: Sex and Society in Eighteenth-Century Britain*, emphasized the connection between the commercialization of the economy and the sentimentalization of culture. Barker-Benfield demonstrated the moral ambitions and religious valences of sensibility within this economic context, but emphasized its gendered element: its goal was the reform of the *man* of feeling.[25] Where *The Culture of Sensibility* has been faulted, it has been for what some see as the reduction of sensibility's complexities to an all-embracing totality, and many subsequent writers have responded to Barker-Benfield by offering less far-reaching, more focused accounts of sensibility.[26] Claudia Johnson's *Equivocal Beings: Politics, Gender, and Sentimentality in the 1790s*, for instance, built on Barker-Benfield's, Kay's, and Mullan's insights to give in some ways a reverse account of the effects of sentiment as the century progressed: "sentimental man," she claims, "having taken over once-feminine attributes, leaves to women only two choices: either the equivocal or the hyperfeminine."[27]

Revisionist political criticism of sentiment has also complicated our understanding of its relation to economic life, highlighting not so much the hidden class agenda of sentimentality as its explicit engagement with the social and economic injustices of its day. In *Sensibility and Economics in the Novel, 1740–1800: The Price of a Tear*, Gillian Skinner claims that sentimental novels did not erase or evade economic reality as earlier criticism implied, but rather participated in its logic and debates both directly and at more profound levels.[28] Similarly, in *The Politics of Sensibility: Race, Gender and Commerce in the Sentimental Novel*, Markman Ellis stresses that "reading sentimental fiction" was held by many "to be an improving experience, refining the manners by exercising the ability to feel for others"; sensibility, according to Ellis, was a tool for the "thorough-going and self-conscious analysis of the emergent consumer-economy of British society and culture."[29] In *The Economy of Character: Novels, Market Culture, and the Business of Inner Meaning*, Deidre Lynch has argued that the boom in novel publishing from the 1760s onward was fueled by readers' appetites for literary characters whose inner lives offered "the imaginative resources on which readers drew to make themselves into individuals, to expand their own interior resources of sensibility."[30] One of the more complex and synthetic arguments to emerge, Julie Ellison's *Cato's Tears and the Making of Anglo-American Emotion*, weaves a cultural history of public, civic emotion, at the center of which are languages of sympathy and the figure of the sensitive man. Ellison too believes that the literature of sentimentality is complexly aware of economics and of its own privilege, investigating "perceived degrees of personal and collective solvency, the price of the individual, and the humiliations of exchange" and revealing the genre's fundamental effects to be organized by race as well as by class and gender.[31]

Alongside these economic contextualizations and politicized, gender-oriented critiques, a parallel group of studies has emerged concerned to show where sentiment and science converged and illustrating how indebted the language and concept of sensibility were to the scientific discourses and epistemologies of the day: among them Ann Jessie Van Sant's *Eighteenth-Century Sensibility and the Novel: The Senses in Social Context*, Robert A. Erickson's *The Language of the Heart, 1600–1750*, and Geoffrey M. Sill's *The Cure of the Passions and the Origins of the English Novel*.[32] These works have demonstrated that sensibility referred to a psycho-perceptual system of the receptivity of the senses and their connection to the mind, as explained by Newton and Locke, that paradigmatically colored the way people thought about consciousness and particularly about moral awareness for most of the eighteenth century. Emphasizing the crossover of empirical science and emerging theories of the nervous system into speculation about moral sensitivity and ethics, these studies have shown us that feelings were seen in the eighteenth century not as strictly opposed to reason but were the very foundation of the empirical quest for moral knowledge.

But scholarship has also shown that, because of the epistemological weight they came to bear, feelings were also the recurring site of the specter of not knowing, and morality and science turned out not to be the easy companions many had hoped. As William Donoghue puts it, "the language of feeling" proved to be "the principal manifestation of skepticism in the eighteenth-century."[33] In *Strange Fits of Passion: Epistemologies of Emotion, Hume to Austen*, Adela Pinch has focused on incidents and accounts of extravagant feelings to show how they repeatedly are characterized as both individual and transpersonal, and that they emerge at moments of epistemological concern over specific questions about society, gender, and aesthetics.[34] Wendy Motooka also insists on the connection between the rational and the sentimental, contending that "it is a mistake to hold these terms in opposition." In *The Age of Reasons: Quixotism, Sentimentalism, and Political Economy in Eighteenth-Century Britain*, she examines eighteenth-century images of quixotism from *The Female Quixote* to Adam Smith, arguing that the trope of "English quixotism criticizes empirical method by exposing its potential circularity"—that is, by highlighting the way that experience produces the reason that is in turn used to rationalize and record experience as history. Novels of feeling and quixotism are for Motooka not only attempts at an empirical morality but often heir to the skepticism of universal reason and objectivity, and they thus engage in a debate about the efficacy of empirical feeling as a ground for moral sentiment, showing that the appeal to personal experience as claim for universal moral truth is, ultimately, quixotic.[35]

And this uncertainty characteristically led to problems of agency. Scott Paul Gordon's *The Power of the Passive Self in English Literature, 1649–1770* reads what others have called sensibility's paralysis as a principled passivity. Where cultural historians have traced the emergence of the "self-enclosed individual" in the seventeenth century, Gordon argues for an accompanying "counter-tradition that resists 'autonomy' and that defers agency from the individual to external nature." Against Hobbes's and Mandeville's claims of universal self-interest, "English Enlightenment culture needed *both* to believe in self-interest *and* to preserve belief in disinterestedness," Gordon claims, for together they enable the social effectivity of an emerging bourgeois ideology.[36] Faced with the difficulty of reconciling the two, Restoration and eighteenth-century writers devised complicated strategies to "preserve the world from the sceptic" and "to re-convince themselves that disinterestedness is indeed possible," one of which was what Gordon calls "the passivity trope." Gordon's study points out not only the conundrums of agency in an age that rooted meaning in a world of unchanging laws, but the "difficulty of belief" in the face of pervasive suspicion and "the difficulty of imagining a solution to the epistemological crisis of knowing what motives generate public behaviors."[37]

Building on the last decade's enriched awareness of sensibility's complex negotiations of morality and subjectivity, gender and commerce, Pinch's, Motooka's and Gordon's studies in many ways return our critical conversation about sensibility and sentimentality to its earlier philosophical concerns, focusing our attention on ways that eighteenth-century discourses of feeling engaged, dodged, and mitigated issues of uncertainty and belief. And yet, while this renewed interest in questions of epistemology and belief would seem to suggest that sentimentality participated in the reconfiguration of faith and knowledge in an early period of secularization, recent critical work has continued to narrate sensibility and sentimentality as phenomena that emerged within a thoroughly secular cultural space which at most affected religion from the outside. In Barker-Benfield's terms, to take but one example, "sensibility rested on essentially materialist assumptions," and proponents of the cultivation of sensibility only "*came to invest it* with spiritual and moral values"; a newly emotional religion "compounded" the power of sentimental fiction, which therefore became "semireligious" just as "sensibility" and the "sentimental" grew somewhat "mystic."[38] Like a great deal of scholarship on the eighteenth-century, Barker-Benfield's language implies the natural division of experience into the categories of the religious and secular. But this division is a conceptual development that takes place, as Asad points out, in the period under study and is therefore more appropriately an object of our critique than an operative critical assumption.[39]

What has struck me from the outset of this project is, in fact, the messy imbrication of religious and secular discourses surrounding sentiment and spontaneity: how, for instance, Shaftesbury will invent a deliberately secularized religious notion like "true enthusiasm" and, yet, how his secular philosophy of the moral sense retains both the language and logic of free prayer with its reliance on spontaneous sentiment. Rather than assuming the division between the secular and the religious, then, one of my methods of inquiry, following Asad, is to interrogate the context in which this division took shape. Taking my cue from Michael McKeon's analysis of the emergence of the novel, I approach religion not as an existent, discrete entity but as a category or "simple abstraction" emerging in the period, in part, because its separation from a purely secular sphere answered to desires and needs, both cultural and ideological.[40] As Hervieu-Léger has suggested, rather than assuming secularization as a decline in religious belief and practice, this study is alert to what she calls the strange fragmentation and redistribution of religion in modernity, listening for unexpectedly religious notes in secular texts, and vice versa.[41] In cultivating a nuanced critical understanding of religion and secularism, my approach to literary and cultural materials is therefore integrative and interdisciplinary, focusing on rhetoric and discourse at the same time that it is deeply historicizing in its sensibility. Esteem for spontaneity was central both to "secular" discourses of sentiment and to religious behaviors and discourses of emotion that preceded it, and careful consideration of the specific ways seventeenth- and eighteenth-century English men and women articulated the meaning and value of spontaneity proves to be an especially effective tool for pulling on the thread of religion's role in sensibility and fate in modernity. This study therefore examines the discourses of spontaneity across a variety of genres in the long eighteenth century with an ear toward their common discourses, evolving logics, and the shared questions to which they are responding. It takes up what Gordon calls the "difficulty of belief" and the "epistemological crisis" of determining moral value at the heart of the culture of sensibility, and seeks to understand its relationship to the adaptation and transformations of religious faith in modernity. A richly historical, rhetorical account and a critical examination of the dialectics of religion and secularism in the emergence of the culture of sensibility is in large part the contribution of this study.

While this rhetorical approach shares certain affinities with Michel Foucault's discursive genealogies of classical and modern *epistemes*, it is more closely related to Jean-François Lyotard's approach to genres of discourse in *The Differend*. Lyotard defines "phrase regimens" as the sets of rules by which different sorts of phrases—phrases of "reasoning, knowing, describing, recounting, questioning, showing, [and] ordering"—are constructed. "Phrases from heterogeneous regimens cannot be translated from one into the other," Lyotard claims, because their identity resides in part in the sort of phrase they are; in "translating" a describing phrase into a questioning phrase, for instance, the identity of the phrase as such would be lost. Various sorts of phrases are, however, "linked one onto the other *in accordance with an end* fixed by *a genre of discourse*."[42] A differend, according to Lyotard, is a conflict, wrong, or double bind that emerges between two parties because "a rule of judgment applicable to both arguments" is lacking: that is, because the parties articulate meaning according to genres of discourse with different ends.[43] When one end or a related set of ends is increasingly asserted as the most legitimate and eventually universal way phrases must be linked to make meaning, individuals either adopt the new ends outright or, forced to translate their experiences and understandings of meaning into the dominant discourse, encounter incommensurabilities between language and their experiences, making their values resemble madness or impossibility. Lyotard's contribution to the linguistic turn in Western philosophy is thus a keen reflective awareness of the ways that meanings and truths borne of particular ends and genres of discourse can become inarticulable and almost unthinkable once other heterogeneous discourses achieve prominence.[44]

This study employs this Lyotardian awareness of discourse—and particularly a sense of the often unforeseen consequences of articulating the meanings of experiences in specific rhetorics and genres—to historicize the rise of spontaneity and the decline of ritual in modernity. That is, its combined historical, rhetorical approach allows us to understand how spontaneity gained currency at a particular moment in seventeenth-century England and how it dialectically evolved across the long eighteenth century. Beginning with the eruptive new esteem for spontaneity in free prayer and its subsequent secular, moral, and aesthetic incarnations, this project demonstrates the shared logic of spontaneity in ostensibly religious and secular forms: that of trying to prove or know goodness as knowledge or possession of fact, at a time when epistemological and economic discourses were inching closer together and increasingly overlapping. As the work of Mullan, Skinner, Ellis, Ellison, and others on sensibility suggests, the quasi-religious, moral discourse of spontaneity is at once enmeshed in and resisting empirical and economic ways of thinking, simultaneously plagued by the amorality of Hobbesian appetite and of the marketplace and anxious for a certainty about goodness—about real "moral value"—that would stand in opposition to it on its own terms of scientific proof, economic quantification, and legitimate possession.

Yet this new way of thinking about the real substance and value of goodness, particularly in its overtly religious manifestations, was also plagued by an abiding sense of uncertainty and by profound resistances within individuals to imagining all human relation in these terms. Experiences of religious faith, prayer, love for neighbor, and responsibility for shaping the self, as well as the traditions that had articulated their meaning, were profoundly compromised by the empirical and economic discourses in which they were increasingly articulated during the seventeenth and eighteenth centuries. Discourses that could speak of the value of uncertainty and of belief as opposed to certainty, of the repetitive shaping of the self rather than a deterministic operation according to natural tendency, and of personal interaction with a God not operating according to predetermined, fixed laws—these were in a very real sense swallowed up by Western modernity's esteem for propositional truth, practical results, and efficiency, and the languages in which these were valued.[45] My argument concerning these emerging modern moral discourses therefore finds parallels in recent subaltern studies that are bringing to critical awareness precisely such pressures to translate and mute the religious in modernity: "For the purpose of writing history," writes Dipesh Chakrabarty, "the first system, the secular, translates the second [the religious] into itself," when, as subaltern studies is increasingly theorizing, according to another scholar, "the shape of life inside religious belief" is "unrepresentable in secular terms."[46] The rumblings of uncertainty—of the precarious position of knowledge and the unavoidability of belief—in both religious and secular eighteenth-century texts invested in the logic of spontaneity, foreshadow many current conversations revising our understanding of the religious, a discussion taken up in this book's conclusion.

In the texts examined in this study, manifestations of spontaneity from enthusiasm to sensibility appear not as secular developments outside religious concerns, but rather as outgrowths of an anxiously self-secularizing religion, of religious concerns articulated within rational discourses of science and consumer culture, ostensibly put to the service of virtue and reform, but nearly paralyzed by self-scrutiny borne of what Conrad Brunström has referred to as an ethos of emotional correctness rooted in a long religious "tradition of experiential reasoning" that "exemplifies rather than rejects the ideological climate" of its age.[47] Secularization appears here not as something that happens to religion from without but as an ongoing yet perpetually incomplete process that takes place first of all from within, a result of religious thinkers embracing forms of rationalization which are themselves simultaneously transcendentalizing and

22   Rituals of Spontaneity

secularizing, a point to which we will return. In the texts I analyze, what Motooka diagnoses as quixotic epistemological hyperactivity, on one hand, and on the other, the passivity associated with waiting for spontaneous emotional experiences and with the anxious paralysis bred by self-scrutiny, look less like what Gordon calls countertraditions and more like a painful paradox about agents and agency internal to the very notion and subjectivity of rational autonomy, to which both ostensibly secular and religious modern subjects are prey. Followed carefully, the story of spontaneity ultimately questions generally assumed distinctions between secular and religious subjects while highlighting their unnoticed differences, and ultimately suggests the startling question of whether the idea of a secular space devoid of uncertainty and therefore of the vulnerability of belief is not the constitutive (and gendered) fantasy both of Enlightenment, and of the modern forms of religion it generates.

Out of the story of spontaneity this study tells, then, comes a remapping of our understanding of sentiment and secularism alike that begins to unravel the puzzling persistence of religion—and of a particular sort of religion—in a modernity that by the best predictions of the secularization thesis should long ago have been done with it. The religious and quasi-secular enthusiasms continually reinvoked by Enlightenment rationality most often function as the vexed sites of attempts to quarantine—through quasi-scientific notions of spontaneous sentiment and emotional response, and through the familiar contours of sentimental narrative—the uncertainty that always lurks in the shadows of language and is a particular plague (ironically) to faith and morality as it strives to legitimate itself in an era of empiricism and early capitalist development. As J. G. A. Pocock has written in another context, "this analysis requires us to remain within the parameters of Enlightenment not completely secularized, not altogether detached from the religious matrix within which it had first taken shape"—and yet it also requires us to consider religion in Enlightenment as something already embedded in secularizing modes of thought.[48] It leads us beyond arguing for either the inherent religiousness or secularity of various enlightenments, toward complicating that binary altogether.[49]

Secularization Made Strange

The case for the centrality of religion to an emerging ideology and subjectivity of secularism in eighteenth-century Britain is likely as surprising to many scholars as the idea of free prayer's incipient secularism would have been to Bunyan or might be to an American evangelical today. Registering the full secularity of apparently religious phenomena such as free prayer as well as the intense, even libidinal connection of secular phenomena to religion is unmistakably difficult, for both conceptual and historical reasons. In the Restoration period a narrative about rational secularization took shape that has echoed through historical accounts to the present day, in which enthusiasm was anathematized as the irrational beast that, during the previous decades' wars of religion, threatened to usher in the apocalypse and which justified the decision after the Restoration to imprison the most dangerous enthusiasts (as was the case with Bunyan) or to forbid them to preach. Following this line of thinking, the Royal Society that Charles II chartered in 1662 tabled all theological debate and—by the account of Thomas Sprat, the Church of England divine recruited by the Society to defend it against charges of promoting atheism—sought to banish from the discourse of the New Science the "mists and uncertainties" of the passions and the luxurious tropes and figures that enflamed them.[50] Scientific authority, in other words, came into rhetorical being articulated against what it framed as a linguistically and logically suspect religion which it occasionally invoked but claimed not to harm or to impinge upon. For the great eighteenth-century historian Ernst Cassirer, the Enlightenment was at bottom "a value system rooted in rationality" rather than in religion or tradition.[51] Though it has since become a commonplace to speak of "families" of enlightenments, some more or less antireligious than others, it has remained customary to associate the cusp of modernity with a conscientious secularization begotten of principled rationalism that first asserted itself in response to seventeenth-century religious violence and enthusiasm.[52]

And yet, as many historians have also pointed out, the Reformation itself, particularly Puritanism and Dissent, had by this time already shown itself to be secularizing in its own right.[53] William Bouwsma's thick description of seventeenth-century secularization documents a gradual process of the separation of politics, economic life, and culture from religious-legal control that was well advanced in mainland Europe by 1600 and which flourished alongside both Protestantism and counter-Reformation Catholicism; even under Puritan rule in England in the 1640s and 1650s, the civic certification of birth, marriage, and death advanced this trajectory of separation.[54] Raymond Tumbleson has demonstrated the vital role that English anti-Catholicism played in "enabling the Enlightenment to erase the ideological legitimacy of the premodern social order," and the work of Knud Haakonssen and others underlines the secularizing and rationalizing tendencies of Dissent.[55] In other words, the rationalized "ideology of objectivity" that Robert Markley has shown to coalesce in the Restoration period had a long religious prehistory. Patrick Collinson affirms that a logocentric rationality and its method of binary opposition seems to have governed virtually all Puritan argument and was "by no means a Puritan peculiarity but rather part and parcel of early modern thought and discourse."[56]

Bouwsma has also rightly claimed that the differences between rationalist and empirical forms of systematization are less important than what rationalism and empiricism share in common, namely "the conviction than an intellectual construction can be something more than the product of a particular culture, and that it is possible for human beings to attain certain knowledge."[57] Both pre- and post-Cartesian rationalism had shared the impulse toward the systematic integration of all experience, and Bouwsma narrates the movement from medieval to early modern thought in terms of the unraveling of scholasticism's "bounding and distinguishing." The collapse of medieval boundaries resulted not in skepticism, however, but as Bouwsma points out, in an expanding reliance on quantitative, mathematical, and economic logic, together with an increasing urgency to systematize and to assert the objective existence of the new boundaries and distinctions in nature.[58] This systematization and division of knowledge, together with the synthesizing countermovement, would accelerate as the Enlightenment progressed. As Theodor Adorno and Max Horkheimer famously put it, "in advance, the Enlightenment recognizes as being and occurrence only what can be apprehended in unity: its ideal is the system from which all and everything follows."[59]

But in the abstraction and systematization into unity, truth was separated further and further from its grounds, and the bifurcation between the world of concrete, given things and the realm of abstract value and meaning ostensibly drawn from them grew wider and wider, in not only Renaissance but particularly Reformation thought. As Carlos Eire puts it, for Calvin "faith was reasonable, it had to make sense," and in Calvin's new, scripturally based metaphysics "the boundaries between the spiritual and the material were more clearly drawn than ever." Thomas Luxon similarly points to Calvin's primacy in maintaining an absolute separation between this world and the next, where (exclusively) Christ's glorified body resides: "no more miracles, no Eucharistic real presence, no ecstatic raptures."[60] The line between the given world and spiritual reality was not, it appears, first drawn by explicitly secularizing people, but by religious reformers working along what they saw as rational lines. Despite commonplace distinctions between Renaissance and Reformation thought, Graham Ward rightly claims that "the Puritan worldview that sought for the primitive is the same worldview wanting to discover the foundational, that which is most certain, and those laws generating that certainty."[61]

This rationalization of religion produced two major outcomes. On the one hand, scriptural literalism gave rise to an ever-proliferating fragmentation of sects and denominations within Protestantism. On the other, it generated what Ward calls "a new discourse about religion," first glimpsed in the work of one of Donne's closest acquaintances, Edward, Lord Herbert of Cherbury. In Herbert's early-seventeenth-century *De Veritate* and *De Religione Gentilium* could be heard the voice of what would become the modern philosophy of religion and the later sciences of religion. In this new mindset, according to Ward, "the right use of reason as outlined by a new theory of knowledge and exercised by each individual in conformity with what is most natural and instinctive in all human beings, would define the nature and essence of religion itself"; "a new relationship between faith and reason was under negotiation," by which truth would come to be seen primarily as "a moral principle applicable across all human cultures, histories and biographies."[62] Ward is matchless in his description of exactly how this later discourse of "true religion" ultimately takes up the logics of spontaneity and "self-authenticating experience" but leaves behind not just quarrelling sectarianism, but eventually the specificity of the Christian religion altogether:

> The true religion has no role for Christ to play other than moral teacher and *exemplum*. The significance of the life of Christ (incarnation, crucifixion, resurrection), the doctrines of the triune God and the sacraments of grace were only secondary truths, to be understood metaphorically as particular expressions of the underlying universals. . . . A cyclical logic is evident in which natural religion provides the condition for understanding revealed religion and vice versa. The conditions for assessing the conformity include recognizing "the breath of the Divine Spirit [which] must be immediately felt." In other words, final appeal is made to a spirituality, a pneumatology, whereby in inner sensations "we feel the Divine guidance." There are "intimate divine apprehensions," a "sense of succour," moments of "intense faith" when we "feel within us His saving power and a sense of marvellous deliverance." Final appeal rests upon subjective judgment of inward emotional states made in accordance with the five universal laws constituting religion. A certain pietism lies waiting in this emphasis upon self-authenticating experience; a "spirituality" is emerging that William James will catalogue in his famous Victorian tome *Varieties of Religious Experience*.[63]

More than a political process or part of scientific method, secularization was in a profound sense the result of a rationalizing process which, this book shows, was active in Puritanism, Dissent, and beyond, but which had been taking place at the heart of western Christianity at least since high Scholasticism and certainly long before the Restoration.[64]

Economies of Faith and the Secularization of Religion

We are still left to explain, though, how an abstracting rationality actually translated into concrete forms and practices of secularization. Economic development has long been understood as the crucial mediating force between Protestantism and secular rationalism, yielding a spectrum of theory and debate. For Marx, Protestantism had been the ideological superstructure that capitalism necessarily produced, custom-fit to supporting its needs.[65] In *The Protestant Ethic and the Spirit of Capitalism*, Max Weber famously reversed that notion, arguing that Puritan clerics defended certain behaviors like methodical labor as tangible outward evidence of one's spiritual status, which in turn facilitated the rationalization of economic behavior that is the basis of capitalism.[66] R. H. Tawney's *Religion and the Rise of Capitalism* later posited the classic compromise thesis, arguing for a more symbiotic and reciprocal relationship and mapping the center mark of the pendulum stroke through which subsequent work would tend to swing.[67]

What Weber, Tawney, and those generally arguing against economic determinism failed to explain, as much as did Marx himself, was how these colossal theological and practical changes were actually effected. David Zaret's *The Heavenly Contract: Ideology and Organization in Pre-Revolutionary Puritanism* is one of the most important and specific studies to step into that gap. Like Weber, Zaret resists economic determinism and upholds the importance of cultural factors in shaping religious behavior. But in his intensive survey of both the economic context of England 1500–1640 and the literature of covenant theology, he argues that early capitalist development provided the language and terminology in which covenant theology was argued and the experiences against which it measured up. Seventeenth-century England's "early capitalist development," according to Zaret, "created a highly differentiated rural economy organized around specialized regional and national markets," and "from 1500 to 1640, contractual transactions in pursuit of profit became a familiar feature of everyday economic life. . . . Notions of reason and reasonableness increasingly referred to a market rationality: what was reasonable in economic affairs was that which was mutually agreed to by contractors."[68] What Zaret identifies as the "emerging market economy" in this period thus cultivated the kind of contractarian worldview conventionally associated with the work of Hobbes, but it equally enabled Puritan theology to shift its teachings into its particularly English seventeenth-century form: "Puritan casuistry relied on lay knowledge of economic contracts in order to teach parishioners how to look for evidence of election. . . . This theology . . . showed that the pursuit of one's ultimate religious interest had the same dimensions of accumulation, exchange, and ownership as the pursuit of one's economic self-interest. Here Puritan theology relied on a very specific model of economic life, one governed by a market rationality."[69] One of the conclusions Zaret therefore reaches is that "the relation between Puritanism and economic life is far more reciprocal than Weber thought it was"; as Zaret points out, it was the widespread practice of laying earnest money that "channeled lay initiative in the direction of seeking evidences of election, and it provided strong encouragement for such activity."[70]

This study together with Zaret's work helps us understand precisely how the reciprocal influence of capitalism and Puritanism upon each other works: rhetoric—language and metaphor—provides the link from logic and practice in the realm of commerce, to logic and practice in devotion. When Karl Polanyi sought to locate the "Great Transformation" in the nineteenth century, he was half right; the demands of capital did tend to subordinate all other discourses to its own, but this rhetorical transformation had thoroughly remade Puritanism and Dissent in a manner that foretold the next three centuries of Protestant evolution as early as the Restoration.[71] We might say that "market rationality" is a redundancy, that is, that the same intellectual motion of continual abstraction is at work in both market practices and the rationalizing theology that made such ready use of economic figures. But crucially, it was the actual adoption of particular economic ways of thinking and behaving that brought people to think of ritual as boring and out-of-date and to speak of the "interest of words in prayer" or of free prayer as the "true token of a truly godly man." This combined economic-epistemological way of thinking that generated the fetishization of spontaneity as a marker of spiritual value and repeatable evidence of grace simultaneously allowed the discarding of liturgy (and of other traditional elements of Christian thought and practice as well) and the embrace of new spiritualities to take place. The lesson of covenant theology and free prayer is not simply that changing the form of a religion changes its content, but that when the forms change, the motivating factor is almost certainly a deep shift in thinking that has already taken place—in this case, through the reimagining and rearticulating of the faith in economic, abstract, rational terms—which changes the content and form by changing the terms in which it is valued.

But the discourse and practice of free prayer, like other spontaneities across the long eighteenth century, also confess the fears and anxieties of having adopted economic, empirical logics. The discontents and hegemonic tendencies of economic discourse have also been the object of some of the last quarter-century's most far-reaching philosophical and cultural analysis. Kurt Heinzelman's *The Economics of the Imagination* has charted the problematic economic metaphors that inform daily speech, social fictions, and literature alike.[72] More genealogically, in his sweeping *Money, Language, and Thought: Literary and Philosophical Economies from the Medieval to the Modern Era*, Marc Shell has powerfully demonstrated that through the very structure of metaphors, literary and philosophical discourses about truth participate in what he calls a "formal money of the mind" or economic form of thought.[73] As far back as the grail legends of the thirteenth century and the shift from economic realism to economic nominalism, Shell identifies money in literary treatments as a "floating signifier" of a hope for universal truth through abstraction or "for a kind of disembodied Word or blank check" and the totality and control that would represent. Yet he also notices that the internalization of economic modes of thought invariably gives rise to "discomforting, but motivating" stings and resistances,[74] much as we see in the life of Bunyan, Shaftesbury, and Smart.

Lyotard shares with Shell this concern for analyzing linkages, whether monetary or linguistic, as contingencies for which speakers are responsible, rather than the inevitabilities as which they often masquerade. It is precisely the interconnection of epistemological and economic genres of discourse and ways of thinking—and their power to dress up their contingency as necessity, the sum of beliefs and volitional linkings as knowledge—that is the focus of his critique in *The Differend*. Lyotard claims that his book and its call for attention to differends is nothing short of an effort to redefine real thought (or "reflection" and "philosophy") as something other than the two adversaries that assail it: "the genre of economic discourse (exchange, capital)" and "the genre of academic discourse (mastery)."[75] *The Differend* as a whole can be seen as the effort to show how these two discourses (economics and knowledge-mastery) are interrelated, and to what effect. For Lyotard, there are realities in experience that are incommensurable with ways of thinking about the world that emphasize efficiency and control and that disallow the time necessary for reflection. The problem with economic discourse in particular, he contends, is the ease with which its imperative for efficiency is coopted in the service of political hegemony. Economic calculation and the "finality of the economic genre ... seem fatal" to philosophy, because "reflection requires that you watch out for occurrences, that you don't already know what's happening. It leaves open the question: *Is it happening?*"[76] Like Deleuze's critique, in *Difference and Repetition*, of patterns of thought and commercial life that condition us to ignore difference and to reduce experiences and others into interchangeable units and "repetition of the same," and like Derrida's critique in "Force of Law" of the injustices wrought by thinking that an abstract rule can supply justice in all cases, the focus of Lyotard's critique is on the wrongs inflicted in real, individual lives by reductive, abstracting turns of thought, however practical and efficient they seem, and the thoughts and ways of being in the world which they render difficult or impossible.[77] It is a primary contention of this study that the very economic and epistemological discourses that so concern Lyotard by virtue of their hegemonic and reductive capability, also make religious experience as such—that is, as distinct from commodified ways of desiring and from rational and empirical models of knowing—harder and harder to articulate in its own terms of relation to God and others (and in Christianity, within the Trinity itself) in faith and in love.

To "understand and to change the tyranny of our world," Shell claims in another place, we must analyze the tokens and behaviors that like money serve as "ideological links between thought and matter" and denaturalize them.[78] The fetishized spontaneous experiences of the Restoration and eighteenth century—spontaneous prayer, benevolent feelings of philanthropy, the emotional response to novels, the inspired compositions of poems, and, inseparable from most of these, the spontaneous giving of money either in donation or purchase—are just such ideological links, constructing relations to people and things in terms of exchange and possession, immediate perception, and objective certainty. This study seeks to make these familiar tropes strange, and to show the logic by which they come to seem natural and inevitably desirable. It also seeks, in Shell's words, to challenge the tyranny of these notions. For I do contend that they come with their own tyrannies, today as they did in the long eighteenth century for the figures in this study: the tyrannies of feeling powerless before emotions one seems unable to change, of continually expecting fresh feelings and novelty from external stimuli, from commodities, and from the people and the quotidian life that surround us and that are diminished by constant scrutiny in these lights. As Ward points out in "The Commodification of Religion, or The Consummation of Capitalism," what is needed, though, is not an escape from economics, but from the particular forms of the circulation of commodities and the reification of persons that capitalism produces. "Capitalism does not have the monopoly on economics, on *oikonomeo*," he writes with a theological cast, "and in that lie all our hopes for cultural transformation."[79]

Spontaneous, Secular Subjects

At its furthest reaches, this study points to spontaneity and secularism as central components not just of modernist ideologies of objectivity and exchange, but of the subjectivities they imply, in ways resonant with Slavoj Žižek's dialectical fusion of Althusserian, post-Marxist ideology critique with Lacanian psychoanalysis. Like Hegel, Žižek sees man as an "animal sick unto death," extorted by the "insatiable parasite" of language and logocentric reason.[80] The self as subject, as a function of language, is sick unto death, because it has by definition always already fallen into believing the temptation of language, that a totalizing system in the symbolic order or an objective, complete account of reality by which all experience can be known, understood, and controlled, is possible. Or, in language we might provocatively borrow from the Genesis account, this is a self that has eaten the forbidden fruit of the "tree of the knowledge of good and evil," which promises a godlike total knowledge, but which instead brings death. In Žižek's terms, the subject is therefore also perpetually plagued by a fundamental antagonism, that is, the "real-impossible kernel" of experience that eludes containment in the symbolic order. More simply, this impossible kernel is that in experience which seems to resist the totalizing, neat system, forever shadowing language and unsettling our attempts at final, abstract meaning.

Žižek's real contribution, through this melding, is to explain what eludes Althusser: that is, to show, via Lacan, how the subject is interpolated by, lured into, or subjected to an ideology and its ways of desiring, in spite of all manner of thoroughgoing ideology critique. The answer for Žižek is that what we come to desire in entering a particular ideology—its notion of totality and its particular pleasures, be they those of various sexualities or of visions of political or religious utopias—is really the allure of the position that system holds open for the self as subject; the fantasy of the subject is itself the "sublime object of ideology."[81] In the ideologies we have come to critique as peculiarly rational and modern, that sublime, imaginary, symbolic space is for an image of the self as a whole, self-contained master. Or, again to borrow the language of the biblical account, the serpent of ideology always speaks with the same forked tongue, hissing the diabolical promise that "you shall be like God" and "you shall not surely die."[82] Calculation and abstract reason promise mastery, we might say, and deliver subjectivity: subjection to the letter and the law, and to the endless antagonisms of gendered hierarchies (the curse of Genesis: "your desire shall be for your husband, and he shall rule over you")—death, not life.[83] In this psychoanalytic reading of ideology, the full radicality of Jesus' pronouncement makes sense, "you cannot serve both God and money."[84] Rather than the marker of all value, money stands as the supremely tempting fruit: the allure of symbolic systems of good and evil and the godlike place for the subject they entail. It is this calculating reason, propelled toward self-deification and the seductive glitter of money, that replaces the contingent fragility and faith of living relation, of walking with God and the other in the cool of the day: that casts the subject out of the relational paradise that is Eden in the Genesis account.

It is in precisely the sense of the lure "you shall be like God" that the modern subject is both adamantly secular and yet never quite willing to leave behind the god or the religion it defines itself as supplanting. As Hervieu-Léger puts it, though "modernity has deconstructed the traditional systems of believing," it "has not forsaken belief," however much it dresses that belief up as necessity and knowledge.[85] The ideology of all meaning as abstract, rational knowledge, so intimately connected to an ideology of value as money and spontaneous emotion as moral evidence, seduces by virtue of the space it creates for the subject as knower *without belief*, of a certainty without the vulnerability of faith and interrelation that is the very substance of religion.[86] In analyzing transcultural relations such as the British outlawing of religious self-torture in India, Asad demonstrates that what is at stake in secularism is not simply a matter of eliminating particular cruelties, but of "imposing an entire secular discourse of 'being human,'" central to which are its ideas about individualism and "detachment from passionate belief." To this way of thinking, objectivity is akin to skepticism, for "only the skeptical individual—always suspicious of his or her own beliefs as well as of others—can be truly free of fanatical convictions."[87] In Ward's related terms, by the twentieth century "secularity as such came to be associated with 'impartiality'; as not itself an ideology but the unbiased judge of all ideologies."[88] The place through and into which the ideology of secularism interpolates subjects, then, is a fantasy position of mastery and skeptical certainty, free of belief and therefore capable of discerning the error of all other beliefs. This is why, again, as Asad puts it, "the concept of the secular cannot do without the idea of religion"; secularism must continually reinvoke the religion whose disavowal constitutes it.[89]

In *Towards a New Christianity?* Hervieu-Léger has provocatively suggested that "the process of secularization is above all a [modern] process of *reconstructing* belief."[90] My study suggests that the reconstruction of belief in modernity takes place primarily through the disguising of belief—and its productive mechanisms and rituals—as knowledge, common sense, and spontaneous desires, through masked rituals of spontaneity, and by the appeal it thereby extends to the subject conceived of as knower and master. The appeal of this position for the subject, which I am describing as essentially secularizing, is, I emphasize, something to which religious thinkers have clearly not been immune; in fact, religious thinkers seem the first to succumb to it. But its trajectory is secularizing nonetheless: it moves meaning into ever more abstract realms, even as it defends its truths as experientially validated and economically logical. "Enlightenment secularism," as Caputo has so aptly put it, is perhaps best defined as "the objectivist reduction of religion to something other than itself."[91] In ever more isolated, anxious, and potentially violent modes of being, it positions the subject as understanding its worth in terms of knowledge and of immunity to the potential error and vulnerability of belief. This is precisely the spot where we can understand how, as a new wave of scholarship is arguing, such fundamentalism is not a primitivism but rather a product of modernity, of a modernity that, to constitute its self and selves, must constantly disavow its uncertainties and faiths. Absent the admission of uncertainty and of responsibility for belief, Caputo prophesies, "God and death-dealing, religion and violence, will never be far apart."[92] But Caputo also enables us to understand how secularism—an ideology of a world of facts, without belief and construction—is itself the ultimate fundamentalism. "At the core of fundamentalism," Caputo maintains, "there lies a repressed fear that faith is only faith and as such a risk with no guarantee of anything, which is the truth about religion"—and, we should expand, about human existence in language—"to which it testifies in the mode of repressing it."[93] The extent to which this repressed fear manifests itself in literary and cultural studies is an issue I take up in the conclusion.

Religion in modernity, in Derrida's terms as well, is most often profoundly informed by such systematization, even as it seems to resist rationalistic tendencies toward abstraction, legalistic formalization, and schematization. In "Faith and Knowledge: Two Sources of Religion at the Limits of Reason Alone," Derrida distinguishes between faith and religion, the later being aligned with a Kantian "reflecting faith" that is formed in relation to reason and the law, and like the secularism that continually reinvokes the religion it disavows, is "bound" to reason and the law by its own counterclaims to certainty, that is, "by the band of their opposition."[94] This secular reason and religion are also, I would argue, connected by the logics of their symptoms, the specter of continually disavowed uncertainties that haunt both their subjectivities. In *True Religion*, Graham Ward provides an astute reading of the emerging secularized, economized religious subject, given its perhaps quintessential voice in Daniel Defoe's *Robinson Crusoe*. In words that are as true when applied to *The Pilgrim's Progress* and Shaftesbury's journals, Ward writes that in *Robinson Crusoe* we glimpse the meeting of Herbert's *homo religiosis* with the implications of *homo economicus*, trying to become fit to be *homo politicus*, but throughout, "the center of concern is the I, the me, the myself" that fills the sentences and pages of the novel.[95] Everything ostensibly serves this self—everything except time and the natural elements, which are indifferent to it, and "it is the *insecurity* of the new modern subject that gives rise to narration itself." The early novel "is founded upon insecurity," Ward writes, and this is why Robinson's calm years are unnarratable. The writing of accounts in Defoe's novel is "an attempt to remain in control, to understand how the finest of details is part of the whole design," and the mastery of one's surroundings and adversities is needed "to express a fundamental self-mastery, an internalized disciplining."[96] From the blank pages for prayer-phrases in Matthew Henry's *A Method for Prayer*, to Bunyan's autobiography, to Shaftesbury's journals, and to an endless stream of sentimental novels, the literature of spontaneity is in large part this sort of accounting, the attempt to make the subject add up. Crusoe's conversion of Friday and his willingness to kill unrepentant savages and criminals are also part of this frantic accounting. Proselytism, religious or secular, takes a libidinal, violent edge in (early) modernity, we might say, as its stakes increasingly include providing evidence, in the form of converts, of the objective, irrefutable truth of the one "true religion," which looks maddeningly less and less possible.

In the face of such ongoing metamorphoses of religion in modernity and the currently rising tide of fundamentalism worldwide, what is called for, Hervieu-Léger argues, is scholarship that stops assuming religion's unilateral decline or advance and that documents the contours of this transformation, that unravels the "cultural and symbolic rationale that lies at the heart" of what she calls the peculiar "religious products of modernity."[97] That is the sort of unraveling the following chapters enact. The first two chapters trace the rationale at the heart of the spirituality and worship of Western Christian modernity, and the third traces the strangely religious contours of the full-blown secularism that will seek to replace religion with an objective "morality." The marvel of this rationale and the religious and secular fundamentalisms it produces is the way that it generates a religion without faith, an ideology disavowing faith and claiming proof and certainty, and yet whose truths are haunted by the specter of belief and the violent irruptions of their epistemological and libidinal disappointments. These are ideologies which cannot seem to begin to articulate the value of faith as faith, of what I have elsewhere called "the benefit of doubt." From the outset of this study, I have also been profoundly interested in ways of thinking, speaking, and living that would attempt to break out of the death-grip of subjectivization and fetish desire. The latter part of chapter 4 and the final chapter examine two such attempts and their various failures and successes. The imaginative rethinking of a religiousness—and a scholarly criticism—that would own up to their faith as faith is also a task I take up in the conclusion.

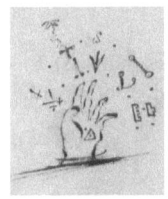

CHAPTER I

The Rejection of Liturgy, the Rise of Free Prayer, and Modern Religious Subjectivity

Q: *Why do not the Presbyterians say the Creed and the Doxology?*
A: Because they are not, Word by Word, in Scripture.
Q: *Why do they not say the Lord's Prayer?*
A: Because it is, Word by Word, in Scripture....
Q: *Wherefore do not the Presbyterians sing Glory to God on high?*
A: Because that was a Song of Angels, made upon *Yool-Day*, and they are not for *Christmas* Carrols....
Q: *Have the Presbyterians any Set Forms at all?*
A: Yes, they have a Form of Godliness, but deny the power thereof.
Q: *What is the sad Effect of the Want of a Form in a Church?*
A: It is just as it was said of the Earth, *Gen.* i. *The Earth was without form, and void, and Darkness was upon the Face of the Deep.*

—From *A Short Catechism, for the Instruction of Young and Old*, By R. C. Philo-Presbyt., Glasgow 1720

When Sir Thomas Holcraft ... went [to his Curate] when his house was on fire, desiring him to pray, the Curate betook himself with much hast [sic] to his Service-book, and finding out the prayer for *Rain in time of require*, prayed according to the form thereof, That God would send *such moderate showers*, &c. Moderate showers Sir *Humnet* ... said the Knight, that will do no good, it is a great fire, a very great fire: howsoever he had none other [than] holy water to quench it: Thus he exposed two things (besides himself) to derision (which should be entertained with gravity and reverence) *Calamity* and *Devotion*.

—John Ley, *A Debate Concerning the English Liturgy* (1656)

Early Modern Backgrounds of Spontaneity—The Crisis of Representation and the Critique of Ritual

When the earliest rumbles of the Reformation sounded among Wycliffites, Lollards, and Hussites in fourteenth- and fifteenth-century England and Bohemia, Christianity in both the East and West had been a liturgical religion for nearly a millennium and a half. A rich practice and literature of worship had blossomed from Sarum to Kiev with no hint of the coming critique of ritual and the ethos of spontaneity that would remake Christian worship entirely. The English church year in particular was characterized by the stunning half year from December to Midsummer's Day. The twelve days of Christmas, with their holly and ivy, wassailing and caroling, were followed by Plough Sunday in early January. Soon after, Candlemas, the feast of the Purification of the Virgin on February 2, marked the formal end of winter. Shrovetide, the Sunday through Tuesday before Ash Wednesday, led into Lent and looked toward Holy Week; beginning with Palm Sunday, it included traditional practices like "creeping to the cross" on Good Friday and lighting candles at a symbolic sepulcher in the church. The week culminated with the celebration of Christ's resurrection on Easter Sunday, from the singing of "Christ is risen" at a predawn liturgy to the coloring of eggs and spring cleaning. A week later, Hocktide brought playful role reversals between the sexes; St. George's Day was celebrated April 23, and May Day ushered in summer with games and Robin Hood plays. The sober Rogation processions preceding Ascension were followed shortly by Pentecost and its lively Whitsunales. After Corpus Christi and Midsummer's Day, the festal calendar slowed as agricultural work increased. Lammas, or Loaf Mass, August 1, marked the beginning of harvest, with the busy autumn season of fairs punctuated mainly by Michaelmas (September 29), by All Saints and All Souls Day (November 1), and by St. Nicholas Day (December 6). As Ronald Hutton describes it in *The Rise and Fall of Merry England: The Ritual Year 1400–1700*, this rich ritual cycle continued and expanded right up to the cusp of the Reformation: "up till 1530 the English calendar of celebrations, like the religion to which so many of them were attached, was still flourishing and expanding rapidly along traditional lines. There was no sign of the changes which were soon to transform both almost out of recognition."[1]

The dramatic decline of the ritual year and of ritual practice in worship which followed resulted not only from Protestant critiques of Catholicism but from deeper cultural shifts in which both early modern Catholicism and Protestantism participated. Reformation controversies of the sixteenth and seventeenth centuries accompanied what has been called a crisis of representation, in which the term *ceremony*, for instance, first began to acquire negative connotations of hollowness and superstition, and in which interrogations of the power of signs, "in particular the communal, repetitive, formal, performative sign," led Reformers to develop an "anti-magical semiotics" defined against a "mystified, sacral, essentialist" understanding of signs.[2] In this Erasmus and Calvin led the way, and it is apparently to Calvin that we owe our abiding association of "superstition" with any form of ritualized behavior.[3] In *Literal Figures: Puritan Allegory and the Reformation Crisis in Representation*, Thomas Luxon describes how early Protestants repeatedly promised to liberate the Christian faith not just from superstitious rituals but from what they worried were "the riddling allegories and equivocating tropes of 'Papist' scholastic theology and hermeneutics"; English Puritans in particular sought to shore up religious meaning by grounding it solely in the Bible and in a literalist approach to its interpretation.[4]

In this literalist approach, ritual acts such as baptism were no longer trusted as working or signifying salvation; rather, to be saved, one must believe—in propositional, clear, biblical language—in God's sole and definitive action in salvation, at most looking for evidence that this has taken place. In sixteenth- and seventeenth-century Calvinism, this evidence most frequently took the form of conversion: an experience of overwhelming worthlessness or infinite debt before God, cured by a sense of relief so strong that it could have come only from outside one's soul.[5] Configuring salvation in these terms, the Reformation religious subject gradually became less a participant in communal, bodily ritual action, and more and more the Cartesian *cogito*, an individual, inward-looking possessor of knowledge drawn from evidence and analysis. If the "Cartesian moment" is that moment when as Francis Barker has asserted the self can be conceived of without the body, it is also the moment when it can be conceived of without ritual; by what might be called a Cartesian logic, the later English Reformation places efficacious signs of salvation elsewhere than church ritual, first in a literalist reading of Scripture, and ultimately in the individual conviction of the particular truths of Scripture and in the self who experiences it.[6] It is not overstating the case to say, as Patrick Collinson has, that "England's wars of religion began, in a sense, with a maypole";[7] between dancing around a maypole and forbidding it lies a gulf of difference in conceptions of community, knowledge, salvation, and the self.

In an increasingly rationalistic, experiential response to this crisis of representation, from the late-sixteenth century onward the more radical English Reformers, first derided as "Puritans" and "precisians" in the mid 1560s, made ritual and, to some extent, liturgy, the target of their reform.[8] After the late fifteenth century, ritual change had come steadily with each accession to the throne. The earlier acts of the Henrican Reformation of 1529–1537 left the ritual year largely intact, but in 1538 royal decrees began to alter local worship significantly, installing Bibles, simplifying vestments, and snuffing most church candles. Such liturgical props reemerged quickly after Henry's death in 1547, however, suggesting to some historians that the "overwhelming majority of the English did not expect, and probably did not want, the reformation which was about to occur."[9] Nevertheless, Edward VI proceeded with an even more radical reinvention of English worship: 1549 saw both the first English Book of Common Prayer and the first Act of Uniformity, which virtually demolished seasonal ritual and forbade the use of medieval service books. The accession of Mary Tudor in 1553, however, brought another enthusiastic if ultimately brief renewal of ritual. Following these fitful changes, her sister and successor Elizabeth then attempted to steer a firm middle course between tradition and reform with the revisions she allowed in the 1559 Prayer Book. And yet, the changes were austere, both colossal and extreme, in the larger context of Christian history. Her Royal Injunctions for the "suppression of superstition," Calvin's bugbear, ordered the clergy to "take away, utterly extinct and destroy all shrines, covering of shrines, all tables, candlesticks, trindals, and rolls of wax, pictures, paintings, and all other monuments of feigned miracles, pilgrimages, idolatry and superstition, so that there remain no memory of the same in walls, glasses, windows, or elsewhere within their churches and houses," and to "exhort all their parishioners to do the like within their several houses."[10] Under political injunctions and the pressures of the crisis of religious meaning that underlay these changes, by 1570, "no parish" in England "admitted to preserving an altar, image, or rood loft," and the transformation of English churches from settings for ritual into preaching houses was virtually complete; "the old religious year had gone for ever."[11]

But the concern to purify religious truth from superstition had an insatiable quality about it, and the revision of English worship had far from come to an end. Long held off by Hooker's *Of the Laws of Ecclesiastical Polity*, seventeenth-century Puritans continually criticized specific ritual practices and, increasingly, liturgical content which they found unscriptural. The celebration of saints' days and festivals, vestments, the imposition of prewritten homilies, the "vain repetitions" of the prayers and collects, as well as "superstitious" gestures and doctrinally suspect language in the ceremonies for baptism, for the Lord's

Supper, for confirmation, ordination, marriage, burial, and the churching of women, all eventually came under attack. Zeal to expunge every trace of Romish superstition resulted in text scrutinizing and "arguments from silence" that forbade traditions such as the exchange of wedding rings and kneeling at Communion, traditions which were not addressed in Scripture and which other Reformers considered *adiaphora* or "matters indifferent." In the vigor with which they rejected ritual, turned to an "anti-magical" semiotics, and revised the liturgy, English Puritans have been said to have "out-Calvined Calvin," becoming a sort of law unto themselves in the world of reformed religion.[12] In 1644 accelerating Puritan ritual and liturgical reform achieved what would be its greatest success; the Puritan-controlled Parliament repealed use of the Common Prayer and issued its own guide for corporate devotion, *A Directory for the Publique Worship of God*. The *Directory* enacted nearly all of the desired Puritan reformations of worship and curtailments of ritual and, importantly, it was felt, provided orthodox guidelines within which ministers could safely exercise their "gifts" for preaching and spontaneous prayer. In June 1647, Parliament pressed even further: it abolished the feasts of Christmas, of Easter, and of Whitsun (Pentecost), going so far as to forbid churches to open on Christmas Day and to discourage the observance of Lent. What Christopher Durston has described as the "frontal assault on the seasonal festivals that had traditionally marked the turning year, the transformation of the rites associated with the important stages in the lifecycle, and the sweeping measures to clamp down on popular leisure pursuits and moral laxity," when taken together, constituted "nothing less than an attempt to bring about wholesale cultural revolution."[13] This revolution ultimately failed, according to Durston, due to lack of support and an eventual crescendo of open scorn, and the Restoration "merely delivered the *coup de grâce* to a generally discredited experiment." Even the formidable Puritan leaders of Dorchester had in the end been defeated by tenacious traditions and the chorus of mocking laughter from the town's "ungodly" inhabitants.[14]

And yet, the Restoration did not restore the Church of England to its pre-Civil War condition.[15] When the crown, the episcopacy, and the Prayer Book were put back in place, when rings were again allowed in marriage and godparents at baptism, it was spontaneous prayer that lingered and became an even greater sticking point between English Protestants than it had previously been. For most of the seventeenth century, only a handful of extreme Separatists criticized liturgical prayer per se; the mainline Puritan stance had amounted to a revision of the script, so to speak, but not an effort to throw it out altogether.[16] The 1661 Act of Uniformity, however, made complete conformity to the Book of Common Prayer a test for church membership, effectively purging Nonconformists and 2,000 Nonconforming ministers from the church and from holding office. Horton Davies has argued that this "Great Ejection" galvanized Puritans and Separatists against the Prayer Book, and that this historical coincidence accounts for free prayer emerging as the dominant Dissenting position.[17] But the polarizing effect of the Act of Uniformity does not explain the emergence of free prayer as a distinctly English Protestant phenomenon, nor would it seem to speak to the appeal of spontaneous prayer that grew more compelling not only in Restoration Dissent but in eighteenth-century Methodism, not to mention in a host of low-church denominations in the intervening three centuries.[18] As late as the year of the ejection, the eminent Puritan Richard Baxter was trying to hammer out a compromise ritual in the form of his Savoy Liturgy, showing that not all Puritans were at this point entirely averse to what some derided as "stinted forms."[19] Given the longstanding Puritan amenity to some degree of liturgy and the enormous political pressures toward conformity, the consolidation of free prayer as Dissenting dogma between 1660–1700 and the slow but certain trajectory by which spontaneous prayer in public worship became more popular and accepted should puzzle us more than perhaps it does. The most dramatic sea change in 2,000 years of Christian worship and practice remains to be accounted for.[20]

The merits of spontaneous prayer over liturgy had been asserted in print early in the seventeenth century, but after the Act of Uniformity, a new pamphlet and sermon war erupted that lasted well into the eighteenth century, and which provides us with a host of primary texts testifying to the discourses and rationales in which the case for spontaneous prayer came to be so persuasive.[21] The epigraphs for this chapter, written at opposite ends of the period it examines, are drawn from this controversy and speak both to the popular level of the debate and to the deep homologies of free prayer with the driving forces of a Restoration culture often embarrassed of it, but in which it ultimately flourished.[22] Like secular critics of enthusiasm, supporters of the Common Prayer like "R. C. Philo-Presbyt." poked fun at the contradictory literalism and devotional oddities by which Dissenters avoided liturgy at all costs. And yet, beneath the laughter evoked by Sir Thomas and his curate flows a serious undercurrent palpable in most free-prayer literature: the sense of real danger on some deep cultural level, to which the curate's traditional church and holy water seem to have no response.

Sir Thomas's fire makes a fit emblem for the profound unease that I argue fuels free prayer, that borne of the intensifying epistemological pressures of the Renaissance and Reformation crises of representation. In this chapter, I contend that in free prayer we see the fruit of these epistemological pressures and of their increasingly frequent articulation within an economic rationality which became only more pervasive in the mid-seventeenth century and in the years following the Restoration. Late-seventeenth- and early-eighteenth-century England experienced the burgeoning of the New Science as well as of the economy, both the first epoch of mercantile capitalism and the emergence of a consumer society, commercialization, and a recognizably modern political economy, developments which made quantificational logic indispensable.[23] These changes represented not so much a break from the Renaissance and Reformation culture of sixteenth- and seventeenth-century England as they did the fruits of the monumental shifts of thought that took place during that time.[24] And as discourses of scientific evidence, of empirical proof and economic abstraction, and of quantification and exchange were disseminated in early modern culture, religious behaviors and concerns were increasingly subject to articulation in their terms. In the sixteenth-century morality play *Everyman*, the hero has his "counting-book" of "reckoning" with him, but as many scholars have noted, its "knowledge" is far from our notion of accumulated data analytically processed, and something more like "acknowledgement"; it is an account book only in a highly allegorical sense, registering the results of sin and the sacraments along the lines of late medieval understandings.[25] But as David Zaret has shown in compelling detail, in response to epistemological pressures and lay anxiety, seventeenth-century Puritan covenant theology came to focus almost exclusively on notions of spiritual "earnests" and the "heavenly contract" that resonated with what had by that time become familiar features of everyday English economic life.[26]

It is in this increasingly commercial, simultaneously rationalistic and empirical context of late-seventeenth-century English culture, I argue, that the logic of spontaneous prayer made sense, and in which we can account for the increasing salience of the logic of spontaneity in both religious and secular spheres in the periods of rationalization and industrialization that followed. As William Bouwsma pointed out, the late medieval and early Renaissance crises of representation did not stall out at their skepticism of the old systems but rather progressed to an even more urgent defense of objective boundaries and quantifiable truths.[27] In "The Secularization of Language in the Seventeenth Century," Margreta de Grazia has shown how this pursuit of certainty led to a skepticism about language itself that dissociated words from God and deverbalized God's message, prompting thinkers from Thomas Sprat of the Royal Society to Hobbes, Robert Hooke, Galileo, and Newton to seek certainty in mathematical knowledge; quantifiable, identifiable substances; and trial, experiment, and experience.[28] As Puritan propagandist Vavasor Powell put it in the middle of the seventeenth century, "*Experience* is like steel to an edged tool, or like salt to fresh meat, it seasons brain-knowledge, and settles a shaking unsetled soule."[29] Paralleling more secular quests for certainty, the Puritan quest for grounding religious knowledge in a literalist reading of Scripture focused ever more intensely on manifest, genuine *experience* confirming salvation and the personal application of scriptural truth. The spontaneous "pouring out of the heart" in prayer was just such an evidentiary experience.

Against the backdrop of Renaissance and Reformation crises of representation and scriptural debates about ritual surrounding the imposition of the Common Prayer, this chapter shows how the language of late-seventeenth-century English free-prayer tracts continually and anxiously appeals to intensifying demands for evidence, exchangeability, and emotional experience to determine the validity of prayer and of the heart that prays. Defenses of free prayer dramatize the process by which rationalistic, empirical, and economic modes of reasoning—what we may call a secular rationality—produce the rationale of spontaneity and free prayer when they are mapped onto the traditionally religious concerns of goodness and salvation and come to bear on a distinctly modern religious subject. When the matter at hand is eternal salvation or damnation, the "unsettled soul" suspicious of ritual and tradition looks for evidence of her spiritual condition as close to the knowing self as possible, not in the objective mathematical language to which the Royal Society aspired but in objective experiences of spontaneous, passionate speech: in the substance of the inmost, most immediate thoughts and feelings, evinced by spontaneous, fervent prayer, which it takes both scientifically and economically as proofs and tokens of grace. If the Restoration witnessed the rise of what Robert Markley has called the ideology of objectivity, it also saw the coalescence of a related ideology of spontaneity. Concerned with the science of the soul and informed by emerging market and commercial logic, the cardinal points of this ideology were authentic and immediate sincerity (as opposed to performance or artifice), pure desire (as opposed to coldness, hypocrisy or a bifurcation between doctrinal knowledge and feeling), freedom (as opposed to form), and novelty and currency (as opposed to the repetitive, the boring, and the out-of-date). In the consolidation of the discourse and practice of free prayer, we see the culmination of Renaissance crises of representation and the fruition of the dramatic Reformation attacks on ritual, when under increasing pressures toward certainty and ever more entrenched economic logics, spontaneity becomes policy: not an option, but, for growing numbers of Protestants, paradoxically an obligation and the *sine qua non* of valid prayer and a saved subjectivity.

"Evidence of the Spirit"—Emotional Proof, Rational Knowledge, Spiritual Worth[30]

In his 1656 tract *A Debate concerning the English Liturgy*, Puritan divine and propagandist John Ley related a story that became archetypical in free-prayer literature, of a "well known Doctor of Divinity" who professed that he "had heard a layman in a leathern jacket pray by heart, without art or book, and with such an evidence and demonstration of the Spirit, as hath made him much ashamed of his own defects and disabilities to perform that duty of devotion in such a manner and measure as he had done."[31] In Ley's tract as in a variety of pamphlets published before and after the Restoration, free prayer constitutes above all an emotionally compelling "evidence and demonstration of the Spirit" and of grace; its emotional, verbal spontaneity both presumes and mediates an ontology of spiritual reality observable through prayer. The Puritan *Directory* had similarly expressed the importance of sincere, visible emotion, providing explicit directions for the manner in which the minister was to pray: "All [of these services] he is to endeavour to performe," it instructed, "with suitable affections answerable to such an holy Action, and to stir up the like in the people."[32] Again and again, free-prayer tracts inveigh against liturgical prayer as emotionally "cold" or "lukewarm," mere "lip-labor" born of "custom and formality." Even more than doctrinal correctness—contend these pamphlets—the element of true prayer lacking in those who use forms is emotional authenticity and sincerity, to which spontaneous, unwritten, and unpremeditated verbal prayer testifies and to which the formulaic repetition of liturgy is inimical.[33] *The Anatomie of the Common Prayer-Book*, published in 1641 and popularly reprinted in 1660 as *The Common Prayer-Book Unmasked*, calls the Prayer Book "a very transplantation of the Essence or nature of Prayer, wherein the words are to follow the affections, and not the affections the words, as it doth in the best set forms."[34] Even in allowing for the possibility of set forms, *The Common Prayer-Book Unmasked* makes emotional spontaneity the heart of prayer.

After 1660 the quest for a precise definition of the "essence" of acceptable prayer became one of the hallmarks of free-prayer literature. John Bunyan, at the outset of his volley in the conflict, *I Will Pray with the Spirit* (1663), formulated a seven-point definition of prayer, which structures the first quarter of the book and echoes through the works of generations of Dissenting writers. "Prayer," he wrote, "is a sincere, sensible, affectionate pouring out of the heart or soul to God through Christ, in the strength and assistance of the Holy Spirit, for such things as God hath promised, or, according to the Word, for the good of the Church, with submission, in Faith, to the Will of God."[35] As his title suggests, the key to prayer is praying "with the Spirit," and over the course of nearly 120 pages, Bunyan underlines again and again that praying with the Spirit means an "affectionate pouring out of the heart" in prayer; a spontaneous, fervent prayer is the result and evidence of sincerity and of an undivided heart, which in turn are evidence that one has been saved according to correct doctrine. Bunyan marshals a troop of scriptural passages (Ps. 66:17-18, 17:1-2; Jer. 29:12-13; Hos. 7:14; Jer. 31:18) to highlight the importance of speaking to God unhypocritically from a sincere heart. "*Sincerity* is the same in a corner alone as it is before the face of all the world," writes Bunyan; "It knows not how to wear two vizards, one for an appearance before men, and another for a short snatch in a corner; but it must have God, and be with him in the duty of Prayer. It is not a lip-labour that it doth regard, for it is the heart that God looks at" (*IWP*, 7–8).

Sincere, pure desire is the condition and basis both of prayer and of the single, undivided subject who, with one heart, one face, does not even know how to pretend to be or to want anything else.[36] This coherent, self-transparent subjectivity, necessary for being heard by God as Bunyan understands him, is a matter of one's deepest longings and desires, which must be purely and only for the "things of God," as delineated in God's word. Bunyan references verses from the Psalms as evidence of David's sincere longing for God, making it plain that the desires of the heart, more than one's actual sins or good deeds, determine whether one's prayers will be heard. "Thou cryest out, that thou art vile, and therefore God will not regard thy Prayers," Bunyan imagines a reader saying; "'Tis true, if thou delight in thy vileness, and come to God out of a meer pretence. But if from a sense of thy vileness thou dost pour out thy heart to God, desiring to be saved from the guilt, and cleansed from the filth, with all thy heart; fear not, thy vileness will not cause the Lord to stop his ear from hearing of thee" (*IWP*, 104–5). If secret delight in sin negates prayer, then delight in God and the genuine desire to be cleansed of moral filth (as opposed to its "meer pretence") validates it. Bunyan points out, for example, how the Pharisees of Jesus' day no doubt phrased their prayers well but were condemned because they fell short of "pouring out" their hearts to God (*IWP*, 38). Without help from the Holy Spirit in purifying and pouring out the heart, he writes, one who prays is "hypocritical, cold, and unseemly" and "abominable to God" (*IWP*, 37).

The hypocrisy God detests, then, is importantly not a matter of saying one thing and doing another, but of saying one thing and feeling another: of a disjunction between the logocentric intellect and the heart, between the propositional truths of abstract doctrine and the emotions which are substantively to mirror and confirm it. Using the "similitude" of two beggars, one poor and starved and the other healthy and lusty,

Bunyan explicitly contrasts prayer from "custome and formality" with emotional speech that accurately signifies a person's genuine condition:

> The two use the same words in their begging ... but yet the man that is indeed the poor, lame, or maimed person, he speaks with more sence, feeling and understanding of the misery that is mentioned in their begging, than the other can do; and it is discovered more by his affectionate speaking, his bemoaning himself: His pain and poverty makes him speak more in a spirit of lamentation than the other, and he shall be pittied sooner than the other, by all these that have the least dram of natural affection or pitty. Just thus it is with God. There are some who out of custome and formality, go and pray; there are others, who go in the bitterness of their spirit: The one he prayes out of bare notion, and naked knowledge; the other hath his words forced from him by the anguish of his soul. Surely, that is the man that God will look at. (*IWP*, 66–67)

In the fear of praying out of "bare notion" and naked knowledge" we hear the scandal of language that the crisis of representation both sensed and tried to remedy: the fear that words themselves can be bare or naked, disconnected from substantive reality. Emotion, particularly a "feeling of misery" which forces words spontaneously from the heart, is put forth as the true substance or the sign and seal of words in prayer, the substance of the self who needs, as we will see in the next section, to possess worth and not to be simply an effect or performance of language.[37] In the spiritual epistemology and ontology of this passage, desirable moral feelings are like physical substances (the "least dram of natural affection") that can be detected and measured. The manner in which prayer is spoken may be taken as evidence of one's true spiritual condition, and a good heart—one saved or elect, sanctified by the grace of God—is both the source or cause of spontaneous, acceptable prayer, and the desired spiritual condition of which free prayer would ideally be evidence.

These themes of corresponding emotional and doctrinal correctness as requisites for prayer recur in the most influential Dissenting devotional works in the Restoration period and into the eighteenth century.[38] In his much-reprinted *A Method for Prayer* (1710), Matthew Henry encourages readers to cultivate the "sincere representation of holy affection," for spontaneous outbursts of prayer are fundamental to daily Christian life: "we must be frequently addressing our selves to God in short and sudden *Ejaculations*, by which we must keep up our Communion with God."[39] Isaac Watts's highly influential *A Guide to Prayer* (1715), self-billed as a "Prayer-Book without Forms," also emphasizes the importance of verbal spontaneity in expressing desire in prayer. Under the heading "What the Gift of Prayer is," he explains that "it is an Ability to suit our Thoughts and Desires to all the various Parts and

Designs of this Duty, and a readiness to express those Thoughts and Desires before God in the fittest manner to profit our own Souls and the Souls of others that join with us." The chief danger of confinement to forms, on the other hand, is that "it much hinders the free Exercise of our own Thoughts and Desires, which is the chief work and business of prayer."[40] Since sincerity requires the "free exercise" of doctrinally correct thoughts and corresponding correct desires, "unhindered" by forms, free prayer is repeatedly figured as liberty and novelty: as freedom from repetition and imposed texts that were boring or out-of-date. The rhetoric of the *Directory* figured liturgy as an imposed "burden" from which people wished to be free (2), and *The Common Prayer-Book Unmasked* similarly speaks of being "tied to those *Prayers*" as a "limiting of the Spirit" (68).[41] This rhetoric of heaviness underscores the paradoxical rationalization that religion undergoes in this period: liturgy and ceremony are heavy and substantial—material and meaningless in themselves—while real religious meaning is verbal, disembodied, and transcendent, yet nonetheless available to measurement and scrutiny.

In the logic of these texts, liturgy is a burden both because it is legally imposed and because it is repetitious, and it is repetition in particular that is taken to stultify genuine, spontaneous emotional response. Like similar tracts, *The Common Prayer-Book Unmasked* pokes fun at the repetitiveness of liturgy: "in this letany [sic] there is, *Lord deliver us* eight times, *hear us we beseech thee*, twenty times: to omit many desires to be delivered from things from which there is not the least appearance, no more than of the *French pox, the danger of being drunk at a Whitsonale*, or *a purse cut at a stage play, and not so much*" (CPU, 27). *Eikonoklastes*, John Milton's 1649 response to the posthumous publication of Charles I's *Eikon Basilike*, more gravely contends that liturgical prayer amounts to tyranny over the emotions: "To imprison and confine by force, into a Pinfold of set words, those two most unimprisonable things, our Prayer and that Divine Spirit of utterance that moves them, is a tyranny that would have longer hands than those Giants who threatn'd bondage to Heav'n."[42] Similar logic would echo through generations of less politically inflected writing. In Watts's *A Guide to Prayer*, repetition is the culprit in liturgical prayer that threatens to dampen the intense emotion necessary for true prayer:

> 'Tis very apt to make our Spirits cold and flat, formal and indifferent in our Devotion: The frequent Repetition of the same Words doth not always awaken the same Affections in our Hearts which perhaps they were well suited to do when we first heard or made use of them. When we continually tread one constant Road of Sentences or track of Expressions, they become like an old beaten Path in which we daily travel, and we are ready to walk on without particular Notice of the several parts of the way; so in our daily Repetition of a Form, we neg-

lect due Attention to the full Sense of the Words. But there is something more suited to awaken the attention of the Mind in a conceived Prayer; when a Christian is making his own way toward God according to the present Inclination of his Soul and urgency of his present Wants; ... While we are clothing the Sense of our Hearts in fit Expressions, and as it were digging the matter of our Prayers out of our own Feelings and Experiences, it must needs keep the Heart closer at work. (51–52)

Earlier disagreements about liturgy debated the particular conditions of the "old beaten Path," so to speak, but Watts concerns himself with the traveler's feelings about the road rather than the condition of the way itself. Even at midcentury, John Phelps in *A Vindication of Free and Unprescribed Prayer* rehearses what are by then old, familiar arguments when he derides forms for their repetition, which is "totally subversive" of both emotional spontaneity and sincerity.[43] The same Anglican who uses the Prayer Book, Phelps exclaims, would never dream of listening to his minister deliver the same sermon every week! By the same way of thinking, "variety" of petitions, he claims, "would be incomparably more suitable, affecting, and interesting" than the "general, vague and indeterminate Petitions" of the liturgy which, he notes, are doomed always to go out-of-date (*VF*, 30, 34). For Phelps as for Watts, being emotionally affected is a homogenous and largely passive experience. Watts does not recommend tending to the path as a means to attentive prayer, but assumes like Phelps does that a different path simply *will* be more affecting. The appeal of the fresh and the new for both writers connects their denigration of the repetition of liturgy less to scriptural arguments than to a commercial mentality that both writers take to be natural.

Emotional proof, rational knowledge, spiritual worth: the tracts and sermons of the free-prayer debate cohere around the logic of a unified, self-transparent, rational subject, whose doctrinal knowledge is confirmed by a sort of emotional empiricism and linked to emerging commercial logic by its appeals to novelty and variety. From this marketplace variety of prayer-words and the consciousness of being either current or outdated, to the "business of prayer" and the avoidance of mere "lip-labour," these texts reference a world in which individuals negotiated a host of socioeconomic calculations every day and came increasingly to view knowledge and meaning in calculable terms. The self that sought to be a whole, unified possessor of a pure heart was a possessor and trader of material goods as well; the Cartesian subject is also and not incidentally the subject of mercantile discourses. To look back to Bunyan's definition of the sincere self in prayer, "It must have God." "Having God" references at once possession—a knowable and certain condition—and a pure and burning desire, illustrating exactly how it is that these discourses of doctrine and emotional proof, evidence and exchange, encompass the terms of quantifiable yet abstract value and the subject who comes to be understood as a function of them. The economic metaphors of the free-prayer pamphlets show how the Restoration rise of spontaneous prayer marks a moment when religious experience is seen perhaps more than ever before through the twin lenses of epistemology and of economics, and how sincere, spontaneous, emotive speech in prayer becomes valuable in view of both. Like the epistemological rhetoric of the tracts, their economic language contributes to the abstraction and reification of religious value and meaning away from the ritual, material, and liturgical; but being imbricated in the material, concrete, and everyday, this economic language is also the site where the disjunctions, paradoxes, and anxieties of free prayer more readily surface.

"The Interest of Words in Prayer"—Epistemological Economies of Spontaneity

One of the most articulate tracts in the free-prayer debate, *A Sober and Temperate Discourse, Concerning the Interest of Words in Prayer*, by Henry Dawbeny, was published in London in the furor leading up to the Great Ejection.[44] Framing its entire discourse in the economic terms of determining the value of prayer, it positions spontaneous emotional fervor as the sort of currency in which all true prayer traded, into which its value could be abstracted.[45] Chapter 1, "The Interest of Words in Prayer considered," begins by proclaiming what is at stake in deciding how to pray—no less than a "performance," which God may or, it is implied, may not hear and respond to:

> So transcendent is the privilege of coming to the *Holy of Holies*, by the *new* and *living way* in the most sublime and spiritual duty of *Prayer*, where the soul talks with its *Creator*, as it were, *face to face*. Such is the nature of that spiritual performance, considered in it self, so momentous the Concerns, for which in it we wait upon the Throne of Grace; so many the directions which our *Holy Father* hath given us in his Word for the *acceptable performance* of it, that we must be concluded *unthankful to God* . . . if we should not warily attend our Souls in so Sacred an Homage, in which so much of our Interest lies.[46]

All of one's true interest is in prayer: from the outset, Dawbeny's argument about prayer seems to foreshadow a lineage of thinkers from Shaftesbury to Francis Hutcheson and Adam Smith, who will defend virtue by claiming that it is one's true interest. One's interest in the words of prayer lies in it being heard or not, or specifically in this text, in its being a "performance" before God that will be deemed either acceptable or unacceptable, and ultimately salvific or damnable. The main criterion for an acceptable performance, Dawbeny goes on to say, is obedience to God's commands concerning prayer, and at the core of those commands, in Dawbeny's understanding (as in that of so many others), is mental and emotional intensity.[47] God's commandment "obligeth us to a performance of [prayer] under such *Circumstances*, as shall neither divert the *intention of our mind*, nor cool the *fervour of our Spirits*, which two things are most essentially necessary to the acceptable performance of our duty in it . . . and without which our performance is but *lip-labour*, and *lost labour*; yea, no other than a most gross *Hypocrisie*, and *mocking* of him *who cannot be mocked*" (*ST*, 2). In the terms of good business sense, emotional fervor is the condition for getting paid for one's work—for not losing one's labor. The author later goes to great lengths to argue that words are not strictly necessary either for us or for God in prayer, but function only as verbal tokens of the sincere desires and emotions that are real value of the words being exchanged. "*Words* are no more than *the desires of our souls interpreted*," writes Dawbeny, "and there being no further use of them in the duty of Prayer, than that by them we might *sacrifice* unto God the devotion of our hearts by the *calves of our lips*. . . . And by the help of them we might interpret the (otherwise not intelligible) desires of our souls unto others" (*ST*, 3).

In these passages the precise connection between the emotional, epistemological, and economic logics coming increasingly to bear on the modern religious subject is clearly laid out. In free-prayer spirituality, the worth of the heart, seen as both scientific object and object of trade, is an emotional value exchanged and known in words that are genuine tokens or "interpreters" that, here, function exactly like money; the value of the soul is abstracted into this currency, and the religious subject is alienated from the labor of prayer and self-construction by virtue of these prayer-words that are seen as not its own.[48] What cannot be articulated in these registers is the worth of silence or sacrament, or of performative, ritual language. The modern religious subject *must* speak, both spontaneously and according to elaborate rules and, for all its critique of repetition, again and again: an anxiety-inducing imperative, as becomes increasingly apparent.

Words uttered spontaneously out of sincere emotional desires not only insure that God will accept an individual's prayer but also "interpret the desires of our souls unto others," and so spontaneity becomes as well the very ground for religious community in public prayer. The minister, *A Sober and Temperate Discourse* asserts,

> needs be no further careful of words in Prayer . . . than [of] the use of other words, to warm the hearts of those that are to joyn with him, and

> to boyl them up to a greater degree of *fervency in spirit*.... And indeed, those *phrases* which do this excellent deed, are experimentally found to be such as the inwardly affected heart of the Speaker immediately dictates to his Tongue.... words coming from the heart of the Speaker, find the nearest and readiest way to the heart of the Hearer ... as if there were a *Sympathy of devout Souls*, which is indeed from the mighty secret working of the same spirit of Prayer acting both, and at the same time preparing the Speakers heart and tongue to dictate and speak, and the Hearers souls to hear, sigh, groan, and to give a fiducial assent. (5–6)

Words become effective and affective, according to Dawbeny, by being immediately dictated from the heart; through an alchemical sympathy of like substances, an affected heart produces words effective and affective to other hearts.[49] Shared emotional intensity, arising spontaneously in the moment of extemporary prayer in the congregation, in this tract as in so much Puritan and Dissenting discourse, becomes the primary indicator of the promised presence of the Holy Spirit and of the unity among believers that Christ promised through that Spirit. Within a framework valuing intense, simultaneous, spontaneous emotional experience as evidence of spiritual authenticity, the particular terms of the writer's disdain for forms—for their contrivance—make sense, and Dawbeny writes that in the end, he "do[es] not conceive the *Interest and concern of words in Prayer such, that there is any need at all, that Forms should be starcht up for all to use*" (*ST*, 57–58). In pragmatic, utilitarian terms, liturgy becomes "unnecessary."

Extemporary prayer and emotional spontaneity are taken, then, as the very possibility for simultaneity and shared experience upon which true community can be based. *A Sober and Temperate Discourse* imagines religious community as based in the Bible but also in the simultaneous experience of homogenous, pure emotion in prayer by people who remain thoroughly individual, whole, and self-contained.[50] This point did not escape criticism even in the seventeenth century. *Liturgy* means literally "the work of the people," and in *A View of the Face Unmasked* (1661) Samuel Wotton complained that practitioners of free prayer "mak[e] our Liturgy no Liturgy, and turn public Prayers into private; every one by this means, as their affections are different, so praying differently.... There are but so many several private prayers made, and not one joynt public prayer at all."[51] But in spite of this obvious liability, the "interest of words in prayer"—the reason they interest so many writers and readers, as well as the profit they gain or lose—amounts to no less than personal salvation and the solvency of the Christian faith, imagined in the abstracting terms of rational empirical epistemology and of an expanding mercantilism and commodity logic. These words are either true or counterfeit currency; the search is for tokens of genuine emotional experience, desire, and sincerity with which one might purchase the pearl of great price, the kingdom of God, or alternatively, which show that one has been redeemed into that kingdom. Either the value of prayer is articulable as this single, abstractable quality of sincerity, of spontaneous fervency, or it has no value that can register in these discourses.

But in contrast to their claims to the objective authenticity and evidential status of sincerity and spontaneity, both Watts and Bunyan refer to free prayer in clothing metaphors that, like Dawbeny's economic rhetoric, suggest an uncomfortable if peripheral awareness of its performativity.[52] Watts writes of "clothing the Sense of our Hearts in fit Expressions" (*GP*, 52), which suggests not only a salubrious, bare sincerity but perhaps a shameful nakedness of raw feeling as well, making prayer some kind of cover for emotion rather than an exchange medium for its real value. In Bunyan's parable of the two beggars related above, it is the formalist who prays "out of bare notion, and naked knowledge" (*IWP*, 67), thereby paradoxically figuring emotional prayer as some sort of clothing, made artifact, or, in the words of *A Sober and Temperate Discourse*, a constructed "performance." At the same time that these texts defend free prayer foremost as emerging spontaneously from a heart touched by God and evidence of this grace, they embody an anxiety about performing spontaneously, thus intimating an uncomfortable awareness of the constructedness of these experiences and the spiritual economy in which they take place.

Like emerging systems of material exchange, this economy is not without its alienations, strained relations, and fear of counterfeiting. The repeated disdain for lip-labor, for pretense, and for "starched up" speech calls up images of workers who often labor without a sincere love for their employers, in which it is possible to pretend to feel a certain way, perhaps far more virtuously than one does. As soon as prayer is abstracted into a semantic worth of "sincerity," there appears a space of alienation from one's prayer, from words in general, and from the relational self that is constructed during prayer; a gulf opens between the assumption that the self should be spontaneous and the actual effort required to perform and evaluate the spontaneous self. This is the familiar conundrum of the split subject of modernity, and we see it here in its specifically religious incarnation. In spite of the Reformation affirmation that one is saved by grace through faith and not by works, and in spite of Calvinist insistence on total depravity, the economic rhetoric of these tracts consistently if unconsciously introduces the idea that free prayer is not just evidentiary experience of grace but—contrary to explicit reformed doctrine—*work*, a task performed in costume or livery, to be appraised by a divine master or employer from whom one hopes, rather anxiously, to be paid grace or salvation. This threat of losing one's spiritual labor is in itself enough to alienate one from oneself or from God; it generates a self-scrutinizing worry that is itself inimical to sincerity. And crucially, in this system one always loses one's labor in some sense: prayer is to be a passionate and sincere "performance," in Dawbney's term, but not belabored or performative. Under epistemological and economic logic, for prayer to have truth and value, the labor of prayer must paradoxically disappear. The fetishized authenticity of true substance—of words and self as objects—displaces the construction and performance of prayer and the self. But the anxiety engendered by the spiritual economy underlying the ideal of spontaneous prayer remains. It had already found expression in the major Puritan document that aimed at legislating and controlling public devotion, and it would come more sharply into view in the private free-prayer guides that were its heirs.

"To This or Like Effect"—Regulating Spontaneity

The paradox of prescribing spontaneous prayer had been from the outset fascinatingly incarnate in the Puritan *Directory for the Publique Worship of God*. In January 1644 Parliament had forbidden the use of the Book of Common Prayer and ordered implementation of the *Directory*, a document which had been painstakingly produced by the Westminster Assembly of Divines. By August of the following year, its implementation was scattered at best, and Parliament found it necessary to pass an additional ordinance ordering the knights and burgesses of the counties to print and deliver copies of the *Directory* "fairly bound up in Leather" to the committees of Parliament, who would then distribute them to constables or other parish officers, levying hefty fines for the use of the Book of Common Prayer and for neglecting and preaching or writing against the *Directory*. Under the second wave of directives, implementation of the *Directory* seems to have been fairly complete by 1649, and it remained in effect until the Restoration. As such the *Directory*'s influence was initially limited but ultimately far-reaching. As Alan Clifford puts it, Christians today "who are used to so-called non-liturgical orders of service have inherited a largely *Directory*-based state-of-affairs."[53]

Written before the strict free-prayer position achieved dominance, the *Directory* attempts to navigate a treacherous strait between form and freedom, direction and spontaneity. Its full title expresses its ambitious scope: *A Directory for Publique Prayer, Reading the Holy Scriptures, Singing of Psalmes, Preaching of the Word, Administration of the Sacraments, and other parts of the Publique Worship of God, Ordinary & Extraordinary*. The antiritual position of the *Directory* is clear in the negative instructions of its opening section, "Of the Assembling of the Congregation," such as injunctions against bowing upon entering a church and against other traditional postures and customs of Anglican worship (*DPW*, 10). The remaining thirteen sections then instruct the ministers in liturgical matters: the public reading of Scripture, prayer, preaching, administering baptism and the Lord's Supper, keeping the Lord's Day, solemnizing marriages, visiting the sick and burying the dead, and organizing observances of public fasts, days of thanksgiving, and the singing of psalms.

In these sections, the strange hybrid form of the *Directory*, mixing sincerity and artifice, spontaneity and control, is apparent in its typeface and physical appearance. Catholic and Anglican liturgical books had long alternated typeface, style, and, in manuscript, ink color to distinguish between rubrics and the actual words spoken by the celebrant. In a similar but significantly altered way, the *Directory* alternates rubriclike instructions in smaller roman type with phrases for prayer in larger italic type (see fig. 1; p. 54). For instance, the *Directory*'s instructions for the "Assembly of the Congregation" read:

> The Congregation being assembled; the Minister, after solemne calling on them to the worshiping of the great name of God, is to begin with Prayer;
> *In all Reverence and Humility acknowledgeing the incomprehensible Greatnesse and Majesty of the Lord, (in whose presence they doe then in a speciall manner appeare) and their own vilenesse and unworthinesse to approach so neare him; with their utter inability of themselves, to so great a Work: And humbly beseeching him for Pardon, Assistance, and Acceptance in the whole Service then to bee performed; and for a Blessing on that particular portion of his Word then to bee read: and all, in the Name and Mediation of the Lord Jesus Christ.* (10–11)

Each section of the *Directory* repeats this pattern of instructions followed by italicized indications for the contents of prayers and exhortations. Consistently preceding the italicized portions are phrases such as "to this effect": "the Minister is to pray to this or the like effect: *That the Lord who hath not left us as strangers . . .*"; "he is to give thanks and pray, to this or the like purpose; *Acknowledging with all thankefulnesse, that the Lord is true and faithful . . .*"; after the marriage solemnization, "the Minister shall . . . conclude the action with Prayer to this effect, *That the Lord would be pleased to accompany his own Ordinance with his blessing . . .*" (44, 46, 63–64). The *Directory* is clearly meant to be used by the minister during the worship service as traditional liturgical texts were, but in a key departure from previous liturgical books, the grammatical form of the italicized text is always such that it cannot be read verbatim by the minister in the assembly. As in the long quotation above, the minister must continually change phrases like "humbly beseeching him for pardon" to "We humbly

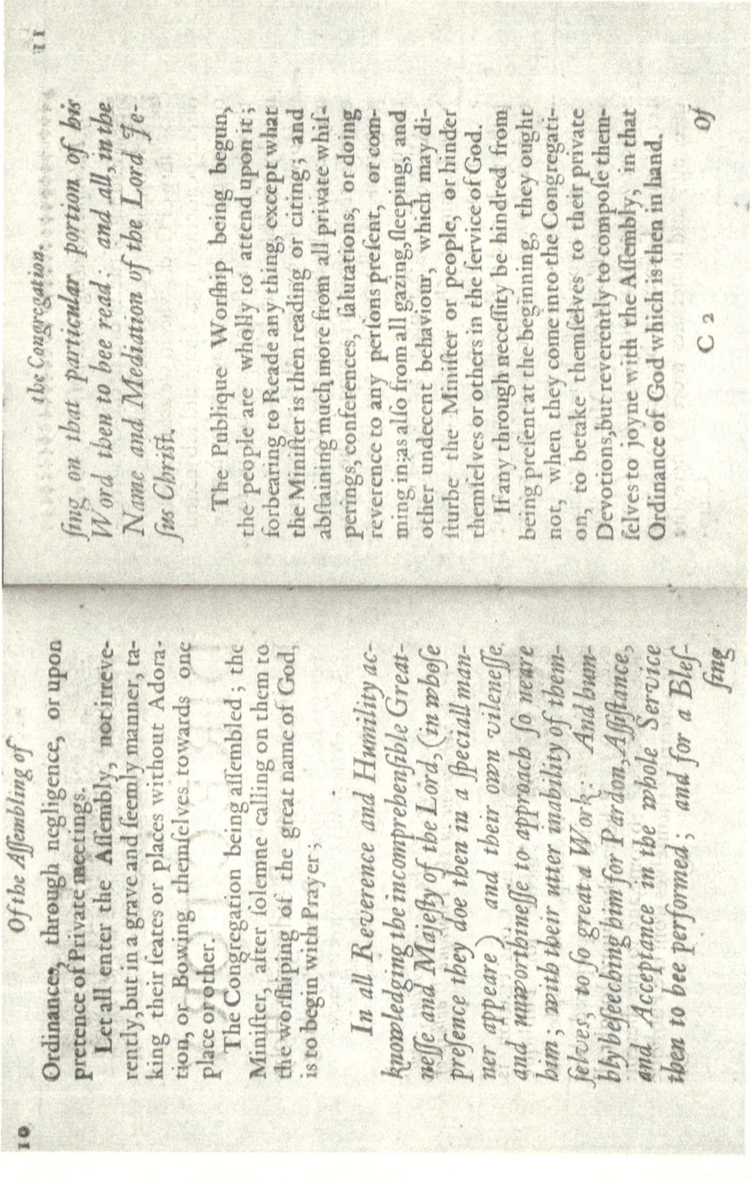

Figure 1 Opening from *A Directory for the Publique Worship of God* (1644). *Courtesy Lilly Library, Indiana University, Bloomington, IN.*

similar method; he provides, for instance, an amazing two and a half pages of verses elaborating on the one phrase "Our Father, who art in Heaven" (*MP*, 163–65), a general topos, he says, from which prayer begins. Many editions of the *Method* were printed as Henry intended, interleaved with one blank page between each printed one, to enable the reader to pen in his own collection of phrases to supplement Henry's own. Like Bunyan's demand for scrupulous sincerity, Henry's lists and blank pages, figures of accumulation and abstraction, combine literally to efface the Lord's Prayer and erase it from Dissenting practice.

Between the ledgerlike pages of Henry's collected phrases and the blank sheets for scribbled lists of readers' personal prayer phrases, one senses a variety of fears: that without this careful accounting the business might go bankrupt, that in the copious, nervous quoting from God's word to talk and talk and talk to God, God might not listen or respond at all. If spontaneous prayer gains value as evidence of the substance and nature of the soul in response to a crisis of representation, that soul is here a membrane or shell, an echoing warehouse whose interior is furnished only with language and ready-made phrases collected with an eye toward coaching devotion. But above all, the anxiety of free-prayer instruction books is about the nature and substance of the self: the self that should be whole and full may be an unsettling odds-and-ends shop, with shelves stocked with something other than "sacred things"—or worse, empty. Even in the well-thumbed editions of Henry's *Method*, most of those blank pages left to be filled by the individual subject are still eerily empty, leaving only the predetermined language and longing of the devotional guidebook as commodity-form itself. The self revealed in free-prayer literature is in every sense a modern religious subject, a subject of language that in abandoning ritual both tries to utter in prayer "*sound Speech that cannot be condemn'd*" and also discovers that in this search for evidence of the soul, rationally conceived, one only ever finds language, in all its iterable liturgicality. The prayer that would be proof of the correctly desiring, spontaneous, and sincere self turns out to be a stockpile of words that come from outside sources, making sincerity, authenticity, naturalness—those cardinal virtues of a soul imagined like an object in the given world—practically impossible, and the freedom of spontaneity, a burden. As Bouwsma puts it, the self-scrutiny of Calvinist spirituality split the self "into observer and observed, audience and actor, neither capable of natural and spontaneous behavior, [but] driven back to theatricality even by [the] effort to escape it."[61] An "empty self," that is, one performed in language and in relation with others—not a coherent object like something found, analyzed, or exchanged in the given world—seems the unthinkable thought of free-prayer spirituality, whose trace we nonetheless find in its literature.

vocabulary—through collecting descriptions of the divine attributes found in Scripture in order to facilitate prayer "On a sudden" (*VF*, 20–21). In this he, like Watts and so many other writers, drew not only on the tradition of paraphrased spontaneity prescribed in the *Directory* but specifically on the work that stands perhaps at the pinnacle of this method for facilitating emotional spontaneity and verbal variety in prayer, Matthew Henry's oft-reprinted *A Method for Prayer, with Scripture Expressions Proper to be Us'd under each Head* (1710).[59]

Following the trajectory of Dawbeny's "interest of words in prayer," Henry's central metaphor figures the suppliant as a busy craftsman, servant, or errand-boy in a spiritual marketplace, bringing his labor in the form of phrases, praises, and requests, before a merchant-God who presumably evaluates the labor and pays wages by granting or denying the laborer's requests. In the language of Henry's *Method*, a rich collection of phrases enables prayer that is full like a merchant's warehouse from which a variety of goods can be brought. "It is desireable that our Prayers should be *copious* and *full*," Henry writes; "This Storehouse of Materials for Prayer may be of use to put us in remembrance of our several Errands at the Throne of Grace, that none may be quite forgotten" (*MP*, [6–7]).[60] In stockpiling and bringing these goods before God, Henry recommends crafting them almost wholly of phrases from the Bible:

> I would advise that the *Sacred* Dialect be most us'd . . . that Language that Christian people are most accustom'd to, most affected with, and will most readily agree to. . . . This is *sound Speech that cannot be condemn'd*. And those that are able to do it may do well to enlarge by way of Descant or Paraphrase upon the Scriptures they make use of; still speaking according to that Rule, and comparing spiritual things with spiritual, that they may illustrate each other. (*MP*, [8–9])

Henry's instructions for prayer sound something like self-help books designed to help people cope with modern life, while entrenching the very mindset that makes coping difficult: frantic speaking and trying not to forget all one's "errands," the desire for self-confirming equivalences of meaning between Scripture and spontaneous prayer, fear of threatened condemnation, and competitive, class-conscious concern for speaking properly and "by the rules" in an increasingly polite public marketplace. Whether for particular favors or God's approval in general, the errand-boy of prayer is self-consciously preoccupied with getting something.

Henry's *Method* culminates with his most fascinating phrase-collection of all, "A Paraphrase on the Lord's Prayer, in Scripture Expressions." Christ's own form of prayer given to his disciples had long been a thorn in Puritans' sides, to be plucked out by being understood as only a general guideline. Henry's strategy is to neutralize the prayer's form in a figures as deformities, weaknesses, and handicaps: seeking to authenticate its goodness and wholeness, yet perennially afraid of its inner divisions, the demand of its repeated performance, and perhaps most of all of its silences.[55]

In this way the *Directory* also looks toward the spiraling anxiety that is one of the enduring legacies of Protestant and English Dissenting spirituality in the Restoration and Enlightenment.[56] More paradoxically than the writers of the *Directory*, Dissenters later wrote a vast literature to instruct those within their camp in the art of praying spontaneously. This literature too begs the question of why free prayer needed coaching, a query many dealt with directly. But it also sets forth as its most common recommendation for achieving true prayer the collection of lists of phrases, usually from Scripture, which once memorized would roll off the tongue and be easily assembled into prayer on the spur of the moment. Where the *Directory*'s very form expresses the implicit knowledge that spontaneity is no real guarantor of (doctrinal or spiritual) truth, these free-prayer guides murmur with the fear that spontaneity may not come at all. While they seek to fill the mind with scriptural phrases, constructing, in Matthew Henry's words, a "Storehouse of Materials for Prayer," they also speak another truth. Besides being furnished with nonorthodox materials, the self that flees performativity and ritual, looking inward for authentic substance, finds itself fluctuating and, in the face of the demands of performance and empirical, experimental repetition, often silent and empty.

A "Storehouse of Materials for Prayer"—Spontaneity and Its Alienations

It is no surprise that, with the weight of authenticity and salvation hanging in the balance, private devotion was often called "wrestling with the Lord in prayer." As John Spurr affirms, "Diary after diary tells us that this was generally difficult, unrewarding work—described as 'restrained' or 'hard'—and only occasionally do we get a sense of prayer flowing easily and of its immense rewards."[57] And so it is also no surprise that in answer to this difficulty devotional guides gradually emerged, instructing Dissenters in how to pray spontaneously. As paradoxical as it seems, Isaac Watts's popular Dissenting *Guide to Prayer* (1715) provided an entire section of "*Directions* how to attain a rich Treasure of Expression in Prayer," mainly from Scripture: "Seek after those ways of Expression that are pathetical," Watts advised, "such as denote the Fervency of Affection and carry Life and Spirit with them" (112).[58] At midcentury, antiliturgy writer John Phelps was still advocating what seems like better prayer through beseech Thee for pardon." The constant repetition of "to this effect" downplays the importance of particular words, reifying transcendent meaning in a familiar maneuver, while constructing a controlled spontaneity for public worship. "To this *or like effect*" makes a double gesture at the minister's freedom in praying, at the same moment that it reduces freedom and spontaneity in prayer to a predictable alteration in grammar, a shifting between pronouns and verb forms and a choosing among synonyms.

The *Directory* stands as a monument both to English Protestantism's participation in a rationalism that had been gaining ground since the high Middle Ages, and to its particular manifestations of the crisis of representation. It challenges a sacramental, ritual semiotics and affirms an understanding of language as a means for communicating known contents of meaning in a variety of equivalent ways; it implies that there *is* a knowable, doctrinally correct spiritual condition of the suppliant before God, which would necessarily, almost mechanically, give rise to a variety of phrases that are correct, equivalent, and interchangeable. The *Directory* does not express anxiety about Scripture's (or language's) ability to contain a single, ascertainable body of propositional truths, but while it hopes for an objective emotional sincerity that could underwrite the truth of language, it crucially doubts the reliability of the rational subject that has enacted this challenge to ritual. In its doubt of that subject, it teeters between liturgy and purely free prayer. For fear that the minister might lapse into doctrinal error, the free prayer that was a vigorously defended liberty and sought-after sign of grace amounted, in the end, to verbal, syntactical freedom within the carefully defined limits of Puritan orthodoxy.[54]

The framers of the *Directory* were not unaware of its paradoxical stance vis-à-vis ritual, either. Its preface obliquely acknowledged the oddity of institutionalizing a prescribed means of praying when Puritan teaching held that converted people would pray aright by the Spirit, but offered it as "some help and furniture" to the minister, so that he might "furnish his heart and tongue with Materials of Prayer and Exhortation, as shall be needful" (7–8). The careful, italicized language of the *Directory*, meant to be paraphrased but not displaced altogether, embodies a sort of anxious, secret checking of spontaneity that is in fact part and parcel of its logic. In spite of the selection of a man who appeared a trustworthy minister of God's word, not only might his prayers stray from sound doctrine, but more than that, they might not flow freely, spontaneously, and affectively at all. In referring to the guide as "help and furniture," the *Directory* portrays what it believes should be a modern, rational, self-transparent, and spontaneous self, operating under what it

Attending to the language of the Restoration free-prayer pamphlets, it becomes clear that enthusiasm, free prayer, and the logics of the emerging secular, commercial culture and polite society with which it seemed at odds are in actuality profoundly interconnected. The paradoxes of the early modern religious subject emerge from the particular epistemological pressures of early modernity and its crises of representation—from the intensifying urgency to find proof of salvation and knowledge of the state and substance of the soul outside ritual and sacrament—and come to fruition in Restoration free prayer and institutionalized Dissent: in a voracious empire and bustling mercantile culture where religion understands itself increasingly in terms of abstraction and trade and, in Graham Ward's terms, becomes simultaneously "globalized and privatized."[62] While these texts do not support explaining free prayer as a function of economic or social determinism any more than as the simple victory (as they claim) of scriptural truth over "Romish superstition," they show the rise of free prayer to be intricately related to the modes of discourse and reasoning that went hand in hand with changing economic and social systems. They point toward a conclusion like Zaret's, someplace between those of Marx and Weber, that resists a totalizing, deterministic explanation but shows that "the relation between Puritanism and economic life is far more reciprocal than Weber thought it was," and that interaction between the two stems from the logic and rhetoric of economic life coming to permeate all forms of rational thought as unarguable common sense or an inevitable bottom line.[63]

Even more strikingly, we witness the anxieties attendant on requiring spontaneity, and the way its evidentiary, economizing logic seems to be at odds with the very notion of personal relation with God or others, perhaps with the very religiousness of religion.[64] This chapter's examination of later-seventeenth-century free prayer enables us to speak of a modern religious subjectivity, coalescing in the Restoration period, that is defined chiefly by its imbrication in modern empirical and economic ways of thinking about the world and about the self. Imagining the heart as both a scientific object and an object of trade, the substance and value of which can be abstracted into the currency of words in prayer, it consequently is characterized by the anxiety and isolation borne of an emphasis on individual spontaneous experience and self-scrutiny, by a conception of community experienced as an anxious comparison of individual experiences as spiritual evidence, by a sense of fragmentation and alienation from one's prayer as labor and performance, and by a declining sense of agency, compared with earlier and early-modern willingness to believe in the constructive self-fashioning of the subject.[65] This modern religious subject engages in the quest for transcendent, spontaneous experience that would be both true proof and knowledge of salvation, beyond question or doubting, but never escapes anxious self-scrutiny of the authenticity of its experiences. Rather, imagining oneself being appraised or examined by God for complete sincerity, complete emotional-rational transparence, engenders a self-conscious anxiety that negates the homogenous subject of knowledge it presupposes.

In the broadest scope, these texts show how the religious self in modernity is increasingly filtered through a concept of speculative reason that inherently tends toward secularization, that is, toward removal of meaning (whether religious, philosophical, or aesthetic) from the *saecula*, the material world of rituals, bodies, and quotidian practices, and into an immaterial, transcendent realm.[66] In these texts, the modern religious subject is thus haunted by the lonely quasi awareness that, in concerning itself with knowledge, certainty, and proof, it has silenced itself, moving away from the realm of language and relation to the other that is always inhabited by uncertainty and faith.[67] The spontaneity required in free prayer ultimately appears as a peculiarly secular sort of religious sentiment borne of increasingly rationalistic ways of thinking about religious faith and practice, a form of sentiment that will sever much of Western Christianity from more than a millennium of its liturgical history, sublimating religious meaning away from the ritual and the liturgical, and from the material world altogether. Moreover, its problems and paradoxes announce emotive patterns that recur in a variety of texts in the long eighteenth century, texts that partake in the logics of spontaneity as proof of moral or aesthetic goodness, from the instinctive responses of the Shaftesburian moral sense and the anxious tears of sentimental novels, to the "spontaneous overflow of powerful feelings . . . recollected in tranquility" set forth as the essence of Romantic poetry. Understanding the ideology of spontaneity in free prayer helps us situate it and these later phenomena as what Talal Asad has identified as "formations of the secular," belonging to the potent ideology of secularism bound up in Renaissance humanism and Enlightenment conceptions of nature and histories of progress, formations that are constantly referenced to a religion which they both structurally need and devalue.[68]

The spirituality of free prayer expresses perhaps nothing so well as the symptoms of that which was lost in the Reformation crisis of representation and its rejection of the vast, varied communal Christian ritual life: faith in the possibility of communing with God through the action of a community rather than the isolated self. In responding to the crisis of representation by shifting the terms of religious value towards acts which were spontaneous and individual, this spirituality paradoxically undermined the grounds of its own validity. The more individualized these spiritual practices became, like the personalized collections of scriptural phrases, the more readily their constructedness—their non-spontaneity—was apparent, opening the believer to a sense of isolation and perpetual, nearly neurotic self-critique: in Henry's words, constantly comparing one's "spiritual things" to those of Scripture and of others, anxious "that they might illustrate each other."

Alternately, the cult of true sincerity and spontaneity led to a profound skepticism that dismissed all prayer and worship as what it can only be, in some manner constructed, volitional, and performative. But the psychological toll of continual anxiety over one's acceptability to God and of a nervous comparison of self, Scripture, and other that we hear whispering in these free-prayer texts also echoes throughout the eighteenth century in seemingly secular texts, from moral sense philosophy to sentimental novels and a discourse of spontaneity in Romantic poetry, that have recourse to a logic of spontaneity for reasons similar to those of free prayer, via the rationalization of goodness. More directly connected to the free-prayer texts, we hear these anxieties speak even more distinctly in the most popular Dissenting text of all time, *The Pilgrim's Progress*, and in the spiritual autobiography of its author, John Bunyan's *Grace Abounding to the Chief of Sinners*. In Bunyan's work we shall see the connection of free prayer to a different sort of spontaneity and ritual: a repetitive, nearly hysterical, symptomatic eruption of anxiety over the self understood as object, and over figuring relation between the person and God in terms of certainty and exchange.

CHAPTER 2

"As Blood Is Forced out of Flesh"

Spontaneity and the Wounds of Exchange in *Grace Abounding* and *The Pilgrim's Progress*

> If a man should see a Pearle, worth an hundred pounds, lye in a ditch, yet, if he understood not the value of it, he would lightly pass it by; but if he once get the knowledge of it, he would venture Up to the neck for it. So it is with souls concerning the things of God; If a man once get an understanding of the worth of them, then his heart, nay, the very strength of his soul runs after them, and he will never leave crying till he have them.
>
> —John Bunyan, *I Will Pray with the Spirit* (1662)

The same year that 2,000 ministers left the Church of England out of resistance to the Act of Uniformity and imposition of the Common Prayer, John Bunyan published one of his earliest books, *I Will Pray with the Spirit, and I Will Pray with the Understanding also: Or, A Discourse Touching Prayer, From I Cor. 14.15*, a 117-page defense of spontaneous prayer and a guidebook to its practice. In it Bunyan's God seems at times a judge hearing petitions which must be by the book, so to speak, before being granted; at others, a physician probing prayers and "searching the heart" to determine the believer's fervor and sincerity.[1] Prayer "according to God's will" is for Bunyan a matter of the "root and spirit" from which it arises, a spiritual-ontological quality of heart coming not from the Prayer Book but from the Spirit, the tests for which are harrowing. Calling God "Father," for instance, evokes not familial closeness but the ultimate trial of sincerity. The threat of insincerity is so grave that

Bunyan discourages readers from praying the "Our Father" or teaching it to their children, since unless they are truly converted, they would be lying: "You say, Our Father, God saith you blaspheme" (*IWP*, 43).

For genuine prayer, on the other hand, Bunyan looks to a "feeling and understanding of the misery" in which words are "forced from him by the anguish of his soul," because prayer that pours forth from the heart sincerely and spontaneously would be, as he imagines it, evidence of God's grace and the sure sign that one's prayer was correct and would be heard (*IWP*, 66–67). As with the free-prayer texts treated in the previous chapter, the central logic of *I Will Pray with the Spirit* is the logic of spontaneity. Bunyan's passionate defense of liberty and newness in prayer, as well as the value he places on painful prayer as costly and authentic, both answer and appeal to discourses of evidence and exchange which Bunyan has himself internalized, discourses which are at the root not just of the larger phenomenon of free prayer but also of the secular moral sense philosophy that would later proclaim itself the "true enthusiasm."[2] Bunyan's anxious, literalist approach to Scripture and the "word coming upon him," for instance, participates in what Robert Markley has called the ideology of objectivity that coalesced with the rise of the New Science in the 1660s and the writings of Boyle and Newton, which saw both the self and the world as fallen, yet scrupulously observed inner and outer phenomena to discern God's truth.[3] Scholarship has likewise linked Bunyan's propositional discourse to the contemporary "propaganda" of the Royal Society and consequent late-seventeenth-century experiments in genre; like the aggressive scientific plans for organizing the world, so attractive in this period, Bunyan's project develops propositional maxims and allegorical, quasi-novelistic fiction as "literary paradigm[s] which unit[e] irreducible facts with anticipated formats" and which "present fragmentary experience as a pathway to an organized, providentially guided society."[4]

Besides serving as authentic experience in a sort of spiritual empiricism, painful spontaneous prayer is also, Bunyan implies, costly, and as the epigraph from *I Will Pray with the Spirit* has it, Bunyan's hope is that an emotionally integrated subjectivity that consistently and sincerely runs after goodness will arise from true knowledge of the "*value*" and "*worth*" of the "things of God." In registering religious meaning in these terms, Bunyan was far from alone. The economic flavor of Bunyan's spiritual epistemology has its roots in Puritan covenant theology, which as Christopher Hill has shown became accepted Puritan doctrine by the 1640s and was so culturally persuasive and pervasive as to have appeared in popular emblem books and to have been preached in Parliament. With its focus on Christianity as the new covenant of grace (as opposed to the old covenant of law and works), in which Christ pays the debt for man's sins, covenant theology conceives of salvation primarily in terms of the binding legality of a contract; in Hill's words, "the relationship of the elect to God is conceived as a debtor-creditor relationship," a paradigm that appears in all Bunyan's works.[5] *The Doctrine of the Law and Grace Unfolded* (1659), Bunyan's most detailed exposition of covenant theology, recounts the gospel entirely in these contractual terms. "The price that was paid for sinners," Bunyan declares, was "agreed upon before the world began." In an elaborate bargain, Jesus agreed to be put to death, submitting his body "to the stroaks of [the Father's] *Justice*," and God the Father agreed to raise him up again; both the conditions covenanted for have been fulfilled, and so "This doth prove us under Grace."[6]

While the image of salvation as the payment of the debt of sin certainly appears in Christian Scripture, it is only one among its many figures for salvation. Covenant theology marks the culmination of a long process by which Christ's death and resurrection are seen increasingly— and ultimately, almost exclusively—in legal, economic terms. Gustaf Aulén's seminal study, *Christus Victor: An Historical Study of the Three Main Types of the Idea of Atonement*, has shown how the "Latin view" of Christ's atonement came to supplant the "classical view," dominant for the first Christian millennium and still definitive in the Christian East, which understands the incarnation of God as itself salvific, and Christ's resurrection as a cosmic, ontological liberation from sin and death that cannot be fully rationalized. In the Latin view, crystallized in Anselm of Canterbury's eleventh-century *Cur Deus homo?* and predominant in the later medieval period, the demands of divine justice must be satisfied through compensation, by merit "earned" by Christ and given to the "credit" of human beings, and the payment of this satisfaction is treated as the essential accomplishment of the death of Christ.[7] Aulén argues that where late medieval theology tended to mitigate the necessitarian strain of Anselm's writings, Protestant orthodoxy actually served to underline the economic aspect of salvation by emphasizing Christ's endurance of punishment as retribution, ultimately following Anselm's view more closely than the usual medieval teaching.[8]

Given the rich mercantile context of seventeenth-century England, it is easy to understand why an increasingly economic understanding of salvation should flower in its soil. As David Zaret has argued in *The Heavenly Contract*, covenant theology made sense from the perspective of the market rationality that was well-entrenched by Bunyan's day. Zaret shows that by the late-sixteenth and early-seventeenth centuries, market forces had increasingly penetrated into the English countryside; the commercialization of agriculture re-created among rural people the cities' vocational conditions, economic autonomy, and practical rationality, which, together with the printing revolution and increasing literacy, paved the way for conceiving of religion in pragmatic, trade-oriented terms. Drawing together the work of economic historians with the vast literature of covenant theology and preaching, Zaret demonstrates that covenant theology continually referred to a vivid world of "early capitalist development" in England in which, in particular, "contractual transactions in pursuit of profit became a familiar feature of everyday economic life."[9] As early as 1601, for instance, a writer on behalf of the Merchant Adventurers claimed that "there is nothing in the world so ordinary and natural unto all men as to contract, truck, merchandise, and traffic one with one another, so that it is almost impossible for three persons to converse together two hours, but they will fall into talk of one bargain or another, chopping, changing or some other kind of contract."[10] Crucially, Puritan preachers pushed the analogy of the covenant further than their brethren on the continent and used the common contractual practice of giving earnest money as evidence of good faith to encourage believers, by analogy, to seek evidences of their salvation, providing potential comfort in the face of doctrines of total depravity and double predestination, as well as welcome outlets for individual initiative.[11] It is this intersection of market rationality with increasingly empirical spiritual epistemology that informs Bunyan's earliest works as well as his posthumously published works written in the 1680s, including *Israel's Hope Encouraged* and *The Saints Privilege and Profit* (1692), and that is at the heart of *I Will Pray with the Spirit* and the perceived value of spontaneous prayer.[12]

The intersection of empirical-economic thought with the creation of new understandings of religious "value" also provides, I contend, the animating tension of Bunyan's literary output and spirituality. Bunyan's spiritual autobiography, *Grace Abounding to the Chief of Sinners* (1666), articulates a spirituality centered on spontaneous experiences of language, particularly fervent prayer and the Scripture "coming upon" Bunyan, sought as evidences of spiritual states such as faith and conversion. It is also perhaps our greatest literary testimony to the psychological toll of imaging religion in this way. For *Grace Abounding* clinks and clangs with economic language, but the effect is far from reassuring. At the heart of *Grace Abounding*, taking up over a third of its pages, is a central trauma dramatizing a wholly other form of spontaneity and what I argue is the combined pressure of increasingly empirical and economic reason brought to bear on devotion with full force: the agonizing, haunting voice Bunyan hears over twenty times an hour, day in, day out, for over a year, coaxing him to "*Sell him, sell him,*" to sell Christ "for this or that." The most obvious feature of this episode, its economic form, has gone virtually untouched in criticism. Where *I Will Pray with the Spirit* holds out hope that knowledge of what the epigraph terms the "worth" of "the things of God" would once and for all fix the heart's desires on those things alone, Bunyan's account of his personal experience in *Grace Abounding* calls the very possibility of such valuation and knowledge into doubt, and questions framing personal relation in these terms. I contend that Bunyan's harrowing experience of hearing a voice repeatedly urging him to "Sell him, sell him" is best understood as a symptom of an early or newly modern religious subjectivity bearing the excruciating cost of a theology that has come to understand itself almost wholly in evidentiary, economic terms. The emotional utterances of prayer that Bunyan imagines should be produced by spiritual knowledge come to be scrutinized as natural phenomena to confirm the correctness of that knowledge. In perpetually surveying his inner experience to determine whether he has a true "understanding of the worth" of "the things of God," sincerity becomes ever more difficult, and Bunyan eventually figures the only true spontaneity in prayer as the passive pain of blood being "forced out of flesh."[13]

If the "Sell him" episode represents the wound of perpetual self-scrutiny and imagining relation to God in economic-epistemological terms, *The Pilgrim's Progress* attempts to suture that wound.[14] From the contract-like roll that Christian receives to the damnation of Ignorance in the dramatic final sentences, the burden of *The Pilgrim's Progress*, I argue, is to banish not only doubt and uncertainty but also the more frightening specter of *Grace Abounding*, the sense of bad faith involved in reducing relation with God to a contract or exchange. Ironically, the very form of *The Pilgrim's Progress* as a commodity, claiming to contain "the truth, as cabinets enclose the gold," is key to the success of its exorcism, because *The Pilgrim's Progress* inveighs against the merchantry of Vanity Fair while participating in and thereby enabling its deeper economic rationality.[15] Where the previous chapter makes it possible to account for the rise of a spirituality of spontaneity in terms of its answering to pressures for quantifiable experiences and proofs of grace, this chapter makes it possible to account for the popularity of *The Pilgrim's Progress* in terms of the degree to which it relieves the guilt and psychological toll of that spirituality, assuring readers that salvation can be certified with Christian's contract-like roll and that they, like Christian and Hopeful, can "buy the truth." The enduring popularity of *The Pilgrim's Progress*— which sold over 100,000 copies in the last decade of Bunyan's life alone and has been second only to the Bible as the most reprinted book for much of the last 300 years—testifies to the degree to which it offers literally the salvation of an emerging market economy and commodity culture: that is, what Graham Ward has called the allure of religious transcendence in the commodity form itself.[16] Together the specific traumas of *Grace Abounding* and their particular suturing in *The Pilgrim's Progress* offer a profound window onto the repercussions of the dramatic changes much of Western religion underwent in early modernity. Passing through covenant theology and its attendant spirituality and trauma, Christian arrives at the very modern destination set out for in Anselm's *Cur Deus Homo?*—a world understood in fully rational, accountable terms. And this world, as many Bunyan scholars have noted, turns out to be a profoundly secular space, a world virtually without God. Yet, in spite of Bunyan's deep imbrication in an increasingly rationalized mercantile culture, the puzzling ending of his autobiography provides a glimpse, I argue in the final section, not of spirituality viewing itself via economic rationalism, but of another sort of religiousness and faith, which *Grace Abounding*, for all its trauma, retains: the hope for a loving relation with God outside fixed "reasonable" certainty and economic exchange. This as much as the commodity-logic this religion embraces may account for its abiding appeal, despite its imbrication in logics with which it is profoundly at odds.

"True Tokens of a Truly Godly Man"—Knowledge and Exchange in *Grace Abounding*

Vincent Newey has called *Grace Abounding* the apogee of the experimental theology tradition, and in its opening paragraphs Bunyan passes quickly over his childhood, education, and first marriage to detail the first experiences of his spiritual awakening in the 1650s in Mr. Gifford's Bedford congregation.[17] The catalyst of this awakening, he tells us, was his overhearing "three or four poor women sitting at a door in the Sun, and talking about the things of God."[18] "Methought they spake as if joy did make them speak," he recalls, and this joy caused their words to stick with him even after he returned to his labor: "my heart would tarry with them, for I was greatly affected with their words, both because by them I was convinced that I wanted the true tokens of a truly godly man, and also because by them I was convinced of the happy and blessed condition of him that was such a one" (*GA*, ¶38:15, ¶40:15).[19] Bunyan then recounts how his early spiritual life was characterized by a series of spiritual qualities and by his attempts to discern whether he possessed these various "true tokens of a truly godly man." In the first episode, Bunyan recalls being startled by a passage in 1 Corinthians 12 mentioning faith: "especially this word Faith put me to it, for I could not help it, but sometime must question whether I had any Faith or no" (*GA*, ¶47:17).[20] In the second instance, he was assaulted by the question of whether or not he was "elected," and eventually, his reading of Scripture brought him to fear he was not "called" or "converted" (*GA*, ¶57:20, ¶71:24). In Puritan spirituality the dramatic conversion experience—an overwhelming sense of guilt, followed by a sense of release so strong that it could only be divine—came to be regarded as the ultimate evidence of election,[21] and being called by Christ became Bunyan's greatest desire and source of anxiety in his account so far: "I cannot now express with what longings and breakings I in my Soul, I cryed to Christ to call me. Thus I continued for a time all on a flame to be converted to Jesus Christ, and did also see at that day such glory in a converted state, that I could not be contented without a share therein. Gold! could it have been gotten for Gold, what could I have given for it! had I had a whole world, it had all gone ten thousand times over, for this, that my Soul might have been in a converted state" (*GA*, ¶73:24).

The emergence of the language of gold and possession at the moment of spiritual crisis dramatizes the way that economic possession became a favorite Puritan and Dissenting figure of desired spiritual certainty. As previously mentioned, covenant theology appealed to a real-world experience of contractual interaction which assumed a formal equality between parties entering into agreements and which thus served to mitigate the anxiety caused by the doctrine of predestination.[22] Instead of the comforting equality of partners in a contract, however, in *Grace Abounding* Bunyan faces the looming inequalities of the soul figured as a commodity before God. Where God probes to know the soul's value in *I Will Pray with the Spirit*, in *Grace Abounding*'s recurring language of commodity-desire God functions frighteningly as both creator (or producer) and discriminating purchaser of souls: "That which made me fear, was this, lest Christ should have no liking to me" (*GA*, ¶75:25). Learning from Scripture that he lacks the "perfect righteousness" that would make him likable to God, a righteousness "nowhere to be found but in the person of Jesus Christ" (*GA*, ¶83:27), Bunyan experiences himself less as a party to a contract and more as a thing before an economic agent who may take no liking to him. Powerless to affect his own value, Bunyan can only examine his inner self for signs that, in a cosmic transaction, Christ's righteousness has been credited to him.

In one of the most famous episodes of *Grace Abounding*, Bunyan recounts hearing a sermon on Song of Songs 4:1, and his response illustrates the toll of religious agency confined to scrupulous examination of self and Scripture. Preaching on the text "*Behold thou art fair, my Love; behold, thou art fair*," the minister urged the "*poor tempted Soul, when thou art assaulted and afflicted with temptation, and the hidings of Gods Face, yet* [to] *think on these two words, MY LOVE, still*" (*GA*, ¶89–90:29). This point of the sermon affected Bunyan intensely, but even in the midst of the experience he began interrogating its authenticity: "the words began thus to kindle in my Spirit, *Thou art my Love, thou art my Love*, twenty times together . . . they waxed stronger and warmer . . . [but] I still replied in my heart, *But is it true too? but is it true?*" (*GA*, ¶91:29). Throughout the account Bunyan is at pains to stress his passivity in feeling the words pass through his heart, and the moments closest to agency on his part are self-questioning and simply "giving place to the Word" (*GA*, ¶92:29).[23] Even at the height of joy Bunyan is careful not to claim that any colossal exchange has taken place but only that he felt his sins "should be" forgiven. And even this assurance was short-lived: "Wherefore I said in my Soul with much gladness, Well, I would I had a pen and ink here, I would write this down before I go any further, for surely I will not forget *this* forty years hence." "But alas!" he laments, "within less then [*sic*] forty days I began to question all again," because he had "lost much of the life and savour" of the experience (*GA*, ¶92–93:30).[24]

In *Grace Abounding*, the quest for such spontaneous, affective evidence of spiritual exchange and the possession of grace leads Bunyan not to the desired one-time conversion but to suspicion of every positive experience as a product of his wish and not of God's will.[25] In this way Bunyan's account poignantly foreshadows the conundrum by which, for most of the Restoration and eighteenth century, inspired by the advances of the New Science, empiricism in moral philosophy promised certainty and delivered nothing so much as skepticism.[26] In a system of thought that seeks knowledge of salvation configured as a moment of exchange, the very certainty to which this knowledge aspires seems self-subverting; the critical vigor that drives one to seek certainty also ceaselessly drives one to question its evidence, especially as it recedes from immediate sense into the mists of memory. In Bunyan's empirical quest for the certainty of conversion, anxiety and guilt paradoxically become the only things that give him peace, because they afford him the opportunity for repeated relief and reassurance. "The guilt of sin did help me much," he confesses in a revealing moment, "for still as that would come upon me, the blood of Christ did take it off again, and again, and again, and that too, sweetly, according to the Scriptures" (*GA*, ¶125:39). This recurring "sense and terror of [his] own wickedness" seems also to have fed a certain masochistic economy of this spirituality, in which the misery of guilt increases the value of the release, even if the many experiences of release never attain to a failsafe certainty.

In *Grace Abounding*, the mindset that seeks "true tokens of a truly godly man" ends with a spirituality of neurotically biting-the-coin, so to speak. As Marc Shell has pointed out, the moment that marks the internalization of economic forms of thought comes when the status of the physical coin as arbitrary symbol and constructed, physical artifact is silently erased and the leap is made into the transcendent realm of "meaning." And yet, he notes, this internalization inevitably produces discomforting, motivating stings and resistances.[27] Bunyan's spirituality marks just such a moment, the near breaking-point of an increasingly rationalized religion which removes meaning from the material realm of ritual and quotidian practice into the realm of feelings coming upon one as "true tokens" of transcendent reality. Repeated phrases such as "My love, my love" register less as particular words than as series of events proving God's favor. Bunyan's repetitive cycle of anxiety and release, testing the metal of experience in search of "true tokens" of the godly self, seems on the verge of the realization that it is not tokens themselves but the good faith of the giver or receiver that is true or false—that the human experience of interpreting language and signs is different from the realm of calculable exchanges governed by laws and contracts.[28] Given Bunyan's scrupulous spiritual epistemology, what is notable about *Grace Abounding* is not the irrational enthusiasm of which Bunyan was often accused, but precisely the full extent to which he enters into the rationalization of his day.[29] The distinguishing feature of his faith is not that it is a crutch or opiate, nor that it allows him to entertain some fantasy of his agency or virtue, but the pained passivity to which it gives rise in the search for such certainty: the quasi paralysis of anxiety, with spiritual agency almost entirely out of reach except in the mental hyperactivity of self-critique. In what could be called Bunyan's schooling in Puritan epistemology, Mr. Gifford urged his congregation "to take special heed, that we took not up any truth upon trust . . . but to cry mightily to God, that he would convince us of the reality thereof," for "clearly there was . . . a great difference between that faith that is fained [*sic*] . . . and that which comes by a man being born thereto of God" (*GA*, ¶117–18:37). Faith here is not a volitional act on the believer's part but a state of knowing conferred by God. Faith has been cashed out as knowledge, and the value of religion is understood more and more in terms of certainty, possession, and exchange. *Grace Abounding* is above all an account of Christian spirituality experienced and articulated in these discourses. This spirituality not only fails to achieve a final, correct calculation of "the worth of the things of God," but its psychological violence engenders its own resistance. This resistance, more even than the quest for certainty, is arguably the heart of Bunyan's autobiography.[30]

"Sell Him, Sell Him"—Wounds, Resistances, Incommensurabilities

In the first third of *Grace Abounding*, Bunyan's cycles of assurance and doubt crescendo until Christ's taking away his guilt "again, and again, and again" by his blood brings what Bunyan believed was real spiritual knowledge: "Now had I an evidence, as I thought, of my salvation from

Heaven, with many golden Seals thereon, all hanging in my sight" (*GA*, ¶128:40). But it is precisely at this longed-for point in the narrative that the great crisis consuming most of the volume erupts: "And now I found, as I thought, that I loved Christ dearly. O me thought my Soul cleaved unto him, my affections cleaved unto him. I felt love to him as hot as fire, and now, as Job said, I thought I should die in my nest; but I did quickly find, that my great love was but little, and that I, who had, as I thought, such burning love to Jesus Christ, could let him go again for a very trifle" (*GA*, ¶131:41). The central trauma of *Grace Abounding* erupts at the site where love is thought in terms of proof and knowledge, and it is after God has given him "such strong consolation and blessed evidence from heaven touching my interest in his love" that Bunyan suffers "a more grievous temptation than before" (*GA*, ¶132:41):

> And that was to sell and part with this most blessed Christ, to exchange him for the things of this life; for any thing: the temptation lay upon me for the space of a year, and did follow me so continually, that I was not rid of it one day in a month, no not sometimes one hour in many days together, unless I was asleep. . . .
>
> It did always, in almost whatever I thought, intermix itself therewith, in such sort that I could neither eat my food, stoop for a pin, chop a stick, or cast mine eye to look on this or that, but still the temptation would come, *Sell Christ for this, or sell Christ for that; sell him, sell him.*
>
> Sometimes it would run in my thoughts not so little as a hundred times together, Sell him, sell him, sell him; against which, I may say, for whole hours together I have been forced to stand as continually leaning and forcing my spirit against it, lest haply before I were aware, some wicked thought might arise in my heart that might consent thereto; and sometimes also the Tempter would make me believe I had consented to it, then should I be as tortured on a Rack for whole dayes together.
>
> This temptation did put me to such scares lest I should at sometimes, I say, consent thereto, and be overcome therewith, that by the very force of my mind in labouring to gainsay and resist this wickedness my very Body also would be put into action or motion, by way of pushing or thrusting with my hands or elbows; still answering, as fast as the destroyer said *Sell him;* I will not, I will not, I will not, I will not, no not for thousands, thousands, thousands of worlds; thus reckoning lest I should in the midst of these assaults, set too low a vallue of him, even until I scarce well knew where I was, or how to be composed again. (*GA*, ¶133, 135–37:41–42)

And under such psychological weight, Bunyan eventually did, he tells us, succumb:

> But to be brief, one morning, as I did lie in my Bed, I was, as at other times, most fiercely assaulted with this temptation, to *sell and part with Christ;* the wicked suggestion still running in my mind, *Sell him, sell him, sell him, sell him,* as fast as a man could speak; against which also in my mind, as at other times, I answered, No, no, not for thousands, thousands, thousands, at least twenty times together; but at last, after much striving, even until I was almost out of breath, I felt this thought pass through my heart, *Let him go if he will!* and I thought also that I felt my heart consent thereto. Oh, the diligence of Satan! Oh, the desperateness of man's heart! (*GA*, ¶139:43)

In the weeks and months after this ordeal, reeling from guilt, Bunyan is haunted by an image of irreversible, damnable exchange found in both the Old and New Testaments: "And withal, that Scripture did seize upon my Soul, *Or profane person, as Esau, who for one morsel of meat sold his Birthright; for you know how that afterwards when he would have inherited the blessing, he was rejected, for he found no place of repentance, though he sought it carefully with tears,* Heb. 12. 16, 17" (*GA*, ¶141:43). For the rest of his account, Bunyan's despair of salvation takes the form of Esau having sold his birthright. Though he managed to convince himself that his sin was not identical to Judas's unpardonable selling of Christ for thirty pieces of silver (*GA*, ¶158:48), Bunyan's sin of selling Christ seemed to him worse by comparison than every sin committed in the Bible: "These thought I are great sins, sins of a bloudy colour, yea, it would turn again upon me, *they are none of them of the nature of yours, you have parted with Jesus! you have sold your Saviour!*" (*GA*, ¶171:51).

The temptation to "Sell him" and its aftermath dominate *Grace Abounding*, and yet criticism has scarcely addressed why the crisis erupts at this point in the text or why it takes the particular form that it does, an insidious invitation to exchange.[31] The horror of this temptation, to Bunyan's mind, lies particularly in it occurring after his receiving "*evidence . . .* touching my *interest* in his love" (italics mine). He reads this trial as a reflection on his own spiritual poverty and pride; it reveals his lack of love and faithfulness precisely where he thought he possessed it and where this evidence should have produced it. What can be clearer to us perhaps than to Bunyan is the extent to which this crisis reflects not simply his inner condition but the larger discourses and logics in which his spirituality and worldview are imbricated. Seeking proof of love and evidence of salvation *qua* exchange, Bunyan's spiritual life erupts in a horrific trauma that takes an uncannily economic form. His defining temptation is not to adultery or murder but to that ubiquitous act of exchange on which the booming mercantile economy of his day was based, and most disturbingly, to an act that is a grotesque mirror image of the conversion—purchase and redemption—which he has desired and desired evidence of from God. Just as the key to right prayer in *I Will Pray with the Spirit* is knowledge of God's value, so its inverted, obsessive fear manifests itself in Bunyan's refusal to exchange Christ for thousands of worlds, "lest I should . . . set too low a value of him."

Erupting after Bunyan had experienced repeated spontaneous assurances taken as evidence of love and tokens of salvation, this episode exposes the centermost fissure or traumatic kernel of a faith that conceives of itself in these economic-epistemological terms. The numbingly repeated "Sell him, sell him" becomes more articulate when set in its theological and cultural context and read as a recurring psychological symptom, a category of experience which Jacques Lacan associates with the repetitive emergence of the real at the same site. For Lacan in *The Four Fundamental Concepts of Psychoanalysis*, repetitive psychological symptoms are often associated with "radical points in the real"—the "real" referring to that which is unsymbolizable in the symbolic order—where "reality is in abeyance there, awaiting attention."[32] These encounters with the real, according to Lacan, are essentially missed because of their originally traumatic nature and their continually re-presenting what is "*unassimilable*" in the subject and the symbolic order (*FF*, 55). The real "always comes back to the same place," the place "where the subject does not meet it" (*FF*, 49), because the "original encounter" with the inassimilable real in the self or other is traumatic; "the real," Lacan writes, "in its dialectical effects [is] originally unwelcome" (*FF*, 69).

If we understand "Sell him, sell him" as the great symptom of Bunyan's theology, the very juxtaposition of these words—violently forced out next to each other, perceived as the words of "the Destroyer" and resisted "til I scarce well knew where I was, or how to be composed again"—suggests the site of what is inassimilable for this theology and for Bunyan. The rupture of the real lies literally between these two words, at the incommensurability of "sell" with "him," between personhood and the logic of adequation and interchangeability. The horror of "Sell him, sell him" is the violence that the first word wreaks on the other, the disjunction between personal relation and possession, and the trauma occasioned by a theology that imagines salvation as simply conversion, and loving relation as exchange and valuation, as setting a price on another, effacing her as a person by making her a known and interchangeable quantity. For Bunyan the greatest temptation is to sell Christ, the greatest sin to set an incorrect value on him; and yet the immense guilt surrounding the episode bespeaks a recognition on some level that to think of salvation in terms of buying and selling is itself tantamount to sin, since to sell the infinite God and personal Christ is to devalue him, and thus the entire theology of salvation as purchase, as conversion, as "having God," and as redemption by sacrifice, itself becomes painfully suspect. Love, which Bunyan thought he had rationally ascertained, is literally inarticulable in this system.

Part of the incommensurability embodied in this episode, then, stems from the disjunction between loving and knowledge-possession, between the subject "I" who owns, appraises and sells, and the "him" who would be loved but is ultimately wronged in being bought, sold, and known as an object—positions which both God and Bunyan occupy at different times in the narrative.[33] This explains why Bunyan's account is consistently vague about what Christ was to be sold for; the temptation was not to sell Christ for money or for something as dear as his blind daughter's sight,[34] but simply "to exchange him for the things of this life, for anything . . . *Sell Christ for this, or sell Christ for that; sell him, sell him*" (*GA*, ¶133, 135:41). It is the larger system of adequation and certainty that is at odds with "him," with love, with faith. At the height of his misery, Bunyan feels the good news of Christ as bad news, as it were, because it speaks to him only of guilt and of the good he has sold:

> Now the most free, and full, and gracious words of the Gospel were the greatest torment to me; . . . for the remembrance of a Saviour, because I had cast him off, brought both the villainy of my sin, and my loss by it to mind. . . . Every time that I thought of the Lord Jesus, of his Grace, Love, Goodness, Kindness, Gentleness, Meekness, Death, Blood, Promises and blessed Exhortations, Comforts and Consolations, it went to my Soul like a Sword; for . . . these thoughts would make place for themselves in my heart; *Ay, This is the Jesus, the loving Saviour, the Son of God, whom thou has parted with. . . . This is the only Saviour, the only Redeemer, the only one that could so love sinners as to wash them from their sins in his own most precious Blood: but you have no part nor lot in this Jesus, you have put him away from you, you have said in your heart,* Let him go if he will. . . . O thought I, what have I lost! What have I parted with! What have I dis-inherited my poor Soul of!
> (*GA*, ¶183:56)

Torment, villainy, loss, parting, disinheritance: after Bunyan has succumbed to temptation, he is haunted by the notion that he has committed the unforgivable "sin against the Holy Spirit" and, like Esau, sold his birthright in one rash moment of hunger. Esau is a compelling figure for Bunyan's experience of religious subjectivity: the subject before language and the law, always evaluating, exchanging, and possessing, always in danger of total destitution, especially if he gives in to his desire for comfort, "selling him" as Bunyan does, simply to be rid of this hounding temptation. Jesus is nowhere portrayed so vividly or at such length in *Grace Abounding* as in this passage, vis-à-vis Esau: not as Byzantium's transfigured victor over Hades or the sexualized lover of late medieval mysticism, but as nothing so much as Bunyan's lack or loss, the perpetual threat of what one might lose forever. As an agent constantly imperiled by the threat of one devastating exchange and an object Christ might take no liking to, Bunyan experiences himself as doubly impoverished. Several critics have interpreted the "Sell him" episode as Bunyan's bid or desire for autonomy from God,[35] but the reverse reading seems more compelling. The excruciating psychological tension of seeing oneself forever isolated as a commodity before God and the haunting guilt of looking at the other through such lenses are precisely what erupt in this episode, and so it is rather the very possibility of an autonomous self who can buy and sell, be bought and sold, that Bunyan's traumatic experience calls into question. In this way, the "Sell him" trauma marks nothing less than the potential undoing of Bunyan's covenant theology and of its entire framework for an understanding relation with God.

But Bunyan misrecognizes this possibility, and for his theology to remain intact he must; he resists the temptation to sell Christ, he tells us, "lest I should set too low a value on him," keeping his economically inflected theology in place. At the deepest level, what is both hidden and revealed in the ceaseless call to "Sell him" is the way in which this theology has sold Christ already. It has made him exchangeable not in indulgences or "superstitious" veneration of the Eucharist but in its very configuration of his dealings with humanity as purchase, atonement, and conversion, regulated by systematic doctrine discernible though a literalist reading of Scripture.[36] But by a logic of wounding that connects the misery of *Grace Abounding* back to *I Will Pray with the Spirit*, Bunyan reads his great spiritual struggle in a way that actually recuperates the two and a half years of depression it causes, as spiritual evidence in the very terms of his theology. In *I Will Pray with the Spirit*, the evidence of spiritual authenticity Bunyan seeks must be so natural as to be like "blood forced out of flesh": "The soul, I say, feels, and from feeling, sighs, groans, and breaks at the heart. For right Prayer bubleth out of the heart when it is over-pressed with grief and bitterness, as blood is forced out of the flesh, by reason of some heavy burthen that lyeth upon it. . . . Again, *It is a pouring out of the Heart or Soul*" (*IWP*, 8, 14). The recurrent free-prayer image of pouring out the heart becomes much more articulate when connected to the violent picture of prayer bubbling out of the soul like blood from a wound. Perhaps no other image in free-prayer literature so accurately captures its ideology of spontaneity and the tenor of the spirituality it produces. The spirituality of spontaneity both engenders and contains its own resistances; it produces a psychological wounding that in the "Sell him" ordeal bespeaks this spirituality's profound incommensurabilities and cries out its nearly inarticulate resistance to the closure of rationalized religion; this bleeding and wounding is then recuperated as evidence of the system's validity.[37]

Bunyan's experience of wounding echoes the contradictory emotion and violence that Debora Shuger finds in the self-divided reader produced by Calvinist passion narratives. "In Renaissance Protestantism," she writes, "violence replaces desire as the fundamental operation of the soul's *practique de soi*," and in these Calvinist texts, "awareness of the opposing surges of intense, contradictory emotions sweeping across this psyche gives rise to an urgent demand for self-control, moderation, and obedience to external authority in order to halt this inner turbulence.... But ... self-control itself turns out to be a form of violence and hence unable to still the eddying repetitions of torture, in which the victim and aggressor exchange roles in a seemingly endless cycle."[38] In just such a cycle, Bunyan returns repeatedly in *Grace Abounding* to the image of blood and payment in the Scripture ("Without shedding of blood there is no remission of sins," Heb 9:22), and yet in this agonized "pouring out" of his soul, that blood is as often Bunyan's as Christ's.[39] In a similar reversal of roles, divine love comes to be understood as a version of human commodity desire. After the striking "I have loved thee with an everlasting love" passage, Bunyan elaborates on his understanding of God's love:

> Yea, the love and affection that then did burn within to my Lord and Saviour Jesus Christ, did work at this time such a strong and hot desire of revengement upon my self for the abuse I had done unto him, that, to speak as then I thought, had I had a thousand gallons of blood within my veins, I could freely then have spilt it all at the command and feet of this my Lord and Saviour.
>
> And as I was thus in musing and in my studies, how to love the Lord and to express my love to him ... thus it was made out to me, *That the great God did set so high an esteem upon the love of his poor Creatures, that rather then [sic] he would go without their love he would pardon their transgressions.* (*GA*, ¶192–93:60–61)

Even at his most tender, God in Bunyan's rendering forgives people not because it is in the divine nature to be loving or kind, but because he "sets so high an esteem upon the love of his creatures": because they possess what he wants, something he can purchase by forgiving their debts, securing their love almost as obligation. Love for God in *Grace Abounding* seems never to be mutual delight in another but, understandably, only the gasp of suffering in momentary relief.

In *The Four Fundamental Concepts of Psychoanalysis*, Lacan links the religious, though perhaps not religion per se, to his notion of the real when he says, "*The gods belong to the field of the real*" (45). Though Lacan repeatedly denies that psychoanalysis is a religion, he affirms that, perhaps like religious experience, psychoanalysis too is an "essential encounter" with the real, "an appointment to which we are always called with a real that eludes us," an encounter that "the subject is condemned to miss," though "even this miss is revelatory" (*FF*, 53, 39). Bunyan's crisis of hearing "Sell him, sell him" day in and day out for over a year, resisting and resisting, finally succumbing, and then attempting to recover from that guilt, is just such an ongoing, near-but-missed encounter with the real, with an experience of self and God that cannot fit into the symbolic order of a theology that particularly in the preceding century had imagined itself in terms of abstraction, knowledge, and exchange. The ideology and fantasy of mercantile culture and of its signature religious form is the fantasy of abstraction and equivalence: that all things are reducible to propositions and contracts, that the relationship to God and persons can be completely abstracted into sin and payment. The real, "impossible kernel" in Bunyan's experience is the radical incommensurability between being exchanged like a thing and relating as a person, in both directions—from man to God and from God to man as man figures it, in the image of man's own social relations.

In addressing the repetitive symptom, at one point Lacan notes somewhat cryptically that "the real supports the phantasy, the phantasy protects the real" (*FF*, 41). In Bunyan's account, the real supports the fantasy in that the symptomatic re-eruption of anxiety about conversion and buying-and-selling always allows the repeated experience of the word coming upon Bunyan afresh and providing a sort of empirical proof of God's favor. In a faith that has rejected the ritualistic and liturgical, its "spontaneous," symptomatic rituals are the ones generated by empiricism and exchange: anxiety and release over conversion, and, as we will see in the next section, the repetition of conversion-as-exchange in the evangelization of others. "The fantasy protects the real" as well, indirectly and unintentionally, in that the fantasy in which there could be final proof of conversion and in which relation to God or the other could be economic—and not an uncertain, dialogic encounter with one who nonetheless remains truly other and inassimilable—allows the real to keep re-emerging at this spot, this suture or symptom. The real supports the fantasy, then, in just the way that *Grace Abounding* is the basis for *The Pilgrim's Progress*. It is the allegorical narrative that Bunyan crafted out of the experiences of *Grace Abounding* that can be understood as simultaneously and overdeterminedly the origin of the English novel and the ultimate fantasy of an increasingly rationalized and secularized religion.

The Pilgrim's Progress—Evangelism and the Salvation of Commodity Culture

After the "Sell him" crisis, Bunyan's inner life gained in stability but was still frequently consumed with cycles of despondency, anxiety, and fear, followed by momentary relief. In day-to-day life, however, Bunyan's spirituality authorized two main behaviors, the study of Scripture and evangelism. Where religious learning takes place not through participating in liturgy or sacrament but almost exclusively through rational argument, Bible study and evangelism become the primary pedagogical tools. They also work to relieve the incommensurability and uncertainty at the heart of *Grace Abounding*. Bunyan relates that he eventually found evangelism his calling, and the labor of converting others to Christ is the focus of much of the final two sections of *Grace Abounding*:[40] "I found my spirit leaned most after awakening and converting Work. . . . In my preaching I have really been in pain, and have as it were travelled [i.e., travailed] to bring forth Children to God; neither could I be satisfied unless some fruits did appear in my work. . . . It pleased me nothing to see people drink in Opinions if they seemed ignorant of Jesus Christ, and the worth of their own Salvation, sound conviction for Sin . . . and an heart set on fire to be saved by Christ" (*GA*, ¶289-91:89). For Bunyan, "bearing fruit" means not the cultivation of virtue in general but replicating in others the conversion and knowledge of spiritual worth he hopes has occurred for himself. The "satisfaction" of this converting work lies at least in part, then, in that it empirically assures him as to his own experience of salvation in a less painful and more repeatable way than strictly personal experience does, keeping the memory of conversion fresh through a never-ending succession of conversions sought perhaps as much out of a desire for one's own salvation as for others.'[41]

It was this calling to evangelism that by Bunyan's account provided the impetus for writing *The Pilgrim's Progress*. After the Restoration Bunyan was imprisoned as one of a handful of ministers considered too dangerous to be tolerated in nonconformity and whom Charles II's government attempted to force to promise never to preach again. In limbo between conforming and, he thought, dying for his faith, Bunyan wrote one of the most effective evangelical tools that Protestantism has produced. Against conventional Puritan opinion that only Scripture was appropriate for converting work, in "The Author's Apology for His Book," Bunyan defended its imaginative, allegorical form almost completely in terms of evangelism:[42]

> You see the ways the fisherman doth take
> To catch the fish, what engines doth he make?
> Behold! how he engageth all his wits
> Also his snares, lines, angles, hooks and nets.
> Yet fish there be, that neither hook, nor line,
> Nor snare, nor net, nor engine can make thine;
> They must be groped for, and be tickled too,
> Or they will not be catched, what e're you do.[43]

This story, he contends, can be as legitimate an evangelical tool as preaching or Bible study because its language contains the same valuable substance of truth that Scripture does: "My dark and cloudy words they do but hold / The truth, as cabinets enclose the gold" (*PP*, 6). In these opening pages *The Pilgrim's Progress* presents the gospel as deeply compatible with value as figured in emerging commodity culture; *The Pilgrim's Progress* is pictured in fact as the dream commodity that promises the perfect convergence of novelty, diversion, truth, knowledge, and feeling:[44]

> This book is writ in such a dialect
> As may the minds of listless men affect:
> It seems a novelty, and yet contains
> Nothing but sound and honest gospel-strains.
>   Would'st thou divert thyself from melancholy?
> Would'st thou be pleasant, yet be far from folly?
> Would'st thou read riddles and their explanation,
> Or else be drowned in thy contemplation?
> Dost thou love picking-meat? Or would'st thou see
> A man i' the clouds, and hear him speak to thee?
> Would'st thou be in a dream, and yet not sleep?
> Or would'st thou in a moment laugh and weep?
> Wouldest thou lose thyself, and catch no harm
> And find thyself again without a charm?
> Would'st read thyself, and read thou know'st not what
> And yet know whether thou are blest or not,
> By reading the same lines? O then come hither,
> And lay my book, thy head and heart together. (*PP*, 9)

In saying that this book "seems a novelty" yet contains nothing but the same old gospel strains, Bunyan reveals a profound truth about *The Pilgrim's Progress* and its popularity, the degree to which the commodity-driven love of novelty is both crucial to and problematic for this spirituality. "Lay my book, thy head and heart together" binds the images in the preceding lines, with commodity, emotion, epistemology, and religion all spun together in a single strand. *The Pilgrim's Progress* stands as the perfect drawing together of these discordant elements, a narrative so comforting and necessary because in reality the strands unwind; their being peacefully entwined is a much-desired fiction.[45]

Christian begins his journey to the Celestial City, then, navigating pitfalls and waiting for the removal of his heavy burden. Not surprisingly, his first major trial is the Slough of Despond: despair, precisely over his lost condition and lack of spiritual worth. Helpful tells him: "This miry Slough is such a place as cannot be mended; it is the descent whither the scum and filth that attends conviction for sin doth continually run . . . for still as the sinner is awakened about his lost condition, there ariseth in his soul many fears, and doubts, and discouraging apprehensions, which all of them get together, and settle in this place; and this is the reason of the badness of this ground" (*PP*, 17). One of the chief functions of this spatialization of spiritual life is to enable the fantasy that spiritual pain and horrible "places" such as the Slough of Despond can simply be avoided.[46] *The Pilgrim's Progress* masks the inevitability of this despair and diminished agency as a response to being perpetually agent or object, Esau or commodity, in a celestial economy of salvation and damnation; one of its haunting thoughts is that this very concept of salvation itself entails such misery.

Just as *The Pilgrim's Progress* masks the deep logic connecting its spirituality to misery, anxiety, and passivity, it also provides a powerful fantasy of the possible certainty of conversion. When the burden of Christian's sin is finally removed at the Cross—that is, when Christ's perfect righteousness is applied to the debt of Christian's sin at the site of his shedding of blood—Christian is given three tokens of this conversion. Two of them, the white garment and the mark on his forehead, are symbols found in Scripture itself and long used in rites of baptism and confirmation. The third, a "roll" or paper "certificate," though, is without scriptural type as a sign of salvation, and its prominence in Christian's journey is due to the role it fills as the much-desired tangible proof of salvation economically construed. Bunyan tells how Christian "would be often reading in the roll that one of the Shining Ones gave him, by which he was refreshed" (*PP*, 38). How dear the certificate is to Christian becomes clear when he loses it: "who can tell how joyful this man was, when he had gotten his roll again! For this roll was the assurance of his life, and acceptance at the desired haven" (*PP*, 41). Elsewhere he calls the roll "my evidence" (*PP*, 43). Most critics have passed over the roll without comment; in the most specific readings, Christopher Hill has called it "a sort of identity card," and Michael McKeon sees it as a certificate of indenture to the Lord of the Hill.[47] In the context of the covenant theology that was so determinative for Bunyan and his first readers, it is almost impossible not to understand it as a contract: the personal addendum adding Christian to the heavenly contract of the New Covenant of Grace. At the gateway to heaven, it is not his heart which will be weighed but this roll, or contract, which Christian must present, the evidence of knowledge and exchange, one of the "true tokens of a truly godly man." In the spirituality of spontaneity, the actual ontological condition of salvation—what that might mean in terms other than an external certificate of conversion or the replication of conversion through evangelizing others—is inaccessible and inarticulable, and ultimately its value is eclipsed by that of its external certification.

Just as the roll upholds the fantasy of final, certified religious conversion, so Christian's foil, Ignorance, serves to uphold the idea that Christian possesses real knowledge.[48] After Hopeful relates the tale of his conversion, he and Christian once again meet up with Ignorance. In the familiar pattern of assurance followed by scrutiny and skepticism, the moral of the ensuing encounter is that Ignorance's feeling regarding his salvation—"My heart tells me so"—is not a valid indication of conversion. Such feelings, we are told, are insufficient "except the Word of God beareth witness" (*PP*, 126), and the only heart-feelings that the word confirms are ones of continual judgment for sin. Again, authenticity equates with misery; Ignorance cannot believe his heart is so totally bad, and Christian tells him that he therefore never had a good thought in his life. Indeed, no figure in the allegory serves to make the good news look like bad news as much as Ignorance. When Christian first meets Ignorance, he asks him what he possesses "that may cause that the Gate should be opened" to him. Ignorance answers, "I know my Lord's will, and I have been a good liver, I pay every man his own; I pray, fast, pay tithes, and give alms, and have left my country, for whither I am going" (108). It becomes apparent that whether or not he has kept his end of the bargain, Ignorance has no contract; like the person who unwittingly prays the Lord's Prayer without perfect conviction, Ignorance lacks the distinguishing mark or "earnest" guaranteeing true knowledge of spiritual worth.

We might go so far as to say that the ontology of this allegory crumbles under the figure of Ignorance, or hangs on the magic contract-roll: the Slough of Despond, the River of Death, these can be successfully traversed without being saved, "in ignorance" and without certified knowledge of conversion. In the journey from the City of Destruction to the Celestial City, the sole distinction between the "true" faith of Christian and the "false" faith of Ignorance is not progress, but parchment: the tiny written roll, a legal document certifying that the trip already actually made was legitimate. Even as the text tries to establish the breach between Christian and Ignorance, it highlights their similarity; both of them physically make it to the Celestial City, while many in the story do not, and Ignorance seems somehow to have gotten rid of his burden. In *The Pilgrim's Progress* a true pilgrim is ultimately distinguishable from a false one only by this magical sign, the roll, a desired, fantastical, evidentiary object that would be the sure seal of salvation or certification of truth. After the emotional roller coaster of Christian's journey, the reader is left perhaps more confident of the pathway to take but, like Bunyan in *Grace Abounding*, also eternally desperate for certification that her own journey is legally approved by God.

It makes sense therefore that the final scene of *The Pilgrim's Progress* is not of Christian but of Ignorance. After the Shining Ones receive Christian into heaven and the pearly gates close behind him, we glimpse Ignorance, having made it across the River of Death, albeit by a ferry. He tells the gatekeeper that he has eaten and drunk in the presence of the king and wishes to enter, but when asked for his roll, he has none. At this, two angels bind him hand and foot: "Then they took him up, and carried him through the air to the door that I saw in the side of the hill, and put him in there. Then I saw that there was a way to Hell, even from the Gates of Heaven, as well as from the City of Destruction" (*PP*, 141–42). The final warning with which Bunyan leaves his reader is the terrifying result of salvation translated into the economic, epistemological terms of his day: that even at the door of paradise, there is a trapdoor to hell, the lack of proof of legal spiritual exchange. Perhaps even more terrifying is that in Bunyan's system such certification never materializes as a literal roll but can only take the form of despair over one's worthlessness, felt with such pain and intensity that it bubbles forth like blood from a wound.

An obvious corollary of the "Sell him" trauma does not appear in Christian's journey, but the centerpiece of *The Pilgrim's Progress* is arguably its crucial reworking, expressing a similarly vexed conscience about exchange at the same time that it reinscribes economic thought in Bunyan's theology and spirituality. The City of Vanity, with its Vanity Fair recalling the great centers of commerce in Bunyan's day,[49] is the most treacherous obstacle between the City of Destruction and the Celestial City, first and foremost because of the greedy consumption that goes on there: "all such merchandise [is] sold, as houses, lands, trades, places, honours, preferments, titles, countries, kingdoms, lusts, pleasures, and delights of all sorts, as whores, bawds, wives, husbands, children, masters, servants, lives, blood, bodies, souls, silver, gold, pearls, precious stones, and what not" (*PP*, 79). Christ himself went through this fair, we are told, with every temptation "to cheapen and buy some of his vanities; but he had no mind to the merchandise, and therefore left the town without laying out so much as one farthing upon these vanities" (79). Where Bunyan was tempted to sell Christ, Christian and Faithful are called by the hawkers to buy: "One chanced mockingly . . . to say unto them, 'What will ye buy?'" and in one of the key moments of the Bunyan corpus, Christian and Faithful, "looking gravely upon him, said, 'We buy the truth'" (80). Truth and knowledge are here not only possessions but commodities; salvation is a matter of making the right purchase. *The Pilgrim's Progress* expresses a certain bad conscience about commodity logic but not a complete break with it; it dreams of correcting and spiritualizing buying and selling, not of declaring them incommensurate with personhood or relation with others. Whereas the central episode of *Grace Abounding* testifies to the incommensurability of economic logic with personal relation, the central episode of *The Pilgrim's Progress* constitutes the self precisely as the buyer and possessor of knowledge, effectively suturing the precise wound exposed at the heart of *Grace Abounding*.[50]

The Pilgrim's Progress is then, in both senses of the phrase, the salvation of commodity culture: it is the salvation it has to offer, the purchase of knowledge as that magical, reified, all-fulfilling object, and it saves mercantile culture and the religion that has internalized its logic from the haunting suspicion of its own bad faith. At Faithful's trial he is accused of having said "that Christianity, and the customs of our town of Vanity"—not its buying and selling—"were diametrically opposite, and could not be reconciled" (*PP*, 83). Though the text expresses disapproval of much that was evil about exchange in Bunyan's day, it never questions the analogy of the market projected onto Christianity and relationship with God (for which Scripture, among other metaphors, does after all supply warrant). Only in its opening pages does the tale betray a weariness of the continual anxieties associated with understanding all of life in terms of buying and selling. Heaven is described as a place of riches and the stable ownership of God: "There are crowns of glory to be given us; and garments that will make us shine like the sun in the firmament of heaven. . . . There shall be no more crying, nor sorrow; for he that is owner of the place will wipe all tears from our eyes. . . . There also you shall meet with thousands, and ten thousands that have gone before us to that place; none of them are hurtful, but loving, and holy, everyone walking in the sight of God and standing in his presence with acceptance for ever" (*PP*, 15). Perhaps nothing in the Bunyan corpus is so poignant as this picture of heaven and exactly what of earthly life Christian hopes will be missing from it: God is the owner of all, there is no longer the anxiety over buying or selling or whether God will "take a liking to him," and the jeering masses of Vanity Fair are replaced by a vast, kind group and "acceptance forever," implying that the warm community so long denied the pilgrim is possible only after commerce is ended.

And yet this version of heaven is where the story starts, and not where it ends, with its warning against Ignorance and its reinstantiation of the economic, epistemological logic it wishes to escape. *The Pilgrim's Progress*, not unlike the Puritan spirituality of which it is the most popular flower, attempts nothing less than the salvation of commodity culture even as it indicts its evils; it is both the culmination of and escape from exchange. It serves as a powerful reminder that ideology is not a simple dream-like illusion or escape, but a "fantasy-construction" that supports and structures our real social relations by "mask[ing] some insupportable, real, impossible kernel" of antagonism within those relations.[51] *The Pilgrim's Progress* is just such a fantasy construction, masking the irreducible tension between religious, personal relation and what Lyotard calls the discourses of economics and mastery.[52] And like all fantasy, the appeal of *The Pilgrim's Progress* lies in the particular place it holds open for the subject.[53] Frontispiece engravings illustrate this from the earliest editions: varying slightly in size and composition, they show Christian on his journey, small and in the background, and in the foreground a massive Bunyan: author, poet, and preacher-hero, imagining the story, and in later editions, dreaming Keats-like over his own book (see fig. 2; p. 86). Bunyan the writer and dreamer of this allegory, as represented at the front of *The Pilgrim's Progress*, is constituted as a whole subject, the shattered self of *Grace Abounding* put back together again by the logic of authorship and narrative, itself supposed to be a work not of art but of spontaneous inspiration. Readers are often presumed to identify with Christian, but the portraits of a heroic Bunyan, prominently displayed in edition after edition of *The Pilgrim's Progress*, reveal that his *authority*, in both senses, is as much the ground of the power of this narrative.

But by attempting to reconcile religion to discourses of economics and mastery, *The Pilgrim's Progress* is also inherently secularizing. Christopher Hill has commented on its profound secularity, and as Gordon Campbell notes, Bunyan's "cruel God does not even appear in the narrative"; *The Pilgrim's Progress* "pictures Christian in a world without God, and is only unattractive in those rare instances in which God intervenes in Christian's life."[54] The pilgrim crosses over not so much from the City of Destruction to the Celestial City as from the Protestant upheavals of the early modern period into a fully modern religious subjectivity, one that inhabits this secular space, this world without God, and imagines itself as "buying the truth" in fully empirical and economic terms. Even so, the enormous evangelical potency of reconciling the religious self to this position of subjectivity and to economic and empirical rationality cannot be overestimated. *The Pilgrim's Progress* ran into twelve editions in Bunyan's lifetime; by 1938 there were at least 1,300 editions, with translations today in at least 200 languages. It has been called "the prose epic of English Puritanism" and "the best *Summa Theologiae Evangelicae* ever produced by a writer not miraculously inspired," with

Figure 2 Title page and illustration of John Bunyan, The Pilgrim's Progress, first edition (1678). Reproduced by permission of The Huntington Library, San Marino, California.

Bunyan lauded as "the Spenser of the people," "the Shakespeare of the Puritans," and perhaps most accurately of all, the "poet-apostle of the English middle-classes."[55]

"Thou Takest No Money for Them"—Hope, Desire and the God beyond Exchange

The spirituality of spontaneity, with its ethos of free prayer, emotional self-scrutiny, and evangelism, appears in this reading both as a symptom of the religious imagination under the dominant economic and epistemological discourses of its day, and as a constellation of resistances borne of this subjection. In the emerging market economy of early modernity, human endeavor and experience were increasingly valued in economic and scientific terms, in terms of abstractable knowledge and value. Religion likewise came to articulate its worth in these terms, to think that knowledge and system were what it was about, so to speak. And yet, Bunyan's tortured spirituality seems to exist as a rupture, crying out that buying, selling, and possessing are incommensurate to personal relation with God and others. In this light, the incessant "Sell him, sell him" is both Bunyan's traumatic symptom, and his finest moment, in which he experiences, however obliquely, a gap in ideology or in representation in the symbolic order, the intimation of a personal other who is not commensurate with knowledge and exchange. Bunyan adumbrates the way religion misunderstands itself in modernity inasmuch as it thinks of itself as defensible only as a system of knowledge, doctrines, and rules—when perhaps what is most religious about religion or what might be most defensible about it is the extent to which it marks the radically personal limits of system, of exchange, and of the symbolic order.[56] In this analysis, the gulf between the secular and the sacred, which as many scholars have noted was incipient in the Reformation itself and came into full flower in the eighteenth century,[57] is based not primarily on the opposed categories it so often claims, reason vs. enthusiasm, objectivity vs. belief, moderation vs. extremism. Rather, early modernity insists on the divide between the secular and the sacred because of the problems the simple abstraction of a discrete religious sphere solves. The production of the religious sphere in binary opposition to the secular is precisely what allows acquisitive capitalism to flourish; it answers to the need and desire for a secular space of human relation, that is, a realm where human relations are governed by systems navigable by calculation and interest, and free of ambiguity, doubt, and the radical responsibility of each act and belief made in the space of epistemological indeterminacy.[58]

Ultimately, it is a problematization of the divide between the secular and the religious that the anxious, systematizing spirituality of John Bunyan points toward. Symptoms often speak a strange, eloquent language around dominant discourses, tracing that which escapes their representations, and "A brief Account of the Author's Imprisonment," a sort of afterword to *Grace Abounding*, speaks with just such an eloquence. After the main account of his spiritual life, recorded ostensibly for others' edification and assurance, Bunyan describes the profound barrenness he felt during his years of imprisonment, in which he could have returned to his family if only he would recant his calling. Confined by conscience to his cell, Bunyan recounts how he was overcome with the sense of God's freedom and his own lack of it in his indefinite incarceration. After seeking evidence of conversion and never finally acquiring it, and languishing in prison with no sign of divine intervention, Bunyan seems to make a decisive break: "Wherefore, thought I, the point being thus, I am for going on, and venturing my eternal state with Christ, whether I have comfort here or no; if God doth not come in, thought I, I will leap off the Ladder even blindfold into Eternitie, sink or swim, come heaven, come hell; Lord Jesus, if thou wilt catch me, do; if not, I will venture for thy name" (*GA*, ¶337:101). Bunyan then considers the similarity between his case and Job's, in which Scripture asks "Doth Job serve God for nought?" and finally ends the book enigmatically: "And as I was thus considering, that Scripture was set before me, Psa. 44. 12 &c. Now my heart was full of comfort, for I hoped I was sincere; I would not have been without this trial for much; I am comforted everie time I think of it, and I hope I shall bless God for ever for the teaching I have had by it" (*GA*, ¶338–39:101).

Verses 12 and 13 from the psalm Bunyan cites address God in startling tones: "Thou lettest us be eaten up like sheep: and hast scattered us among the heathen. Thou sellest thy people for nought: and takest no money for them."[59] After Bunyan's spiritual energies have been consumed literally for years over desiring to be redeemed by God and over his own sin in agreeing to sell Christ, how he would find this verse comforting, speaking as it does of God making a losing bargain, and to his people's detriment, is particularly opaque, except when read against the backdrop of a spirituality simultaneously resisting and enmeshed in economic epistemology and the emotional empiricism that springs from it. Bunyan is comforted only when external evidence for his gaining something by "venturing with Christ" is gone, and when he thinks of God not as taking a liking to people, desiring their love, and forgiving sins as an act of exchange, but like Bunyan himself, as performing an act completely inscrutable by the laws of the market. It is in its very inscrutability as an act of exchange—"taking no money for them"—that Bunyan is comforted: in the moment in which he can almost imagine a direct conversation with Christ and dealing with him outside the thought of either his status as a commodity before God or his own commodification of God. In this oblique way, something in Bunyan's own spirituality testifies to that which is inarticulable in the ideology of salvation-as-exchange: the hope and desire for relation to the sacred other as something besides a subject-object buying-and-selling, for conversation that is not being scrutinized as proof, for prayer that is not about getting something. That hope—that love's inability to articulate itself as either certain knowledge, evidence, or ownership—is expressed perhaps nowhere as clearly as in Bunyan's cryptic reference to "Psa. 44. 12. &c" and the empty white space of the page that follows it.

In the larger scope of literary history, the unspoken hope of Bunyan's rationalized faith may account for his appeal as much as the other cultural work his texts perform. Above all, such a hope serves to mitigate the shutting down of prayer that the ideology of spontaneity so often threatened. Fear of insincerity had actually prompted Bunyan to dissuade readers from praying the "Our Father" or teaching it to their children. As Michael McGiffert has observed, such fear of hypocrisy and self-delusion has "desperate consequences" when pressed to its logical conclusions, plunging one into endless suspicion of insincerity and undermining all possibility of the assurance needed for and sought in prayer.[60] Bunyan's spirituality seems to have retained a hope for love and relation outside exchange that mitigated these desperate consequences and made it possible, however difficult, to pray. But paradoxically, it was not Puritan or Dissenting enthusiasts who pushed the logic of spontaneity to its most "desperate consequences." That would be left to a consciously secular philosophy that launched the most vehement attacks against religious fanaticism and claimed the rational high ground of "true enthusiasm." With this true enthusiasm came psychological ruptures that were, equally, sublimations of the secularized religion that went before: the pains of "Sell him, sell him" and "blood forced out of flesh" taken to new levels.

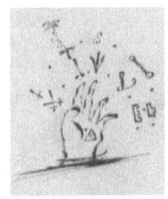

CHAPTER 3

"True Enthusiasm"
Moral Sense Philosophy and Fissures of the Secular Self in Shaftesbury's Private Writings

> *To solve the Phœnomena* in a true sence: not the Phœnomena of the Skyes or Meteors; not those in Mathematicks, Mechanicks, Physicks; not those wch by solving or unfolding ever so skillfully one is neither Better, nor happyer, nor wiser, nor more a Man of sence or worth, of a more open free understanding, liberal Disposition, a more enlarg'd Mind or a more generouse Heart; but those wch being not unfolded, nor well resolvd, contract & narrow a Man's Genius, cause a real Poorness in the Understanding, disturb, distract, amaze, confound, perplex, lead away, like those dancing Fires of the *Ignis Fatuus*, plung into Abysses; & cast into endless Labrinths.
>
> Let this be thy Philosophy. & leave the other Phœnomena for others.
>
> —Shaftesbury, Ασκηματα[1]

Legacies of Moral Sense Spontaneity

Eighteenth-century Britain has been said to have almost single-handedly invented modern moral philosophy, and the story of how this came about begins in the tumultuous years following the Interregnum.[2] The Restoration "revolt against enthusiasm" coincided both with the reaction against Thomas Hobbes and his materialist account of intrinsic human selfishness, if not against the calculating mercantile spirit of which it was born, and with the birth of the Royal Society and rise of the New Science. The Plague Year, the saving cataclysm of the Great Fire, and the rebuilding of St. Paul's Cathedral on the design of Sir Christopher Wren—a part secular, part religious temple celebrating a perfectly ordered universe—make ready ciphers for the moral revolution that took place alongside them. The architect of the new moral philosophy was Anthony Ashley Cooper, John Locke's most famous student and eventually the third Earl of Shaftesbury, and the edifice he raised, or at least for which he left provocative blueprints, was his notion of the moral sense.[3]

If enthusiasm, with its symptomatic Civil War, regicide, and anarchy, was a plague that only cynical Hobbesian worldliness could burn away, Shaftesbury undertook to clean up the moral aftermath of both without falling prey to Locke's indictment of innate ideas. Shaftesbury famously wrote to Michael Ainsworth that "it was Mr. Locke that struck the home blow" to morality, throwing "all order and virtue out of the world, and [making] the very ideas of these . . . *unnatural*, and without foundation in our minds."[4] In search of the foundations of natural virtue, beginning with his earliest treatise, *An Inquiry Concerning Virtue* (1699),[5] Shaftesbury offered the solution of a "moral sense": spontaneous and prereflexive, it allowed human beings to "experience right and wrong with all the swiftness of the senses," navigating the gulf that seemed to have opened in the seventeenth century between matter and spirit, particulars and universals, empiricism and rationalism,[6] "solving the inner phenomena," as the epigraph proposes, as surely as Newton and Galileo had solved those of mathematics and astronomy. Shaftesbury himself used the term *moral sense* only rarely, but it is no accident that his popularizer, Francis Hutcheson, picked up the phrase to encapsulate Shaftesbury's contribution. The moral sense indicated morality through an instinctive response upon reflection; in Shaftesbury's words, "*Actions* themselves, and the *Affections* of Pity, Kindness, Gratitude, and their Contrarys, being brought into the Mind by Reflection" become objects of this sense in their own right, producing "another kind of Affection towards those very Affections themselves," much like the response to a beautiful work of art.[7] In his account of the eighteenth-century notion of "the beautiful soul," Richard Norton has rightly stressed the "thoroughly rational strain" in Shaftesbury's thought and pointed out that Shaftesbury has wrongly been considered a "sentimentalist," one who believes that morality is ultimately a matter of feeling as *opposed* to knowledge.[8] Like the enthusiastic free prayer that preceded it, the moral sense Shaftesbury has in mind entails not only emotional response but a rationalized way of thinking about feeling, an ideology of spontaneity that quantifies spontaneous affective responses as evidence in a systematic account of spiritual worth and moral goodness.

But however natural the moral sense was supposed to be, it paradoxically was not easy, and like Bunyan's sense of misery in prayer, this served to increase its value: "It is not instantly we acquire this Sense by which these Beautys are discoverable," Shaftesbury warned in *The Sociable Enthusiast*, but "Labour and Pains are requir'd, and Time to cultivate a natural Genius."[9] The leisure that could afford moral cultivation rings with class connotations, and Robert Markley rightly positions Shaftesbury's philosophy as Whig and aristocratic.[10] Reminiscent of David Zaret's contextualization of covenant theology, Terry Eagleton has argued that Shaftesbury's moral sense appeals to an "instinctual economizing of the mind" that was well-advanced at the dawn of the eighteenth century. To believe that "to do good is deeply enjoyable, a self-justifying function of our nature beyond all crass utility" shored up a middle-class rationality by mitigating its uglier tendencies at the same time that it appealed to its logic—a feat that in part accounted for the paradoxical appeal of an aristocratic philosophy to rising middle and professional classes, particularly in the Scottish Enlightenment.[11]

While Shaftesbury's inquiry into virtue shares the logic of spontaneity with his Puritan and Dissenting predecessors, it breaks with them not, as Shaftesbury claimed, by replacing their fanaticism with reason, but by following the ideology of spontaneity into a pointedly secular register. His first venture into print, the 1698 preface to the *Select Sermons of Dr. Whichcote*, criticized religion for emphasizing "spirit" over human nature, "*as if*," he prodded, "*Good-Nature, and Religion, were Enemies*," and it launched a secularizing tendency that characterized all his works.[12] If religion and good nature were not enemies, in Shaftesbury's mind they were clearly unequal allies. The following year the question at the heart of the *Inquiry* was "How far Virtue alone could go; and how far Religion was either *necessary* to support it, or able to raise and advance it." Virtue was disinterested, and yet, in bringing happiness, it was man's truest interest, and all that was needed was to convince him of this fact.[13] Almost a decade later, "A Letter Concerning Enthusiasm" (1708) continued the rhetorical work of sorting out virtue from religion in a way that indicated that religion and good nature were far from friends. In the "Letter," religion appears almost entirely as falsity and enthusiasm. The site of worked-up emotion and of melancholy opinions which grew up "in an ill mood" and were "kept up by Solemnity," the enthusiasm Shaftesbury eschewed was the "Ridiculousness of an Extreme," the source of panic and prejudice, propounded by "ill Physicians" who tamper with the body's natural humors. It is a "Distemper," and in order not to inflame it more, it should be coolly tolerated by rational men who are, he contends, the only *true* enthusiasts.[14] This trope of "true enthusiasm" recurs again and again in Shaftesbury's writings as a favorite figure for genuine goodness, leading Lawrence Klein to speak of Shaftesbury's "transvaluation" of enthusiasm into the foundation for morality and sociability.[15] The appeal of Shaftesbury's moral philosophy rests not only on its claim to empirical observation of affections but perhaps even more so on this transvaluation: on the extent to which it quarantines epistemological uncertainty, violence, and emotional excess as particularly religious ills in order to eliminate them from an increasingly secular virtue that nonetheless retains a quasi-religious authority.[16] Shaftesbury's "true enthusiasm" is perhaps our best emblem for the subterranean connection of explicitly secular discourses to the religiousness they both deny and retain.

A philosophy sublimating empirical ambition into a discourse of moral objectivity, a style emanating nobility and appealing to aspiring middle classes, and a rationally measured "true enthusiasm" replacing fanatical religion: the moral sense proved to be a virtually irresistible theory, and British moral philosophy—and through its influence, philosophy in Germany and France—was dominated by the idea of moral beauty and its sensory-rational perception for most of the eighteenth century.[17] The path of moral-sense philosophy was paved by Shaftesbury's chief systematizer and defender against Mandeville, the Irish Presbyterian minister Francis Hutcheson.[18] Hutcheson's enormous influence on eighteenth-century thought resulted from his treatises on beauty and virtue, published in the 1720s, in which, the first claimed, *"the Principles of the Late Earl of Shaftesbury are explain'd and defended . . . With an Attempt to introduce a Mathematical Calculation in Subjects of Morality."*[19] The perception of a grateful readership was that these treatises developed Shaftesbury's intimations of the moral sense into a defensible theory.[20] As a result, Hutcheson was unanimously elected Chair of Moral Philosophy at the University of Glasgow in 1729, a post he held until his death in 1746, lecturing daily before luminaries of the Scottish Enlightenment including Adam Smith and David Hume. No doubt part of Hutcheson's appeal lay in how he confidently dismissed what was perceived to be Shaftesbury's irreligion as unfortunate *"Prejudices he had receiv'd against Christianity"* and set about legitimating Shaftesbury's rational moral sense and Christian theism in terms of each other.[21] For real Christian virtue to exist at all, the "Universe must be govern'd," he taught, by such *"general Laws,* upon which we can found our Expectations, and project our Schemes of Action."[22] The *Inquiry's* "attempt to introduce a mathematical calculation in subjects of morality" was the outgrowth of this Newtonian logic, prompting Hutcheson, apparently without hesitation, to provide readers with formulae for virtue (see fig. 3; p. 95): "The *Quantity of Love* toward any person," for instance, "is in a compound Proportion of the apprehended *Causes of Love* in him, and of the *Goodness of Temper* in the Observer. Or $L = C \times G$."[23]

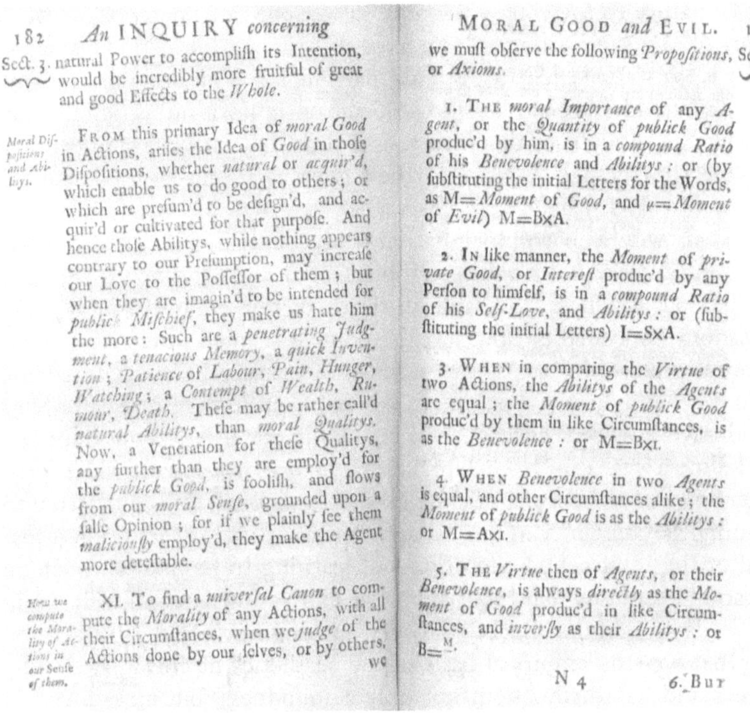

182 *An* INQUIRY *concerning*

Sect. 3. natural Power to accompliſh its Intention, would be incredibly more fruitful of great and good Effects to the *Whole*.

Moral Diſpoſitions and Abilitys.

FROM this primary Idea of *moral Good* in Actions, ariſes the Idea of *Good* in thoſe Diſpoſitions, whether *natural* or *acquir'd*, which enable us to do good to others; or which are preſum'd to be deſign'd, and acquir'd or cultivated for that purpoſe. And hence thoſe Abilitys, while nothing appears contrary to our Preſumption, may increaſe our Love to the Poſſeſſor of them; but when they are imagin'd to be intended for public Miſchief, they make us hate him the more: Such are a *penetrating Judgment*, a *tenacious Memory*, a *quick Invention*; *Patience* of *Labour*, *Pain*, *Hunger*, *Watching*; a *Contempt* of *Wealth*, *Rumour*, *Death*. Theſe may be rather call'd *natural Abilitys*, than *moral Qualitys*. Now, a Veneration for theſe Qualitys, any further than they are employ'd for the *publick Good*, is fooliſh, and flows from our *moral Senſe*, grounded upon a falſe Opinion; for if we plainly ſee them *maliciouſly* employ'd, they make the Agent more deteſtable.

How we compute the Morality of Actions in our Senſe of them.

XI. To find a *univerſal Canon* to compute the *Morality* of any Actions, with all their Circumſtances, when we *judge* of the Actions done by our ſelves, or by others, we

MORAL GOOD *and* EVIL. 183

we muſt obſerve the following *Propoſitions*, or *Axioms*. Sect. 3.

1. THE *moral Importance* of any *Agent*, or the *Quantity* of *publick Good* produc'd by him, is in a *compound Ratio* of his *Benevolence* and *Abilitys*: or (by ſubſtituting the initial Letters for the Words, as M=*Moment* of *Good*, and μ=*Moment* of *Evil*) M=B×A.

2. IN like manner, the *Moment* of *private Good*, or *Intereſt* produc'd by any Perſon to himſelf, is in a *compound Ratio* of his *Self-Love*, and *Abilitys*: or (ſubſtituting the initial Letters) I=S×A.

3. WHEN in comparing the *Virtue* of two Actions, the *Abilitys* of the *Agents* are equal; the *Moment* of *publick Good* produc'd by them in like Circumſtances, is as the *Benevolence*: or M=B×1.

4. WHEN *Benevolence* in two *Agents* is equal, and other Circumſtances alike; the *Moment* of *publick Good* is as the *Abilitys*: or M=A×1.

5. THE *Virtue* then of *Agents*, or their *Benevolence*, is always *directly* as the *Moment* of *Good* produc'd in like Circumſtances, and *inverſly* as their *Abilitys*: or B=$\frac{M}{A}$.

N 4 6. BUT

Figure 3 Opening from Francis Hutcheson, An Inquiry concerning Moral Good and Evil, *second edition (1726), pp. 182–83, under the marginal heading "How we compute the Morality of Actions in our Sense of them." Photo courtsey of The Newberry Library, Chicago.*

When a pious Scotsman objected to Hutcheson that an act could be virtuous only if it were done expressly for the love of God, Hutcheson replied at length that actions could be innocent, "nay virtuous," with "no actual *Intention* of pleasing the Deity."[24] Hutcheson made Shaftesbury's moral sense seductive as proof of the reasonableness of Christian morality, but he did so by an essentialist logic that, paralleling the ouster of liturgy in favor of the spontaneous essence of free prayer, made personal theism and the particular tenets of Christianity ultimately unnecessary. This lack of necessity grew more obvious in the works of Hutcheson's most influential student, Adam Smith, who inherited Hutcheson's chair at Glasgow. In *The Theory of Moral Sentiments* (1759), which was to see six editions in his lifetime (Hume reproached him with its popularity),[25] Smith articulated the moral philosopher's task as finding the proper balance of benevolence and self-love, and went so far as to shift Christianity's unilateral "Love thy neighbor as thyself" to a more moderate calculation.[26] "As to love our neighbor as we love ourselves is the great law of Christianity," he wrote, "so it is the great precept of nature to love ourselves only as we love our neighbor, or what comes to the same thing, as our neighbor is capable of loving us"—which is, the *Theory* tells us, not all that much.[27] The proximity of this view to its Hobbesian and Mandevillean opposition is surely the unthinkable thought of the *Theory*, as it must have been to midcentury religious thinkers who welcomed the *Theory* as a long-awaited rational defense of virtue, whatever its costs.[28]

What would become apparent only several generations after Shaftesbury was that, by fighting Hobbes on his own ground of scientism and making goodness calculable in terms of self-interest, moral sense philosophy conceded most at just the point it seemed to triumph. That is, moral philosophy across the eighteenth century followed this logic down a seemingly irresistible path toward a utilitarianism Shaftesbury would have despised, encapsulated in the dictum that Jeremy Bentham lifted almost verbatim from Hutcheson, "*that Action* is *best*, which procures the *greatest Happiness* for the *greatest Numbers.*"[29] Not unrelated to the utilitarian tendency of this thought was the paradoxical notion it fostered of the sentimental education—of learning to be natural. Such an education meant, in Shaftesbury's phrase, cultivating natural genius or, in the words of Edmund Burke's *Enquiry*, making one's taste—the natural taste that was the empirical basis of the aesthetics he formulated—"by degrees and habitually attain not only a soundness, but a readiness of judgment."[30] As the *Enquiry*'s logic of the masculine sublime and feminine beautiful illustrated, part of what passed for natural in this educational process was an aesthetics of gendered and sexualized desire that would later seem to undo the very chivalry and ethics that the sentimental education aimed for. What connected utilitarianism and the sentimental education that seemed to oppose it was the intensely interested individual subject and its sexualized desire that lurked, to differing degrees, beneath a discourse of moral naturalness and objectivity. The universalization of privileged male feeling naturalized an appetite for mastering the beautiful and assaulting the sublime with ever-increasing force, such that the sentimental gave way to the gothic and the Byronic by the same discernible logic that Richardson's novels came to be a key source both for Rousseau and for the Marquis de Sade.[31]

The connection of moral sense philosophy and its reliance on spontaneous responses to eroticized irreligion and violence that we see in Sade was not, however, an aberration sprung up at the far reaches of Enlightenment.[32] This chapter argues that Shaftesbury's soon-to-be-published private writings provide a window into the psychological structures that both fuel and are fueled by this rationalization of goodness and its ideology of spontaneity, not just in their paradoxes but in their affective costs and aftershocks, particularly regarding the secularism that is central to them. In contrast to the famously appealing public persona of politeness, wit, and raillery, the Shaftesbury of the private notebooks resembles what one writer has aptly called a "Nehemiah Wallington stalking society in a Stoic's toga."[33] The densely written pages of Shaftesbury's notebooks certainly evoke Puritan graphomania, with Shaftesbury railing against himself with a cruelty that rivals Wallington's or Bunyan's and is explicitly connected to his efforts to internalize the philosophy he publicly expounded. Written during Shaftesbury's most ambitious and intellectually productive years, in many cases anticipating and revisiting the essays of the *Characteristicks*, the notebooks which Shaftesbury labeled the Ασκηματα or "Exercises" represent what is in every sense Shaftesbury's project, the architecture of the secular, moral "Self" along rational, natural lines.

And yet, those lines are never straight. For Laurent Jaffro, the translator of the Ασκηματα into French, the notebooks express a certain dialogism and development, but without seeming to progress as intended; Jaffro has likened them to a wilderness, embodying the "art of an English garden in philosophy."[34] Or we may think of the Ασκηματα as a secular corollary to *Grace Abounding*, a generation removed. They provide an almost ideal psychoanalytic text of Enlightenment, a strange epic of modern subjectivity that in some ways telescopes the legacies of the moral sense in the century following Shaftesbury's death. Faced with the notebooks' dramatic difference from the *Characteristicks*, Shaftesbury's biographer Robert Voitle has compared the critic's task with that of an archaeologist reconstructing a building from its ruins, who discovers at the site "a totally different sort of stones which do not seem to fit in with the materials he has been using."[35]

As such, it is not surprising that even book-length studies drawing on these manuscripts have yet to give us a precise, critical understanding of their place in Shaftesbury's oeuvre.[36] Stanley Grean's elegant 1967 volume, *Shaftesbury's Philosophy of Religion and Ethics: A Study in Enthusiasm*, is oddly reminiscent of Hutcheson in its efforts to recuperate Shaftesbury for mid-twentieth-century Protestant theology. His attempt to show that the Shaftesbury corpus is united by an insistence on love and dialectical method forces him to use the Ασκηματα in a highly selective way, quoting only a few early passages that are far from representative.[37] Following J. G. A. Pocock's work on politeness in the eighteenth century, Lawrence Klein devotes two chapters to the Ασκηματα in *Shaftesbury and the Culture of Politeness* (1994). In the service of his dual project of making Shaftesbury the origin of a culture of politeness and putting politeness at the center of Shaftesbury's thought, Klein like Grean is forced in part to harmonize the notebooks with the public works, and in part to read them as evidence of a "severe personal crisis" that is fundamentally irreconcilable with his larger oeuvre.[38]

Instead of either reconciling the disjunction between Shaftesbury's public and private texts or letting the latter stand as virtually uninterpretable, I seek, beneath their real dissonances, to listen for the notebooks' deeper homologies with the public writings, and by surfacing their terms, to show that, while they are vastly different from the *Characteristicks*, they are nonetheless intimately related to them by a mappable logic. This chapter thus shows how Shaftesbury's quest for spontaneous love of his fellow man, declared at the beginning of the notebooks, leads by a discernible path to his angry paralysis at the roadblock of intractable, naturalized emotions and to a gendered loathing of the vulnerable permeability of his body. The unruly spontaneity, lack of mastery, and resistance to reason that bodily desires present leads Shaftesbury in turn to a ritualistic "Regimen" of severe psychological *ascesis*, what we may think of as his perverse ritual of spontaneity: the disavowal of intimacy and the self-conscious splitting of his "Self" from his body and desires, in an attempt to master them. Rather than this mastery of desire, the Regimen cultivates in Shaftesbury an aggressive sexualization of philosophy which threatens him with psychological unraveling and leads, finally, to a metaphorical sexual assault on the "Deity" who in the opening entries was the necessary guarantee of universal moral order. Shaftesbury's disgust at his body and the image of the violation of God in the Ασκηματα parallels a similarly visceral disgust with Christ graphically manifest in his final notebook. Together, they illustrate how ideologies of masculinity, national superiority, and class privilege are connected to a libidinally invested, frequently vengeful or violent secularism that echoes in the works of Hume, Richardson, and Sade, and how they share a sense of self defined by mastery. In the Ασκηματα, the body, the feminine, and the religious coalesce as the site of a violent fantasy that is the symptom of an ideology of masculine total control. Shaftesbury's secular "true enthusiasm," and with it the moral sense tradition through Hume and Sade, is in Derrida's words mutually "bound" to rationalized religion "by the band of their opposition," expressing a disavowed uncertainty that enthusiasm's empiricism and scriptural literalism had also attempted to elide.[39]

"A Common Father of Mankind"—God and Man, Love and Loathing

In his early twenties and after returning from the Grand Tour, between 1689–1695 the young Anthony Ashley Cooper followed in the steps of his controversial grandfather, the first Earl of Shaftesbury, and involved himself in Whig politics, standing for Parliament in 1695 and serving in the House of Commons until July 1698. The adherence to principle that his tutor Locke had encouraged meant that in Parliament he was often accused by fellow "country Whigs" of a lack of party spirit. This uncomfortable political wrangling was compounded by the asthma that began to plague him during these London years and which was his professed reason for declining to stand for Parliament a second time.[40] In the same month that he left the House of Commons, his mother died, and after her funeral Shaftesbury traveled to the Rotterdam home of his longtime correspondent, Quaker and political radical Benjamin Furly, for what he would call his "first and second Retreat & Studdy in Holland": retreats from the contentious world of shifting London alliances, from family sadness and discord, into reading and self-scrutiny, recorded in a bare, personal style such as we have for no other seventeenth- or eighteenth-century philosopher save perhaps Pascal.[41]

The two closely written volumes of these notebooks correspond roughly to these retreats. Fewer than half the entries give date or place, but the inscriptions in the first volume indicate that its first half was written in Rotterdam during his retreat of July 1698 through April 1699, with subsequent entries written in 1699–1700 after his return to England, in London, Chelsea, or at his family home of Wimborne St. Giles, Dorset. Shaftesbury became the third earl following his father's death in November 1699, and Voitle refers to the years 1700–1702 as the time when Shaftesbury was above all "Lord of the Manor," absorbed in estate improvements and in renewed political involvement, now in the House of Lords. Late in 1702 Shaftesbury's health again declined, and desiring to withdraw from the tension surrounding his younger brother's campaign for Parliament, in August 1703 he returned to Rotterdam, taking up his notebooks again and staying with Furly through the autumn of 1704.

On the spine and on the title page, Shaftesbury labeled these journals in Greek uncials ΑΣΚΗΜΑΤΑ (*ah skee' ma ta*), plural for ασκημα or "exercise." These notebooks very much are *Exercises*, like bits of homework aimed at mastering a body of knowledge or particular skill. In places they show evidence of revision or of transcription from a previous draft, while at others the writing seems more spontaneous. Marginal notes link passages to previous and subsequent pages, and in the second volume Shaftesbury begins to refer to "the parchments," a pocket-sized condensation of principles from the Ασκηματα, which still exists, smudged and well-worn, among the Shaftesbury papers.[42] This intensive rereading and distillation point to the central place these books occupied in Shaftesbury's life. As early as December 1699 Shaftesbury was thinking of these personal philosophical labors as a greater service to his country than court and parliamentary corruption allowed. In one of the latest entries, he exhorts himself to be grateful for the illness and party maneuverings that drove him from politics, inasmuch as they drove him into the more important arena of inward health, that is, into these retreats and stoic self-scrutiny.[43]

In the sense of ασχησις (asceticism), these exercises seem to have been written very much as part of a set discipline.[44] Shaftesbury's pattern was to write four pages quarto on a given topic, sometimes more, and then at his next sitting to begin a new heading on the following page.[45] Whenever he revisited a topic, apparently to save paper and preserve continuity with the earlier exercise, he began at the end of the previous entry on that topic, wrote to the bottom of the page, and then inserted a direction to a later opening (e.g., "inf:114"), indicating that the entry continued at that point. This method makes for a complicated manuscript, but it physically maps how Shaftesbury moved from one topic to the next and then circled back again, picking up previous threads and pressing in new directions, offering a marvelous sense of philosophical movement and psychological trajectory that is completely lost in the only previously published English text, the expurgated and highly inaccurate Benjamin Rand edition of 1900.[46] Given the psychological trajectory these notebooks reveal, the forthcoming publication of the Ασκηματα in their entirety in the Shaftesbury Standard Edition should generate a welcome body of criticism bringing to light their hitherto ignored complexity and disturbing richness.[47]

From their opening pages, the Ασκηματα evoke a range of affinities and differences between secularized "true enthusiasm" and its Puritan anti-self. Just as the central trauma of *Grace Abounding* erupts at the moment where Bunyan seems to approach certainty of his love for Christ, so the intense inner journey of the Ασκηματα begins in the opening lines with the question of love and the difficulty of loving one's fellow men:

> To have *Naturall Affection:* not that w[ch] is only towards Relations; but towards all Mankind. to be truly φιλανθρωπος, neither to scoff, nor hate; nor be angry; nor be impatient wth them; nor abominate them; nor overlook them: and to pitty in a manner, & love those that are the greatest miscreants; those that are most furiouse against thy self in particular, and at the time when they are most furiouse. How is it in a Mother, or a Nurs, towards sickly children? . . . What is more amiable than such affection? . . . When is it, therefore, that Thou shalt become, as it were, a common Father of Mankind? (*A*, 10)

In these opening sentences, the central question of the Shaftesbury corpus and of post-Hobbes, post-Restoration England is announced: how is one to be virtuous, how to love one's fellow man with a love which, if it is to be real, meaningful, or possible at all, must be a *natural* affection? The natural affection Shaftesbury imagines is very much reason's love, a principle which he arrives at as part of a universalizing, abstract rationality and which, above all, he seeks to make constant within himself. Only a few lines later, he asks,

> When shall this happy Disposition be fix'd, that I may feel it perpetually, as now but seldome? When shall I be intirely thus affected, & feel this as my Part grown naturall to me?—It shall then be, when thou no longer seekest for any thing they seek; when thou no longer rivall'st them, or wouldst partake of their Goods; when thou no longer wantest anything from them, or canst be worsted by any thing that may happen to Thee from them. in short; it is then only that thou canst truly *Love Them* when thou expect'st neither thy Good nor thy Ill from them. for, whilst that is, we must of necessity be jealouse of them & suspect them; flatter & court them; be one while in great familiarity with them, at another time in open Enmity; to day in favour, tomorrow in disgrace; this moment warm & affectionate, the next, cold & indifferent; asham'd of what wee just before were proud of; and sick of those wee before so highly relish'd. (*A*, 10–11)

Alongside this vision of virtue, we see from the outset that which it wrestles against, inconstancy and a tendency not to be amiable but to be sick of others, to scoff, abominate, be angry and impatient. To be at all vulnerable to others—to need of them, desire their approval, feel competitive with them—is a barrier to love, for here, as throughout the Ασκηματα, love is conceived of in terms of the immutable laws of a Newtonian universe. The rational self Shaftesbury imagines cannot suffer or be vulnerable. "Remember then," he writes at one point, "Whilst I am my Self, I cannot be hurt" (*A*, 233). To love others and what they esteem is inevitably "*to be Enviouse; to repine, & long; to be often disappointed & griev'd; to be bitter, anxiouse, Malignant; suspiciouse & jealouse of Men, & fearfull of Events* (all wch is Misery:)" (*A*, 38). And so, in trying to love all men, he seeks also to be above them and their pleasures, in order to "take care of them" (*A*, 12). From the opening pages, Shaftesbury's quest for φιλανθρωπια is haunted by rivalry, contention, and at times a disgust which seems a given, even as he thinks it unnatural and wishes, via a certain paternalism, to escape it.

It is in this context of seeking a constant, natural emotional state from which to love mankind that Shaftesbury's analogous rendition of god takes shape.[48] Shaftesbury begins the Ασκηματα by imagining himself a "common Father of Mankind," words he uses for the divinity only paragraphs later, calling him the "supream Parent, a common Father of Men & all other Beings" (*A*, 15). This Deity is the keystone of the notebooks, and the opening entry on "Naturall Affection" is by a discernible logic followed, not preceded, by one on "Deity," one of the longest entries and most revisited topics. For Shaftesbury there must be a "System" and "**Great Whole**" for the universe to be rational or intelligible, and the Deity is the "producer" and "administrator" of this system. "One & Simple, infinitely ~~Intelligent Rationall~~ Wise, & perfectly Good," a "Supream Eternall Mind or Intelligent Principle belonging to this Whole," and the "Great Master & Organist," the Deity is everywhere synonymous with order and nature.[49] It is this alignment of the Deity with an ultimate principle of reason and order that explains why Shaftesbury continues to disdain atheism long after he has abandoned Christianity as only marginally better than druidic human sacrifice, referring to Marcus Aurelius and Epictetus as the "Divine Men" and even praying to them.[50] Against Hobbes's accusation that "faith" most often signifies "*a premeditated & stubborn Resolution of giving Reason the Lye*," Shaftesbury affirms that the faith he has in mind is "*a premeditated & stubborn Resolution to give every thing the Lye besides Reason only.*" Without this faith in Reason, "all must be *Atheisme*" (*A*, 247), and true religion for Shaftesbury is reason. The god that is so crucial to the Aσκηματα is the god who is arrived at from the viewpoint of the rational observer, seeking order in the universe; without this Deity, there is no presumption of material or moral order to study and master. In the realm of moral affections, the Deity is above all the perfect object of desire that would regulate all feelings aright: "**O Soul!** think how noble will be thy State . . . when all those other inferiour secondary Objects are lov'd according to their order, never but *last;* and the **First Object** *first,* . . . with an Affection above all other Affection besides" (*A*, 152).

Shaftesbury's conception of this desirable, reasonable Deity takes shape particularly vis-à-vis his disgust with the piety of common humanity. Again and again he formulates his conception of Deity over and against "the vulgar," "vulgar devotion," and their "sordid shamefull nauseouse Idea of Deity" of which he wishes to purge himself. He forbids himself to sing even such hymns as the Stoics recommend, because until his idea of divinity is correct, worship may be dangerous or "even fatall" (*A*, 100). What seems most repulsive about the vulgar idea of God is his sensory accessibility: the idea that the Deity would allow himself to be seen or heard by a common person. And Shaftesbury is equally revolted by his own desire for this sort of direct divine contact. "Dost thou, like one of those Visionaryes, expect to see a Throne, a shining Light, a Court & Attendance? is this thy Notion of *a Presence?* . . . —Wretched Folly!" (*A*, 92). He elsewhere relates how he eagerly desired such a direct communication from God in his youth and would have obeyed it at once, yet this is but one of many desires which only "seem" natural and which he eventually puts away as not becoming a man.[51] If "**He** be *here*," he asks himself, "actually present, a Witness of all thou dost, a Spectator of all thy Actions, & privy to thy inmost thoughts; how comes it that thou liv'st not with Him, at least but as with a Friend? . . . is this living with a Benefactour? a Father? a Superiour, who is more than Magistrate, more than People, more than Friends, Relations, Country, Mankind, World? . . . This is, in effect, to believe, & not believe" (*A*, 92). Not the God of "the meerest Enthousiasme," Shaftesbury's Deity is "a Being infinitely more perfect than all that they conceive or think" (*A*, 103). More real, more aware, more authoritative and courtly, this Deity should therefore be more affecting than the vulgar God, just as enthusiastic free prayer was to be more affecting than liturgy; Shaftesbury's enthusiasm is a sublation of theirs, his Deity their image of patriarchal authority raised to the most abstract plane. Anticipating Smith's "impartial spectator" and "man in the breast," this Deity is a silent witness of his actions and thoughts, a lawgiver and "Ruler" whose laws Shaftesbury seeks, and crucially, "his Generall" in whose presence a "Souldier" is so affected that he cannot think of his own sufferings (*A*, 93, 98).

It is this inability to suffer that, as the opening passage of the Ασκηματα indicates, is central to the self that Shaftesbury desires to be, a lover of men but immune to the slings of commerce with them. To Shaftesbury's mind, the divinity himself cannot suffer, particularly by the esteem or disesteem of his creatures. "What is it to Deity itself, whether prais'd or disprais'd; acknowledg'd, or disown'd?" he asks, "Can Deity suffer? is it His Ill? how can this be? . . . if Deity suffer not; what else can suffer? . . . how canst Thou be worsted, or injur'd?" (*A*, 111). Divine perfection resides in remaining untouched by that of which it is master, and all that remains is for Shaftesbury to be fully convinced of this divinity and therefore immune to harm. Neither a direct command nor a vision of a heavenly throne can once and for all fix his natural affections for his god and his fellow men, "Nor can anything else besides *the Reason of the thing*," he writes, convince him "*that his Administration is intirely Just & Good*" (*A*, 93). Like Bunyan's dream of the "knowledge of the worth of the things of God" that would fix his desire once and for all, it is a reasoned certainty and a consequently whole self, immune to doubt and sorrow, that the *Exercises* aim for.

But the sentence that follows this postulation of certainty is one of the most excruciating in all the Ασκηματα: "*Why, then, am I miserable?*— . . . Hence all those Expostulations with Providence, & Sentiments w[ch] we endeavour to stiffle but cannot. Thus the Vulgar" (*A*, 93). While Shaftesbury can imagine a god who does not suffer and who even is so awe-inspiring as to cast out consideration of his own pain, he does indeed suffer, it is clear from the notebooks, a great deal—from an asthma which he expects to suffocate him at any moment, from friends who draw him into relationships he abhors, from desires for fame and sexual intimacy—and this misery is the rock against which his efforts to be a "common Father of Mankind" crash time and time again.[52] Where Bunyan's image of God scares him into silence for fear of saying "Our Father" with imperfect sincerity, the Deity who would guarantee nature's laws and order the universe as a perfect system is ultimately a god of necessity, one with whom there is no point expostulating, no point speaking with or praying to at all. Regret, resistance, and wishing things were otherwise are irrelevant to such a system and to a Deity who, if he allows an individual to suffer pain, disease, or death, must do so for the good of the whole, which only he can see. Nearing the end of his first retreat, Shaftesbury reaches an impasse: knowing all this, he is still miserable, and his affections are *not* "natural," that is, reverent and resigned before god and "the Whole."

It is here, where the reasoning subject is thwarted by its own physical and emotional pain, that the logic connecting Shaftesbury's early neo-Platonism to the intense stoicism of the exercises comes sharply into focus. The work of the exercises takes place in a period of illness, unsatisfied desire, disgust, and unrest, all of which pain Shaftesbury greatly, while the Deity he has fashioned is necessarily indifferent to his sufferings and would seem to fault him for suffering to begin with. In *Formations of the Secular*, Talal Asad observes that secularism is characterized by a "discourse of being human" that assumes an autonomous subject who operates based on a "utilitarian calculus of pleasure and pain," where there is no sense to be made of suffering, no way of imagining one's relationship to it other than minimizing it.[53] In this way of thinking, pain becomes an excess outside rational subjectivity, at the same moment that the aesthetic emerges as a category for the pursuit of a contained, sanitized secular excess. Both moments of secularism converge in the Ασκηματα. The exercises bring Shaftesbury to a conception of truth and Deity which allows for no creative, negotiated relationship with pain; pain and the longing to be freed from it are both an affront to self-mastery and, as we shall see, to masculinity. Thus the notebooks come to be about what Shaftesbury calls a "Regimen" for bringing his aestheticized sentiments in line with immutable Providence, for arriving at natural affection—that is, resignation and the lack of vulnerable desires—and the ability to feel this spontaneously.

The Regimen—"However Terrible It May Appear"

> Begin therefore and work upon this subject. **Collect. Digest. Methodize. Abstract.** How many Codes, how many Volumes,

Lexicons, how much Labour and what compiling in the Studdy of other Laws? but in the Law of Life, how?[54]

Early on in his first retreat Shaftesbury asks himself, "How long is it that thou wilt continue thus to act two different parts, & be two different Persons?" (*A*, 59), and the Regimen we see in the Ασκηματα aims away from being two different persons, and toward self-identity. "*Integrity Intire*," he underscores: "in Limbs?—No.—Skinn?—No. but Affections" (*A*, 339). To expel the misery that sticks in the throat of natural affection is the Sisyphean task of this quest for wholeness, requiring nothing less than what Shaftesbury refers to as surgery or amputation. Troublesome thoughts and feelings are again and again cut off, disallowed as irrational in hopes that they will cease to exist. As Asad argues, pains and desires are excesses placed outside secular subjectivity, and they become in Lacanian terms a horrifying, religiously inflected real, threatening the symbolic order from outside, yet crucial to its framework.[55]

This process of amputating initial responses in search of the "natural" also appears in Shaftesbury's published works, though in the softer aesthetic terms of shaping moral and aesthetic "taste." This aestheticization of the self occurs at the site of the secularization of virtue into morality and serves in part to palliate the difficult submission which must go hand in hand with an idea of a determined system of natural order. But it is also a way of negotiating the paradox that Shaftesbury shares with the free-praying enthusiasts he abhors and that echoes through Hutcheson, Smith, and Burke: the paradox of learning to be natural. "Is there Studdy Science & Learning necessary to understand all Beautyes else? and for the Sovereign Beauty is ther no Skill or Science requir'd?" he asks, anticipating the *Sociable Enthusiast:* "observe how it is in all those other Subjects of Art or Science: what difficulty to be in any degree knowing; and how long 'ere a true Tast is gain'd: how many things shocking, how many offensive at first, w[ch] afterwards are known & acknowledg'd the highest Beautyes. But it is not instantly that this *Sense* is acquir'd, and these Beauties discoverable. Labour & Pains are requir'd, & Time to cultivate a Naturall Genius tho' ever so apt or forward" (*A*, 182–83).

The "labor and pains" which Shaftesbury undertakes in search of natural affection are in many ways "shocking," not least in their drive for total self-command and nearly sadomasochistic denial of suffering. He admonishes himself to remember that the management of emotions in daily "Trifles" is not at all trifling, for in so doing he becomes "a Legislatour to [him]self," "establishing that Economy or Commonwealth within" which "alone . . . leads to true Religion" (*A*, 71). He allows himself no "Complaining murmering discontent [or] rebellio[n]": "no

Indulgence: no . . . mis-calling or disparaging Heavens Distributions: no Nick-naming of Providence—*hard Providences. dark Providences Affections Tribulations Calamityes Crosses.*—What *Crosses* to one who stands not cross to Providence? What *Affliction* to one who wills only as That wills?" (*A*, 216–17). Shaftesbury's "true religion" is very pointedly a circumvention of the cross, a submission to Providence so profound that it is not crucifixion but heroic self-mastery. Such management of the self allows for no relaxation, requiring relentless vigilance and constant attention to keep from catching fire with desire for something other than what is. In more than one place Shaftesbury figures this vigilance as inserting wedges in a machine to keep it from shaking, imagining the self and its passions as a great piece of machinery, primed for malfunction if any part works its way loose.[56]

In the Ασκηματα it is paradoxically the pressure to be whole and spontaneously so, in accord with a universal system, that creates the split self that would master its own emotions. This splitting is embodied in the manuscript itself: what is in the first volume the single category of "Self" in the second splits into two categories, the "Self: Natural" and "Self: Economical" or "Artificial." In search of the natural self, Shaftesbury imagines himself with clothing removed and even limbs cut off, dissecting and asking again and again **"What am I?"** and finally answering in a bold hand, **"A Mind"** (*A*, 284–85). Cutting against the grain of his public ideals, sociability is here most often "false" and associated with the artificial, economical self, "a laughing talking Entertaining Part that dos all with Others, that admires & is ravish'd, wonders, praises censures, rejoices, greives and takes on (as they say) with others," that is "a faithless, corrupt, perfidiouse, mutinouse, sacrilegiouse Part" (*A*, 301). For this part, "vizt: the familiar conversible, *sociable* part (for so it will be call'd) I can find Companions enow, a large Society," he repines, "but for this better, the *truly sociable*, where shall I find a Companion Helper or Associate?" (*A*, 301–2). In the quest for emotional continence, the "friendly" part is split off from self and society, and the part of the self that seems most natural is taken as artificial.

At the heart of this solitary Regimen are methods for interrogating and controlling desires which Shaftesbury adapts from the ancient Stoics. "There is nothing more usefull in the management of the *Visa*," he writes, in words that would find gentler form in "Soliloquy," "or that helps to fight more strongly ag^t the striking Imaginations, than to learn a sort of custome of putting them into words, making them speak out & explain themselves as it were *vivâ voce*, and not tacitely & murmeringly; not by a Whisper & indirect Intimation, imperfectly, indistinctly & confusedly, as their common way is" (*A*, 97).[57] Once the self is split and the *visa* (distracting ideas and images that incite desire) are given voice,

Shaftesbury's aim is to defeat them rationally through various techniques: the "inversion" of mistaken desires or what he sometimes calls "the contraryes," or the application of εκκλισις and ορεξις, aversion and desire, as antidotes to unwanted inclinations.[58] Inversion is for Shaftesbury the primary tool for "molding of the *Visa*" and desires (*A*, 126)—and quite literally for the production of self as aesthetic object.[59] Inversion amounts to a sort of deconstruction of one's desires, aimed at convincing oneself that what one seems to want is in fact abhorrent, and that what one may shun—intense mental labor, the cutting off of desire—is in fact desirable. The pages of the Ασκηματα are filled with this exercise in inner interrogation, using inversion like a scalpel to remove desires he finds shameful.[60] Whenever desires resist inversion, Shaftesbury's strategy is to use "aversion" (εκκλισις) to "curb desire" (ορεξις) or, much less often, to use desire or encouragement to curb his aversion to the Regimen or his despair of progress. Aversion is the method Shaftesbury uses most frequently to try to curb his sexual appetite and the desire for social interaction that whets it; it is "in a reall sence *Dejection, Mortification* & nothing less . . . the depressing extinguishing killing that wrong sort of Joy & enliven'd Temper: the starving supplanting that Exuberant Luxuriant Fancy . . . and the introducing a Contrary Disposition; vix^t; the wean'd, allay'd, low, sunk; that wch creates a mean & poor Opinion of outward things, diminishes the Objects, & brings to view the viler but truer side of things" (*A*, 171). In "the viler but truer side of things" we see the negativity and suspicion toward which this asceticism tends; everything that presents itself as "Friendlyness, Humanity, Amicable-Pleasures, social Joys, Sympathy, Naturall Affection, Endearment, Tenderness, or Love" becomes potential "Poyson," "Corruption," and the "Dissolution of all" (*A*, 171).[61]

This paranoid vigilance does not prevent slips of control, though, and, if anything, exacerbates them with a sense of weariness, veering into a downward spiral of despair. Toward the end of the first volume, Shaftesbury castigates himself for abandoning self-control in an apparently sexual encounter which threatened to undo the progress of his first retreat.[62] Upbraiding himself with his broken resolutions, in a stunning passage he constricts his Regimen into a new and harsher law, "however terrible it may appear":

> See whither the Same *Impetuouse Impotent Temper* has led thee! Was it for this thou retiredst? is it this thou hast brought home? . . . Begin now. Consider thy Shameful Fall. See what is absolutely necessary in the Case: what with these *Wounds*, these *Sores*. . . . Bear with the Regimen, the Prescription, the Operation. Bear with the *Dejection Mortification Weaning*. . . . Cutt off Joy. Cutt off Tenderness of a certain kind. Cut off Familiarity Inwardness & that Sympathy of a wrong kind.

> Learn to be with Self; to talk with Self. Commune with thy own Heart. ... See what thou hast got by seeking Others, is this *Society*? is It genuine & of a right kind, when It is *that fond Desire of Company, that seeking of Companionship, & want of Talk & Story*? ... Mistake not, Friendship has nothing to do here.... remember that *real Friendship* is not founded on such *a Need*. Friends are not *Friends* if thus wanted. This is Imbecillity, Impotence, Effeminacy: and such is all that *Ardour & Vehemence* in behalf of Others.
>
> How is this *being a **Friend**?* How possible on these Terms, to be a Friend & Lover of Mankind? How be a Brother? How a Father, & that *common Father of Men*? How *the Tutor* & not *Tormentor* & *Tyrant* of the Children?
>
> But, Be this so no more. And that thou may'st not return ever more to those *Ardours* & *Vehemences*; know the Condition & Law, however terrible It appear:
> *To take Pleasure in Nothing.*
> *To do Nothing with Affection.*
> *To promise well of Nothing.*
> *To Engage for Nothing.* (*A*, 143, 176–77)

In this passage, and more and more as the notebooks progress, Shaftesbury isolates himself from others; everyone outside himself becomes suspect, a potential source of contamination with wrong affections. In the face of his permeability to others' desires and his inability to resist contamination with them, Shaftesbury moves beyond discipline to a "cutting off" of all pleasure and engagement. Increasingly, he wonders why he would admire anything—a celebrated beauty, a palace, a feast, a carnival—besides virtue, and he distances from himself every possible object of pleasure. Shaftesbury's rational quest to become a loving godlike father of all mankind ends in this "terrible law," in the "viler but truer side of things," and ultimately in a vision of the "monstrosity" of everything and everyone around him (*A*, 79). According to Asad, secular, rationalist logics produce a discourse of being human centered around individualism, skepticism, and detachment from passionate belief, and it is this skepticism—the conviction that only the vigilantly skeptical person can truly be free of deception and destabilizing fanaticism—that "introduce[s] instability at another level: that of the secular, autonomous subject."[63] In reading the Ασκηματα, we see how Shaftesbury's rational, skeptical process of ceaselessly calling himself into question culminates in the complete inversion of the spontaneity and naturalness on which his moral epistemology and subjectivity are based. The φιλανθρωπος ends up in complete isolation, sublimated into the abstract transcendent "Nothings" of that terrible law, with communion across difference coming to be both loathed and yet hauntingly desired in the subject's destabilizing dreams and paranoid fantasies.

Mastering the Body—Disembodiment and "Dark Dreams" of Desire

The second volume of the Ασκηματα, corresponding to Shaftesbury's latter retreat to Holland in 1703–1704, is marked by a similar intensification of the "terrible law" set out in the first volume and by an unremitting tone of beating himself: "Begin then. Not (as before) to leave off again anon, begg Pardon for a while, lye down & rest . . . . . . from What, thou Wretch! from Good? from Rest itself?" (*A*, 190). This self-flagellation produces the opposite of its intended effect, igniting recurrent nightmares and fantasies which Shaftesbury is unable to quench. The second entry in volume 2 (see fig. 4; p. 110) is one of the most stunning, and the first to make extensive use of a set of private symbols by which Shaftesbury removed from language the desires most troublesome to him:[64]

> Φευ, Φευ. ******* The Chasme! . . . View the Past. . . .
> . . . . Dreams. Dreams . . . a Dark Night. dead Sleep. Starts. disturbing Visions. faint Endeavours to awake . . . . a sick Reason. Labyrinth. Wood. Sea. . . . . Waves tossing. Billows. Surge. the driving of the Wreck. . . . . Giddy Whirlwinds. Eddyes, and the over-whelming Gulph.
> How emerge? When gain the Port, the Station, Promontory? . . . Awake. rouse. shake off the Feters of the Enchantress. begin.
> Again retir'd. See, what Providence has bestowd on thee! Once more in thy power to be sav'd; to redeem thyself; to raise thy self from this Sink, these Dreggs, this Guise of a World, to Manlyness, to Reason & a naturall Life; to come on again on the Stage as an Actor, not as a Machine: but as knowing the Author of the Peice, as consciouse of the Design, to joyn in the Performance the Disposition & Government: to be a Spectator, a Guest, a Friend; and with the same Friendlyness to retire and thank the Inviter . . . . But O, these Dreams! this Sleep! . . . . No more. Dye all together thou Wretch: not thus. (*A*, 2:194–95)

Shaftesbury's salvation in this entry is explicitly to be "redeem[ed]" to "Manlyness, to Reason & a naturall Life," and yet Shaftesbury seems unaware that it is the unrelenting control of reason that produces its own resistance in the forms of these haunting dreams. Hearkening back to the epigraph, it is the unrelenting drive to "*solve the Phænomena*" that *has* "plung[ed] into Abysses" and "cast into endless Labrinths" the subject who meant to avoid them. Slavoj Žižek has provocatively suggested, following Lacan, that it is in dreams that we are confronted with the real of our desires; rather than escaping from reality into dreams, we most often awake from dreams to escape from our unfaceable desires into the reality we construct for ourselves in language and ideology.[65] Shaftesbury's

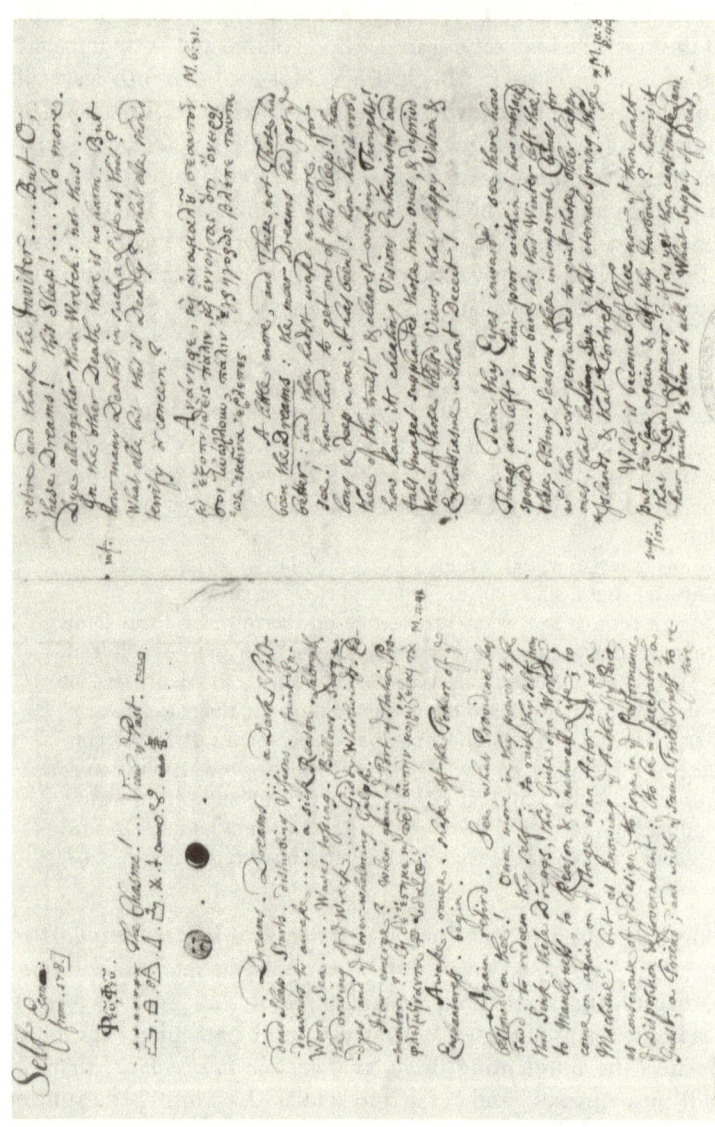

Figure 4 Antony Ashley Cooper, Third Earl of Shaftesbury, Ασκηματα manuscript, pages 2:194–95. The National Archives (Public Record Office) PRO 30/24/27/10 pt. 2. Photograph by Hugh Alexander.

dreams bear this out, presenting a litany of haunting desires that fall outside his ideology of disembodied rationality and total self-command; the dark, the nonlinear, the bodily and oceanic, the overwhelming winds and giddy circling of waters threaten the dissolution of subjectivity. "Begin: take up the Clew. continue the Thread," he warns himself, "and see that it break off no more. no more unraveling: but wind thyself up. collect thy self with all thy might within thy Self." But he asks almost immediately, in a large, bold hand, **"What am I? Who? Whence? Whose?** . . . . to what or whome belonging? with w^t or whome belonging to me, about me, under me?" (*A*, 2:200).

The passage continues, more and more dizzying, circling around the identities of manliness and nobility, trying to think of them ever more abstractly, ever more removed from the vulgar world. In urging himself to "collect [him]self" and "Wind [him]self up," he gestures at the unraveling that is evident in his prose; as the notebooks go on there is less and less a sense that the questions and inversions are getting anywhere, except in the indirect revelation that his dreams and appetites are not submitting to his rational "convictions." Shaftesbury's repeated sexual "falls" and the breach of self-control they represent lead him to a loathing for sexual, bodily permeability that seems to go far beyond any conscious attempt to cultivate aversion toward it. In an early passage, troubled over homosexual desires, for page after page he writes of the sexual body in terms of disease and disgust:

> How happy had it been with Thee, hadst thou kept to these Rules! Now see! whither a certain Lightness & Transport has led Thee! & what Passions are grown from those strong Indulgences in Friendship! Wretch! . . . If Thou canst not think of these as *Sores*; all is Corruption & Sore to the Bottom of thy Mind. . . . But it is in thy power to think of these as *Sores*, & treat them as such. therefore remember after any weak Sensuous, as after Dreams & Fancyes of the Night or after any overpowering Encounters, any of those high florid Luxuriant Thoughts, any of that treacherouse Joy, those Desires Loves, impotent Wishes, Hopes, Excursions, Rovings; remember how this running Ulcer is to be treated. remember how it is that the purulent Matter gathers, that the Part inflames, that the Fungus's and proud flesh arise, & that at last the Part mortifyes & grows insensible. Is the Feeling meanwhile to be indulg'd on this occasion? is the Itch to be satisfied, or the Patient allow'd to appease the Eagerness of it by scratching, or but by tampering or feeling? is not the Part to be bound up close, & kept from the Air? and when it is open'd to dress, are not Incisions, Cauteryes & other things to be us'd, & all this patiently & even cheerfully endur'd through hope of the Cure? How then? Wilt thou tamper with thy self? wilt thou indulg? wilt thou spare thy Flesh, & fly from the Fire, the Steel, the Operations & sharper Remedyes? or are the

other Wounds something, but these Nothing? is it no matter how it is *within*, or whether thou liv'st allways with a Macerated corrupted Mind? Would'st thou willingly go out of the World because of such a Body that is incurable; & not because of such a Mind? ... is there not a wors Lameness, a wors Deformity, & Filth? (*A*, 83, 168)

For Shaftesbury, the cutting off of sexual permeability is an amputation preferable to the subjective death that such penetrability represents, and the loathing of self and other, of desire as filth, weakness, and deformity in the Ασκηματα, is in service of the impossible autonomous subject position of the "common Father of Mankind" he desires to occupy. "Remember, still, what thou art to them; & they to thee," he reminds himself, "What are their Friendships for one another? consider w^t they are capable of: and what a little time is sure to bring about" (*A*, 132), that is, either enmity or intimacy, equally detestable. In a passage that turns the "sociable enthusiast" and philanthropy on its ear, Shaftesbury elaborates a method for turning desires for others into revulsion. "Whenever a certain Fondness comes upon Thee, such as invites & draws towards Familiarity & Intimacy," he advises himself,

> Remember what has been said above ... the Fight, Enmity & Opposition of Principles; what it is that is plac'd as a Gulph between us. remember Hipocrisy, Imposture, Imposition, Intruding: Who *They* are; and what *I my Self* am. that we now talk to one another mask'd, & in disguise. that I take not Him for Him; nor he Me for Me. He pleases himself with a Specter; and I, my self with another Specter.... Strip us; set us Naked before one another; and see how each will stare & be amaz'd. see how we shall then view one another. How will he bear the sight of my Opinions? or how I his, when I see them bare-fac'd and naturall? How dos he appear to me in his Anger, in his Pleasure, in his Lust? How in a Title, with an Estate, in Reputation or Disgrace, in Prosperity or Adversity? how amongst his Domesticks? how in ordinary provocations? how in Sickness? how in any Cross or Disappointment? how many ways intollerable? And am I more tollerable, as I stand with him? can my Opinions, or such Affection as mine, be bore with? am not I a Monster to him? (*A*, 133)

For the subject as autonomous, disembodied mind, the body figures, in psychoanalytic terms, as the horrible fantasy "supplement"—precisely because it is vulnerable and permeable—by which the symbolic or ideological system's failure is taken into account in advance.[66] The body becomes the site of masking and deception; to be physically naked masks, Shaftesbury imagines, the deeper nakedness of desire and intention that remains hidden, and by virtue of which lovers would be loathsome to each other. In much the same terms that that liturgy was vilified in free-prayer literature for its ritual physicality, in the secular cult of moral sense and spontaneity, the body is linked to "pomp, *ceremony*, shew" and all "unnatural" things Shaftesbury wants to be rid of. Just as vices come to be seen as "Incumbrances & Growths," "as it were, Parts of thy Self, & sticking to thee: Wretched Things" (*A*, 2:198), so the body comes to be seen as alien to the self: "a truly Wise Man thinks his Body no part of himself nor belonging to him even whilst in it! only he takes Care of it as of a Lodging an Inn, a Passage-boat, or ship, a Post Hors" (*A*, 230). Later in the Ασκηματα Shaftesbury's pressing question becomes how to "redeem" himself from "the carcass": that "helpless weak impotent Thing, full of Wants, Ails, Necessityes, Cravings" (*A*, 279). "*I* (the real *I*)," he writes, "am not a certain Figure nor Mass, nor Hair, nor Nails, nor Flesh, nor Limbs, nor Corps; but **Mind, Thought, Intellect, Reason**" (*A*, 278). The divorce of the self from the body is at the service of protecting the self from the weakness, permeability, and vulnerability to the other that the sexual, hungry body represents.

And yet, it is the very effort to make the self impenetrable that fuels a violent enjoyment of the other, who is both disavowed and obsessively desired. In seeking to constitute himself apart from the body and from others, Shaftesbury had earlier reminded himself of "what it is that is plac'd as a Gulph between us" (*A*, 133). This "Gulph" that the rational subject constructs as a protective moat, the forbidden intersubjective space of desire and relation, is precisely that which returns as the "overwhelming Gulph" of giddy, labyrinthine desire in his haunting "dark" dreams, which the subject of the Ασκηματα would rather "Dye all together" than be plunged into.[67] Subjectivity-threatening desire returns not only in dreams, but even more vividly in Shaftesbury's violent, sexualized fantasies of his inner life and of revenge on the Deity who seemingly does nothing to rescue him.

"Monstrous Copulations"—Others, Fancy, and the Violation of God

At one of the more disturbing points in the Ασκηματα, Shaftesbury compares talking to others about his Regimen to passing about phlegm and stools: "Man! what have we to do with this? Take thy Physick, purg, vomit, that thou mayst be well & come abroad: but what have wee to do with Stools? why talk to us of Flegme?" (*A*, 154).[68] In a similar image of disgust, the dreams and false *visa* that haunt the second volume of the Ασκηματα are detestable because they are the deformed results of "monstrous copulation" and miscegenation: "The Apparitions, Specters, compound-Visa, Monsters of Monstrouse Copulation, Species mix'd. Dragons, Mules. Publicke & Private: the Hors & Ass. amphibiouse Animalls: dubiouse Ones: Batts: Centaurs: Chimeras: Sphinxs . . . . How long deluded? How long impos'd on by these Forms? Go to the

Anatomy. dissect: separate, according to Art, and with the Instruments that are given. divorce the unnatural Pair. divide the Monster" (*A*, 241). In Shaftesbury's thinking all copulation is in some sense monstrous, evincing an uncontrollable and vulnerable desire for the other, but his specific revulsion at "unnatural" unions hints why it is particularly his homosexual desire that troubles him. Particularly the desire to be penetrated would be as perverse to Shaftesbury as wanting to display his own excrement, testifying as it does to the body's permeability and the subject's lack of complete self-containment. Such penetrability or subjection to another would directly threaten his essential masculinity. "One of these two must ever be," he claims:

> that a **Man** has his Fancyes in right Discipline; turning, leading, & commanding Them or They Him. Either They must deal with Him, take him up short (as they say) teach him Manners & make him know whome He belongs to: Or this will be **His Part** to teach the Impostress Fancy & her Train; shew Her what She is herself & whome She has to deal with.
> This is to be *a Man*. (*A*, 274–75)

"Man," the supremely masculine subject position of the "common Father of Mankind," is a matter of controlling and commanding, precisely that which is not "*Childish. Womanish. Bestial. Brutal*" (*A*, 334), and in the latter parts of the Ασκηματα, "Effeminacy, Tenderness, Niceness" is a threatening "disease" growing "Wors & Wors" (*A*, 341).[69] In an almost drunken, spatially irregular passage, the self and its very linguistic coherence threaten to "dissolve" in effeminacy: "Even when Attention, the Προσοχη, strict Attention is but suspended, w^t else is it? What but *Dissolution?* . . . . See the Effects too . . . . all Dissolution . . . . . . Instrument down, unstrung . . . . . Dissolution of Liquors; of the Blood . . . . . Dissolvd in Effeminacy *Diffluere Luxu, Voluptatibus, Otio*.[70] Every loss of Attention, every Relaxation, every time of the τα Παθη [passions] of any kind . . . All this, *Dissolution*" (*A*, 339).

To represent his inner world of desires and the Regimen that would remedy them, Shaftesbury most often evokes gendered, material images of permeability, excess, and the materiality which he seeks to escape. In one of the most chilling later passages, we see the precise means by which dominating, sexualized desire is not evacuated but reinscribed in Shaftesbury's intellectual life. Reflecting on "entertainments," Shaftesbury decrees to himself that his entertainment is not to be the usual social or sexual intrigue but "penetrating" into the hearts and motives of others. While he is to keep his own self whole and inviolate, he is to "Pierce into the Bottom-work of their Minds," he tells himself, into the dark Chambers & Corners of their Hearts; their Principles of Judgment; their decisive determining Thoughts & Rules of Action; their Spring Source Origine of Affection, Hatreds Loves, Appetitions Aversations; their Genuine Fancyes, Imaginations, Opinions, Δογματα, Decrees, Judgments; nor those they sett out to shew, before others. To penetrate, to dive & search into their Ways, Moods Dispositions, Humours Feelings: . . . Nothing to do with Secrets, their Family or State-Secrets, their Secret Tales, Projects, Interests Amours, or any other Secrecyes: but to disclose by their good leave (or whether they give leave or no) the secret & hidden mistery of all their Life & Action; the springs & Wheels of the Machine & see into their Breasts layd open . . . . Be these thy Entertainments & Discourses with thy Self (tho' in Company:) these thy Fables; when needs there must be Fables, & Discourse of that kind: this thy Table Talk within, with self. & let alone that other. . . . (*A*, 378–79)

Shaftesbury's disembodiment of the self actually enables a profoundly sexualized fantasy: not so much that of loving as of penetrating the other, psychologically and intellectually, without being oneself at all vulnerable or revealed. An obvious component of the pleasure of this intellectual entertainment lies in its similarity to rape: "to penetrate" the "secret & hidden mistery of all their Life & Action"—"whether they give leave or no."[71]

The corollary threat of being overcome by one's own desires is likewise violently sexualized. In these volumes of inner soliloquy that takes place in suffering and, as it were, in the place of the prayer and "expostulation" with the Deity it has foreclosed, the only other persona who appears in 400 pages and with whom Shaftesbury speaks—and, we may say, the chief other at whom his inversions and self-splitting arrive—is the voice of his desire, Φαντασια or (Shaftesbury's preferred translation) Fancy, literally the power of the mind to place objects before itself, usually, in the Platonic tradition, giving rise to false pleasures.[72] Like Pleasure, she is feminine, and the most vivid inner conversations Shaftesbury records are with her. In his method of giving voice to his desires, she becomes the persona he imagines speaking, and he coaches himself in how to get the better of her, depending on what class of woman—a wench, a servant, or a refined lady—she takes the form of at the moment. Sometimes the exchanges are more rational and argumentative, but more often they resemble compelling depictions of domestic violence, abusive interrogations in an effort not to let her have her say. The encounter is continually portrayed as an all-or-nothing affair of domination or submission, and his violence is justified by the perpetual threat of her dominating *him*.[73]

Rambling, accelerating, spiraling out of control, one of the late dialogues with Fancy is one of the most brilliantly telling passages in the notebooks. Rebuking Fancy, Shaftesbury writes:

> **O Sophistry!** Artifice, & deep lay'd Design! So Artfull as to appear all Simplicity: so natural as to seem allmost Nature itself . . . O, Imposture! powerfull charming, perswasive Dame, η παντας τους ανθρωπους πλανωσα [the deceiver of all men]. W^t an Offspring? W^t a Brood engenderd? what Machines, Hosts, Gyants! . . . . . *Loves. Appetites. Desires.*
> . . . . . . Opinion, Fancy, all. All from this Sophistry . . . . . "Irresistable Powers! Gigantick Forms! Whence all your Strength Dimensions Weapons & Array? the pointed Steel, the Viper-Teeth & Scorpion-Stings . . . . What Sting? and Whence? . . . . . . Opinion, Fancy . . . . Ω Φαντασια. Thine is the Sting. thine all the Force. thine the Dominion Power. From Thee this Empire Without Thee all faints languishes & dyes. *Loves Appetites, Desires,* all live in Thee.
> "To Thee I come then. With Thee is my Concern, Thee alone." Tis Thou must form Me, or I Thee . . . . *Loves Appetites, Desires, Fears, Horrours, Anguishes,* and all yee Hosts of Passions: stand by: retire, & wayt aloof the Issue of this Conflict. If I am overcome, the Field the Place is yours: sack pillage plunder ravage. But if I prevail; retire for ever: yee are Nothing, nor have no Pretence.
> *Responsare Cupidinibus* [To resist or respond to lust]—No such Thing. but *Visis,* Φαντασιαις [to images, to fantasies]. this is the Thing. and thus it is right said. Here the Resistance . . . . . The Father (Opinion) subdued; the Children fall of Course . . . . . . Sampson's Lock. Achilles's Heel . . . . Here strike. No dealing but this. this way only vincible, penetrable, tractable. this way & in this sence *Responsare Cupidinibus.* To bear up. To be a Match for 'em. *Give em* (as they say) *their own* and send 'em back as they came. (*A,* 308–9)[74]

Beginning with Nature as his first term and as a system operating by fixed laws, Shaftesbury has been seeking the principle that would govern him in natural affection, that is, in resignation before an impassible Deity of order and system, of abstract, disembodied reason, to whom one cannot talk or pray, especially about one's suffering. In searching for this lawlike resignation before what is, he is faced with his misery and fights to subdue it by giving voice to the desires that "effeminately cry and whine" about their unhappiness and by then expostulating vehemently with them. Here, in one of the most heated of such exchanges, addressing Fantasy, Shaftesbury suddenly echoes the ending of the Lord's Prayer—"For thine is the kingdom and the power and the glory"—and in the next breath, St. Paul's evocation of the God "in whom we live, and move, and have our being" ("all live in Thee"; *A,* 309).[75] Rhetorically, the Fancy with whom Shaftesbury so long does battle becomes God, partly the Christian God whom the vulgar desire and whom he despises, and partly the Deity who, in refusing to impart certainty, causes the suffering of unfulfillable desire. The one Shaftesbury castigates is not initially recognized as God because she is the feminized subject of his railing, but the psychological trajectory of this anger and desire for domination over the Deity is unmistakable. In the course of the passage, the "Loves Appetites, Desires" that Fancy begets are masculinized and transformed into lust (Cupid, cupidity), whose father is Opinion, that is, the formerly feminine false vision or visa and Fantasia. Slipping momentarily into the god-position, Fancy is masculinized as false Opinion, and through stoic inner battle, overcome: "this way only" is he/she "vincible, penetrable, tractable." In the self of the Ασκηματα, split within itself, split from prayer and the Deity, and from its own desire, we see Shaftesbury's fantasy and desire feminized and abused, transfigured as God, remasculinized, and, in a crucial word in all its many valences in the Ασκηματα, *penetrable*—mastered, overcome.[76]

This implicit gesture of penetrating God, the image of a sexually violated God, recurs in various keys and modalities throughout the moral literature of the eighteenth century that is heir to Shaftesbury's public writings and clearly also to a shared deeper logic. And this image is, I would argue, crucial for understanding the troubled relation of Enlightenment subjectivity to religion, which much recent scholarship is trying to articulate.[77] Richardson's *Clarissa* is perhaps the most obvious example, echoed and reworked throughout so much sentimental fiction in its quasi-pornographic mode: its climax the absent but everywhere fetishized scene of Clarissa, the earthly "angel" and "divine woman," rhetorically deified through hundreds of pages of Lovelace's letters, lying finally lifeless and mute, violated by him. More literally the image appears in the works of Richardson's most infamous admirer, the Marquis de Sade. The earliest account we have of Sade's sexual behavior is a document discovered in 1963, the deposition given on 19 October 1763 by Jeanne Testard, a prostitute whom Sade had procured the day before. According to Testard, once they reached his quarters, Sade's first question was whether she were religious, and specifically if she believed in God, in Jesus Christ, and the Virgin; she replied that she did, and observed her religion as best she could given her profession.

> To which the individual replied with horrible insults and blasphemies, saying that there was no God, that he had proved it . . . that he once had sexual union with a girl with whom he had taken communion, that he had made off with the two communion wafers, had shoved them into that girl's sexual parts, and had sexual congress with her, all the while saying: *If you are God, avenge yourself.*[78]

This scene, in which Sade puts the wafer, the body of Christ, up the woman's vagina, follows it by his own penis and, as Sade's biographer Neil Schaeffer puts it, "presumably embugger[s] Christ," is played out in heterosexual and homosexual permutations in almost all Sade's writings, particularly in *Philosophy in the Bedroom* (1795) and his earlier, more methodically scientific and brutal *The 120 Days of Sodom* (1785).[79] Closer to home as it were, almost twenty-five years before Sade's first arrest and in Shaftesbury's direct philosophical lineage, there is Hume's famous letter to Lord Kames, which he ends by saying that he is busy "castrating" the Treatise, "that is, cutting off its noble Parts."[80] What he is cutting off, ostensibly out of respect for Bishop Butler, is the attack on miracles; the phallus of the *Treatise*, then, is in a profound way its sexualized attack on religion seen through the eyes of proof and necessity, on the possibility of proving God's being.[81]

Shaftesbury's *Exercises* suggest ways to particularize and historicize these representations of sexualized assaults on God in otherwise seemingly secular texts: by understanding them as manifestations of the way a certain form of abstract rationality and subjectivity, oriented around mastery and control, constructs and must construct what we may call the god-term or god-position. What Shaftesbury calls the Deity is first a guarantee—perfectly objective, unassailable, and disembodied—of his own subject position within what Robert Markley has identified as the ideology of objectivity that flourished during the Restoration period. Under scientists like Boyle and Newton, this ideology began with a theistic and ascetic bent, yet became the basis for the aggressive, materialistic imperialism of the Restoration. The "fiction of objectivity" and of objective language, Markley writes, is a fiction that "aspires to the status of a metaphysic," a fiction that in the late seventeenth century enacts a "secularization" of previously "theological justifications for order and stability."[82] The Deity of the notebooks is very much a secularized God, the one who appears necessary to thinkers through Kant precisely as the guarantee of an ideology of reason, abstraction, and certainty.

But if Žižek's psychoanalytic account of ideology is to be believed, ideology, which seeks to secure a total knowledge of the world through ideological quilting points or what we might think of as master signifiers, is the result of fantasy construction, that is, it is both borne of a fantasy of totality—of total knowledge without uncertainty or antagonism—and borne of the fantasy-structures of desire that attempt to suture the impossibility of that closure. Fantasy itself, according to Žižek, is a mechanism by which an ideology takes its failure into account in advance; it is always sexualized, enabling the subject symptomatically to fetishize a particular signifier that becomes "permeated with enjoyment," and structuring desire as a sort of endless Möbius strip which it is impossible to fulfill or escape from. Fantasies supplement ideology, giving us a libidinal investment in remaining blind to ideology's failings, serving as plugs in the gap of its incompleteness. Thus both positive fantasy and its loathed, paranoid supplement, point to the location of that incompleteness, not simply in the lack of the subject itself, but in the lack in the other, the great Other who is supposed to know and in whose name the ideology is authorized.[83]

When one reads Shaftesbury's preface to Benjamin Whichcote's sermons and sees the appeal that a quite secularized Christian neo-Platonism held for him, one might be prompted to ask why Shaftesbury resolutely rejected confessional Christianity, especially since the English church had become significantly rationalized by his day. Reading passages of the notebooks, on the other hand, in which Shaftesbury prays to Epictetus and Marcus Aurelius and barely contains his disgust for Christianity, we might more easily wonder why a god appears at all in these texts, that is, why Shaftesbury did not become an outright atheist.[84] The answers are closely related. Shaftesbury despises atheism for the same reason he eventually condemned Locke's work, because throwing out either a rational creator or innate ideas threatens to throw preordained, constant order out of the world as well; the Deity as abstract, disembodied total knower guarantees the only sort of moral knowledge that can be meaningful to Shaftesbury from within his moral-empirical mindset. It is in the service of this ideology of objectivity that reason's Deity becomes a quilting point and that the specifically Christian dimensions of theism, belief in the incarnate Christ and communion with him, are disavowed. Upholding the explicit system of objective moral certainty, the fantasy of the Ασκηματα is perfect control of one's desires, the spontaneous mastery of "natural affection." Part and parcel of this fantasy, both its foil and its lure is sexualized as Φαντασια, Fancy and the eroticized, ever-incomplete quest for her domination. But as Lacan has it, "what is foreclosed in the Symbolic"—that is, for Shaftesbury, institutionalized Christianity—"returns in the Real" of the symptom and of desire. It is this return in the real of the symptom and desire that we see in the spiraling passage where Fancy becomes divinized and "penetrable" as the Christian God of St. Paul and the "Our Father" of the gospels. The sexualized attack on the Deity, rather than a cool walking away from God, reveals the way that a libidinally invested secularism is a key fantasy supplement for various Enlightenment ideologies that put at their center a place for the masculine subject of mastery and control. More than a simple return of the repressed, though, the reappearance of specifically Christian tropes in violent, sexualized contexts in Shaftesbury,

Richardson, Sade, Hume, and others confesses a specific loathing for Christ that is a component of this ideology, and that is evidenced in the notebook he took up after he had set the Ασκηματα aside.

"Christ! Wretched Model"

Though inscriptions indicate that Shaftesbury was rereading the Ασκηματα as late as 1708, he stopped writing in the notebooks with regularity around 1705.[85] The last major entry was added at St. Giles in January 1706/7, and it hints at why: it intimates a desire on Shaftesbury's part to break out of endless self-flagellation, to "Be diffident" and even cynical but to move outward toward "Action" in the world (*A*, 387).[86] Action meant work on his public philosophical writings aimed at the improvement of his fellow men, which he painstakingly revised and published as the *Characteristicks* in 1711. By the time it appeared, Shaftesbury had turned 40, married, and only just months before produced the long-awaited heir to his estate. By this time, Shaftesbury was also in what he suspected was his final illness, and in hopes of lengthening his final days, he and his wife left their infant son in the care of their steward and traveled to Naples. There Shaftesbury devoted himself to two tasks: to preparing detailed instructions for the illustrations of the second edition of the *Characteristicks*, and to making notes for what was to be its sequel, *Second Characters* or "Plasticks, an Epistolary Excursion in the Original Progress and Power of Designatory Art," a treatise which was to mirror in aesthetics what *Characteristicks* attempted in morality.

Traveling in Italy and compiling notes on the works of the great masters, Shaftesbury at one point compiled a list of the chief "discouragements in art." Pronounced among these, in Shaftesbury's words, was how the great masters, especially his admired Raphael, were "forced" to make their livings by painting Christ:

> Cheif support of painting wt?—X^t!—Wretched model! Barbarean No Form, no grace of shoulders Breast (here cite the Poet's finest verses of *Apollo* Jove) no *Demarche*, Air, Majesty, Grandeur, a lean un-comely Proportion & Species, a mere *Jew* or *Hebrew* (originally an ugly scabby people) both Shape & Phyz: with half Beard peaked not one nor t'other, Lank clinging Hair, sniveling Face, Hypocritical Canting Countenance, & at best Melancholly-Mad & enthusiastical in the common & lower way, not so well as even the Bacchinals & Bacchaates.[87]

In a way perhaps unequalled in the works of Shaftesbury or his philosophical heirs, we see here the interconnected logic of class prejudice, aesthetic taste, misogyny, anti-Semitism, and antireligious sentiment, culminating in and brought to bear on the person of Christ. Formulating what he hoped would be a "thoroughly moral aesthetic" and reviewing the works of the great masters he most admires—Raphael, the Carracci, Poussin, da Vinci, Michelangelo—Shaftesbury quite nearly worships their formal beauty and genius, and is everywhere overcome with disgust at their explicit subject, Christ, so completely at odds with the entire system of meaning in which he is invested.[88] In traditional Trinitarian teaching, Christ appears in every way as the unthinkable, disgusting "Thing" in Shaftesbury's system: God in a body, vulnerable, crucified, effeminately penetrated, subject to all manner of violence and "unnatural" affections from his creatures, and from the wedding in Cana to the thief on the cross "expostulated with" from first to last. Shaftesbury's language late in the Ασκηματα of penetrating God cannot help but invoke both desire and loathing, both a hypermasculine fantasy of violating his self-fashioned Deity of mastery, and this abject crucified Christ, in a way that is exactly symptomatic of the logocentric drive for certainty and totality in the symbolic order and of the forms of desire it generates, inseparable from the fantasy-supplements of loathed figures—woman, the Jew, and here Christ—that mask the larger impossibilities of the perfect, totalizing, closed system.[89]

What is perhaps clearer to Shaftesbury than to the many religious writers who, following Hutcheson, attempted to co-opt his moral sense as "proof" of Christian theism,[90] is the radical incommensurability between this Christ and the ideals of the rational, all-controlling Deity of reason. God secularized as rationalism's Deity is anything but worldly. He, most definitely he, is the result of despising the world and the body in all its humility, vulnerability, and interrelation with others, its association with repetitive praxis, with eating and longing, with faith and ceremony and ritual, with different sorts of knowledges and loves inaccessible to pure reason and delegitimated by it.[91] This Deity is the guarantee of the subject's position in a system of moral ideology, but it is eventually the position that subject would assail as well. To move toward challenging this Deity would seem an integral part of the logic of masculine mastery and subjectivity, part of what has been called the characteristic "outbidding" of reason, its perpetual movement toward ever-greater mastery and abstraction.[92] But anger more than ambition accounts for the vehemence of this attack on God. Alienated from the porous body and from the silent, absolutely abstract Deity who is indifferent to his pains and desires, the sexualized subject of reason and of the symbolic order feels assailed by both and, in the form of the fused loathed supplement of God-in-a-body, attacks both with a vengeance—feminizes both, needs both; eschews, desires, and loathes both God and the body. At the intersection of those violences, Shaftesbury finds the particular God he has foreclosed uncannily already there, having submitted to the very violence that the libidinal economies of rationalism would seem inevitably to want to inflict on him.

In an equally profound sense, this Christ whom Shaftesbury loathes from the position of the subjectivity of mastery is closest of all to Shaftesbury's repressed or second self throughout the Ασκηματα. Christ is the masculine subject dissolved in effeminacy, the "*Wretch!*" and wretchedness with which Shaftesbury has a hundred times reproached himself. In his final months, having an endless stream of paintings brought to his *palazzo* by the art dealer Signor Porchinaro, seeing most of his art in Neapolitan churches and the monasteries of San Marino and Mount Oliveto, the suggestion would have been hard to avoid: Christ suffocating on the cross, St. Anthony wrestling with the demons in the desert, his modern namesake wrestling in a desert of reason and abstraction, smothered by asthma. If the self as *philanthropos* and common father of mankind never materializes in the notebooks, but is everywhere threatened by its crucifixion, its subjective destitution, its disintegrating into a feminized wretchedness outside of the symbolic order and language, it is no wonder that Shaftesbury devoted his final months not just to *Second Characters* and a theory of aesthetics, but to designing the visual images that would appear in the second edition of the *Characteristicks* and that, more than any of his writings, attempt to concretize and unify the self that felt itself excruciatingly divided and dissolving. First among these was an image of their author. On the first page of the *Characteristicks*, we see Shaftesbury enrobed as a philosopher-god, with his political and aristocratic titles inscribed beneath his engraving, appearing like Bunyan most whole in a didactic, evangelistic stance, as a voice in print culture proclaiming to others their illness, and offering his solution. However much they proclaim politeness and wit as remedies for the ills of early eighteenth-century English culture, the *Characteristicks* and its images serve above all to create a whole self in a way that the Ασκηματα could not. But like the Ασκηματα behind the *Characteristicks*, behind the *Characteristicks*' engraving of Shaftesbury was a truly singular portrait of the self-splitting produced in the quest for this fantasy of totality.

CODA TO CHAPTER 3

"Divide Yourself, Be Two"
Images of the Modern Subject

> Torn in two, a Janus-faced being, Shaftesbury captures the period's most profound contradictions and anticipates its most characteristic developments in moral philosophy.
>
> —Michael Prince, *Philosophical Dialogue in the British Enlightenment*[1]

In the first edition of Shaftesbury's *Characteristicks* (1711), only a single emblematic engraving appeared, which Shaftesbury referred to in letters as "the Old Device" or "the round Figure," and which functioned as the frontispiece.[2] But during 1711, as his health deteriorated and he and his wife traveled to Naples, Shaftesbury grew more and more intent on designing a whole set of emblematic figures for the second edition, which would ultimately appear after his death, in 1714. As art historian Edgar Wind has put it, Shaftesbury was accustomed to seeing the artist not as a creative genius but as an "amanuensis," a "manual executant who carries out in visible material the ideas dictated to him by the philosopher,"[3] and his detailed instructions for the emblems include letters, a small diary containing about twenty pages of notes on the illustrations, and instructions he sent to the printer and engraver, so specific as to demand that "there must be nothing added" to the emblems outside his instructions "which can possibly make a sense or meaning."[4]

Felix Paknadel, in his oft-cited article "Shaftesbury's Illustrations of *Characteristics*," has collated these instructions together with the engravings and offered compelling, comprehensive reading of the emblems. The

Figure 5 Emblem designed by Shaftesbury and engraved by Simon Gribelin for "Soliloquy: Or Advice to An Author," in the second edition of Characteristicks *(1714).*

triptych for the centerpiece of the collection, "Soliloquy," written in 1707, is illustrative of the care and meaning with which Shaftesbury invested these engravings (see fig. 5).[5] It illustrates the notion from Shaftesbury's long practice in the Ασκηματα that, following the teachings of the ancients, one should "RECOGNIZE YOUR-SELF," which "was as much to say, *Divide Your-self*, or *Be* TWO. For if the Division were rightly made, all *within* wou'd of course, they thought, be rightly understood, and prudently manag'd."[6] The theme uniting the three panels is therefore the mirror in which one should look to recognize his true self. In such a mirror a man will see two faces, one virtuous, the other "rude, undisciplin'd and headstrong";[7] these are represented by the two boys in the panels on opposite sides of the mirror. The boy on the left is according to Shaftesbury's instructions "well-proportion'd, natural, genteel and well-pois'd," recalling the "Natural Self" of the Ασκηματα; he gestures toward himself and examines himself intently in a hand-mirror. The boy on the right recalls the "Artificial or Economical Self" and is "less comely," standing in a "timorous posture ... in the passion of fear," under a dark and cloudy sky, assailed by harpies that symbolize Fancies. The Fancies over the natural self, in contrast, fly away in confusion. In striving to be the better self, one must confront the Fancies plaguing the artificial self, and in the words of *Soliloquy* familiar from the earlier notebooks, embark on "our Sovereign Remedy" of soliloquy, in which the mind "apostrophizes its own fancies, raises them in their proper *Shapes* and *Personages*, and addresses 'em familiarly, without the least Ceremony or Respect."[8] In the center panel of the emblem looms a large looking-glass of what Shaftesbury called the "fashionable sort," hanging over a modern book and reflecting nothing, because the interior of the room, the mind, fed on fashion and the moderns rather than the ancients, is dark.⁹ The emblems for the other essays were similarly detailed and didactic.

The first of the new illustrations, however, which was to appear on the opening page of the first volume, was more straightforward: a portrait of Shaftesbury engraved by Simon Gribelin (see fig. 6). In it, a magisterial Shaftesbury appears wearing a toga and long curled hair or a light-colored wig, standing beneath a canopy, with one hand resting on a pedestal bearing volumes of Plato and Xenophon and the other clutching a book to his chest. Visible behind him through an arch is a manicured landscape, indicating his rank and wealth. The image is one of stately grace and control, one which Marcus Brainard has interpreted as standing in for the whole aim and design of the *Characteristicks*: in

Figure 6 Engraving of Shaftesbury by Simon Gribelin, prefixed to the second edition of Characteristicks *(1714).*

Shaftesbury's words, to "correct *Manners* and regulate *Lives*" by inviting readers to "undertake the quest for self-knowledge" that the author in the portrait has clearly undertaken.[10]

Behind both *Soliloquy* and Gribelin's engraving of Shaftesbury, though, was a stunning painting, one likely as intricately designed as anything Shaftesbury ever commissioned, a full-length portrait, previously dated 1700–1701, by the artist John Closterman, who created and col-

Figure 7 Portrait of Shaftesbury by John Closterman, 1704–1705[?]. Image by the National Portrait Gallery. Reproduced by permission of Lady Shaftesbury, Wimborn, St. Giles.

lected for Shaftesbury during the last dozen years of his life (see fig. 7; p. 126).[11] Almost 8 feet by 5 feet, the massive painting from which the engraving was reversed is regal and dramatic in its stark color scheme, dominated by the pale blue-grey flowing toga and royal crimson drapery. In it Shaftesbury appears sober and radiant, younger than in the engraving, with warm, light brown hair where the engraving seems to suggest a powdered wig, a glowing complexion, bright blue eyes, and a white linen undershirt open almost halfway down his chest. The most striking feature of the portrait, where only an open archway would appear in the engraving, is an unidentified second figure. Behind Shaftesbury and to his left, the second man appears roughly two-thirds his size but still so large and in detail as to preclude a symbolic or generic figure.[12] Dressed in day attire of the same blue-grey color as Shaftesbury's toga, he is older, with light or powdered hair, more tightly curled, and carries over his right arm the white and crimson robes of the House of Lords.

With the provenance of the painting in continuous family descent, that a major figure in such an imposing portrait should be unidentified is itself quite curious. Most scholarship has echoed the opinion of the tenth Earl of Shaftesbury, expressed when the portrait appeared in the National Portrait Gallery's Closterman exhibition in 1981, that the second figure is likely a senior member of Shaftesbury's household; Voitle and Leatherbarrow have suggested his steward John Wheelock.[13] Read in this way, the painting portrays a servant bringing Shaftesbury his parliamentary robes and beckoning him from philosophy to public duty, dramatizing the tension between the *vita activa* and the *vita contemplativa*. In the portraiture of the day, however, servants almost never appear unsubservient on such a scale, and without exception, the servants in other Closterman portraits appear below and much smaller than their masters, usually in profile; the figure is almost certainly not a servant.[14] Moreover, the two figures wear the same color fabric and bear a marked family resemblance: the cleft chin, the asymmetry of the eyes and their identical dark blue color, the protuberance of the end of the nose, the bow of the lips, the crease to the left of the mouth, the bit of a second chin. Shaftesbury's closest living male relative at the time, his younger brother Maurice, would thus seem a likely candidate for the second figure, but he can be ruled out. The attendant is clearly older than Shaftesbury, where Maurice is younger, and an earlier double portrait of the brothers also by Closterman shows Maurice with a scar on the left side of his chin, clearly absent in this later portrait.[15] The sharp, dark divide between the two figures, however, with the older man crossing a threshold, could in the artistic idiom of the day suggest that this was a figure appearing from the past, perhaps a departed relative. The inclusion of a deceased forbear would more commonly have taken the form of a portrait on the wall behind the sitter, but mythical characters and other figures from the past appearing through the liminal space of an arch or doorway would nonetheless have been part of a pictorial vocabulary with which Closterman, like Shaftesbury, was conversant.[16]

The provocative suggestion arises, then, that the second figure might be Shaftesbury's grandfather, the first earl. Existing portraits show him with curled blond hair, and after the Restoration he served in the House of Lords, so the robes he carries would be his own. Moreover the dramatic vertical divide between the two figures also fittingly calls up Shaftesbury's complex relationship to his grandfather. The Ασκηματα and Shaftesbury's early letters indicate the profound influence of the first earl in directing Shaftesbury's education and inspiring his political activity. Between December 1699 and January 1700, though, when Shaftesbury returned to London from his first retreat and suffered one of his early "falls," he distilled his Regimen into a set of rules for conduct with others, and under rules regarding "simplicity" and deportment with others, he added: "And Remember the treacherous Pleasure: *reviving chearing entertaining moving affecting imprinting*: Imitation of G^d F[ather]—Perniciouse! Ruinouse! All this cutt off. no Pleasure in pleasing: none in being hearkened to: none in amusing astonishing: no, nor profiting—What *Profiting?* (wretch!)" (*A*, 3). These sentences are bracketed, with "Hence Φυρειν" written vertically in the right margin: "Hence, defilement." However much Shaftesbury prized his grandfather's Whig ideals, it is clear from this passage that he came to see "imitation" of his grandfather's vivacious social manner in public life as "pernicious and ruinous," leading to the sexual "defilement" that so disturbed him and in which he always seemed to become embroiled when returning to London and Parliament.

We might then see the second figure, the first earl, as a noble but nonetheless tempting presence, ever beckoning his grandson away from his philosophical endeavors to the "treacherous pleasures" of social and political life, tempting him to exchange his philosopher's garment for a parliamentary robe—certainly an unusual representation of the ancestor to whom Shaftesbury owed his title and education. More positively perhaps, though he is positioned below his grandson, the first earl is stepping up into the plane where Shaftesbury stands. He has removed his robes and, with his left hand open in a relinquishing motion, seems to be deliberately heading towards the philosophical realm, eager to take up study in the exalted intellectual sphere to which he led his grandson. This reading would resonate with the only other reference to the first earl in the Ασκηματα, in which Shaftesbury encourages himself to be grateful for his grandfather's having "la[id] the Foundation of [his] Education" (*A*, 1:196). But even in this more charitable reading, the divide between the two is stark and complete, and the second figure stands distinctly below

Figure 8 Portrait of Shaftesbury by John Closterman, detail of first figure.

Figure 9 Portrait of Shaftesbury by John Closterman, detail of second figure.

Shaftesbury, literally with a dark cloud over his head, not unlike the dark boy or unnatural self in the emblem for "Soliloquy." And as resonant as this reading may be, it still begs the question of why the first earl would have gone unidentified in a portrait that still hangs in his home and has been continuously held by his descendents for 300 years.[17]

It may be, in fact, that the most unlikely understanding of the second figure—virtually unthinkable in terms of historical precedent or available portraiture idiom—affords, for its very strangeness, the most satisfying and compelling reading of the portrait. Given the uncertainty of three centuries, as well as the larger Shaftesbury oeuvre, some speculation is warranted. Immersed in Shaftesbury's labyrinthine private writings in conjunction with his philosophy, I have found myself unable to resist the notion that the second figure is Shaftesbury himself, and that together the two figures dramatize that self-conscious self-splitting that is everywhere referenced in both his public and private writings.

The two figures are seen from opposite angles—the first figure from his right side, the second, from the left and with his head tilted, from slightly below—but the physical similarity, especially in facial detail, is, as mentioned, quite striking: the figures are clearly meant both to be seen as connected and yet also to be differentiated (see figs. 8 and 9). The figures may even be thought of as wearing the same undergarment, with Shaftesbury's simply opened at the neck. Without too much license, we can imagine the second figure as Shaftesbury's "Artificial or Economical Self," the desirous second-self against whom he is forever railing in the Ασκηματα. This self is more worn and worldly, more appetitive and plump, wearing either a wig or fashionably powdered hair, looking over his shoulder in angst at the cares of the world: Shaftesbury as he so often was, and wished not to be. The larger, more attractive figure would then be Shaftesbury's "Natural Self," that ideal subject of "natural affection" that is from the outset the goal of the Ασκηματα project. This figure is literally at home with the ancients, at ease with them, and clothed as they. The fabric of attire for the outside world he has remade into the grander philosopher's robe, and the crimson garment of the House of Lords he has exchanged for the truer nobility of this crimson-canopied interior life. The left hand of the artificial self, which bespeaks the call of the outside world, is limp and empty, while the left hand of the natural self grasps to his chest as its dearest possession a small, dark greenish-brown book—which bears an uncanny resemblance to the very volume in which Shaftesbury inscribed the first half of the Ασκηματα.

Once we entertain this interpretation, it is almost impossible to resist seeing the two portrait figures also as the two selves in the "Soliloquy" and its emblem. As in the engraving, the self on the right of the portrait is overshadowed by dark clouds and averts his eyes from the viewer. One of the harpies flying around the darker boy wears a monarch's crown and carries a royal scepter—and certainly Shaftesbury's parliamentary life was plagued with many rifts with crowns of England and Europe. And just as in the emblem, the figure on the left is brighter, lighter, more "comely and well-proportioned," and looks directly at the viewer—or, as in a mirror, at himself. For, ultimately, the intended viewer of the painting, thus conceived, is the one who commissioned it in all its cryptic complexity and in whose house it hung. Unlike the large "fashionable mirror" in the middle of the "Soliloquy" emblem, hanging over a "modern book" and reflecting nothing, this grand portrait, hanging in Shaftesbury's increasingly reclusive home, would have functioned for Shaftesbury quite literally as a mirror: the mirror not of modern books but of philosophy, in which, as he wrote in "Soliloquy," he could see both the ancients—in the clearly labeled volumes of Plato and Xenophon—and his two selves, the opposing selves which he had interrogated in such excruciating detail in the Ασκηματα.[18] This portrait-mirror would face him daily with the central question of his Regimen and his great ritual of spontaneity: do you want to be that "artificial," appetitive self, or this "natural" virtuous philosopher-god?

And this was precisely the sort of high moral, didactic aspiration Shaftesbury nurtured for painting. Shaftesbury concurred with most late-seventeenth- and early-eighteenth-century painters in maintaining, as John Barrell's *The Political Theory of Painting from Reynolds to Hazlitt* relates, a hierarchy of genres that placed history painting at the top and portraiture near the bottom, viewing portrait painters as "hack artificers" and portraiture as effeminate and degenerate, despite the portrait's ascendance in practice.[19] What Shaftesbury lamented about most portraiture was that "the mere face-painter" and the "wretched business of face painting" were socially and artistically detrimental; the portrait was, in Alison Conway's words, "incapable of instructing the viewer in high moral principles, as promoting only sensual appetite as a universal experience."[20] Closterman's long relationship with his patron, however, was exactly that of the artistic amanuensis Shaftesbury desired. Wind documents the creative relationship between Shaftesbury and Closterman spanning a decade and the "eclectic method by which a work of art was produced in this collaboration, Closterman collecting the material and assisting in the designing, Shaftesbury supervising the work and directing its progress, so as to make it expressive of his philosophical ideas."[21] We know that Closterman executed specific instructions from Shaftesbury for the highly symbolic details of his previous portrait of him with his brother Maurice. It is completely plausible that Shaftesbury designed this later work for Closterman's execution with the intention of providing everything that, to his mind, most portraiture lacked. Shaftesbury's final notebook of 1710–1711, *Second Characters*, includes a vivid reminiscence of "my Painter (Closterman), going into his Picture when in the Dark & standing long before it"—perhaps a lovely image of Closterman working on this complex, weighty portrait.[22] The interpretation I am suggesting is all the more persuasive inasmuch as it makes this painting, almost certainly designed by Shaftesbury in close collaboration with his longtime artistic amanuensis, a counter precisely to that which Shaftesbury found "wretched" about "mere face painting." This is a portrait capable of promoting something beside the "sensual appetite" portraiture encouraged; it is portraiture as vigorous, even stoic moral instruction, admonishing the viewer to leave appetites of the sensual world behind for a life of high moral principle.

Read in the light of both Shaftesbury's public and private writings, Closterman's portrait of Shaftesbury appears as perhaps our most stunning Enlightenment representation of the split self of modernity: the self who begins by asking in the Ασκηματα, "How long is it that thou wilt continue thus to act two different parts, & be two different Persons?" and, in its quest for "Integrity Intire," ends by commanding in *Soliloquy*, "*Divide Your-self*, or *Be* TWO," in hopes that "if the Division were rightly made, all *within* wou'd of course, they thought, be rightly understood, and prudently managed." In this representation we sense the "self-shattering" that Cynthia Marshall has called "a deep, constitutive impulse within the early modern subject, an undertow that pulls against the drive that [Stephen] Greenblatt identified as 'self-fashioning.'"[23] The self in the portrait is a unified subject predicated on what seems like the condition of its impossibility, its own self-division, as well as the division between self and other. In this sense the second-figure-as-grandfather and the second-figure-as-other-self may not be incompatible readings;

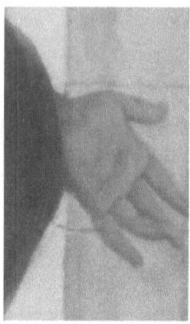 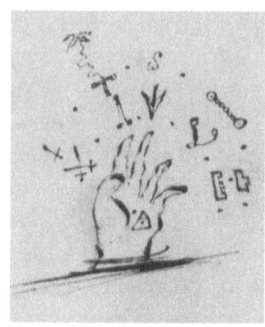

Figure 10 Portrait of Shaftesbury by John Closterman, detail of hand.

Figure 11 Shaftesbury's "Parchments," page 26, detail. The National Archives (Public Record Office). PRO 30/24/27/11. Photograph by Hugh Alexander.

the other presents the same threat to wholeness and naturalness that one's appetitive second-self does.[24]

In this portrait we may also glimpse the way in which the split self of modernity is also a self of renunciation, a self that is defined by the impossibilities and antagonisms that its symbolically structured appetites, desires, and fantasies continually present and preclude. The strangely open left hand of the second figure seems to reference one of the only sketches we have by Shaftesbury himself (see figs. 10 and 11). On the last page of the "parchments," his pocket-sized condensation of rules from the Ασκηματα, Shaftesbury drew a left hand flinging away all the pictographic symbols of sexual desire, political strife, and material cares that plagued him. The portrait bears no year but has traditionally been dated at the same time as Closterman's famous double-portrait of Shaftesbury and Maurice, 1700–1701, the plan for which Shaftesbury had disclosed to Closterman in a letter written during his first retreat to Holland. This conclusion appears unfounded for several reasons, not least of which is the fact that the Shaftesbury in the toga appears considerably older and more full-faced than in the portrait with his brother, which would seem to be an earlier painting.

The parchments bear the inscription "Holland 1704 Coming away & on Shipboard," and it would not be unreasonable to suppose that, just as Shaftesbury returned from his first retreat with an elaborate, philosophically informed design for Closterman to execute in the portrait of him with his brother, he returned from the second retreat, more advanced in his determination to withdraw from the world, more practiced as the notebooks attest in the art of self-splitting and self-scrutiny, with a design in mind that echoed the spirit of renunciation in the parchments, with its hand flinging away desires and distractions.[25] This interpretation locates the splitting of the self with astounding precision, at the moment when (what will retroactively be figured as) the artificial self in the world is interpolated by the rational ideal of wholeness and self-control, and projects an ideal ego—the "Natural Self" that we see as Shaftesbury in the portrait—as the *true* self and the "sublime object" around which its ideology and fantasies are shaped. In the moment we see captured in the portrait, it comes to loathe its pangs and permeability, and casts away, in nonlinguistic symbols or off the edge of the canvas, the desires, lusts, and ambitions that make it permeable, mutually interdefined with and vulnerable to others.

Finally, we also see in this fascinating portrait the centrality to the modern self of religion and of the book form. Almost directly in the center of the painting is neither figure but a bound volume: it is not at all hard to believe, the Ασκηματα, Shaftesbury's equivalent of Christian's roll, their exercises and asceticism distinguishing the legitimate from the illegitimate self. The centrality of this book in the portrait cannot help but reference a ubiquitous Reformation portraiture that so frequently included a Bible as constitutive of the sitter's identity, and in Closterman's painting it evokes a disavowed yet for Shaftesbury necessary religious past in the same way that secular "true enthusiasm" evokes the Puritans and free prayer. The book Shaftesbury clasps to his heart might, as Voitle has suggested, be the *Meditations* of Marcus Aurelius,[26] but it is in either case a holy writ, an object in his private devotion to the ancients to whom he prays, of whom he is a votary or perhaps a priest. In this mirror of modernity we see the self split, an object of renunciation and fantasy, but also simultaneously secularized and deified, in the toga of both the philosophers and the gods that were so overdeterminedly meaningful for the neoclassical eighteenth century. This portrait is secular, and it is religious, in the way that secularism characteristically invokes religion to negate and sublimate it. It presents Shaftesbury as he would like to be seen, one of the few divine *virtuosi* of a rationalized inner life. It is the painting and the self that he would put in the place of Raphael's *Transfiguration* or any of the masterworks on the "[w]retched model," Christ.[27]

But the book as object also figures in this self in another way, that is, in the way that the single Shaftesbury of the engraving that accompanied the second edition of the *Characteristicks*, as it accompanies most of its reprints today—that is, the authorial, unified Shaftesbury that we speak of—is very particularly a product of print culture. The profoundly divided, fragmented self of the Ασκηματα achieves unity only in this way: only as the ethereal, disembodied yet potently represented and reproduced, witty yet wholly didactic voice, not so much of sociability as of impersonal public command. In *The Bonds of Love: Psychoanalysis, Feminism, and the Problem of Domination*, Jessica Benjamin explains how the pleasure of domination and submission in sadomasochistic relationships tends toward a certain numbness or exhaustion, after which a new idealized figure to whom to submit must be found.²⁸ In the Ασκηματα, Shaftesbury's painful submission to an idealized, rationalized figure of the Deity breeds its own resistance but also, at the end, tends towards this numbness. And as Shaftesbury turns away from these notebooks to the *Characteristicks*, the new idealized figure in whose eyes Shaftesbury seeks recognition is his reading audience.²⁹

Like Bunyan, confined and fearing death, Shaftesbury finds his "calling" and his salvation in evangelism, in a didactic pose toward a mass reading-public. This is true not only because rational argumentation has come to be seen as the primary medium of moral pedagogy and change, but because this stance itself serves to unify the self as an invulnerable, authorial function of the printed text. Shaftesbury comes to us as the author of the *Characteristicks* more than of the notebooks, just as Bunyan comes to us more the dreamer of *The Pilgrim's Progress* than the traumatized individual of *Grace Abounding*. The suturing work of the *Characteristicks*, reprinted and reread throughout the eighteenth century, seems to have been at least as effective as that in any Protestant narrative. In fact, we might argue that the secular, objective observer of material and psychological fact eventually comes to be a more appealing fiction than that of Bunyan's Christian, so much so that its status as fiction is effaced. A corollary masking of the "fictional," fabricated status of the self is precisely what takes place in the movement from the Closterman portrait to the Gribelin engraving: the literal erasure of the "artificial, or economical, self," the presentation of a virtual reality as real, the author of a new philosophy, based both in the ancients and in the spontaneous movements of affections and the moral sense. This process of erasure—what Markley describes as the "suppress[ion of] the actual processes of transforming the diabolical," that is, the doubled, the haunted, the desirous and bodily, "into the noble and spiritual"³⁰— is itself one of the defining activities of both the ideology of objectivity and that of spontaneity. The noble and spiritual, and the only Deity that will seem compelling in a secular public sphere, ultimately appear as an aesthetic icon of aristocratic celebrity, as what Foucault calls the author function, a secular godlike image, mass-produced and consumed in the commodity print-form, proclaiming what will be the gospel of the market's reified desires: the gospel of the *virtue* of natural ease, emotional spontaneity, and "true enthusiasm," best embodied, it seems, in buying something. Ultimately the ministers of this gospel will be not the high churchmen of philosophy, though, but the more evangelical Grub Street writers and printers of sentimental novels. At the middle of the eighteenth century, they too were haunted by a living figure of England's seemingly inescapable enthusiastic past, Christopher Smart.

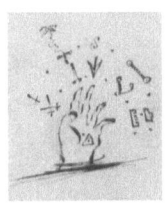

CHAPTER 4

At the Sign of the Bible and Sun
John Newbery, *The Vicar of Wakefield*, and the Ghost of Christopher Smart

> To name as a "cult" the form in which a story was told and received is to suggest one of the culture's innermost origins and proselytizing power. Its sacred beings were deified authors and factualized characters, its rituals expressed by a system of signs, gestures, and words, at first responses to the figures on the page, read in a closet, perhaps aloud to oneself, like prayers, the page often held tremblingly or bedewed with tears. Then these rituals were carried out into the relations between cultists, or, hesitatingly, in the expectations of courtship, then more assertively in marriage and childrearing. Explicitly embracing Protestant pietism, the cult combined this with the "natural religion" illustrated by Shaftesbury's apostrophes. . . . It was the cult of a group of people enjoying literacy, privacy, intimacy, servants, and other distancings from economic distress, and free to concentrate on their own emotional pleasures and pains in their vaunted distinction from the world.
>
> —G. J. Barker-Benfield, *The Culture of Sensibility*[1]

Where Shaftesbury defined his philosophy as a rational, secular, barely theistic "true enthusiasm," his followers such as Francis Hutcheson were more anxious to reconcile religious faith with reasonable virtue. But more even than moral philosophy, the literary culture of sensibility served to popularize the psychoperceptual system of the receptivity of the senses and their connection to the mind that lay at the foundation of moral sense thinking. For hosts of readers and writers, sentimentality echoed with religious valences, and sensibility offered a science of the soul.[2] Just before the final installment of *Clarissa* appeared, Samuel Richardson explained to Lady Bradshaigh his purposes in writing the novel by quoting George Herbert: "A Verse may find him who a Sermon flies / And turn Delight into a Sacrifice—Of this Nature is my Design. Religion never was at so low an Ebb as at present: And if my work must be supposed of the Novel Kind, I was willing to try if a Religious Novel would do good."[3] In Richardson's mind *Clarissa* investigated the highest doctrines of morality and Christianity, and his express intention was to bring about a "reformation" by conveying "the great doctrines of Christianity" in the form of a novel.[4]

And yet, in recent years Florian Stuber has challenged the consensus nearly unquestioned since Richardson's day, that his great novel *is* a religious, Christian work. Its "Providence" is a calculus of rewards and punishments, Stuber observes, and its analysis of moral phenomena mainly psychological; it is "informed by a secular humanism which may be justified by, but which is not dependent upon, the Christian system."[5] Richardson also opined to Lady Echlin that "Instruction, Madam, is the pill; amusement is the gilding. Writings that do not touch the passions of the light and airy, will hardly ever reach the heart."[6] Sensibility was the natural mechanism which Richardson relied upon to reach light-minded readers, a passive, instrumentally responsive goodness which Janet Todd has shown was popularly figured from the 1720s onward in the figure of the Aeolian harp.[7] Relying on this passive mechanism, the social and personal reformation offered through novels of sentiment was implicitly religious but, more importantly, polite, attractive, and entertaining. The question that *Clarissa* and other sentimental novels beg, rather, is not whether they are religious, but what the larger cultural significance is of the particular religiousness they express.

This religiousness embodies elements both of the secularized religion we see in *The Pilgrim's Progress* and of the religiously haunted secularism we see in Shaftesbury's notebooks. As Ian Watt put it, *Pamela* is both "the first true novel" and "something that was new and prophetic in quite another sense: a work that could be praised from the pulpit and yet attacked as pornography, a work that gratified the reading public with the combined attractions of a sermon and a striptease."[8] The sermon and the striptease certainly made for odd companions, and despite authors' ambitions for the genre, the compromised condition of sentimental literature as a tool for reform was apparent to many in the period. William Warner has pointed out that in the prevalent antinovelistic discourse of the mid-eighteenth century, critics accused novels, like the market, of breeding imitation, desire, and automatism.[9] Julie Ellison has likewise shown that, along with its ethical aspirations, the literature of sentimentality is complexly aware of economics and of its own privilege, delving into the Bunyanesque questions of "perceived degrees of personal and collective solvency, the price of the individual, and the humiliations of exchange." The paralyzed affect of sentimentality complements, in her view, the stoic hypermasculinity of politics and commerce in the period and actually enables it; sentimentality is the flip side, as it were, of Shaftesbury's stoicism.[10] Together Ellison and Warner paint a picture of readers and writers of sentimental literature oftentimes uncomfortably aware of their imbrication in the economic practices and market ways of thinking that they wish to reform and who, perhaps as much as they would like to remedy the excesses of wealth with virtue, would like even more to reconcile the two.

At "the Sign of the Bible and Sun," the literary enterprise of children's literature pioneer John Newbery provides an ideal location at which to examine both the moral aspirations of the ideology of spontaneity in its commercial literary form and the vexed consciences of writers uneasy about the reconciliation of morality, religion, and consumer, market logic. This chapter shows how Newbery, an entrepreneurial dynamo known for his benevolence as much as his busyness, built a bookselling empire around the great theme of improvement, efficiently abridging and consolidating useful information on every conceivable topic in volumes popular for their fancy "flowery and gilt" binding. Like John Wesley and other "improvement evangelists" who published magazine-like compilations of edifying devotional material, at the Bible and Sun Newbery became famous for selling moral children's stories and religious gift books whose appeal was not unlike that of the Newbery name itself, a representation of successful, reasonable, market-friendly morality. If part of Newbery's appeal lay in supplying evidence that profit, politeness, and piety were all of a cloth, the sting of the most important works of Newbery's two mainstay writers, Oliver Goldsmith and Christopher Smart, was the recognition that they were more fundamentally at odds.

Neither of them disposed to be thrifty, Goldsmith and Smart came by various paths to see the literary market around them as driven by economic interest in a way that was inimical to the virtuous sensibility it proclaimed, and for both men, this meant a religious turn. Setting both writers in the context of Newbery's shop and the literary world in which it operated, this chapter shows how the novel that Goldsmith worked on outside his commissions for Newbery, *The Vicar of Wakefield*, takes aim at passive, impotent sentimentality and secular moral philosophy as equally incapable of helping people deal with sorrow and injustice. Goldsmith points to his eponymous hero's daily life of private prayer and family devotion as the religious source of a "true sensibility" capable of resisting greed and vice, but the religious praxis that Goldsmith sets at the heart of his reform of sentimentality and market-shaped desires is compromised by both. Unwilling to counter the "harmless delusions" the Primrose family absorbs from bookselling culture—either the women's romance reading or his own delusions of authorial grandeur—the Vicar and his piety are doubly effaced by the literary market; for novels cultivate fantasies of wealth and rank, while also making it virtually impossible to represent repetitive practices like daily prayer. Able only to sentimentalize piety and to make prayer take place offstage, the forward momentum and market sensibility of the novel form literally does not have time to represent the repetitive praxis that Goldsmith recommends as the shaping force of virtue.

Smart's reaction to Newbery's literary world was more radical, though, and serves as something of a foil to Goldsmith's. After what he considered a miraculous recovery from illness, he refused to continue writing secular hack work for Newbery and came to feel it was wrong to resist the urge to pray, pulling friends like Samuel Johnson to their knees when and wherever the impulse struck him. As a result, Newbery had Smart incarcerated in various insane asylums for seven years, during which Smart penned his sprawling *Jubilate Agno*. Where the constraints of the novel form dictate that Goldsmith cannot represent the Vicar's repetitive daily prayers and have his novel be salable, this poem meditates on the polite market tastes that dictate that Smart himself cannot pray spontaneously in public, however sensibly moved, and remain hirable. The central recognition of Smart's poem is that the chief evil of market sensibilities is that they impinge on one's voice and agency. In response to that realization, Smart wrote *Jubilate Agno* at the painstaking ritualistic pace of two to three lines per day over the course of four years, proclaiming its "playing on everything in delight" as a creative self-construction by which "a man speaks HIMSELF from the crown of his head to the sole of his feet," outside the logic of "the coffin and the cradle and the purse."

Jubilate Agno and *The Vicar of Wakefield* thus make sense in light of the market environment their authors inhabited in their work for Newbery and their variously religious responses to market-friendly sensibility and morality. And they also shed light on each other. Goldsmith's novel and his sentimental Vicar throw the real resistance of Smart's religious worldview and praxis into relief, and Smart's incarceration for spontaneous public prayer reveals the real limit of the culture's embrace of spontaneity and its willingness to reform market-driven desire, governed by politeness. Smart and his *Jubilate* resist the logic of coffin, cradle, and purse by reading the world not in the consumptive mode of abridgement but in proliferation, in a way predicated on the endless dissemination of meaning in language, using words to explore the variegated creation and so speak to God. Where Smart's poem traces the contours of what faith imagined as something other than exchange or certainty might look like, Goldsmith's novel locates religion in its conventionally sentimentalized form, where it becomes what Graham Ward has called a special effect, an aura of transcendence around a commodity form, catering to commodified modes of desire, bound by its rituals of spontaneous sentiment, and incapacitated as effectual resistance.[11] Inasmuch as its idea of morality remains rationalized and mechanical, and inasmuch as address to God and the quotidian praxis of faith remain outside the logic of its form, religion as we see it in sentimental literature is profoundly secularized. In the end, the Vicar is not just the novel's hero, but a figure haunted by Smart's ghost, performing important cultural work for Goldsmith and his readers: wishfully remaking his coworker's impolite piety into a polite, publicly palatable religiousness in which novels can still be read and prayer is referenced but invisible, acceptable in the novel form only inasmuch as it has submitted to the logics it embodies.

Smart, Goldsmith, and the Newbery Literary Enterprise

The quirky autobiography of John Newbery's son Francis, "The Life of the Author, written by Himself," is spent mainly in self-praise, but it pauses long enough to give a moving account of the esteem in which Francis's father was held at the time of his death. "Few men have died more generally or sincerely lamented," he claimed:

> All the newspapers of the time spontaneously burst forth in expressions of commendations of his character, and of regret at his loss. . . . He was of an active and cheerful disposition, possessing a fund of natural humour, and a most benevolent heart, which indeed carried him into excess, for he was so indiscriminate in his charities that he never passed a beggar without bestowing something. In his address he was polite, and in his manners and conversation so agreeable that he seemed to have been born and bred a gentleman. He was scarcely ever seen without a book or a pen in his hand, and his mind was ever occupied for some good purpose. With such qualities he could not fail to be beloved by all who knew him and he ranked among his friends, men of the first literary talents.[12]

Goldsmith included a similarly warm cameo of his publisher as a good Samaritan in *The Vicar of Wakefield*: "This person was no other than the philanthropic bookseller in St. Paul's Churchyard, who has written so many little books for children: he called himself . . . their friend; but he was the friend of all mankind."[13] Francis and Goldsmith both marveled at Newbery's constant state of activity, most famously captured by Samuel Johnson in *The Idler*, no. 19 and its description of "Jack Whirler," "whose business keeps him in perpetual motion." With "more business than he can conveniently transact in one house," he keeps two offices and "by this ingenious distribution of himself" between them, "contrive[s] to be found at neither," and "overwhelmed as he is with business, his chief desire is to have still more."[14]

This energetic, whirling, affable yet business-minded Newbery built a printing enterprise in a bustling midcentury London publishing world for which he was ideally suited. The seventeenth-century growth of literacy and the emergence of a public sphere in English print and politics, along with the lapsing of censorship and the Licensing Act in 1695, had combined to produce a professional literary subculture that by the late seventeenth century was popularly referred to as "Grub Street."[15] This pejorative term had first been applied to the London print market in the political upheaval and anxiety of the 1640s and 1680s, and in *Grub Street: Studies in a Subculture*, Pat Rogers has mapped the specific geography of Grub Street and the images it provided to Augustan elites who likewise worried about the debasing effect of a pluralist print marketplace. More recently Paula McDowell, in *The Women of Grub Street*, has given us a view of this English literary marketplace from below as it were, emphasizing the emergence of "heterogeneous collectivities" within this subculture and the democratic possibilities that a diverse market presented.[16]

McDowell's Grub Street of promise and potential was no doubt the version that appealed to John Newbery. Born to farming parents east of Reading in 1713, Newbery was a bright student, gifted at language, and at age sixteen he engaged himself as assistant to William Carnan, printer and proprietor of one of the earliest provincial newspapers, *The Reading Mercury and Oxford Gazette*. Carnan died in 1737, leaving behind his widow and three young children and willing his business to his brother and to Newbery, a testament to the industry Newbery had displayed and the trust he had gained in his eight years with Carnan. Newbery was twenty-four at the time and, in the words of his biographer, soon "began to pay his respects to [Carnan's] widow." In 1738 or 1739 they married, eventually having three children of their own.[17]

In July 1740, three months after the birth of their first child, Newbery set out from Reading for a tour of England that began in London and took him through St. Alban's, Bedford, Leicester, Grantham, Lincoln, Hull, York, Lancaster, Sheffield, Nottingham, Darby, Liverpool, Birmingham, and Manchester. On this journey Newbery kept a memorandum book, recording the miles he traveled each day, the inns where he slept, and occasionally the name of a fellow traveler or curious local gossip. But the pocketbook is most remarkable for the entrepreneurial mind it shows at work. Several entries show him picking up self-protective business practices, for instance, detailing a plan for insuring debt-collection by making several parties liable through a series of endorsements rather than a joint note. Everywhere Newbery was gathering ideas for money-making ventures: "At my return advertize all sorts of the haberdashery and cutlery goods that I keep to be sold wholesale as cheap as in the country where made, only paying 2½ per cent. commission, and write on door, goods sold by commission from the makers per John Newbery & Co., for ready money only, *and so excuse one's self from trusting.*"[18] By far the most interesting notes are ideas for books that he thinks would sell well. These entries express the sense of humor characteristic of many of his later title pages, together with his sense of readers' desires for efficient self-improvement. "Print (Price 6d.) A collection of curious Mottos from Greek, Latin, French, and English Authors, for the use of Poets and Puppeys, by Lawrence Likelihood," runs one entry; "Put Mr Walker on Printing an Abridgement of ye History of the World (but not call it an abridgement) . . . Likewise, A Body of Divinity, compiled from Usher Fiddes and Stackhouse's Bodys of Divinity." He imagined printing a translation of "the Alcoran of Mahomet" with "notes on the extravagances thereof," and a defense of the liturgy of the Church of England to be given to friends at his own expense at Christmastime.[19]

This pocketbook was truly the mind of the young "Jack Whirler" at work. In 1744 Newbery moved his offices to London, for a while under the old Carnan sign, the Bible and Crown. But in 1745 he opened in St. Paul's Churchyard what was to be his shop for the rest of his life, under his own sign, of the Bible and Sun: above a closed Bible with a sun rising behind it appeared the words "FIAT LUX," likening literary enlightenment to God's creative word in Genesis. His business there was as diverse as his notebook suggested it would be, and in his first ten years in London Newbery printed books and periodicals on almost every conceivable subject.[20] In the later 1740s Newbery's titles included volumes on earthquakes and science, songbooks, tithing tables, as well as a book that would go through nine editions by 1762, *A Pretty Little Pocket-Book*, which included letters from Jack the Giant Killer and that promised "infallibly" to "make Tommy a good Boy, and Polly a Good Girl." In 1750 Newbery printed an ambitious work meant to help clergy manage the massive output of printed homilies in England, *An Index to the Sermons published since the Restoration.*[21] Similar offerings continued on into the 1750s and 1760s, with titles in logic, rhetoric, grammar, and spelling; engravings of St. Paul's, the Tower, and Westminster Abbey; collections of songs, children's books, and lettered blocks. In 1758 Newbery brought out *The Evangelical History of our Lord Jesus Christ* as well as a Bible abridged for children, and in his later years he printed defenses of Christianity as well as a series of religious gift books including *The Christian's New Year's Gift* (1766) and *The Whitsuntide Gift: or, The Way to Be Happy, a Book Necessary for All Families* (1767). And alongside these titles, Newbery embarked on the scheme in which his heirs were ultimately most interested: the sale of over thirty medicines, the most famous of which was Dr. James's Fever Powders, for which he acquired the sole rights of sale.

Newbery's successful business, despite his famous flitting from scheme to scheme, suggests that he was a man with his finger on the pulse of a broad-based reading audience. Taken together, Newbery's titles and patent medicines harmonize around the great theme of improvement: purchases that promised easy cures and instant well-being. In an uncannily modern way, the Newbery catalogue evokes a mindset of compiling the expanding knowledge of the world into efficiently edited volumes of essential information. Within this ethos of improvement, the catalogue also conveys the conspicuously moral worth of wealth; the reader of Newbery's children's books is always kept aware of the poor and of the important benefits of wealth. In *The History of Little Goody Two-Shoes*, for instance, Margery's father was "seized with a violent fever in a place where Dr James's Fever Powder was not to be had, and where he died miserably," and in "Blossoms of Morality," little Theophilus tells his father that he pities "poor little boys whose parents are not in a condition to purchase them such a nice gilded library as that with which you have supplied me from my good friends at the corner of Saint Paul's Churchyard. Surely such unhappy boys must be very ignorant all their lives, for what can they learn without books."[22] Foreshadowing later advertising tactics, Newbery was the master of product placement, of "puffing" his works in each other's pages and creating a brand-name aura around the Bible and Sun, which became associated with special "flowery and gilt binding." In time the much-advertised "fine Dutch paper" and packaging of his children's books was at least as appealing as the moral improvement they offered.

Newbery was to situate himself at the center of the London book trade for over two decades, and, as his son pointed out, this acquainted him with "men of the first literary merits." He loaned money to Samuel Johnson at least seven times between 1751 and 1760, and at various times he employed Hugh Kelly, Griffith and Giles Jones, William Guthrie, and Benjamin Martin.[23] But sometime in 1750 Charles Burney introduced Newbery to a man who would become one of his most famous and controversial writers, Christopher Smart. Smart was, in his best known biography's title, a scholar of the university—at Pembroke College,

Cambridge—where he lectured on philosophy and rhetoric and was esteemed for his poetry in both English and Latin. He had moved to London in 1749 full of Cambridge bravura and anxious to connect himself with a publisher and with the entertainments of Vauxhall Gardens.[24] Newbery hired Smart in 1750, and Arthur Sherbo speculates that Newbery's willingness to engage him so soon after he arrived in London was due in part to Burney's recommendation and in part to the reputation his poetry had already achieved. On 25 March 1750, Smart had become the first winner of the Seatonian prize in religious verse for his poem *On the Eternity of the Supreme Being*. He would go on to win the Seatonian prize five of the first six times it was offered, and these poems, written according to the contest rules in praise of "one or other of the Perfections or Attributes of the Supreme Being," achieved a surprising popularity, each going quickly through two to three editions, and after the first, all but one by Newbery.[25]

These religious poems never made either man much money, certainly not enough to live on, and in his early London years Smart was not mainly occupied with religious writing but was in his own way as much a Jack Whirler as his employer.[26] In 1750 he contributed humorous pieces to Newbery's Oxford-Cambridge monthly miscellany *The Student*, and in 1751 he and Newbery collaborated on the hilarious and risqué *The Midwife, or The Old Woman's Magazine*, which Newbery eventually published in two volumes under his nephew's name, presumably to avoid its connection to the children's books enterprise.[27] Smart was living beyond his means in this period, borrowing money and earning extra income by writing children's rhymes for Newbery's *The Lilliputian Magazine* and performing his *Midwife* "Oratory" pieces in drag in the Castle Tavern and Haymarket Theatre. In this period Smart was continually involved in the fracas of literary puffing and sniping, and when Smart's collected *Poems on Several Occasions* were printed and sold exclusively by Newbery in 1752, they received a handsome ten shillings per copy together with a fair amount of criticism, some of it deserved but much of it sheerly vindictive.[28] Alongside all this he kept up his prolific output for various magazines, much of it in the satiric mode of his beloved Horace, and eventually found himself penning love poems to Newbery's stepdaughter, Anna Maria Carnan.

That summer Smart and Anna Maria secretly wed, a rash step which nevertheless seems not to have caused Newbery to withdraw support for either of them, but which made money making all the more important for Smart, and all the more difficult, since as a result he lost his fellowship at Pembroke and the stipend it brought him.[29] It also made the critics' wars more earnest for him, and when John Hill blasted *Poems on Several Occasions* in Ralph Griffith's *Monthly Review*, Smart lashed out in his scathing rebuttal "The Hilliad."[30] Anna Maria had been living with the Newberys in Canonbury House, Islington, and after their marriage the couple had taken up rooms there together.[31] Here Smart lived under specially designed conditions that Newbery maintained for his writers, many of whom, like Smart, were erratic spenders and often on the brink of arrest for debt. At Canonbury Newbery paid in advance for his writers' room and board and made a small library available to them, keeping careful accounts of the advances he paid and of the money they owed.

While most nineteenth-century accounts painted Newbery as the great benefactor of literary geniuses, Smart's most recent biographer Chris Mounsey has suggested that these arrangements amounted to a "drip-feeding" scheme to "keep authors in thrall to him" and that Newbery the "ruthless" businessman "seems to have been capable of anything that yielded a profit."[32] The truth seems likely in between. No one grew rich writing for Newbery; both Smart and Goldsmith slipped further into debt with Newbery the longer they worked for him, and both were eventually arrested for debt.[33] But Smart like Goldsmith was a famously profligate spender, and both seem to have been constantly asking for advances and spending the money on high living. If Goldsmith's experience is any indication, Newbery was no "callous, cantankerous, bloodsucking" Ralph Griffiths, chaining hacks to their desk every day from 9 a.m. to 2 p.m. under the watchful eye of his wife,[34] but neither was he a Thomas Davies or William Griffin, gullibly doling out advances to Goldsmith on a song and nearly sinking his business in the process. Smart may have been, as has been suggested of Goldsmith, as much "the victim of the booksellers' *generosity*" as of any hard-nosed business tactics. In any case, Smart and Goldsmith enjoyed a high degree of freedom working for Newbery and were quite productive with him, working on their own projects alongside what were to them less desirable tasks.[35]

With Anna Maria expecting a child, and income from *The Midwife* trickling off, in 1753 Smart took on yet more hack work from Newbery, including editing chores on his popular songbook *The Muses Banquet* and the jestbook *Be Merry and Wise*, and somehow managed to keep up his act as Mrs. Midnight.[36] Smart was less productive in 1754, and his second daughter was born in October of that year; then and in the next, Newbery was loaning money to Smart and to his wife, and Smart was still racking up tailor's bills. The year 1755 was an even less productive period for Smart, and both this year and the previous one are thin for the Newbery catalogue overall. Smart may have been busy at this time editing two more collections which Newbery brought out in 1756, *A Collection of Pretty Poems for the Amusement of Children Three Feet High* and *A Collection of Pretty Poems for the Amusement of Children Six Foot High*,[37] but he was certainly devoting herculean efforts to his prose translation of the complete *Works of Horace*, which came out in December 1755. That Smart seems to have written this under economic duress is borne out by his later superseding it with a verse translation because he thought the prose version would hurt his memory; apparently Smart was so in debt with Newbery by this time that he saw little of the proceeds from the translation and afterwards complained that Newbery had cheated him.[38] This financial tension between Smart and Newbery seems to have prompted Smart to take up still more work with Thomas Gardner and Edmund Allen for their new periodical, *The Universal Visiter*, which was to appear in February 1756. From the start Smart had troubles coming up with his monthly contribution to the magazine, and soon friends David Garrick, Burney, Johnson, and others either offered their services or were asked to contribute in Smart's stead. That spring, Smart suffered his third and greatest fever since coming to London along with some sort of breakdown that meant he was no longer able to produce for either *The Universal Visiter* or for Newbery, and was admitted to St. Luke's Hospital for the curably insane in May 1757.[39]

It was also in 1757 that Newbery became associated with a writer who would ultimately surpass Smart in productivity and popularity, Oliver Goldsmith. Their partnership was a salvation for them both: after nearly two years of recycling Smart's old works without a mainstay writer, Newbery had finally found a productive and witty replacement, and Goldsmith relished a release from his hack writing for the loathsome Griffiths.[40] Born in Ireland to an Anglo-Irish Protestant minister in a financially troubled family, even as a child Goldsmith was famously witty, bright, and unattractive. Attending Trinity College, Dublin as a sizar, forced to serve meals to boys who were as insulting as they were his intellectual inferiors, Goldsmith developed a whimsical social bravura borne of insecurity. His need for acclaim seemed to outweigh his family obligations, and despite repeated efforts, he could never settle into any of the careers—the church, law, or medicine—that relations sacrificed to make possible for him. He arrived in London in 1756, after having completed the Grand Tour on foot and later in life than most of his peers, with a chip on his shoulder and an enormous appetite for achieving fame and success.[41]

Goldsmith wrote his first pieces for Newbery's *Literary Magazine* in late 1757 or early 1758, and his relationship with Newbery seems only to have grown in the following two years.[42] In January 1760, he moved from shabby lodgings in Green Arbor Court to a house kept by one of Newbery's relatives, and from that time he also spent periods in Islington writing much as Smart had, on Newbery's expense account. After being arrested for debt to his landlady, likely sometime in 1762 he moved into Canonbury House, down the hall from Smart's children who were then under Newbery's care. It was shortly after this time that he also proposed a benefit for Smart, possibly in anticipation of his being released from the asylum.[43] In 1760 Goldsmith began writing his famous *Chinese Letters* for Newbery's *Public Ledger*, two a week for a guinea apiece, which Newbery compiled in 1762 as *The Citizen of the World*. Between 1760–1762, Goldsmith churned out a host of profitable projects, editing, translating, prefacing, and contributing to compilations that fit Newbery's earlier dreams to a letter: *A History of England*, *The Life of Christ*, *The Life of the Fathers*, Sarah Scott's feminist-utopian novel *Millennium Hall*, as well as Newbery's *Compendium of Biography* and colorful reviews for *The Critical* and *The Monthly*.[44] More stunning than this is that during these two to three years he also managed to complete, without advances and on his own time, a novel clearly dear to him, *The Vicar of Wakefield*.[45]

Goldsmith finally achieved the literary fame that he had desired when, in 1764, Newbery published his long poem *The Traveller* and Johnson hailed it in *The Critical Review* as "a production to which, since the death of Pope, it will not be easy to find anything equal."[46] It was likely Goldsmith's rising fame that prompted Newbery to publish *The Vicar of Wakefield* in 1766, though it did not show a profit until its fourth edition.[47] By that time Goldsmith was writing less and socializing more and seems no longer to have been under Newbery's financial thumb; in a moment of hubris after the success of *The Traveller*, he had set himself up as a physician, counting on his literary fame to attract patients. At Newbery's death in 1767, Goldsmith's reputation had reached the point that he could easily secure work from other booksellers. Even with lean seasons, Goldsmith's income between 1767–1772 averaged 400 pounds a year, a great deal for a writer at that time. And yet his debt still increased. In the years before his death in 1774, his arrears to Griffin and Davies were so great that, as Elizabeth Eaton Kent put it, he was likely better off drudging for Griffiths at a pound a week than when his earnings topped 1,000 pounds.[48]

Like not a few wealthy men in his day, Newbery dictated in his will that a dozen poor men of the parish should bear his coffin to the grave, and that they would each be paid half a guinea apiece for this service: a fitting image for someone known both for generosity and business sense.[49] Given his long and varied career, it is hard to imagine that Newbery could have been either as beneficent as Newbery-Medal lore might lead one to believe or as financially ruthless as Washington Irving or Mounsey have made him out to be.[50] Rather, the significance of Newbery's career lies in his being celebrated as a bit of both; Newbery was a genuinely self-made man, a true household name with men of letters as with parents and children, at a time when the reconciliation of business sense and a moralizing benevolence underwriting a sentimental view of family life was particularly appealing. Bookseller to children, careful account-keeper of disorganized literary geniuses, philanthropist generous to his pallbearers: everything in Newbery's life had a moral cast, and everything was also about the pound, about the fantasy that improvement of the spirit like the body could be gained by buying the right book and taking the right pill. "Buying the truth" was at least as old as *The Pilgrim's Progress*, and the scope of Newbery's career at the Bible and Sun seems designed to underline what Gillian Skinner has called "the inescapable link between eighteenth-century sensibility and the economic."[51] It was exactly this easy connection that worried Goldsmith, and a critique of which lay at the heart of the work that was dearest to him.

"Harmless Delusions"—*The Vicar of Wakefield*

In the 1960s and 1970s, Goldsmith criticism was dominated by the desire to claim Goldsmith for the knowing ranks of the wry literati and establish his writings as satiric reproofs directed against the excesses of sensibility.[52] And much of Goldsmith's writing is critical of sentimentality. His oft-quoted late work, "An Essay on the Theatre; or, A Comparison between Sentimental and Laughing Comedy" (1773), takes direct aim at "weeping comedies," the theatrical counterparts of the sentimental novels of the age, for "flattering every man in his favourite foible" and commending vice rather than ridiculing it. Audience responses to sentimental plays, Goldsmith implies, are generally less about acquiring virtue than about reassuring spectators of their sensibility and virtue.[53] To this weeping comedy Goldsmith opposes laughing comedy which, like Shaftesbury's persona in "Letter Concerning Enthusiasm," employs among other means the curative "art of laughing" as a real method for reform. This criticism of weeping comedy runs in the same vein as Goldsmith's plays from the period. *She Stoops to Conquer* and *The Good Natur'd Man* complain of the poverty, hunger, debt, and crime generated by the luxury and waste of mercantile culture, and one of the recurring concerns of the Goldsmith corpus is curbing the acquisitiveness that generates poverty and violence. From his early writings for Newbery to *The Deserted Village*, Goldsmith addressed the reform of socioeconomic injustices, and his main critique of sentimentalism was that it seemed able to do little to change the acquisitiveness at its root. "The dullest writer talks of virtue, and liberty, and benevolence with esteem," opined Altangi in *The Citizen of the World*, "tells his true story, filled with good and wholesome advice; warns against slavery, bribery, or the bite of a mad dog, and dresses up his little useful magazine of knowledge and entertainment, at least with a good intention."[54] As John Bender has shown, it was also the reformist dimension of *The Vicar of Wakefield* that occupied the press when Goldsmith's novel first appeared; newspapers and magazines often excerpted it, and chapter 27 on "a reformation in the gaol" was by far the favorite selection.[55] Bender rightly asserts, too, that "the ironies that mid-twentieth-century critics have found in *The Vicar of Wakefield* are generated not by flaws in the character of Dr. Primrose but by contradictions that mark reformist thought during the 1760s,"[56] particularly, we should add, regarding religion and the market.

In a sort of reverse maneuver from Shaftesbury's secular transvaluation of enthusiasm, Goldsmith's novel uses its eponymous divine to sublimate what Goldsmith sees as a passive, impotent sentimentality and related secular philosophy into a religious sensibility, or a sentimentality that is supplemented and fortified by religion. Goldsmith ultimately offers a religious critique of sentimentality that is in itself very sentimental, and it is the contradictions within this position that complicate the novel's aims and make up much of the larger cultural significance of the book. The Vicar Primrose is held up as both victim and hero against a backdrop that clearly resembles the bookselling world in which Goldsmith was working between 1760 and 1762, when he was writing the novel alongside his commissions for Newbery.[57] The "Advertisement" on the opening page of the novel seems aimed at any of a number of critics and magazine writers with whom Goldsmith was familiar: it predicts that the book's virtues will not be understood by those "fond of high life," who "mistake ribaldry for humour," who prize wit and "have been taught to deride religion," and who will thus "laugh at one whose chief stores of comfort are drawn from futurity" (*VW*, 14). The novel thus reacts precisely against the self-aggrandizing satire characteristic of the "fame machine" culture of book reviewing in which Goldsmith shrewdly participated.[58]

"The hero of this piece," the Advertisement also declares, "unites in himself the three greatest characters upon earth; he is a priest, an husbandman, and the father of a family . . . ready to teach, and ready to obey . . . simple in affluence, and majestic in adversity" (*VW*, 14). And the adversities the Vicar weathers are particularly the fruits of greed and economic injustice. In the second chapter, Dr. Primrose discovers that the merchant with whom he has lodged his money has skipped town, leaving depositors less than a shilling to the pound. The family is left nearly destitute, the oldest son's engagement is broken off, and the family moves from their Wakefield estate to a modest farm in a distant parish. Like the opening chapter on their Wakefield life, the fourth, "*A proof that even the humblest fortune may grant happiness, which depends not on circumstance, but constitution,*" emphasizes that the rituals of daily life that make for the family's happiness remain unchanged by their new circumstances:

The little republic to which I gave laws, was regulated in the following manner: by sun-rise we all assembled in our common appartment; the fire being previously kindled by the servant. After we had saluted each other with proper ceremony, for I always thought fit to keep up some mechanical forms of good breeding, without which freedom ever destroys friendship, we all bent in gratitude to that Being who gave us another day. This duty being performed, my son and I went to pursue our usual industry abroad, while my wife and daughters employed themselves in providing breakfast, which was always ready at a certain time. I allowed half an hour for this meal, and an hour for dinner; which time was taken up in innocent mirth between my wife and daughters, and in philosophical arguments between my son and me.

As we rose with the sun, so we never pursued our labours after it was gone down, but returned home to the expecting family; where smiling looks, a neat hearth, and pleasant fire, were prepared for our reception. Nor were we without guests: sometimes farmer Flamborough, our talkative neighbor, and often the blind piper, would pay us a visit, and taste our gooseberry wine; for the making of which we had lost neither the receipt nor the reputation. These harmless people had several ways of being good company, while one played, the other would sing some soothing ballad, Johnny Armstrong's last good night, or the cruelty of Barbara Allen. The night was concluded in the manner we began the morning, my youngest boys being appointed to read the lessons of the day, and he that read loudest, distinctest, and best, was to have a halfpenny on Sunday to put in the poor's box. (*VW*, 33)

Alongside its romanticization of country virtue, this passage underscores the activities that are held up as both the pillars of the family's domestic happiness and the catalyst for the reform of the gaol later in the novel: private prayer and the communal reading of Scripture and sermons. When his house burns down and his daughter Olivia runs off with the scoundrel squire, Mr. Thornhill, the Vicar repeats what has been, throughout, the novel's mantra of hope: "We shall yet be happy," (131), and this hopeful perseverance is linked throughout the story to these private devotions.

Even when the Vicar is jailed for debt by his daughter's seducer, he tells us that "after my usual meditations, and having praised my heavenly corrector, I laid myself down and slept with the utmost tranquility till morning" (*VW*, 143), and his sympathy for his fellow inmates and the power of his sermons to them stems from this personal piety. "Finding all mankind in open arms against them," the rough characters in the gaol were, the Vicar tells us, "labouring to make themselves a future and a tremendous enemy," and though they assail him with all sorts of "execrations, lewdness, and brutality," he pities their "insensibility" and seeks, in the words of the chapter's title, a "reformation in the gaol" (144). The key to this reformation lies in his "giving sensibility" to these "wretches divested of every moral feeling" (149), and this he does by reading to them from the Book of Common Prayer and exhorting them in a homily. "I therefore read them a portion of the service with a loud unaffected voice," the Vicar recounts, "and found my audience perfectly merry upon the occasion. Lewd whispers, groans of contrition burlesqued, winking and coughing, alternately excited laughter. However, I continued with my natural solemnity to read on, sensible that what I did might amend some, but could itself receive no contamination from any" (145). Some of the inmates shake his hand afterwards, which emboldens the Vicar to repeat his homily the next day, "for it had ever been my opinion, that no man was past the hour of amendment" (146). In the days that follow, the men play all sorts of tricks on him, turning his wig and placing obscene joke books in his papers. "However I took no notice of all that this mischievous groupe of little beings could do," the Vicar tells us, "but went on . . . My design succeeded, and in less than six days some were penitent, and all attentive" (148). To help his fellow prisoners pay their rents in the gaol, the Vicar has his son fetch him some materials and sets the inmates to making wooden pegs to sell to local tradesmen (149). Not yet the purely "social gospel" of the late nineteenth and twentieth centuries, the Vicar's religion is a somewhat traditional piety whose worth is conceived in terms of "giving sensibility," if not sacraments and grace, and, if unable to set the economic injustice of debtor's prison aright, at least working to alleviate it.[59]

In the novel, piety offers this sensibility particularly where moral philosophy has failed to do so, and recognizing this particular contrast helps make sense of what is today one of its more opaque scenes. When it seems the Vicar can sink no lower, his younger daughter Sophia is suddenly abducted and his older son George is thrown into gaol with him. Almost unable to stand, the Vicar props himself against a wall and, to an audience that must expect him to collapse in despair at any moment, gives a chapter-long sermon on the necessity and benefits of religion, its refrain "religion does what philosophy can never do." Philosophy, the Vicar tells his fellow inmates, provides no answer to the real pain of our lives, nor can philosophy mitigate the material miseries of the gaol or lack of the necessities of life: "Let the philosopher from his couch of softness tell us that we can resist all these" (*VW*, 162). Here the novel reflects directly on what Goldsmith portrays as the failure of moral philosophy and the quasi-stoic tone it had reached by the early 1760s in Smith's immensely popular *Theory of Moral Sentiments*. With Shaftesbury it might invoke an abstract notion of the harmonious whole, or with Smith it might tell readers to resist the impulse to crime based on the potential disapproval of the impartial spectator, but its admonition to resign oneself to suffering because it must be for the good of "the whole" is cold comfort in the face of real misery. Goldsmith seems not far from Barker-Benfield's realization in the epigraph that this sort of philosophy of sentiments provides comfort mainly to those who are suffering only a twinge of guilt at the thought of others' suffering: to those members of London literary circles whom Goldsmith both envied and criticized, who increasingly enjoyed "literacy, privacy, intimacy, servants, and other distancings from economic distress" and the freedom to "concentrate on their own emotional pleasures and pains in their vaunted distinction from the world." Philosophy, like the weeping comedies Goldsmith criticizes, fails chiefly in its inability to impart the sensibility that would enable one either to resist greed or to bear its injustices without resorting to crime or violence.

Through hilarious turns of plot in the final chapters, the family's misfortunes are reversed. Rescuing Sophia and returning her to her father, Mr. Burchell confesses his love for her and reveals his true identity as Mr. Thornhill's uncle, the wealthy Sir William Thornhill. The Vicar sanctions their marriage, Olivia is again courted by the humble Mr. Williams, and the family is saved from destitution. Exhausted by oscillations between despair and relief, the Vicar asks their permission to withdraw, and sounds again the novel's recurring note of piety and prayer: "leaving the company in the midst of their mirth, as soon as I found myself alone, I poured out my heart in gratitude to the giver of joy as well as of sorrow, and then slept undisturbed till morning" (*VW*, 182). The Vicar is careful to point out that on release from prison he renews his family's "ceremonies" at the dinner table, and he ends his account of the joyful final scene by adding that "it now only remained that my gratitude in good fortune should exceed my former submission in adversity" (184). In case we miss Goldsmith's point from the title or Advertisement, it is underlined yet again. In the busy early time of his career with Newbery, in a novel he was writing on the side of his commissioned works, addressing the great themes of economic injustice and social reform that also consume his most popular works like *The Traveller* and *The Deserted Village*, Goldsmith makes his hero a vicar, like his father, and like his brother to whom *The Traveller* is dedicated and whose life is described there in glowing terms similar to the Vicar's. He aims his joint critique of moral philosophy and sentimentality at their inability to reform the heart, to keep one from worldly vanity and greed and to give perseverance and hope, which, in the terms of the novel, are rooted in the practice of piety in everyday life: around the table, in prayers and Bible reading, in contented daily work, and in the ceremonies of greeting around rising and retiring. Through both tears and laughter, the same mechanism of sensibility upon which Richardson relies, Goldsmith hopes to set up the Vicar's life as an all-compelling example that will inspire a reformation in the lives of his readers, just as in the lives of the inmates. Offering "true sensibility" where the "true enthusiasms" of moral philosophy and sentimentality had failed, *The Vicar of Wakefield* has as much an evangelical design on its readers as *The Pilgrim's Progress*, only in a more comedic and secular register.[60]

Even so, Goldsmith's novel confesses a quasi awareness that secularizing values and excessive consumption are closer to the Primrose household than is ideal. As Maureen Harkin has pointed out, *The Vicar of Wakefield* attacks not just luxury and material excess, commercialism and consumerism, but also the effects of the culture of professional writing and criticism in which he was an exemplary participant. For Goldsmith, Newbery's industry of hack writers pandering to critics and educated readers who lack religious conviction runs the risk of reducing everything to industrial-style consumption and production; "the problem" for Goldsmith, as Harkin puts it, "is that the republic of letters is also a realm of commerce."[61] And it is the women in the Vicar's family, Timothy Dykstal points out, who are especially susceptible to the temptations of consumerism.[62] Much of the "innocent mirth" that passes between the Primrose women stems from their weakness for fashion and adornment, aimed at attracting wealthy, handsome husbands. In the opening chapter, the girls' interest in moneyed matches and dramatic professions of love—and in the course of events, the root of Olivia's near ruin—can be traced back to Mrs. Primrose's reading romances during her pregnancies and insisting on romantic rather than traditional family names for her daughters. And she passes this legacy on to them more than just in name. Her daughters adopt her reading tastes, devouring sentimental tales of love and adventure by which they later erroneously judge their suitors' worth and sincerity. Goldsmith pokes fun at Sophia's enthusiasm for a romantic epitaph by Gay (*VW*, 46), and Olivia takes her novel reading for a real education in life and philosophy, protesting to the Vicar that she has indeed "read a great deal of controversy"—"the disputes between Thwackum and Square, the controversy between Robinson Crusoe and Friday the Savage," and "the controversy in Religious courtship" (45).

In the course of the novel, this sort of reading yields both mundane and catastrophic consequences. In quotidian terms, the women's desire to attract dashing romantic suitors forces the Vicar to wage a low-key but constant battle against their concern for their appearance and desire to display themselves during worship. When the family relocates to the country, for example, he has to chide them into not wearing their finery to church, adding, "I don't know whether such flouncing and shredding is becoming even in the rich, if we consider, upon a moderate calculation, that the nakedness of the indigent world may be cloathed from the trimmings of the vain" (*VW*, 34). In time, their romantic, reading-induced vanity brings the central tragedy in the novel: Olivia's false marriage with Mr. Thornhill, which nearly reduces her to prostitution. When Olivia is finally taken in by Mr. Thornhill's attentions, the Vicar repines that it is not surprising "that such talents should win the affections of a girl, who by education was taught to value an appearance in herself, and consequently to set a value upon it in another" (43). To underline the point, the family hears that the pair has run off just moments after the Vicar complains about the sentimental elegies the family loves listening to: "the great fault of these elegists is," he says in words like Altangi's, "that they are in despair for griefs that give the sensible part of mankind very little pain. A lady loses her muff, her fan, or her lap-dog, and so the silly poet runs home to versify the disaster" (90).

Goldsmith faults the Primrose women's reading tastes for distracting them from the serious realities of life, and yet the Vicar too is implicated in their preoccupations. He admits he allowed their lavish clothes in the past and finds, for instance, that his wife remains attached to her crimson paduasoy "because I formerly happened to say it became her" (*VW*, 34). When Mrs. Primrose entertains inflated notions of the social status of their family—thinking that Mr. Burchell's poverty cannot "entitle him to match into such a family as ours"—and in turn passes on expectations of wealthy, noble suitors to Olivia and Sophia, the Vicar recounts only that he "could not but smile to hear her talk in this lofty strain: but I was never much displeased with those harmless delusions that tend to make us more happy" (31).

The novel as a whole, however, certainly questions whether those delusions really are harmless—and only the women's. The Vicar continually brings up with pride his many pamphlets defending perpetual monogamy in the "Whistonean controversy."[63] At one point he is recognized in public by another clergyman (or so he thought) as "the great Primrose, that courageous monogamist, who had been the bulwark of the church." "Never did my heart feel sincerer rapture than at that moment," the Vicar proclaims, and he launches into conversation with the old man about their shared passion; "no lovers in romance," he declares, "ever cemented a more instantaneous friendship" (*VW*, 73). This friendship turns out to be as spurious as Thornhill's love for Olivia, and the Vicar's passion for sermons and tracts—the mass of printed religious material the likes of which flowed through Newbery's shop—is shown to be not far removed from her love of romances. The implication is that they may be equally problematic, that the Vicar is as distracted from the real problems in his family by dreams of literary fame and religious publishing as others are distracted from real evils by sentimental ballads and novels. So flattered is he by the stranger's acclaim of his authorial greatness that he is swindled out of his only horse, a loss the family can hardly afford at this point. Commercialized, print-commodified religion, hoping to evangelize via the mass media, the novel seems to say, is as dangerously subject to egoism and as impotent a substitute for real reform as is shedding a tear at a play.

Yet even as the Vicar's interventions in religious controversies through tracts is ridiculed in the novel, it is precisely the print-commodity form of the novel itself that undoes Goldsmith's proposed religious reform of sentimentality. For ultimately, the daily, heartfelt yet ritualistic private prayer and family devotion that Goldsmith upholds as the source of real sensibility are virtually absent in the novel, referred to in general or in retrospect, but always, as it were, offstage. The text of the Vicar's moving prison sermon is included, but what certainly cannot appear in the novel is its daily repetition for the week following; the actual inclusion of the repetition of the sermons or, more crucially, any of the Vicar's private devotions or the family's daily reading from the Book of Common Prayer, would bog down the plot of the novel unbearably. The forward momentum of the novel and the interest it must elicit certainly cannot realistically represent the ritual aspect of the devotion Goldsmith promotes as the antidote for consumerism, vanity, and greed. In the novel he can only gesture at it obliquely and never portray it directly, keeping the Vicar's practice of piety shrouded in an ultimately nostalgic, sentimentalized appeal. The novel's portrayal of the Vicar's faith accomplishes less a vindication of religion against secular philosophy or sentimentality than its subjugation to their terms. The reference to religion becomes merely a seal of transcendence on the print commodity; as Ward puts it, religion becomes a "special effect" and "baptises" the commodity form with the allure and illusion of easy transcendence.[64] Goldsmith's Advertisement acknowledges as much, admitting that the novel cannot really "convert" those who are not converted already.

This sentimentalized remnant of religion in the novel is contemporary with Sterne's *Life and Opinions of Tristram Shandy* (which Goldsmith, incidentally, disliked) and anticipates by only two to six years Sterne's portrayal of the parson Yorick in *A Sentimental Journey* (1768), who represents perhaps a more conscious recognition of the real condition of sentimentalized religion. Like *The Vicar of Wakefield*, *A Sentimental Journey* is poised on the edge of a rituality and piety it can only sentimentalize and commodify. Fêted about Paris as a curiosity because of his faith, Yorick is finally sickened at the self-gratifying display of his "*beggarly system*" and decides to leave.[65] Passing through the French countryside on his way back to England, he stops for dinner with a peasant

Bourbonnois family who become the sacramental center of the novel; their dinner is "a feast of love" and his entries on the encounter are eucharistically called "The Supper" and "The Grace." When the meal is over, the father of the family gives a knock on the table, everyone clears the dishes, washes and changes clothes, and proceeds to sing, play, and dance. Yorick "fancied [he] could distinguish an elevation of spirits different from that which is the cause or the effect of simple jollity.—In a word . . . thought [he] beheld Religion mixing in the dance." He might have feared that his imagination was misleading him, he tells us, except that "the old man, as soon as the dance ended, said, that this was their constant way; and that all his life long he had made it a rule, after supper was over, to call out his family to dance and rejoice; believing, he said, that a chearful and contented mind was the best sort of thanks to heaven that an illiterate peasant could pay—," to which Yorick added, "—Or a learned prelate either."[66] Yorick can enshrine the supper and the grace episodically into his sentimental journey, but he cannot move to the French countryside and partake of this rituality without being someone other than the sentimental traveler he is or without writing something other than a novel, and so he goes on, with "The Grace" followed immediately by the famously funny "Case of Delicacy" involving the end of the novel and of the *fille de chambre*. The real "story" of the novel is not (and cannot) be with the peasant family and their daily ritual of singing and dancing, but with the consciousness of the outsider Yorick, to whom they are attractive in a particularly sentimentalized, religious way.

Similarly, the real story of *The Vicar of Wakefield* is not so much the narrative of the Primrose family and their piety as that of the outsider who comes to appreciate their goodness, Sir William Thornhill, whom Brissenden has called a "melancholy man of feeling" and "symbol of alienation, the dispossessed conscience of a sick society."[67] For most of the novel Sir William travels in disguise, searching for a woman who, "a stranger to my fortune[,] could think that I had merit as a man" (*VW*, 181), and his wealth and marriage to Sophia are at least as responsible for saving the Primrose family from ruin as is their virtue. Befriending them as Mr. Burchell early in the novel, Sir William relates his life story to the Vicar in the third person, telling how he had carried his benevolence to excess as a youth. He loved all mankind, he recounts, "for fortune prevented him from knowing that there were rascals," and like the heroes of so many sentimental novels, he gave to all who asked and, more realistically perhaps, "grew improvident as he grew poor; and though he talked like a man of sense, his actions were those of a fool" (29). As with the prodigal son, his friends dwindled along with his money, and he learned that "a man's own heart must be ever given to gain that of another"; like Goldsmith, he traveled through Europe on foot, and now by the age of thirty, Goldsmith's age at the time he was writing the novel, he has recovered his fortune and grown both richer and wiser (30). A reformed sentimentalist, Sir William comes to his senses and to the rescue of the abused Vicar and his family. His is a sublimated sentimentality, more savvy, making a better exchange—giving not money for virtue but hearts for hearts—looking for true sensibility and finding it in the Primroses.

In the world of the novel, Sir William will presumably marry Sophia and enter into the family's life of happy piety and simplicity. But we again are not shown that in the novel, and Goldsmith remains in London, paying his homage to his father's and brother's lifestyle but living more like the preconversion Sir William and more caught up in the fame machine than the Vicar could ever have been. The miraculous rescue of the virtuous Primroses by the worldly wise, reformed man of feeling in the second half of the novel is a disjunction to be sure, presenting almost a rival hero to the Vicar and seemingly admitting, in Jonathan Lamb's words, the "impossibility of reconciling notions of primitive innocence with the facts of civilized society."[68] But it is not a writerly failure on Goldsmith's part as criticism has sometimes claimed.[69] Rather, it is only from the perspective of Sir William that the Vicar and his family can have the full meaning Goldsmith creates for them: the salvation, in novel form, of a secular cult of sensibility that comes nostalgically to lament its lostness. The extravagant generosity that the young Sir William shares with many of his fictional forebears is tempered at the moment it turns to religious sanction; religion reappears within the naturalistic discourse of sensibility as the cure for its deficiencies and regulation of its excesses, a commodified seal of the transcendence it never quite reaches either in life or the novel. As Lamb puts it, like *Clarissa* and *Humphrey Clinker, The Vicar of Wakefield* idealizes the "marginal condition of characters who have chosen to maintain their integrity above all odds," standing "as a reproach to a polity which has no use for innocence"—"but it cannot represent to the times what the times lack."[70]

Goldsmith's position, closest in the novel to that of Sir William, reproaches both the culture of greed and the sentimentality that is powerless to mitigate it, but does so in the form of sentimental fiction that cannot represent precisely that which Goldsmith argues the times lack: the conscious praxis and rituals of daily life that resist either the secular logic of "philosophy" or the appetites and desires cultivated by Newbery's shop and the print market of his day. Perhaps most strangely of all in a work advancing a religious reform of sentimentality, prayer is referenced, but direct, personal address to God is as absent as in Shaftesbury's writing; in a novel aimed at affecting readers' feelings, the assumption seems to be that actually glimpsing the Vicar in his *prie-Dieu* on stage, as it were, or actually hearing his prayers would not be affective and is not really thinkable in terms of polite sentimentality or the form of the novel. By a mindset analogous to that behind the many abridgments that Goldsmith worked on for Newbery, religion sentimentally reproduced is reduced from the real repetitiveness of its practice to a few essential markers. If, as Maureen Harkin has argued, the problem Goldsmith wrestles with in *The Vicar of Wakefield* is that the republic of letters is also a realm of commerce, the religion he offers as its remedy is afflicted with the illness it is supposed to cure. As Brissenden appraises it, the implications of *The Vicar of Wakefield* are thus as pessimistic and as elegiac as those of *The Deserted Village* and *The Traveller*.[71] As much as Goldsmith hopes for reform and for novels to inspire religious improvement, *The Vicar of Wakefield* pinpoints the exact sticking points of both sentimentality and sentimentalized religion: their inability to enact real agency and reform, ritual, and the repetitive praxis of everyday life from within the culture of commodified novelty—an inability Goldsmith seems to have known firsthand. That these are the central fissures of sentimental literature and sentimentalized religion is underlined on every count by the more drastic response of Goldsmith's coworker to their shared Grub Street context.

"Without Going to Italy or France"—Impolite Spontaneity

Goldsmith, we will remember, came to London in time to slip into Smart's chair, as it were, as Newbery's chief writer, when it became plain that Smart's absence would not be a short one. The details of Smart's illness and incarceration were likely well known to Goldsmith. Smart's previous bouts of sickness were reported in several newspapers, and Goldsmith arrived in London in February 1756, just as Smart was fairly publicly collapsing under the weight of his writing commitments to Newbery and to *The Universal Visiter* and coming down with his third calamitous fever in the half dozen years he had worked in London.[72] Weeks long, this fever threatened to be fatal, and though Smart did recover, it was the great watershed of his life. In June of that year, Newbery published Smart's poem of thanks, "Hymn to the Supreme Being, On recovery from a dangerous Fit of Illness." Prefaced to it was the usual product placement that may have made Smart wince as much as readers today: a dedication no doubt prompted by Newbery, thanking Dr. James who, "under God," through his Fever Powders "rescued me from the grave."[73] Smart often complained that once he entered the Grub world he never had time to revise his poems properly, but this poem is glowing and elegant. In it Smart declares his reprieve from death a miracle which has brought him to the healing balm of penitence: "Brisk leaps the heart, the mind's at large once more, / To love, to praise, to bless, to wonder and adore."[74] He promises to "work, conceive, and speak" to God's "endless glory" and asks that Charity—the love which is higher than "Faith, hope, [and] devotion"—grow deep-rooted in his heart, in order

> That I may act what Thou hast giv'n to know,
> That I may live for THEE and THEE alone,
> And justify those sweetest words from heav'n,
> THAT HE SHALL LOVE THEE MOST
> TO WHOM THOU'ST MOST FORGIVEN.[75]

What exactly this illness entailed in terms of Smart's mental condition is unclear, as are the sins of which he sees healing as the sign of forgiveness. But what recovery entailed was, for Smart, unmistakable, as the tone of the poem suggests. When Smart recovered, Newbery and Anna Maria were relieved that their friend Samuel Johnson could quit covering for him with *The Universal Visiter*, and Newbery quickly made plans for Smart to finish his long-promised collection of verse fables. But Smart refused. He refused to honor his other journalistic commitments as well, writing nothing that was not directly "for THEE and THEE alone."[76] By every account, Smart began to take seriously St. Paul's exhortation in the Epistle to the Philippians to "Pray without ceasing" and cultivated attention to the desire to pray, which, as Hester Thrale Piozzi told it, "he held it as a duty not to controul or repress."[77] Piozzi went on to describe how, "beginning by regular addresses at stated times to the Almighty, he went on to call his friends from their dinners, or beds, or places of recreation, whenever that impulse towards prayer pressed upon his mind." Although, as she was sure to stress, "In every other transaction of his life no man's wits could be more regular than those of Smart."[78] As she put it in an earlier account, once "the Idea struck him that every Time he thought of praying, Resistance against y^t divine Impulse (as he conceived it) was a Crime; he knelt down in the Streets, & Assembly rooms, and wherever he was when the Thought cross^d his Mind—and this indecorous Conduct obliged his Friends to place him in a Confinement."[79] Samuel Johnson's comments on Smart's "insane" public prayer are more famous:

> Madness frequently discovers itself merely by unnecessary deviation from the usual modes of the world. My poor friend Smart shewed the disturbance of his mind, by falling upon his knees, and saying his prayers in the street, or in any other unusual place. Now, although, rationally speaking, it is greater madness not to pray at all, than to pray as Smart did, I am afraid there are so many who do not pray, that their understanding is not called into question.... I did not think he ought to be shut up. His infirmities were not noxious to society. He insisted on people praying with him; and I'd as life pray with Kit Smart as any

one else. Another charge was, that he did not love clean linen; and I have no passion for it.[80]

Regardless of such assertions of his relative sanity, beginning in May 1757 Smart was incarcerated against his will in at least two private madhouses, St. Luke's Hospital and Mr. Potter's asylum in Bethnal Green, for the better part of seven years. Though the conditions at these institutions were not so horrible as in Bedlam Hospital, in *Jubilate Agno* Smart does refer to the common madhouse experiences of being visited like a circus curiosity by local citizenry, and to violent treatment: "For they work me with their harping-irons," Smart wrote, "which is a barbarous instrument, for I am more unguarded than others," most likely referring to a device for force-feeding purgatives to inmates (B.124). If as Piozzi claims, in other matters no man's wits were more regular than Smart's, and id as Johnson says "his infirmities were not noxious to society," we are left to articulate more precisely the reason his behavior merited the drastic and expensive step of long-term incarceration in midcentury London.

This study is certainly not the first to question the diagnosis of Smart's madness, but those which have questioned it have tended to gloss over the specifically religious register of that which, in every account, occasioned Smart's incarceration: spontaneous public prayer.[81] In Smart's own plain, playful words in *Jubilate Agno*, "I blessed God in St James's Park till I routed all the company."[82] Clement Hawes has most recently highlighted the political implications of behavior that, like Smart's, evoked seventeenth-century enthusiasm, and forty years ago Devlin pointed out the alarming resemblance Smart's behavior shared, in his contemporaries' minds, with other conversions and enthusiasms, those of the Methodists.[83] In sentencing a Methodist preacher (erroneously, it turned out), the Lord Chancellor Northington wrote in 1757: "Bigotry and enthusiasm have spread their baneful influence far and wide, and the unhappy objects of the contagion almost daily increase. Of this, not only Bedlam, but most of the private madhouses, are melancholy and striking proofs."[84] Smart lived at a time when Methodism could be equated with madness, and spontaneous prayer in public was not the sort of sentiment that appealed to the culture of sensibility, however much it, like free prayer, shared sensibility's fundamental logic. Thomas Keymer has interpreted Johnson's comments on Smart's incarceration as a tacit admission that diagnoses of madness such as Smart's amounted to "a label used to scapegoat crimes against politeness,"[85] and Newbery may have been especially sensitive to this religious impropriety because Smart's wife, Anna Maria, was Roman Catholic.[86]

In *Poor Kit Smart*, Smart's most religiously sympathetic biographer Christopher Devlin nonetheless concurred that his behaviors were offenses against reasonable decorum. He paints a portrait of Smart as a pious Anglican who in his sickness suffered some sort of spiritual experience wholly foreign to his former life and who subsequently was afflicted with "alienations of mind" and a compulsive urge to pray that clearly was "not from God."[87] However much his behavior was perceived by others as disruptive, to my mind too much emphasis has been placed on the illness as a radical break or disjunction for Smart, when his behaviors before and after his illness are clearly related. The religious sentiments of *Jubilate Agno* strike an amazing harmony with the notes sounded in the Seatonian poems and are in the main conventionally orthodox, soundly incarnational, and Trinitarian; the "cherub Gratitude" and joy in God's myriad creation are the touchstones of his faith before and afterward. Smart seems to have been pushed to a point of crisis by the pressures of a life-threatening sickness and the literary market's hold on his life and, consequently, to have repented of what he came to see as misplaced allegiance to that market which amounted to an enslavement of both heart and mind and a lack of attention to God. With heart and mind "at large once more" to "love, to praise, to bless, to wonder and adore," Smart actively resisted the indenture of his inner life by seeking to flesh out his deepest convictions in his everyday world of work: by refusing to write for his own aggrandizement and, most disturbingly to his contemporaries, by praying freely in public and inviting them to join him. Smart's conviction that he should not resist the urge to pray is clearly of a cloth with not only his religious convictions and gratitude for his recovery but with the ideology of spontaneity that is the object of this study. His effusions of public prayer are part and parcel of a longstanding imagination of religion and moral goodness in an empirical mode which, by his day, had blossomed in a cult of sensibility whose favorite image, the Aeolian harp, was also one of his own. His seemingly peculiar conviction that he should not resist the urge to pray is, in a profound sense, exactly what we should expect of a genuinely religious persuasion expressing itself in the culture of sensibility, in a soul which understands itself as an Aeolian harp vibrating to the winds of the spirit.

Smart's dropping to his knees, in Grub Street, in 1756, and praying until he "routed all the company," and his being incarcerated for it, stands therefore as a perfect emblem of the vexed status of spontaneity in mid-century English culture. Edward Young, the famous reverend and author of *Night Thoughts*, was still living and may well have known Smart.[88] In 1742 he had prefaced that poem with a claim to its spontaneous and almost enthusiastic pouring forth, and two years after Smart entered the asylum, he wrote his *Conjectures on Original Composition*, praising the inspired literary genius in terms that anticipate Wordsworth's "spontaneous overflow of powerful feelings." In a culture that was more and more invested in the idea of quasi-divine, inspired poetic originality, the incarceration of one of its most acclaimed poets for spontaneous public prayer marks the real limit of the culture's embrace of spontaneity. The spontaneity that was its hope for reform and virtue was by midcentury carefully circumscribed, limited to fairly passive, secular expressions manifested in the polite conventions that emerged, as J. G. A. Pocock, Brean Hammond, and others have pointed out, to govern an increasingly commercial society and expanding middle class, and which were perhaps best embodied in the impulse to buy *The Whitsuntide Gift: or, The Way to Be Happy* in Newbery's shop and read it to one's niece or nephew.[89] Sentimentality and sensibility were yoked to politeness, and the urge to reform the vices of consumer culture into virtue was often indistinguishable from the desire to reconcile the two. In this climate, Smart's behavior serves almost as a necessary limit-case, a bursting of a boil, as it were, in the culture of sensibility, that marked just how far the inner light of sentimentality would not be allowed to lead.

Much of the criticism of *Jubilate Agno* in the sixty-five years since its first publication understandably has sought to unearth its particular religious form and content: its antiphonal structure, its theology, its connection to the Psalms, to Robert Lowth's *De Sacra Poesi Hebraeorum* and to Freemasonry, numerology, and the occult.[90] In the 1960s and 1970s attention turned to its poetics and theory of representation, most notably in Patricia Meyer Spacks's treatment of Smart's "poetry of vision" and Geoffrey Hartman's well-known *English Literary History* essay exploring its metaphysics of presence.[91] More recent work has helped to situate Smart in his historical context. Harriet Guest's *A Form of Sound Words* has positioned Smart's poetry in terms of religious verse in the period and its stylistic negotiations of address and authority, and Clement Hawes in *Mania and Literary Style* has shown Smart's rhetoric to be drawn from a "subterranean 'manic' counter-discourse" that in reaching back to seventeenth-century enthusiastic prophecy taps into a host of related political, class, and gender conflicts.[92] But it remains to bring the religious and material, historical analyses together: to situate the religion of *Jubilate Agno* and the behavior that occasioned it as disruptively religious, precisely in the larger cultural context of Grub Street and Smart's career with Newbery.

However bold or unusual Smart's decision to pray at his pleasure and to write only religious works, the great rupture of Smart's career, I would argue, is not here. The real break for him came in his first years of incarceration and isolation from Newbery, his family, and the world of literary ambitions. Thrown out of that familiar sphere and into St. Luke's Hospital, Smart chronicles in detail the particular terms of that rift as he came to understand it over the space of lonely weeks, months, and years.

It is this new understanding of what sets the polite sensibility of the world of the Bible and Sun at odds with the faith to which it seemed still attached, I contend, that remakes his faith and poetics dramatically.

It was only during the second year of his confinement that Smart began the poem that reflected the new architecture of this reshaped piety.[93] Where Sterne's parson Yorick, like many eighteenth-century pilgrims, took his sentimental journey to the continent "in pursuit of knowledge and improvements," Smart wrote in the madhouse that "there is a traveling for the glory of God without going to Italy or France" (*JA*, B.35)—or as he would put it still later in the "Hymn for Epiphany" published after his release, "Lo! I travel in the spirit, / On my knees my course I steer / To the house of might and merit / With humility and fear."[94] In the asylum, Smart declared, "For I am the Lord's News-Writer—the scribe-evangelist. / . . . For by the grace of God I am the Reviver of ADORATION amongst ENGLISH-MEN. / . . . For things that are not in the sight of men are thro' God of infinite concern" (B.327, 332, 334)—his implication being that God's news is not man's, or Newbery's, that the liturgy is somehow opposed to the newspaper. Active where sentimentality waxed passive, socially humble where it kept up appearances, Smart's new poetic voice emerges in *Jubilate Agno* amid lines vast and varied, full of keen observation, pathos, and humor, and celebrating resilience and resistance in the bleakest of circumstances:

> Let Ethan praise with the Flea, his coat of mail, his piercer, and his vigour, which wisdom and providence have contrived to attract observation and to escape it. . . .
> Let Romamti-ezer bless with the Ferret—The Lord is a rewarder of them, that diligently seek him. . . .
> Let Huz bless with the Polypus—lively subtlety is acceptable to the Lord. . . .
> For the two Universities are the Eyes of England.
> For Cambridge is the right and the brightest.
> For L is love. God in every language. . . .
> For to worship naked in the Rain is the bravest thing for the refreshing and purifying the body. (*JA*, A.36, 43, 84; B.615–16, 523, 384)

Written under extremely ascetic conditions—without the drink and sex he formerly enjoyed to excess, with a simple diet and narrow compass of activity—this poem evokes the personal intensity of Shaftesbury's Ασκηματα, but in a completely different scale and key. Like the Ασκηματα, *Jubilate Agno* was written as a kind of ritual and exercise, with Smart carefully crafting two to three lines per day during the last four years of his incarceration. But this rituality was the result not so much of the ideology of spontaneity and the religious effusions surrounding his recovery, as of their rethinking. During his imprisonment for what was the very definition of free prayer, Smart, whose doctrinal leanings had already been soundly Anglican, apparently received a copy of Robert Nelson's high-church devotional guide, *A Companion to the Festivals and Fasts of the Church of England*, and he conceived the idea of writing new hymns for all the major feasts of the year, a plan which he completed after his release.[95] This marked not a conversion to a more staid, ritually ordered Christianity, but a faith more effusive and radical even than his praying in St. James Park had been. *Jubilate Agno* reveals that in the asylum Smart developed his own profoundly liturgical vision of the world, in which the strange beauties of people and animals are revealed equally by habitual, careful attention to them and by "playing on them in delight," by actively pursuing the felicitous ambiguities of language in their names, descriptions, and associations. What can aptly be called the liturgical spontaneity of *Jubilate Agno*, with its chorus of bizarre and surprising conjunctions, its leaps and arcana, is a product of a conscious interplay between selves, objects, and language that came from Smart's reconsideration of the London world that had exiled him to Bethnal Green, of his relation to it and to its values. It is precisely the world of Jack Whirler, of frantic production and spending, and of impotent, sentimentalized virtue that is the context of Smart's incarceration for disruptive prayer—and of the composition of *Jubilate Agno* as a poem of the recovery of agency, praxis, and prayer outside the parameters of politeness. It is as though the literature of active ritual or resistance that Goldsmith aspired to, literature outside the logic of the market, of consumption, and of display, could only be produced by a man swallowed up in the belly of Grub Street and vomited forth into the madhouse, isolated and away from its modes of valuing, appraising, and orchestrating life into delineated patterns of productivity and consumption. The very issues that trouble Goldsmith's novel—the opposition of the market and sentimentality to personal agency, praxis and piety to voice and prayer—direct the arc of the longest, most coherent portion of the extant manuscript, fragment B, the heart of the poem as we know it.

"The Coffin, the Cradle, and the Purse"—Ritual, Agency, and Self-Speaking

Early in fragment B of *Jubilate Agno*, Smart made reference to his only friend during his confinement, "a cat, surpassing in beauty, from whom I take occasion to bless Almighty God" (B.68), and at the end of the fragment, over the course of about a month in the summer of 1760, Smart penned the famous passage which Benjamin Britten would set to music two centuries later, which includes these lines:[96]

> For I will consider my Cat Jeoffry.
> For he is the servant of the Living God duly and daily serving him.
> . . .
> For there is nothing sweeter than his peace when at rest.
> For there is nothing brisker than his life when in motion. . . .
> For the divine spirit comes about his body to sustain it in compleat cat. (B.695–96, 738–39, 742)

In this section it is in the endearing performance of Jeoffry's most catly rituals—stretching, purring, kissing another cat in kindness—that Smart envisions the divine spirit coming about him to sustain him in authentic creatureliness. Earlier in the fragment, Smart also mentions people being sustained in their complete creatureliness, but in reference to voice and prayer, the cause of his incarceration. Smart extols the virtue of loud prayer to purify oneself and one's surroundings at the same time, and goes on to explain the goodness of sound and of the voice:

> For the AIR is contaminated by curses and evil language. . . .
> For the AIR is purified by prayer which is made aloud and with all our might.
> For loud prayer is good for weak lungs and for a vitiated throat.
> For SOUND is propagated in the spirit and in all directions. . . .
> For a man speaks HIMSELF from the crown of his head to the sole of his feet.
> For a LION roars HIMSELF compleat from head to tail.
> For all these things are seen in the spirit which makes the beauty of prayer. (B.221, 224–26, 228–30)

The loud voice of prayer echoing indecorously through St. James Park is better for weak lungs or a sore throat, Smart implies, than the many medicines Newbery sold and made available to his sick son-in-law, and in this passage, prayer is about agency and self-construction. In full-voiced prayer, one makes one's weakness strong, one blesses what is contaminated by cursing and evil language, and one "speaks [one]self compleat" both as a testimony to one's innate creatureliness but also as an act of self-construction—choosing to bless rather than to curse—and this realization that one speaks or performs oneself is, to Smart, the beauty of prayer. The "HIMSELF" that the man speaks or the lion roars is various and innate, as Smart's reveling throughout the poem in the "innumerability" of God's creatures suggests, and yet it is also a roaring of one's will; it is both out of his nature, made by God's "*fiat*," and by his own creative doing.

In the lines that immediately follow, Smart elaborates this notion of human-divine cocreation through voice in the figure of the echo, an image of Smart's precise view of voice and agency as both limited and radically free in constructing with its given materials:

> For applause or the clapping of the hands is the natural action of a man on the descent of the glory of God.
> For EARTH which is an intelligence hath a voice and propensity to speak in all her parts.
> For ECHO is the soul of the voice exerting itself in hollow places.
> For ECHO cannot act but when she can parry the adversary.
> For ECHO is the greatest in Churches and where she can assist in prayer.
> For a good voice hath its Echo with it and it is attainable by much supplication.
> For the VOICE is from the body and the spirit—and is a body and a spirit.
> For the prayers of good men are therefore visible to second-sighted persons. (B.233–40)

As we might expect from someone who gave himself over to impulses to pray, Smart begins these lines insisting on the naturalness of speaking—people, like the earth, he suggests, have a propensity to speak. But he then negotiates the problematic relation of natural propensity to personal agency through the concept of the echo. Echo, he writes, is the power of the human voice to exert itself in the hollow spaces, to repeat the creative word into Milton's empty chaos, as it were, and this is why the "prayers of good men" are efficacious and visible to seers: these prayers are both spirit and body, both language and substantive action. Echo is a sort of liturgical and even Eucharistic principle in creation, and in ascribing body and spirit to the words of prayer, Smart highlights the way that language and the spirit in which it is uttered are real and constructive, especially of ourselves and our inclinations. The reference to prayers being visible echoes a theme in the "Let" verses corresponding to this passage: "Fish and honeycomb are blessed to eat after a recovery," and "Broil'd fish and honeycomb may be taken for the sacrament" (B.236, 243). A pet notion of Smart's seems to have been celebrating the Eucharist not with bread and wine as at the Last Supper but with broiled fish and honey, the food which Christ ate on the beach with his disciples after his resurrection and which was proof to them that he was not a ghost but a truly risen body-and-spirit. For Smart, the voice of Eucharistic thanks echoes through all creation and makes the daily rituals of eating sacramental, the miraculous substance of love and resurrection life.

The constructive efficacy of the voice, its echo, is according to Smart greatest in prayer. This assertion is puzzling in light of his spontaneous prayer but makes sense in the context of the larger poem, not to mention in light of the agency necessary to overcome the passivity and silencing of prayer that develops under an ideology of spontaneity in Bunyan and Shaftesbury. For Smart the self-creative power of the voice addressing and blessing God in efficacious and presumably spontaneous prayer is linked, through the trajectory of the lines that follow, to sacraments, music, and liturgy:

> For the feast of TRUMPETS should be kept up, that being the most direct and acceptable of all instruments.
> For the TRUMPET of God is a blessed intelligence and so are all the instruments in HEAVEN.
> For GOD the father Almighty plays upon the HARP of stupendous magnitude and melody.
> For innumerable Angels fly out at every touch and his tune is a work of creation.
> For at that time malignity ceases and the devils themselves are at peace.
> For this time is perceptible to man by a remarkable stillness and serenity of soul.
> For the Æolian harp is improveable into regularity.
> For when it is so improved it will be known to be the SHAWM.
> For it would be better if the LITURGY were musically performed.
> For the strings of the SHAWM were upon a cylinder which turned to the wind.
> For this was spiritual musick altogether, as the wind is a spirit.
> For there is nothing but it may be played upon in delight.
> For the flames of fire may be blown thro musical pipes.
> For it is so higher up in the vast empyrean.
> For [nothing] is so real as that which is spiritual. . . .
> For GLASS is worked in the fire till it partakes of its nature.
> (B.244–58, 261)

The Jewish Feast of Trumpets, celebrated in the seventh month, in October, when these verses were written, is a recurring topos in *Jubilate Agno* which is, in a sense, its own feast of trumpets, celebrating the "blessed intelligence" and instrument of the voice. Here, musical instruments are "blessed intelligence[s]" like the earth and people. God plays on the shawm or harp, and the Aeolian harp, like a person, is not static or inert but can be harmonized and tuned, like a real harp or shawm.[97] In this sense Smart's image of the Aeolian harp directly counters the popular sentimental usage that Janet Todd records, where the individual is the passive instrument for divine inspiration.[98] This tuning or harmonizing, this improving of the spontaneous sounds into musical regularity, Smart connects to the liturgy, which, he asserts, should be musically performed: that is, in prayer, people turn themselves to receive the divine spirit, and through their self-speaking they also tune themselves as instruments to a sound that is pleasing to their ears and to God's. Prayer is not evidence of a hoped-for spiritual state like conversion or election; for Smart it is a workshop, a foundry. Through the medium of language in prayer, in blessing and addressing God and receiving the wind of the spirit, a person is worked like glass in the divine fire until she partakes of its nature, that is, experiencing *theosis*, that radical spiritual ideal which Smart would have encountered in Irenaeus and the church fathers.[99]

But it is the provocative line "For there is nothing but it may be played upon in delight" that points to the key work of liturgy and prayer for Smart, where agent and object are conflated and doubled. For Smart, in liturgy and worship people are both the instruments that God delights to play on, and they are the active, creative voices that through poetry and prayer play on everything in delight, as Smart does throughout the *Jubilate*. In this light, an enigmatic verse in fragment D makes sense: "Let Ready, house of Ready rejoice with Junco The Reed Sparrow. Blessed be the name of Christ Jesus Voice and Instrument" (D.175). Jesus, in Smart's Trinitarian theology both God and man, is himself both voice and instrument, a creature who makes harmonious sounds out of a combined agency, the *synergia* or cooperation of his will with God the Father's.[100] This sort of synergistic relation, where two genuinely different persons and wills communicate and cooperate outside a onesided, unidirectional subject-object relationship, epitomizes what Hawes has called the "intersubjectivity" of *Jubilate Agno*, outside the "violent reifications often involved" in identifications proprietarily understood. This is the hope of Smart's poem and perhaps of his prayer as well: a form of subjectivity that both speaks itself complete and plays as it is played upon in delight.[101] "For all the inventions of man, which are good, are the communications of Almighty God," he writes at one point; "For Action and Speaking are one according to God and the Ancients" (*JA*, B.401, 562). Knowledge and truth are not things operating like natural laws in a given universe for Smart, but they are the product of this profoundly interrelated mode of being, in which man's words and creations are what allow God to speak, and vice versa. This sort of speaking in prayer he views as itself real action, a making and doing, and the inventions of man are both himself and his linguistic creations. "For ignorance is a sin," he startlingly declares, in two different places, "because illumination is to be had by prayer" (B.421, 570). Prayer is illuminative not so much in asking for and receiving a body of knowledge, in the sort of book one might read at Pembroke College or buy from Newbery at the Bible and Sun, but, in the context of the poem, this growing so bold as to speak with God in language is itself creative and illuminative, its own *fiat lux*.

This illumination in prayer is to be had, crucially, by faith, as strong creative prayer depends on a radical, volitional belief, not in Shaftesbury's Deity, the creator of a static, predetermined "whole," but in an intersubjective God who himself in his essence speaks and is spoken with, both "Voice and Instrument." "For Faith as a grain of mustard seed is to believe, as I do, that an Eternity is such in respect to the power and magnitude of Almighty God / . . . For Eternity is like a grain of mustard as a growing body and improving spirit" (*JA*, B.368, 372). Smart's is not a faith reimagined as knowledge, but faith such as can only take place in the space of indeterminacy opened up by language. Faith for Smart is to imagine and speak the self as "growing body and improving spirit" for all eternity, precisely in relation to an infinite God, who nonetheless allows himself to be dealt with in this way—and who is in his being triune and relational.

The image of faith as the seed of spiritual growth is by turn at the root of Smart's love for flowers,[102] the subject of a long passage in fragment B:

> For the doubling of flowers is the improvement of the gardners talent.
> For the flowers are great blessings.
> For the Lord made a Nosegay in the meadow with his disciples and preached upon the lily.
> For the angels of God took it out of his hand and carried it to the Height.
> For a man cannot have publick spirit, who is void of private benevolence.
> For there is no Height in which there are not flowers.
> For flowers have great virtues for all the senses.
> For the flower glorifies God and the root parries the adversary.
> For the flowers have their angels even the words of God's Creation.
> For the warp and woof of flowers are worked by perpetual moving spirits.
> For flowers are good both for the living and the dead.
> For there is a language of flowers.
> For flowers are peculiarly the poetry of Christ.
> For flowers are medicinal.
> For flowers are musical in their ocular harmony.
> For the right names of flowers are yet in heaven. God make gard'ners better nomenclators.
> For the Poorman's nosegay is an introduction to a Prince.
> For it were better for the SERVICE, if only select psalms were read.
> For the Lamentations of Jeremiah, Songs from other scriptures, and parts of Esdras might be taken to supply the quantity.
> (B.492–512)

The first line of this section alludes to Christ's parable of the talents, in which servants are given by their master various amounts of money and left to their own devices as to how to work with and increase their talents, an image of the cultivation of the substance of the self that increases and flowers as a great blessing. Christ himself picked the disciples to form a sort of bouquet that was his creative and, again, synergistic offering to God. Such bouquet offerings are made here by both Jesus and poor men alike from living things, flowers which are both beautiful and medicinal, both healing what is ill and providing some beauty or blessing that was lacking before. Finally, flowers are the "particular poetry of Christ," which leads Smart to associate them with the rejuvenation of the liturgical services on which he was so keen; Smart suggests that psalms and sacred texts need to be selected, arranged, and translated—again, a new work, made with texts that are already there from the pen and tradition of others—as a liturgical bouquet of beauty and medicine for the times.

Though we cannot be sure Smart had in mind any one of the popular collections or "nosegays" of songs or advice of his day, it is certainly the relationship between sentiment and piety that he is rethinking here.[103] Confined to the madhouse for spontaneous prayer, and writing a massive liturgical poem as part of a daily ritual of combined fervent prayer and intellectual exercise, Smart imagines liturgical poetry and prayer as beauty and medicine—though not medicine against his own "madness" or religious mania. It is the line sandwiched in the middle here—"For a man cannot have publick spirit, who is void of private benevolence"—that sounds as a ringing indictment of the culture of politeness and sensibility, and the sort of general love for all mankind sought in Shaftesbury's moral philosophy and notebooks, a love that nonetheless stumbles on the rock of private affect: on its inability by sheer will to bring forth the flowers of personal, "private" love for the particular persons and creatures in one's life.

In the lines that follow, the illness to which this ritual of poetry and prayer is opposed, for Smart, is particularly that of the marketplace and the ways its sensibilities deform a person's agency and silence the voice and cultivation of the private benevolence that for Smart is the only source of real public spirit. The devil—like human commerce—is "against a man," Smart declares, because both devil and commerce mitigate against the exercise of the voice:

> For the voice is always for infinite good which [the Adversary] strives to impede.
> For the Devil can work coals into shapes to afflict the minds of those that will not pray.
> For the coffin and the cradle and the purse are all against a man.
> For the coffin is for the dead and death came by disobedience.
> For the cradle is for weakness and the child of man was originally strong from the womb.
> For the purse is for money and money is dead matter with the stamp of human vanity.

> For the adversary frequently sends these particular images out of the fire to those whom they concern. (B.274–80)

The coffin, the cradle, and the purse are emblems of that which Smart sees as silencing the voice, making one passive, vain, and dead: the silencing of conversation between persons and God, the illness of the body, the frailty of the mind—all that is opposed to life, to speaking oneself, to singing, to the creative awareness that plays with delight on all things in their particularity, and through this, partaking like glass in the fire of the divine nature of the creative word.

Crucially, these lines connect the "death [that] came by disobedience" to money, which "is dead matter with the stamp of human vanity." In the subsequent lines Smart explains that he has been tormented with the specters of illness and death and has overcome them, but it was the purse that had plagued him and would continue to haunt him after his release: "For the purse is for me because I have neither money nor human friends" (*JA*, B.283). The gulf between being the Lord's newswriter and being Newbery's is the calculating quest for money and human vanity because, Smart goes on to muse, money grubbing and profiteering are opposed to God's boundless goodness. In a passage in fragment B meditating on the planets, Smart reflects on the ways God subsumes all human idea of virtue, and on Venus, he writes: "For the Planet Venus is the WORD PRUDENCE or providence. / For GOD nevertheless is an extravagant BEING and generous unto loss. / For there is no profit in the generation of man and the loss of millions is not worth God's tear" (B.379–81). Like the God Bunyan glimpses in Psalm 44 at the end of *Grace Abounding*, the God to whom Smart sings his *Jubilate* is not prudent by the market's standard: there is no "profit" in his making of people, and no calculable "loss" to him in their demise. Yet this God loves so much—thus the reference to Venus—that he does much more than shed sentimental tears on behalf of lost humanity. In God's provident, extravagant generosity, there is no notion of equivalent, substitutable worth. For Smart, profit making and the pursuit of wealth and fame are linked with death; the self is not a matter of the production or possession of dead matter but of its cocreation in effusive, liturgical relation to God. Like Jeoffry, Smart "counteracts the Devil" not in work but in play, after hours, with his real "business": "For when his day's work is done his business more properly begins. / For he keeps the Lord's watch in the night against the adversary. / . . . For he counteracts the Devil, who is death, by brisking about the life" (B.717–18, 720).

Much has been written in recent years about Smart's ambivalence toward Newtonian science in the *Jubilate*, and Mounsey's biography speculates as to the reasons Smart would have had for resenting Newbery; but the scope of this poem's resistance and critique is broader than both and yet very precise.[104] Written against the backdrop of the discourse of spontaneous desires and the way they work to silence human activity into the exchange of "dead matter," *Jubilate Agno* is a radical working-through of faith under the empirical and economic pressures that Newton and Newbery represent, trying to recuperate human agency and goodness as an active communion with God. As in Puritan devotion, prayer is the site where these epistemological and economic anxieties come to a head. Where Watts and Henry coaxed anxious readers into a mandated spontaneity and where the *Directory* had tried to regulate it, where God was largely absent in *The Pilgrim's Progress* and Bunyan found it fearsome and hard to address Christ correctly, and where Shaftesbury found expostulating with God pointless and impossible to imagine, in the ritual of praying and writing *Jubilate Agno* Smart created an imaginative space where nature and the soul's work upon it meet. This space is made possible for Smart by the nature of language and the space it allows for "playing on everything in delight" before a Creator who is "an extravagant BEING and generous unto loss." For Smart things have "right names," but his playing on them and bouquet making in poetry is a construction of himself in cooperation with God—with his givenness but also as a product of the rituals he enacts. "For I have translated in the charity," Smart writes, "which makes things better and I shall be translated myself at the last" (*JA*, B.11). The room that language affords for interpretation and translation is, in *Jubilate Agno*, the room for faith and for an improvement very different from that sold at the Bible and Sun: for prayer, praise, and virtue which, in the end for Smart, is always gratitude and charity, and "makes things better."[105]

For Smart, the world is praying all the time: speaking to its Creator, speaking of creation, voluminously speaking its own creation as loving, articulate intelligence, in something like the epic diversity to which *Jubilate Agno* is committed, in Keymer's words, as the "nearest possible approach to valid description of the created world."[106] But at the Sign of the Bible and Sun, this is a madness, an unabridged enthusiasm for which there is no market, not compared with that for *The Gentleman Tradesman's and Traveller's Pocket Library* or *A Sixpennyworth of Wit*. It is no doubt Smart's most pathetic folly that after his release from Potter's asylum he expected to be God's "reviver of adoration amongst Englishmen" by publishing his translations of the Psalms, his *Hymns and Spiritual Songs*, and *A Song to David* (his "translation" of *Jubilate Agno*) in the marketplace he knew so well.[107] By that time, Smart was widely regarded as mad, a diagnosis that tainted all the critics' reviews. Their sneers drove Smart to recrimination and despair, caught as he was between writing as his only livelihood and his desire to maintain his religious and intellectual integrity. When his Psalms and *Hymns* were quickly forgotten after their publication in 1765, in financial desperation he redoubled his efforts at a verse translation of Horace that, unlike his prose translation for Newbery, would do justice to his well-loved author. Extravagant and "generous unto loss" like the God of *Jubilate Agno* and his coworker Goldsmith, Smart was never able to live within the means his writings supplied him. Though Newbery had seemed willing to help him on his release, this aid ceased, and when Newbery died in 1767, his will made no provision for his son-in-law and specifically protected Anna Maria's inheritance from Smart's interest.[108] Smart spent his final years in frantic attempts to augment his income, begging a guinea here and there from a friend, and was repeatedly arrested for debt. When he was arrested a sixth time, on 20 April 1770, not even his remaining friends Thomas Carnan and Charles Burney were willing to pay his bail, and Smart died in the King's Bench Prison the following year.[109]

Goldsmith too had been arrested for debt and threatened with imprisonment several times before; and when he died less than three years after Smart, he was certainly further in debt, but to men who were willing to bank on the marketability of the more popular writer's reputation and continual stream of proposed histories and plays. This willingness of booksellers to advance and readvance money to Goldsmith is emblematic of the difference between the religious resistance to the market-driven culture of sensibility that he offered in *The Vicar of Wakefield* and that which Smart came to as a result of his illness, recovery, and incarceration. In this way Smart and Goldsmith, working for Newbery in the same literary market, illuminate each other perfectly. At just the time that Smart was beginning to write *Jubilate Agno* in Potter's asylum, Goldsmith was writing in his seat as Newbery's chief writer under the same conditions that Smart had worked, better perhaps than those at Griffiths', but at a breakneck pace nonetheless, with the sober reminder of Smart's children living literally next door to him at Canonbury to call to mind the consequences of not being able to produce or of being unacceptable to polite society through religious behavior deemed unusual.

It seems more than coincidence that sitting in Newbery's offices, Goldsmith dreams up the friendly Vicar, with his love for *private* prayer—so private, in fact, that it is never shown to the reader—and for domestic tranquility, who is unfazed by confinement, in debtor's prison, even there preaching and setting the economic injustices of the world aright. Writing this novel on his own time, as it were, grappling with the same societal problems as Smart and inclined toward similar solutions, Goldsmith created the Vicar as an embodiment of the nervous if noble fantasy that the tastes of the market he wrote for and his own religious ideals (like those of his family and readers) were compatible. The experience of his friend certainly provided incentive for fearing they were not. Both men indicted "the coffin and the cradle and the purse," and both arrived at religious faith and the rituality of prayer and daily life as potent means for shaping a subjectivity that resists the death-in-life of greed and consumption. But Goldsmith made his Vicar friendly to the "harmless delusions" of polite society in a way Smart himself was not, taking the edge off religious resistance to consumer values by sentimentalizing it in a way that was apparently impossible with Smart's praying aloud in St. James Park and asking others to join him. Smart's spontaneous prayer and incarceration led him to a sort of breakout from religion limited to the enthusiasms of free prayer or of the market, to imagining ritual poetry and liturgical prayer as a way for shaping and cocreating himself. Goldsmith's investment in sentiment and sensibility, that ideology of spontaneity in its most market-friendly incarnation, ultimately erased the rituals of daily life that his book put forth as a remedy to sensibility's shortcomings, and legitimated the rituals of consumption and novel reading that engender the delusions about self, money, and sex that the novel hints are anything but harmless.

Setting *The Vicar of Wakefield* and *Jubilate Agno* in light of each other and in their shared context, we see how in the mid-eighteenth century religion remains a site for articulating the discord between the desire for goodness and the mechanisms of commercial society. But we also see that the religion that Goldsmith proposes as a supplement to the culture of sensibility and secular philosophy is already an extremely secularized religion, whose worth is understood in terms of imparting sensibility, the faculty of moral perception empirically conceived, and which appears as the "special effect" or aura of transcendence in the commodity form of the novel itself. In his work on *The Vicar of Wakefield*, John Bender has made use of Raymond Williams's notion of art as the medium of cultural emergence.[110] What emerges in *The Vicar of Wakefield* and other sentimental novels is a peculiarly secularized form of religion that understands itself as resisting a cold, material world whose values it has already internalized. Similarly, Michael McKeon has written that the simple abstraction of the novel conceals the greater cultural significance of the conditions of the novel's possibility.[111] To my mind, the cultural significance of the religion we see in *The Vicar of Wakefield* is that it has completely imagined itself in the terms of sensibility and the ideology of spontaneity: of imparting "true sensibility." What haunts *The Vicar of Wakefield* is the specter of Christopher Smart, a poet praised by Pope and as "regular in his wits" as any man, dropping to his knees in the streets of London, blessing God with full-throated fervor and not allying himself with any commercially sanctioned sensibility.

If the great authorial portraits of Bunyan or Shaftesbury can be taken to represent the modern secularized subject's fantasy of narrative or rational wholeness, Smart was the icon of its fragmentation, its religious constructedness, and the Vicar an attempt to exorcise his ghost. We can speak of several generations of writers—Boswell, Johnson, Piozzi, Frances Burney, Robert Browning—as haunted by him as well, recounting his questionable incarceration in tones that betray a sense of collective guilt. Goldsmith himself came closer to being an icon of authorial celebrity in his day, in part accounting for the willingness of booksellers to pay him advances on a song. But at two and one-half centuries' remove, it is Newbery himself whose image remains with us most vividly, in the Newbery Award for children's literature: a Bunyanesque "golden seal" of desired moral value and aesthetic appeal that takes the form of a medal or coin affixed to a storybook's cover, a guarantee of market success and a fitting testimony to the way these desires still operate in reading markets today. The desires and conundrums that circulated at the Sign of the Bible and Sun—spontaneity, resistance to market values and delusions about the self, liturgical prayer, self-creation, and the problems of secularism and of institutional religion—intertwine and intersect, as wel shall see in the next chapter, even more directly in the works of William Wordsworth, the trajectory of his poetry across a long writing career, and his reception history.

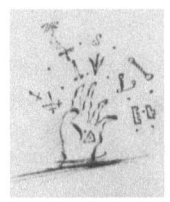

CHAPTER 5

Wordsworth's "Spontaneous Overflow" and the "High Service Within"
From *Lyrical Ballads* to *Ecclesiastical Sonnets*

> And hark! how blithe the throstle sings!
> And he is no mean preacher;
> Come forth into the light of things
> Let Nature be your teacher.
>
> She has a world of ready wealth,
> Our minds and hearts to bless—
> Spontaneous wisdom breathed by health,
> Truth breathed by chearfulness.
>
> One impulse from a vernal wood
> May teach you more of man;
> Of moral evil and of good,
> Than all the sages can.
>
> —William Wordsworth, "The Tables Turned" (1798)[1]

Where Smart's spontaneous outbursts of prayer lurk at the margins of literary history, *Lyrical Ballads* has long provided students of English literature with the quintessential picture of poetic inspiration, and Wordsworth's 1800 "Preface" to *Lyrical Ballads* famously locates authentic feeling and a respectable spontaneity at the heart of true poetry:

> I have said that Poetry is the spontaneous overflow of powerful feelings: it takes its origin from emotion recollected in tranquility: the emotion is contemplated till by a species of reaction the tranquility

gradually disappears, and an emotion, similar to that which was before the subject of contemplation, is gradually produced, and does itself actually exist in the mind. In this mood successful composition generally begins, and in a mood similar to this it is carried on.[2]

In *The Mirror and the Lamp*, M. H. Abrams pointed out that "overflow" bespeaks an expressionistic aesthetic, and Abrams like generations of readers took "spontaneous" to mean the natural as opposed to the artificial, conventional, or contrived.[3] This understanding certainly echoes in the poetic theory of the younger Romantics who admired Wordsworth's early work so intensely. "The mind in creation is as a fading coal," Shelley would write in *Defence of Poetry*, "which some invisible influence, like an inconstant wind, awakens to transitory brightness." "If Poetry comes not as naturally as the Leaves to a tree," Keats proclaimed, "it had better not come at all."[4]

The weight of spontaneity for Wordsworth, though, before it was aesthetic or artistic, was moral. The lines taken as the epigraph for this chapter show how this trust in spontaneous emotional response sprung from a lineage of English writers across the eighteenth century and their Newtonian hope of perfecting the science of moral philosophy, grounded not in the arid philosophizing satirized in "Expostulation and Reply," but in the felt, observable impulses of nature. Using logic familiar from seventeenth-century enthusiasm, *Lyrical Ballads'* spontaneous ideal invoked free prayer as its model, approving a mode of poetic enthusiasm and echoing the critique of ritual and forms as stultifying. In the words of "Lines Written at a Small Distance from My House":

> No joyless forms shall regulate
> Our living Calendar:
> We from to-day, my friend, will date
> The opening of the year.
> . . . .
> And from the blessed power that rolls
> About, below, above;
> We'll frame the measure of our souls,
> They shall be tuned to love. (*LB*, 17–20, 33–36)

Twenty years later, though, Wordsworth would directly criticize the free-prayer movement in *Ecclesiastical Sketches* (1822, later *Ecclesiastical Sonnets*). "Their forms are broken staves," he wrote of the Marian exiles whose Puritanism eviscerated the English ritual year; "their passions steeds / That master them."[5] In 1842 Wordsworth published a note to "Musings Near Aquapendente, April, 1837" that praised the Oxford Movement, making explicit an appreciation for liturgy that appeared in his poetry as early as *The White Doe of Rylstone*, written in 1807–1808 and published in 1815.⁶ And yet, even in friendship with Frederick William Faber and acquaintance with John Keble and John Henry Newman, Wordsworth remained somewhat aloof from the Tractarians who continually courted his public support. And he almost certainly came to view his reserve toward the high churchmen as fortunate. Once Newman and Faber converted to Roman Catholicism in 1844, Henry Crabb Robinson records how an incensed Wordsworth vowed to include a note in future editions "expressing his regret that he had ever uttered a word favourable to Puseyism."⁷

The transition from the "spontaneous overflow" of *Lyrical Ballads* to the celebration of the church year in *Ecclesiastical Sonnets*—the seeming about-face from invoking free prayer to taking up liturgy and church building as images for poetic composition—could easily be assimilated to a host of Wordsworth studies that divide his corpus into early and late works and which rehearse the critical commonplace of Wordsworth's "late orthodoxy" as a regrettable treason against his youthful radical idealism.⁸ In arguing for the vital connection between the "spontaneous overflow" of emotion and Wordsworth's later concern with ritual, this chapter takes on a double challenge, both that of unraveling this seemingly paradoxical reversal and that of countering the mistaken notion of dramatic discontinuity between the early and late Wordsworths.⁹ Beginning with *Lyrical Ballads*, its prefaces and early reviews, in this chapter I show how in the early poetry and its reception we see Wordsworth's empirical approach to moral concerns, alongside a growing awareness of the lack of moral certainty provided by spontaneous sentiment. In *Lyrical Ballads* and in the poem he began shortly after its appearance, *The Prelude*, Wordsworth shows an increasing conviction that an ideology of spontaneous moral sentiment, rationality, and empiricism tends to foster one of two outcomes: either the paralysis and self-indulgence that he like other critics of sentimentality shunned, or the libidinal violence of rationalism that, as we have seen, colors the works of Shaftesbury, Hume, and Sade and that, for Wordsworth, was epitomized in the Terror and the Napoleonic wars. In response to the twin dangers of paralysis or egocentric violence, in "Tintern Abbey" and *The Prelude* of 1805 we see Wordsworth already exploring a positive role for ritual in the agency that is exercised in shaping the self and its spontaneous responses to the world.

Turning from this reading of *Lyrical Ballads* to *Ecclesiastical Sonnets*, in the latter part of this chapter I demonstrate how a concern for practices that shape one's approach and responses to the world leads Wordsworth, not unlike Smart, to a qualified recuperation of ritual as a site for a circumscribed but all-important individual agency: for a particular, creative relationship with memory, the past, and community, and a gentle shaping of a self from which something besides passive melancholy or violent greed can emerge. Ritual and construction become major categories of Wordsworth's middle and later thought, I argue, because and not in spite of the moral trajectory inaugurated in the *Lyrical Ballads*. The all-important connection for Wordsworth between ritual and the need to embrace it in freedom accounts for his leeriness of the high churchmen who turned ritual into a movement and system, and reveals the late Wordsworth as radically concerned both for individual liberty and vital though circumscribed agency, as in his younger years.

This chapter therefore situates Wordsworth's famous "spontaneous overflow of powerful feelings . . . recollected in tranquility" not in the purely political context that has come to dominate Wordsworth studies—that of the French Revolution and its aftermath—but primarily and more richly in this study's account of the history of sentiment and the Shaftesburian moral sense to which it, like so many forms of literary sensibility, bears a familial resemblance. This history of moral sentiment does not, as some scholarship seems to suggest, stand apart or provide an escape from political and material contexts, but is itself, as Wordsworth's poetry insists, part of the cultural and societal context in which the French Revolution took place. The ideology of spontaneity and sentiment was a living part of the culture and psychology in which its actors and critics weighed their responses, part of a scientifically conceived, print-commodity-fed will for perfection that, as Marie-Hélène Huet has pointed out, was itself part of the fabric of revolutionary rhetoric and ideals.[10] It was also secularizing, and in going through and beyond spontaneity's quest for certainty, Wordsworth struggled to recover a religiousness that was not secularized into a system of moral knowledge and insisted more and more on a structure of uncertainty, faith, and freedom as part of the inherent dignity and religiousness of human nature. This examination of the role of uncertainty, faith, and ritual in the Wordsworth corpus therefore revises, at least in Wordsworth's case, the narrative of Romantic secularism echoed in various forms since Abram's *Natural Supernaturalism*. By the chapter's end, it also prompts a reflection on how the critically fashionable picture of Wordsworth as evading history and political responsibility is produced only by evading his most insistently historical and religious poems, the *Ecclesiastical Sonnets*, and their place in the larger arc of his thought.

"Let Him Sound the Key-note"—*Lyrical Ballads* and the Quest for Moral Certainty

Wordsworth's famous definition of poetry from the 1800 "Preface" to *Lyrical Ballads* has so long been quoted as the manifesto of English

Romanticism that it is hard to hear either its sonority with moral philosophy at the end of the eighteenth century or the way it was perceived by its original readers as participating in that conversation. The brief "Advertisement" that preceded the first edition of *Lyrical Ballads* in 1798 was itself couched in empirical language, simultaneously aesthetic but also moral: "The majority of the following poems are to be considered as experiments," Wordsworth claimed, and "were written chiefly with a view to ascertain how far the language of conversation in the middle and lower classes of society is adapted to the purposes of poetic pleasure."[11] The key question that introduced readers to *Lyrical Ballads* was whether ordinary language could meet poetic, aesthetic ends, ends that were widely held to be synonymous with moral, improving ends.[12] The pair of poems "Expostulation and Reply" and "The Tables Turned" underscored the connection between spontaneous, senselike knowledge of things and morality, which was asserted through the volume as a whole, and even spoke directly to the philosophical tradition that flowed from Shaftesbury, Hutcheson, and their followers. In "Expostulation and Reply," where the philosopher Matthew urges William to pay attention to books and academic discussion, the younger man chides the philosopher for dissociation from the body, his most objective, direct receptor of the world, and its natural, passive responses: "Our bodies feel, where'er they be, / Against or with our will" (*LB*, 19–20). In "The Tables Turned," the younger man invites his older friend to quit his books, "Or surely you'll grow double" (*LB*, 4)—a reference not just to hunching over a book and to the sort of philosophical self-scrutiny that counseled as Shaftesbury did to "*Divide Your-self*, or *Be* TWO," but to the maddening self-division Wordsworth describes in *The Prelude*.[13] The poem makes a sharp distinction between an art and science that "murder[s] to dissect" and a more visceral, though still empirical perception of the material world that would teach more of "moral evil and of good, / Than all the sages can" (*LB*, 28, 23–24). In the same vein, Wordsworth's long addition in the 1802 "Preface" to *Lyrical Ballads* put an empirically, experientially based morality at center stage. "The pleasure which I hope to give by the Poems I now present to the Reader . . . is in itself of the highest importance to our taste and moral feelings," it claimed, and our moral feelings, influencing and influenced by our judgments of poetry, will in this dialogue "be corrected and purified." "Upon the accuracy with which similitude in dissimilitude, and dissimilitude in similitude are perceived," he averred, "depend our taste and our moral feelings" ("Preface," 165, 173).

Despite the fact that some modern critics have gone so far as to dismiss any discernible connection between the prefaces and the *Lyrical Ballads* themselves, it was this language of experiment and observation in search of poetic, moral knowledge to which virtually every reviewer of *Lyrical Ballads* responded in one way or another—and with the "strangeness and aukwardness" Wordsworth predicted.[14] Review after review weighed in as to whether he had "accomplished his purpose" or whether his philosophical "experiment" gave the poems an "artificial and antipoetical" property.[15] Even pieces that complained that philosophy was not the domain of poetry accepted the empirical model of trying to establish aesthetic and moral value. Robert Southey, for instance, denounced the "experiments" as failures because they treated humble, lower class characters who made inherently "uninteresting subjects."[16] John Stoddart's review of the second edition of *Lyrical Ballads* for *The British Critic* seems best to capture the interest but uncomfortable uncertainty the volume provoked for many readers. He credited the poet with a "purity of expression" that in individual poems was "generally interesting" and achieved the purpose of arousing "true feeling," but complained that "whether the particular purpose is, in every case, *worthy* of a Poet, will perhaps admit of some doubt." The most notable effect of the poems, Stoddart opined, consisted in "a gentle agitation of contending emotions." Pleasure came from this, but the contradictory emotions remained, leaving aesthetic and moral conclusions elusive.[17]

The seemingly uncertain moral trajectory of the *Lyrical Ballads* remained a problem for reviewers across the next three decades, even as Wordsworth's public esteem rose. With the publication of *The Excursion* in 1814, two trends in readers' responses emerged. Less favorable reviewers, chief among them Francis Jeffrey at *The Edinburgh Review*, but also milder voices like John Herman Merivale at *The Monthly Review* and the unnamed writer for *The Monthly Magazine*, ridiculed the "mysticism" by which the poet "vainly endeavor[ed] to combine certain points of faith with human reason."[18] More favorable readers read the poem as holding out hope for the moral knowledge *Lyrical Ballads* seemed to promise but to most minds had not delivered. Looking for assurances of Wordsworth's moral and religious orthodoxy, reviewers in 1815 praised *The Excursion* for its piety, and then, to varying degrees, attempted to read that faith back onto *Lyrical Ballads* and *Poems in Two Volumes*. *The Eclectic Review* excused what the reviewer deemed the extreme sensuality of the early poems in terms of the profound devotion which the poet now seemed to be revealing.[19] Even in reviewing *The Excursion*, the writer for *The British Critic* felt plagued by the lingering moral uncertainty of *Lyrical Ballads* and urged the poet to greater clarity. Calling Wordsworth's poetry "the shadow of his philosophy," he warned that "there are few who have music enough in their souls to unravel for themselves his abstruser harmonies: only let him sound the key-note, and the apparent confusion will vanish: . . . till then they can delight and improve those only, who have fancy . . . and leisure enough to work out with him the speculations and feelings consequent thereupon."[20]

Throughout the 1810s and 1820s, favorable reviews tried, with noticeable effort and anxiousness, to hear Wordsworth's "key-note" and to co-opt his poems for straightforward religious orthodoxy, and in so doing they repeatedly figured Wordsworth's relation to the earlier poetry in terms of reformation and repentance.[21] At least a few readers felt justified in extrapolating from the repentance of the main characters in *Peter Bell* and *The Waggoner*, both published in 1819, the repentance of the poet himself.[22] The anonymous writer for *Blackwood's Edinburgh Magazine* felt emboldened by *Peter Bell* to venture a moral theory of Wordsworth's development as a poet. Despairing of public acclaim due to the poor reception of his earlier works, Wordsworth's genius (so the conjecture ran) led him to a newly serious consideration of moral questions, and the result was that *Peter Bell*'s "mollifi[cation] into tenderness and repentance" made for a poem technically equal and morally superior to anything in *Lyrical Ballads*.[23] In the wake of *The River Duddon* in 1820, *The Monthly Review* proudly claimed credit for its role in reforming Wordsworth to a "sincere and benevolent piety," and *Blackwood*'s praised the orthodoxy of the sequence, counting Wordsworth fortunate to have "lived to throw into shade the errors" of his earlier pieces.[24] *Ecclesiastical Sketches* and *Memorials of a Tour* seemed to many the capstone of Wordsworth's poetic arch reaching upward toward religious and moral orthodoxy. John Wilson would claim Wordsworth "profoundly versed in the knowledge of all sentiments, feelings, and passions, that ever dignified, adorned, or purified man's heart." "Indeed, his poetry is to him religion; and we venture to say, that it has been felt to be so by thousands," and could surely be trusted to impart solid moral truths of human nature to the nation's youth.[25] As late as 1842, *The Eclectic Review* praised Wordsworth as an established genius but still called on him to repent of his former "excess" and "raptures . . . altogether inexplicable" in *Lyrical Ballads*, which the writer called a "juvenile and most injudicious production," the crime of which was aggravated by his refusal to quit reprinting them and to remove them from his corpus altogether.[26]

In a very real way, though, Wordsworth was *not* repenting of the earlier poems, but literally publishing them anew, and the trajectory toward orthodox moral certainty was based in some cases in accidents of publication history. Published in 1819, *Peter Bell* for instance was composed in 1798 and if anything was of the same cloth as *Lyrical Ballads*, not its renunciation. It was also clearly the effect of readers' desires to elide the moral *uncertainty* the poems continued to present. Yu Liu has characterized the poems of *Lyrical Ballads* as "the repeated representations of morally ambiguous situations." They represent an exploration of moral uncertainty, Liu suggests, that grows not from a "self-protective desire to escape from politics to poetics" or an ideological reversal of his earlier idealism, but from an analogical working-through of the central question raised for Wordsworth by the demise of the French Revolution and explored in his previous works and especially in *The Borderers*, that of the paradoxical origination of "sin and crime" in the effort to do good. In Liu's reading, this reevaluation allowed Wordsworth to understand and accept the failure of the French Revolution, while retaining his social and political commitments to liberty and equality.[27]

The nagging moral uncertainty that Liu identifies in *Lyrical Ballads* and that disturbed readers in the decades after its publication results also, I argue, from Wordsworth's critique of sentimentality and his engagement with the long moral tradition that sought to ground morality in spontaneous emotional responses. In *Lyrical Ballads*, Wordsworth's interrogation of natural feelings led him to see moral agency and responsibility as centrally concerned with *shaping* those spontaneous responses. The volume is marked by a concern for the status of moral beliefs *as beliefs*, rather than as passive responses to natural stimuli, and this concern raised the question of how one maintains moral beliefs against despair, without resorting to crime or violence to bolster them. In turn it also led to an emphasis on repetition and ritual that, with liberty and equality, would link *Lyrical Ballads* to the later poems, including *Ecclesiastical Sonnets*.

Spontaneity, Repetition, and the Cultivation of Love

Within the empirical-moral framework referenced in the prefaces and "Expostulation and Reply," *Lyrical Ballads* already attempted something of a corrective to the particular ills of sentimentality that were rooted in this framework as well. "Lines left upon a Seat in a Yew-tree" drew a picture reminiscent of *The Man of Feeling*, of one who "Fixing his downward eye . . . many an hour / A morbid pleasure nourished, tracing here / An emblem of his own unfruitful life" (*LB*, 27–29), implying that the chief sin of sentimentality lay in pride and that its looking inward for all moral confirmation (as outward for fame and approval) stemmed in fact from selfish arrogance. The final lines of the poem sought to mediate between inner and outer indications of moral truth in a way responsive to both, coaching the reader to keep his feelings unsullied by solipsism and self-pity. The morbidly self-absorbed man of feeling is thus set forth as a warning against contempt of others and an admonition that "true knowledge leads to love," that "true dignity" resides in the tension generated by simultaneously revering and suspecting one's self and one's desires (*LB*, 56–60).

Wordsworth's criticism of sentimentality, not unlike Goldsmith's in *The Vicar of Wakefield*, shares a sentimental acceptance of the value of spontaneous emotional responses while criticizing the vitiation of those responses by consumer culture. In the prefaces to *Lyrical Ballads*, Wordsworth positions his poetry against the dulling forces of the capitalist market, both the monotonous work of urban occupations and the frantic novels he more famously groused about. The poet's task, he asserted, is to cultivate in readers a subtle sensitivity to things besides the "gross and violent stimulants" that these forms of labor and reading provide ("Preface," 159). Wordsworth's quest for a permanently appealing poetry, perhaps too easily attributed to what Keats diagnosed as the egotistical sublime, is defended in the "Preface" as a moral stance against a consumer market of poetry enjoyed primarily in terms of novelty. "If the views with which [these poems] were composed, were indeed realized," Wordsworth claimed, "a class of Poetry would be produced, well adapted to interest mankind permanently, and not unimportant in the multiplicity and in the quality of its moral relations" (154). This critique of market-deformed literary and moral tastes opens up the "Preface" to the larger difficulty that takes shape in *Lyrical Ballads* and that animates much of the later poetry, that of determining "how far this taste is healthy or depraved"—that is, which responses are natural and spontaneous, and which have been deformed by the market (154).

This critique leads Wordsworth to the sort of paradoxical ritual of spontaneity we see in Edmund Burke's "Preface" to the second edition of *A Philosophical Enquiry into the Origin of Our Ideas of the Sublime and Beautiful*, in which Burke defends his aesthetics in terms of natural responses and yet rebuffs his critics by saying that "wrong Taste" is owing to a lack of "cultivat[ion of] that species of knowledge which makes the object of Taste by degrees and habitually attain not only a soundness, but a readiness of judgment."[28] By a similar course Wordsworth calls "an *accurate* taste in Poetry" an "*acquired* talent" only a few lines after he has appealed to readers to judge his poetry by their own genuine feelings and not the opinion of others ("Preface," 177). It is in fact his awareness of the eerily agentless pressure that the market and its forms of labor and consumption exert on individual experience that ultimately vitiates the notion of the spontaneous for Wordsworth and provides the impetus for him to explore the nature of human agency somewhere between passive naturalness and transparent, rational autonomy. In terms of the history of sentiment in eighteenth-century Britain and the moral philosophy everywhere referenced in his work, it is in this concern for human agency amidst the naturalization of feelings and morality that Wordsworth's poetry is truly if quietly radical. Faced with the dilemma of having to determine true goodness in a world where the status of taste as "healthy or depraved" is perpetually in question, Wordsworth proposes that the key lies in considering "in what manner language and the human mind act and react *on each other*," traced out in "the revolutions not of literature alone but likewise of society itself" (154–55, emphasis added)—that is, in how both the mind and its environment operate with paradoxically natural yet free, self-propelling, and interactive agencies.

Because of the difficulty of articulating a concept of partly natural, partly shaped responses, a conflicted rhetoric of agency is the most notable feature of "Lines Written in Early Spring" and its exploration of naturalness, passivity, and action. The opening lines describe the experience of "hear[ing] a thousand blended notes" in a grove, and the second stanza commences by ascribing agency to Nature in this experience: "To her fair works did nature link / The human soul that through me ran; / And much it griev'd my heart to think / What man has made of man" (*LB*, 5–8). The poem centers around the notion that it is *reasonable* to lament "what man has made of man," and, consonant with an empirical search for goodness and moral value, it begins with a fairly objective account of "hearing" natural sounds and the claim that it is Nature's agency linking his soul to her works and prompting these responses. The subsequent stanzas, however, complicate that sense of agency with the speaker's response to his responses, as it were, his questioning of their inevitability:

> Through primrose-tufts, in that sweet bower,
> The periwinkle trail'd its wreathes;
> And 'tis my faith that every flower
> Enjoys the air it breathes.
>
> The birds around me hopp'd and play'd:
> Their thoughts I cannot measure,
> But the least motion which they made,
> It seem'd a thrill of pleasure.
>
> The budding twigs spread out their fan,
> To catch the breezy air;
> And I must think, do all I can,
> That there was pleasure there.
>
> If I these thoughts may not prevent,
> If such of my creed the plan,
> Have I not reason to lament
> What man has made of man? (*LB*, 9–24)

Moving from the ostensibly passive experience of hearing, the third and fourth stanzas point to more active and subjective processes: the speaker's "faith" that every flower enjoys the air it breathes changes in the next stanza to the motions of the birds "seem[ing]" a thrill of pleasure. Belief shapes experience, such that in the next stanza the speaker's belief takes on a propositional urgency; he feels he *must* think, regardless of other indications, that "there was pleasure there." The final stanza realizes with deceptive simplicity the moral complexity of the poem. The line "If I these thoughts may not prevent" references the thoughts of the preceding stanza ("I must think") that have taken shape in response to "seem[ing]" experiences, which were themselves shaped by conjecture and belief after sensation. It is only by the poem's end that these thoughts are unpreventable, that the creed's plan is evident, and that the speaker has "reason" to lament what man has made of man. In the context of the larger quest to articulate a natural morality based in spontaneous response, "Lines Written in Early Spring" realizes the progress from sensation and sentiment to the delicate, responsive agency involved in forming beliefs, and eventually to the production of cultivated sensations and even of reason and knowledge itself. The tenor of much recent criticism would favor reading the nature imagery of this poem as a "validating" idea that covertly asserts the "*rightful* existence" of the speaker's beliefs, thus obscuring his own role in their construction.[29] But the revelation of this poem is much more subtle and profound. A particular sort of moral agency emerges in the poem, in the profound recognition that moral feelings and judgments emerge from *beliefs* that take shape dialectically with early experiences and emotions prior to the thoughts, ideologies, formal creeds, and subsequent perceptions they produce.

Wordsworth's effort to balance both concerns—to explore and account for human agency, while engaging with the long tradition of understanding morality in terms of natural laws and spontaneous, instinctive responses—is one of the most potent forces emerging in *Lyrical Ballads* and shaping subsequent poems. The volume's investment in the "incidents of common life" stems from an empirical sort of data collection regarding affective experiences, tracing in them the "primary laws of our nature" as they are shown by "the manner in which we associate ideas in a state of excitement," spontaneously and without premeditation ("Preface," 156)—and especially in the emotive responses of people removed from the deforming forces of consumer culture. Such people, Wordsworth argues in the "Preface," have continual experience with the objects on which language is based, and "being less under the action of social vanity" they convey feelings simply and directly: "Accordingly such a language arising out of repeated experience and regular feelings is a more permanent and a far more philosophical language" than elevated poetic diction which separates us from our usual sympathies ("Preface," 156–57). In other words, key to Wordsworth is the idea that this common language is both free from corrupting influences and is daily *cultivated* in its natural state; his concern is both natural feeling and the shaping of feeling.

In fact, Wordsworth first sounds the theme of the "spontaneous overflow" of emotion in the context of claiming to have cultivated his thoughts and sensibility, and the concept of spontaneous overflow seems much less spontaneous in the longer passage's emphasis on ways that "habits" and "repetition" both "modi[fy] and direct" influxes of feeling:[30]

> I believe that my habits of meditation have so formed my feelings, as that my descriptions of such objects as strongly excite those feelings, will be found to carry along with them a *purpose*. If in this opinion I am mistaken I can have little right to the name of a Poet. For all good poetry is the spontaneous overflow of powerful feelings; but though this be true, Poems to which any value can be attached, were never produced on any variety of subjects but by a man who being possessed of more than usual organic sensibility had also thought long and deeply. For our continued influxes of feeling are modified and directed by our thoughts, which are indeed the representatives of all our past feelings; and as by contemplating the relation of these general representatives to each other, we discover what is really important to men, so by the repetition and continuance of this act feelings connected with important subjects will be nourished, till at length, if we be originally possessed of much organic sensibility such habits of mind will be produced that by obeying blindly and mechanically the impulses of those habits we shall describe objects and utter sentiments of such a nature and in such connection with each other, that the understanding of the being to whom we address ourselves, if he be in a healthful state of association, must necessarily be in some degree enlightened, his taste exalted, and his affections ameliorated. ("Preface," 157–58)

While tethered to a quasi-scientific ideal of mechanical impulse, this passage nevertheless tugs toward a claim to agency, to having actively formed his feelings so as to claim for them moral weight. Wordsworth legitimates his spontaneous responses in the familiar terms of natural sensibility at the same time that he proclaims their cultivation and construction. In perhaps the most potent phrase generated in the "Preface," Wordsworth comes to affirm that poetic pleasure "is a task light and easy to him who looks at the world in the spirit of love" (167). Such a spirit allows the world and others to speak themselves, as opposed to the unilateral agency of "murder[ing] to dissect." It is in shaping and cultivating this initial spirit of approaching the world that one's agency primarily lies, for as "Lines Written in Early Spring" illustrates, this way of looking contains in it a germ or plan that generates perceptions, creeds, knowledges, and even the very notion of that which constitutes reason.

Alongside the concern with spontaneity, one of the deep themes and central concerns of *Lyrical Ballads* is thus the question of how—in the face of demanding influences like the commercial ones already noted—individuals cultivate and maintain a particular spirit of approaching the world. Relevant to this question was the lengthy note to "The Thorn" that accompanied the *Lyrical Ballads* of 1800–1805, which included a paragraph on repetition that Wordsworth claimed spoke to other poems in the volume as well. Repetition of words, he wrote, does not necessarily constitute meaningless tautology. Indeed, the perpetual variation of words or, by implication, an endless stream of seemingly novel poems, may by their very novelty constitute the greatest "tautology." On the contrary, Wordsworth insisted, literal "repetition and apparent tautology are frequently beauties of the highest kind."[31] They may mark a "consciousness of the inadequateness of our own powers, or the deficiencies of language," but words may also be repeated "from a spirit of fondness, exultation, and gratitude" in which "the mind luxuriates in the repetition of words which appear successfully to communicate its feelings" as in passages from the Bible and various national poetries.[32] The repetition of words in poetry is owing to multiple agencies—both agency naturalized as a preexistent "craving in the mind" and that of a more willful mind "luxuriating" in the successful communication of its feelings to others—and subsequently becomes an image for how one poetically, almost liturgically, cultivates looking at the world in a particular way. "Lines Written in Early Spring" underscores the point that thinking and feeling are in themselves profoundly tautological, that is, that experience and knowledge are themselves products of repeated beliefs and practices.

Connecting repetition as it does to self-shaping agency, the note to "The Thorn" speaks most to the final poem in the collection, "Lines Written a Few Miles above Tintern Abbey." As much recent criticism has emphasized, the poem is dated one day short of the ninth anniversary of the fall of the Bastille.[33] Wordsworth's note dictated late in life to Isabella Fenwick is generally read as affirming the arch-romantic view of the poem's having been born as it were full formed from the poet's experience and imagination, and evidence has been produced pointing to at least some revision and the use of books.[34] Yet Wordsworth's note actually highlights how the poem was composed over several days on a journey between Tintern and Bristol, and written down upon arrival, bespeaking a lengthy composition process, and the poem likewise relates a complex view of repetition and agency. The focus on repetition that pervades the poem is inaugurated in the first of the poem's five sections, narrating Wordsworth's return to the Wye valley after what Kenneth Johnston calls the "five missing years" (1793–1798) of national upheaval and personal change; four times the sensations of the visit are described with "again," marking both nature's repetitions and the speaker's conscious relationship to the past.

The second section sets out the "belief" upon which the poem hinges in the middle section: that from Nature come restorative pleasures "As may have had no trivial influence / On that best portion of a good man's life; / His little, nameless, unremembered acts / Of kindness and of love," as well as heightened states of consciousness "In which the affections gently lead us on" and "We see into the life of things" (*LB*, 33–36, 43, 49). To the autosuggestion that this may be "but a vain belief," the speaker replies only by stating the fact of his repetition of an act, the agency and naturalness of which are left unclear: "How oft, in spirit, have I turned to thee / O sylvan Wye! . . . / How often has my spirit turned to thee!" (*LB*, 50–51, 56–58). In the "now" of the speaker's return to the Wye valley in the penultimate section, "the picture of the mind revives again," suggesting how the mind will inevitably change yet still retain from this experience "life and food / For future years" (*LB*, 65–66). This idea of the mind's change over time kindles a disturbing joy at the intermittent sense of "something far more deeply interfused" pervading all things:

> . . . Therefore am I still
> A lover of the meadows and the woods,
> And mountains; and of all that we behold
> From this green earth; of all the mighty world
> Of eye and ear, both what they half-create,
> And what perceive: well pleased to recognize
> In nature and the language of the sense,
> The anchor of my purest thoughts, the nurse,
> The guide, the guardian of my heart, and soul
> Of all my moral being. (*LB*, 103–12)

At just the point where this stanza of the poem seems most to ascribe agency for the speaker's moral being to Nature, it complicates it. Nature is quite actively "the nurse, / The guide, the guardian" of his heart, but also "The *anchor* of [his] purest thoughts," an anchor which he must metaphorically tie on and let down at a spot he chooses in order to stabilize moral meaning. Nature for Wordsworth is famously "half-creat[ed]" and perceived by the senses, and here it is also "the language of the sense" in the richest of ways, the space like a lake or ocean, of flowing indeterminacy, in which the agency of anchoring—repeatedly—is necessary but free.

By the end, "Tintern Abbey" moves even further beyond grounding moral dictates in Nature. The poet expands his belief in the restorative, illuminative power of Nature so far as to claim that, even if he were not "thus taught" by Nature, he would not "Suffer [his] genial spirits to decay." He claims that because his sister is there and because he does not wish her to despair or to face old age without hope, his faith is enlivened, becoming nearly evidence of things unseen—not an abstract proposition but the living sensation of "*Knowing* that Nature never did betray / The heart that loved her" (*LB*, 123–24, emphasis added). The poem ends with a prayer for his sister, and with it, *Lyrical Ballads* culminates in an image of liturgical "service" as willed returning. The speaker prays that the moon shine on her, that the wind blow freely against her, and that if she should encounter suffering, she would remember his having held to their cheerful hope for her sake, and herself renew and repeat this act of believing. This deliberate holding on to hope on both their parts is seen as itself strengthening and sustaining. "Nor, perchance, / . . . wilt thou then forget," he prays:

> That on the banks of this delightful stream
> We stood together; and that I, so long
> A worshipper of Nature, hither came,
> Unwearied in that service: rather say
> With warmer love, oh! with far deeper zeal
> Of holier love. (*LB*, 151–56)

Through the connection of agency to repetition that shapes perception and reason, the final section of "Tintern Abbey" very particularly owns up to the status of the speaker's moral beliefs as beliefs: as hopes for which there is some, though inconclusive, evidence, and to which he clings, at least in part volitionally and repeatedly, in the emotionally deepening recursions of thought and memory. Prayer—both his petitions for his sister and his standing and worshipping in the "service" of Nature—is the site of agency in the way it was for Christopher Smart: a self-constructing act of belief, an exercise of memory in service of hope, and a compassionate ethical stance toward the other (in Smart's words, "translating in the charity"), unwilling to see her suffer pain or despair. And the speaker is crucially "unwearied" in service that is willed, repetitive, and liturgical. Near the end of the expanded "Preface" to *Lyrical Ballads*, Wordsworth made a related gesture toward the complex relations he was discovering between repetition and agency. "All men feel an habitual gratitude," he wrote, "and something of an honorable bigotry for the objects which have long continued to please them: we not only wish to be pleased, but to be pleased in that particular way in which we have been accustomed to be pleased. There is a host of arguments in these feelings" ("Preface," 178). In an age which still hoped to arrive at natural proof for a moral code, feelings of "habitual gratitude" contain "a host of arguments" in that, if, as Wordsworth comes to believe, the mind both half-creates and perceives the world, then it is responsible for the habits by which it shapes the way it half-creates, either "Unwearied in that service . . . with far deeper zeal / Of holier love," or in "joyless forms."

The inability of the early poems to arrive at Wordsworth's early aim, a morality fully grounded in Nature and in knowledge that would have been the basis of *The Recluse*, has led Kenneth Johnston to see in *Lyrical Ballads* "the triumphs of a failure," a volume haunted in advance by "the multilayered and deeply felt presence of the failed *Recluse*." "It is precisely the *dubiety* of thought and belief, of teaching and of faith," he writes, that underscores the secular, "natural religion" of "Tintern Abbey."[35] In my reading, even the early poems enter into this failure and find through it an alternate path that the later poems follow. Wordsworth's "experiments" in the tradition of the ideology of spontaneity bring him back to ritual and repetition via a concern for learning to look at the world and others "in the spirit of love." This is the moral weight of *Lyrical Ballads*, expressed in its own terms: the human dignity and responsibility in actively engaging with Nature to shape one's half-creating perception of the world and others. Already in *Lyrical Ballads*, and after the moral, spiritual crisis narrated in *The Prelude*, the question for Wordsworth is not whether to ground moral knowledge in spontaneous response or in responses liturgically shaped, so to speak. The question is rather what sort of liturgy to have—what repetitive, formative habits of reading and looking at the world. The recurring motifs of *Ecclesiastical Sonnets*—asceticism, church-building, liturgy, and ritual—continue the trajectory launched in *Lyrical Ballads* and traceable through *The Prelude* and *The Excursion*, in which the quest to articulate a limited, real human agency finds its fullest expression in "litanies of everyday life" effecting what Wordsworth provocatively called "revolutions" or "victories in the world of spirit," which for him were not ethereal but concretely embodied in religious history.[36]

Freedom and "Abject Sympathy with Power" in *Ecclesiastical Sonnets*

Ecclesiastical Sonnets ranks with *The White Doe of Rylstone* and *The Excursion* as the most neglected and even critically despised of Wordsworth's major works, in part because these poems respond less well than others to the particular sort of Marxist deconstruction or political historicizations to which Wordsworth scholarship of the last quarter century has been drawn.[37] Regina Hewitt has made an admirable attempt to historicize *Ecclesiastical Sonnets* in this way, in the context of the Church Building Act of 1818. "Only by considering the political matrix that generated *Ecclesiastical Sonnets*," she writes, "can readers satisfactorily account for Wordsworth's attaching his reformist vision to a conservative program."[38] Interesting in itself, this reading is nevertheless strained.

The larger themes of building and self-fashioning throughout the Wordsworth canon beg the question of whether the "political matrix" of the Church Building Act alone "generated" the sequence. Moreover, in eagerness to contextualize the sonnets in an immediate sense, Hewitt misreads their central metaphor, identifying the "Holy River" sought by the speaker strictly with the English Church. The final sonnet makes quite plain that the "Stream" toward which the poems' detailed history directs us is not primarily that of the institutional English Church but the Holy Spirit, the "living Waters" mentioned by Christ in the Gospels, welling up in thirsty souls to eternal life.[39]

In fact, the sequence references political and religious contexts without the idea that those are mutually exclusive. Written in 1821 and published in 1822 as *Ecclesiastical Sketches*, the first edition was accompanied by a note explaining that it was occasioned by a friend, Sir George Beaumont, building a church on his property, and it would be amended and republished by Wordsworth throughout the next twenty years. The first sonnet indicates the sequence's direct relation to *The River Duddon*, which Wordsworth had published in 1820 after intermittent composition between 1806 and 1820. In *The River Duddon*, Wordsworth explained in the opening of the *Ecclesiastical Sonnets*, he had set out to follow that literal river and with it "the nobler Stream to trace / Of Liberty" (*ES*, 1.1.5–6). He declared a similar set of tasks at the beginning of the latter sequence, searching for a river running through church history:[40]

> Now seek upon the heights of Time the source
> Of a HOLY RIVER, on whose banks are found
> Sweet pastoral flowers, and laurels that have crowned
> Full oft the unworthy brow of lawless force;
> And, for delight of him who tracks its course,
> Immortal amaranth and palms abound. (*ES*, 1.1.9–14)

This river is presumably that of *spiritual* liberty, which like the political liberty to which Wordsworth had devoted so much of his thought, is crucially opposed to "lawless force." The sequence, eventually totaling 132 sonnets, traces the river through three sections: "From the Introduction of Christianity into Britain to the Consummation of the Papal Dominion," "To the Close of the Troubles in the Reign of Charles I," and "From the Restoration to the Present Times."

The lacuna between parts 2 and 3, eliding the eleven years of the Interregnum, is in a profound way the abyss around which, like the French Revolution in *The Prelude*, the sonnets take shape. In the revolutionary Puritan rule of 1649–1660, neither Roman Catholics nor secular illuminati but English Protestants quashed spiritual liberty, in the name of illumination and spontaneous divine insight. Across Wordsworth's most ambitiously historical work, violence—"the unworthy brow of lawless force"—is what the river is shown to oppose and resist: druidic sacrifice, slavery in the Roman Empire, Diocletian's persecutions, barbarian attack, the Saxon, Danish, and Norman conquests, serfdom, the dissolution of the monasteries, and both Catholic and Protestant executions during the Reformation. In the spaces between accounts of heroic resistance to force is a version of the question at the heart of *The Prelude*, that of how and why rational people surrender their liberty and enslave themselves to various despotisms.

Throughout the sequence, the act most opposed to violence is prayer. Prayer is "man's rational prerogative" (*ES*, 2.33.13), the tool with which historical actors enact hope, ask for divine aid, and by humble effort seek to resist violence nonviolently and to effect positive change incrementally. In an early sonnet, for instance, the speaker describes the total destruction of the Old Bangor monastery by the Saxons and "mourn[s] / The *unarmed* Host who by their prayers would turn / The sword from Bangor's walls" (*ES*, 1.12.4–6). Faced with the choice to "swerve / From their known course" of peace, "or vanish like a dream," they choose nonviolence, and their memory is preserved only in the place names of a few indignant hills and streams (*ES*, 1.12.9–10). The fragile power of pacifism and the inner peace needed to resist violence is a recurring note throughout. "Religious awe" gives a person the fortitude to "swerv[e] not" and, like the tethering anchor of returning to nature in "Tintern Abbey," enables one to "contend / With the wide world's commotions" (*ES*, 3.9.5–7). Importantly, Wordsworth claims that in his contemporary times it is through prayer in quiet chapels that modern people, like the monks at Bangor, "Find solace which a busy world disdains" (*ES*, 3.17.14). By the time the river reaches the modern day, the plague of business and busyness—a rationalized violence not unlike Interregnum Puritanism—has been clearly figured as the next and perhaps greatest onslaught against the river of spiritual liberty and living water, an attack which the modern religious person, Wordsworth implies, must actively resist.

Ecclesiastical Sonnets is thus centrally concerned with recuperating understandings of labor, effort, and self-fashioning from the world of commerce and "all its industry." This resistance takes the form of an alternative industry: personal and, as in Smart's poetry, associated with both silence and the cultivation of the voice. Part 1 of *Ecclesiastical Sonnets* contains the most personal poems in the sequence, in which the poet appears to speak in his own voice and directly relates his pursuit for a principled, resistant peace to that of the early Saxon monastics. Sonnet 21, "Seclusion," imagines a converted "war-torn Chieftain" quitting the world for the monastery, "not to dwell / In soft repose," he stresses, but slowly, daily to repent and to make war, as it were, on his own violent pride, gradually undoing longstanding patterns of thought:

>   . . . Within his cell,
> Round the decaying trunk of human pride,
> At morn, and eve, and midnight's silent hour,
> Do penitential cogitations cling;
> Like ivy, round some ancient elm, they twine
> In grisly folds and strictures serpentine;
> Yet, while they strangle, a fair growth they bring,
> For recompense—their own perennial bower. (*ES*, 1.21.6–14)

A lifetime of "living by the sword" seems here to necessitate a violent ascesis directed at a malignant, prideful self, but one that, as it strangles violent pride, paradoxically renovates the self as a perennial peaceful "bower" in which to dwell. The "penitential cogitations" that deck the chieftain like ivy recall similar images from *The Prelude*, by now more than fifteen years old for Wordsworth: the one, of "depraved" Cambridge professors, "tricked out like aged trees / Which, through the lapse of their infirmity, / Give ready place to any random seed / That chuses to be reared upon their trunks," and the other, more like the chieftain, an ash tree at Cambridge, "exquisitely wreathed" with ivy from the ground almost to the top and therefore miraculously green, even in the middle of winter.[41]

In the very next sonnet, Wordsworth calls up his own habits of life and places them alongside the penitent chieftain and the larger history the sequence relates: "Methinks that to some vacant hermitage / *My* feet would rather turn—. . . . Tired of the world and all its industry" (*ES*, 1.22.1–2, 14). Through the juxtaposition of this sonnet with the one on the chieftain before and that on Venerable Bede afterward, Wordsworth creates a space for retreat as something besides indolence or "soft repose." In "Reproof," Bede serves as a Virgil who would guide him out of both the world's industry and indolence, and into a constructive vision of solitude and ascetic struggle in which the self is gradually transformed by labor and "penitential cogitations."[42] In retreat from urban ecclesiastical centers but living in community at Jarrow monastery in northern England, Bede engaged in "diligence" and an "unrelaxing use / Of a long life," where instead of tutors he heard "the billows beat / On a wild coast, rough monitors to feed / Perpetual industry" (*ES*, 1.23.12–13, 7–9). The sonnet expressing awe at Bede's having (in the words of Wordsworth's note) "expired dictating the last words of a translation of St. John's Gospel" and at his industry on behalf of others, together with the four subsequent sonnets, follows the benefits of this labor trickling through the culture and inspiring other "unbought" labors to build monasteries and to save "classic lore . . . / . . . for all posterity" (*ES*, 1.24.1,

1.25.13–14). They paint an imaginative picture of commerce and industry transfigured, with people working "like congregated bees," seeking the "general mart of Christendom" and returning to their cells with spiritual and literary treasures "like richly laden merchants" (*ES*, 1.24.2, 1.25.4–5). The pious King Alfred the Great, trained by monastics and a sort of public counterpart to Bede, careful with his time and zealous for the education and spiritual care of his people, is in Sonnet 26 the boast of "remote Jerusalem, / And Christian India," though "small his kingdom as a spark or gem" (1.26.12–13, 11).

Monastics more than monarchs, though, are also the noncommercial, unsentimental heroes of the second section of *Ecclesiastical Sonnets*. Instrumental in resisting violence and in cultivating virtue in the everyday life of the nation, monks and nuns spread a "gentler life" around their "holy spires" in the midst of economic injustice, "relax[ing] or break[ing] these iron chains" of the "villain-service" and "legalized oppressions" of serfdom, and even from their cells playing the role of conscience in political life, by "fervent exhortations from afar / Mov[ing] Princes to their duty, peace or war" (*ES*, 2.3.12; 2.4.3–10, 2.5.6–7).[43] And yet, in part 2 Wordsworth is also at pains to point out the pitfalls of monasticism, which are temptations in the position he would craft for himself as well. In the first section he had condemned the monk Dunstan, for instance, an "Enthusiast" who from his "Benedictine coop" masterminded ambitious plots and abused the influence of the Church (*ES*, 1.28.2, 6). In the second section, he blames the dissolution of the monasteries under Henry VIII only partly on the "selfish rage" of the spoilers, and at least equally on "Monastic Voluptuousness," on the monks' "ease" and "cumbrous wealth," and especially on their willingness to be served rather than to serve, while falsely proclaiming their spiritual superiority over "the pious, humble, useful Secular" (*ES*, 2.20, 2.18.1–2, 2.19.6).

This last evocative phrase brings together the secular and the sacred, the ritual and the natural, in a way that is emblematic of the resacralization of everyday life central to Wordsworth's project of resisting relentless pressures for its economization and instrumentality. Throughout the sequence, the temptation for monastic and secular alike is to abandon piety, humility, and useful (spiritual and worldly) labor, for the accumulation of wealth and power. The threat of power is represented in this religious history most often by the papacy, both in the individual's lust for power, and the insidious appeal of the institution to common people who are drawn into supporting it. Wordsworth is careful to critique the way the papacy contrived to increase its worldly powers during the Crusades to the Holy Land: "Enthusiasts" for the Crusades unwittingly became accomplices of mounting papal sway, and souls weighed down by the despair of war were "ill fortified" against the appealing fantasy of church power (1.35.13–14, 1.36.12–13). In a characteristically Wordsworthian moment of disgust, the scandal of "Papal Dominion" reaches its height when the Emperor Frederick Barbarossa kneels to be crowned (as was thought) by Pope Alexander III:[44]

> Black Demons hovering o'er his mitred head,
> To Caesar's Successor the Pontiff spake;
> "Ere I absolve thee, stoop! that on thy neck
> Levelled with earth this foot of mine may tread."
> Then he, who to the altar had been led,
> He, whose strong arm the Orient could not check
> He, who had held the Soldan at his beck,
> Stooped, of all glory disinherited,
> And even the common dignity of man!—
> Amazement strikes the crowd: while many turn
> Their eyes away in sorrow, others burn
> With scorn, invoking a vindictive ban
> From outraged Nature; but the sense of most
> In abject sympathy with power is lost. (*ES*, 1.38.1–14)

In *Ecclesiastical Sonnets*, it is crucially this "abject sympathy with power" that leads good men to approve injustice and violence, whether in the name of secular or religious powers. Wordsworth unflinchingly points out, for instance, how during the Reformation the "unreflective herd" allowed Protestant kings simply to subsume papal authority and become even more absolute in their power: "with spiritual sovereignty transferred / Unto itself, the Crown assumes a voice / Of reckless mastery, hitherto unknown" (*ES*, 2.28.13–14).

The image of a pope crowning an emperor cannot help but recall for us (as it could not have for its first readers) the image of Napoleon in book 10 of *The Prelude*, at its nadir and "catastrophe":

> . . . when, finally to close
> And rivet up the gains of France, a Pope
> Is summoned in to crown an Emperor—
> This last opprobrium, when we see the dog
> Returning to his vomit, when the sun
> That rose in splendour, was alive, and moved
> In exultation among living clouds,
> Hath put his function and his glory off,
> And, turned into gewgaw, a machine,
> Sets like an opera phantom. (*P* 1805, 10.931–40)[45]

These passages and the arcs of *Lyrical Ballads*, *The Prelude*, and *Ecclesiastical Sonnets* are related on the most profound levels; the recognition of what *Ecclesiastical Sonnets* calls the "abject sympathy with power" is both the emotional bottoming out and the central philosophical, moral revelation of *The Prelude*. In book 10 Wordsworth describes the moment when, in his hope for a rational, empirically verifiable moral theory and its ultimate trial in the French Revolution and the Terror that followed, he realized that, like noble affections, treacherous "sympathies with power" spontaneously well up within the human breast:

> ... amid the awe
> Of unintelligible chastisement
> I felt a kind of sympathy with power—
> Motions raised up within me, nevertheless,
> Which had relationship to highest things.
> Wild blasts of music thus did find their way
> Into the midst of terrible events,
> So that worst tempests might be listened to: .... (*P* 1805, 10.414–21)[46]

Wordsworth places the great moral, philosophical breakthrough of the poem at just this moment: in the realization that it is precisely because *both* sorts of sympathy well up in human hearts—heterogeneous sympathies that writers from Hobbes, Shaftesbury, Mandeville, Hutcheson, and Smith had wanted to claim as either selfishly or benevolently homogenous—that people have the responsibility to shape those desires:[47]

> Then was the truth received into my heart,
> That under heaviest sorrow earth can bring,
> Griefs bitterest of ourselves or of our kind,
> If from the affliction somewhere do not grow
> Honour which could not else have been, a faith,
> An elevation, and a sanctity,
> If new strength be not given, or old restored,
> The blame is ours not Nature's. (*P* 1805, 10.422–29)

It was not philosophical or ideological error, Wordsworth asserted, that brought the apocalypse of the Terror, but "a reservoir of guilt / And ignorance, filled up from age to age, / That could no longer hold its loathsome charge, / But burst and spread in deluge throughout the land" (*P* 1805, 10.436–39). In the context of the revolution, that "ignorance" is surely of this heterogeneous nature of the spontaneous inclinations of the heart and of the reasoning mind.

In the context of book 10, this "reservoir of guilt" also takes on a very specific meaning, that of guilt in the face of failing to manage one's spontaneous impulses, good and ill. This recognition of immense though limited freedom to shape one's inclinations, and its tragic abdication to either political or consumer forces, prompts in *The Prelude* a sober humility and compassion for humanity's self-inflicted ills. Similarly, in *Ecclesiastical Sonnets* Wordsworth laments the ease of doing evil, even from good motives, which springs from these contrary feelings that seem perpetually to arise in the heart. In lines that echo the ending of "Lines Left upon a Seat in a Yew-tree," this divided nature of the self is the reason that even the sternest denouncement of injustice must come, not from a spirit of self-righteous critique but from a spirit of compassion and love:

> O Man,—if with thy trials thus it fares,
> If good can smooth the way to evil choice,
> From all rash censure be the mind kept free;
> He only judges right who weighs, compares,
> And, in the sternest sentence which his voice
> Pronounces, ne'er abandons Charity. (*ES*, 2.1.9–14)

Prayer is the way to resist violence, for Wordsworth, because liturgy and ritual are crucially the ways human beings can intervene in and shape in themselves those modes of desiring and gazing, and thus effect change in the community or nation. Especially as we will see in the last part of the sequence, the self exists as a church constructed to house a ritual of observing and appreciating the world and others with a heart of love, in awareness and hope that can weather inevitable suffering without recourse to violence, bitterness, or despair. The sequence makes clear that for Wordsworth ritual practices are no panacea, but that the mode of embracing a particular ritual is all-important. Liturgy is not the point in itself but, like the physical church, is ideally a way of stepping into the living waters—in the terms of *The River Duddon*, into the river of liberty limited and flowing within its banks. For Wordsworth, not forms but the faith with which they are embraced brings holiness, and one lives out faith in God's goodness in rituals of daily life that serve in turn to cultivate both love and faith. In the final two sonnets, all of the churches, from mountain chapels to King's College, Cambridge, and all of the selves in the poem, participate in salvation as holy constructions: not first as houses of sacrifice, but as places of incarnation and transfiguration.

Church Building and the "High Service Within"—The Agency and Subjectivity of Love in *Ecclesiastical Sonnets*

Ecclesiastical Sonnets surveys church history seeking the ways people have sought "never to abandon Charity" in the face of external and internal attack—both from the Angles, Vikings, popes, and emperors who seek power, and from an indeterminate and contradictory set of impulses that can bend one toward abject sympathies with power. In the case of external onslaught, the chief way the Church's faith has managed to survive, for Wordsworth, is through her liturgy; throughout the sequence, it is song and ritual that resist power and keep the holy river running so that others, even the conquerors, may come to its waters. In a beautiful sonnet on Canute, the eleventh-century Danish King of England who came to appreciate English institutions and safeguard its Church, Wordsworth asserted that it is liturgy and music that can make the charms of violence and power pale by comparison:

> A pleasant music floats along the Mere,
> From Monks in Ely chanting service high,
> While-as Canùte the King is rowing by:
> "My Oarsmen," quoth the mighty King, "draw near,
> That we the sweet song of the Monks may hear!"
> He listens (all past conquests and all schemes
> Of future vanishing like empty dreams)
> Heart-touched, and haply not without a tear,
> The Royal Minstrel, ere the choir is still,
> While his free Barge skims the smooth flood along,
> Gives to that rapture an accordant Rhyme. (*ES*, 1.30.1–11)

The last three lines of the sonnet shift to the present moment and urge the reader with the "suffering Earth" to be thankful that the "sternest clime / And rudest age" are still subject to the pleasures of "heaven-descended Piety and Song" (*ES*, 1.30.12–14). Similarly, ritual and song enable the English Church to weather the Norman invasion; the "tapers of the sacred quires" are not extinguished, and even a "thraldom" that studiously sought to "expel / Old laws, and ancient customs to derange" wrought no fatal change in English "Creed or Ritual" (*ES*, 1.31.11–14).

It is by this logic—that of resisting and managing the inner and outer onslaughts of unruly sympathies—that the third section of *Ecclesiastical Sonnets*, covering the age of ritual's decline, from the Restoration to the present, focuses on liturgy and ritual. In "Patriotic Sympathies," Wordsworth contrasts abject sympathies with power with the aim of this section, cultivating the "kindred agitations" of "filial love" (*ES*, 3.2.5, 11). In the 1805 manuscript of book 10 of *The Prelude*, Wordsworth had already described his relationship to Nature in terms of two contrasting rituals or ways of adoring Nature, that of his youthful devotion and that of his love for man after the Terror: "How different ritual for this after-worship, / What countenance to promote this second love" (*P* 1805, 10.393–94). Where the first sort of worship seemed all "beatitude" and optimism, the more mature worship takes place in light of the conundrum of human moral and emotional responses. The "troubled human heart," prophetically sensible of "offences [and] punishment to come," trembles at the prospect of retribution but also implicitly at the dread freedom that man has because of the vying sympathies he is called to manage (*P* 1805, 10.397, 405).[48]

Echoing these sentiments from *The Prelude*, in the third section of *Ecclesiastical Sonnets*, the ritual year of the Church is likened to the prophetic cycle of the zodiac, in which individuals envision the future and see what they are brave or hopeful enough to see. After a dozen sonnets, the section breaks off its narrative of past history to take up issues in the English Church of Wordsworth's day, and in "The Liturgy," he writes:

> Yes, if the intensities of hope and fear
> Attract us still, and passionate exercise
> Of lofty thoughts, the way before us lies
> Distinct with signs, through which in set career,
> As through a zodiac, moves the ritual year
> Of England's Church; stupendous mysteries!
> Which whoso travels in her bosom eyes,
> As he approaches them, with solemn cheer.
> Upon that circle traced from sacred story
> We only dare to cast a transient glance,
> Trusting in hope that Others may advance
> With mind intent upon the King of Glory,
> From his mild advent till his countenance
> Shall dissipate the seas and mountains hoary. (*ES*, 3.19.1–14)

The ritual cycle of the church year is that "stupendous mystery" by which individuals actively participate together and manage their mixed responses of "hope and fear." This agency is exercised together, in the context of church worship, but it is always individual and fragile, leaving no room for the role of commanding evangelist, the figure which Bunyan and Shaftesbury cut for themselves and by which Wordsworth felt both drawn and repelled. Rather, traveling the course of the year in the "bosom" of the Church, the individual eyes the familiar events in the life of Christ with "solemn cheer," and rather than forcing them on others, "Trust[s] in hope that Others may advance" of their own accord and follow the living chain of those devoted to this "mild," incarnate "King of Glory," until he comes again.

This respect for the agency of others is again underlined in the context of ritual, in a group of sonnets Wordsworth added to part 3 in 1842, on "Aspects of Christianity in America." These poems celebrate American believers for originally having fled the continent due to the imposition of "Rite and Ordinance abused" but now, as if counterexample to the violence of Interregnum enthusiasm, returning to use of the Book of Common Prayer of their own accord, "Led by her own free choice" and piety (*ES*, 3.14.1, 9). These sonnets, like many in the section, express the paradox of limited agency that appears throughout the Wordsworth canon, the paradox of engaging by one's own will a limit other than momentary inclination. This agency is directly linked to the peaceful overcoming of violence in the next poem in the group, where Wordsworth praises American efforts to retain unity with the Anglican episcopacy after the Revolutionary War as attempts "in filial love to reunite / What force had severed" (*ES*, 3.15.5–6). Similarly, he enjoins godparents to be mindful of their solemn responsibility and to resist the "disheartening custom" of taking this relationship lightly: "Shame," he pronounces, "if the consecrated Vow be found / An idle form, the Word an empty sound!" (*ES*, 3.21.6, 13–14). Invoking free-prayer arguments stretching back into the seventeenth century, Wordsworth suggests that if forms become, in Saint Paul's words, "vain repetitions," it is the fault not of the forms but of those whose lives make them "vain."

The strongest claim Wordsworth makes for church ritual, however, is that it can be used to help the individual, through agency and memory, to "weave a crown for hope," rather than for an emperor. Opening out onto mediations on ritual in general, "Rural Ceremony," for instance, celebrates the July custom of rushbearing, in which Westmoreland children bring rushes to cover the church floor and in their procession make more sublime figures than kings with scepters, embodying an innocent connection with their ancestors stretching back into pre-Reformation times. The poem ends by speculating that the spirits of Hooker and Laud, early defenders of English liturgy, must be pleased by their decorative procession, a thought that turns the following sonnet, "Regrets," to those who stripped the Church of festive practices like decking the halls at Christmastime:

> Would that our scrupulous Sires had dared to leave
> Less scanty measure of those graceful rites
> And usages, whose due return invites
> A stir of mind too natural to deceive:
> Giving to Memory help when she would weave
> A crown for Hope!—I dread the boasted lights
> That all too often are but fiery blights,
> Killing the bud o'er which in vain we grieve.
> Go, seek, when Christmas snows discomfort bring,
> The counter Spirit found in some gay church
> Green with fresh holly, every pew a perch
> In which the linnet or the thrush might sing,
> Merry and loud and safe from prying search,
> Strains offered only to the genial Spring. (*ES*, 3.33.1–14)

Those "graceful rites," some of which had survived the Puritan critique of ritual and in which the Oxford movement was, at the time of *Ecclesiastical Sonnets*, reviving interest, are significant in terms that resonate with the moral trajectory of the Wordsworth canon. Via that religious-imaginative faculty that perceives the given world from which it half creates the self and its future, by participating in such rites people weave a crown for hope. Wordsworth seems here acutely aware of the way the "boasted lights" of spontaneous emotion and illumination "too often are but fiery blights" that "[Kill] the bud" of hope with the determinism, passivity, and violent-tending despair that variously inhabit the free-prayer guidebooks, the works of Bunyan and Shaftesbury, and the literature of sentimentality.

This lack of hope, the frantic despair of optimism dashed by the ideology of spontaneity which engendered it and by the determinism toward which it leans, are the feelings Wordsworth also associates with his experience of the aftermath of the French Revolution. "I read her doom," he wrote in book 10 of *The Prelude*, "Vexed inly somewhat, it is true, and sore, / But not dismayed, nor taking to the shame / Of a false Prophet; but, roused up I stuck / More firmly to old tenets, and to prove / Their temper, strained them more," so that these "opinions," like the parasitic ideas around his professors' minds, did "every day / Grow into consequence, till round my mind / They clung, as if they were the life of it" (*P* 1805, 10.796–804).[49] Lines after these famously connect the rational, empiricist attempt for moral certainty not to the hope it promised, but, by virtue of a disappointed quest for certainty, to despair:

>   . . . Thus I fared,
> Dragging all passions, notions, shapes of faith,
> Like culprits to the bar, suspiciously
> Calling the mind to establish in plain day
> Her titles and her honours, now believing,
> Now disbelieving, endlessly perplexed
> With impulse, motive, right and wrong, the ground
> Of moral obligation, what the rule
> And what the sanction, till, demanding proof,
> And seeking it in everything, I lost
> All feeling of conviction, and, in fine,
> Sick, wearied out with contrarieties,
> Yielded up moral questions in despair,
> And for my future studies, as the sole
> Employment of the inquiring faculty,
> Turned towards mathematics, and their clear
> And solid evidence— . . . (*P* 1805, 10.888–904)

Wordsworth's emotional numbness, borne of seeking moral certainty, bears a family resemblance to anxiety over free prayer and conversion, to Bunyan's turn from inner evidence to narrative, and to Shaftesbury's turn from angry despair and subjective unraveling to shaping public, visual images of self and perfect truth illustrating the *Characteristicks*. In demanding proof everywhere, Wordsworth loses "all feeling of conviction"—a feeling which, he seems to imply, lies at the bottom of all search for truth, without which proof does not carry its sought-after force. In the lines that follow, he rehearses the well-known narrative of his rescue from this mental desolation even as the political situation in France deteriorates: through Nature and "human love," particularly friendship with Coleridge and with Dorothy, who "whispered still that brightness would return" (*P* 1805, 10.904–30). It is their daily interaction with "human love" and looking at the world "in the spirit of love," that preserves what could properly be called *faith in truth*: that gives what he calls in 1805 "strength and knowledge full of peace," and in 1850, "sweet counsels between head and heart / Whence *grew* that genuine knowledge fraught with peace" (*P* 1805, 10.925; *P* 1850, 10.352–53, emphasis added).

It is in the context of part 3's discussion of ritual that *Ecclesiastical Sonnets* most solidly affirms this faith in loving, nonviolent truth. Despite the violent change the Church has weathered, "Regrets" is followed by the sober hope of the more well-known "Mutability," the full significance of which can only be registered in its context in the sequence. It begins with the assertion that the awful notes of societal and spiritual dissolution paradoxically make a "musical but melancholy" scale "whose concord shall not fail" (*ES*, 3.34.3–4). Yet "Truth fails not," he maintains, even though "her outward forms that bear / The longest date do melt like frosty rime" (*ES*, 3.34.7–8). "Mutability" is not against forms for their being mutable; on the contrary, forms are the faith that the living perform to "crown" the hope they believe in as truth:

> Truth fails not; but her outward forms that bear
> The longest date do melt like frosty rime,
> That in the morning whitened hill and plain
> And is no more; drop like the tower sublime
> Of yesterday, which royally did wear
> His crown of weeds, but could not even sustain
> Some casual shout that broke the silent air,
> Or the unimaginable touch of Time. (*ES*, 3.34.7–14)

The image of the tower once topped with its thatched roof calls to mind not only the mutability of the sonnet's title and the reeds of the rush-bearing ritual, but the previous sonnet's "crown for hope," underlining not the inevitable dissolution of all, but the way that crowning truth is the perennial activity of each living generation: crowning it through the rituals of belief and everyday life. The sonnet that follows, "Old Abbeys," also laments the fall not of rituals but of the monastic houses in which they took place. As a younger man he had considered the fall of the great "Monastic Domes" without due regret, but as an older man he claims to appreciate the particular holiness they represent: that spirit not of scrupulous criticism of others but of a repentant reflection on "our past selves" that teaches us in love "to tolerate the infirmities / And fault of others," to "forget them or forgive" (*ES*, 3.35.1, 5, 7–8, 10). A humble love for others as they tackle the (re)construction project of themselves is what he wishes to glean from these holy sites. "Your spirit freely let me drink," he asks in the final line, "and live" (*ES*, 3.35.14).

The emphasis on ritual leads, then, by a discernible logic to the related focus on the construction of churches, buildings which like old abbeys are locations for daily practices where the spirit of love and forgiveness, those "rivers of living water," can be entered into and imbibed; it is by this path that the sonnet sequence eventually arrives at the building of new churches mentioned in Wordsworth's prefatory note. New churches are being built, he writes, because "the time / Is conscious of her want" and thus constructs "due channels which the Flood / Of sacred truth may enter" (*ES*, 3.38.9–10, 6–7). Sonnets 39–41 muse on the site of a new church, where "oaks of Druid memory" shall "shelter the Abode / Of genuine Faith" and Nature cover it in moss and the incense of morning fog "through centuries yet unborn" (*ES*, 3.39.7–9, 3.40.14). In a profound sense, the responsibility one has for *faith*, for struggling to believe and to enact something good in the midst of uncertainty, is for Wordsworth the truth of the holy river of church history. These constructed spaces are important as the site of what Wordsworth views as the epic human struggle, against violence, pride, and despair, for faith and hope:

> ... Encinture small,
> But infinite its grasp of weal and woe!
> Hopes, fears, in never-ending ebb and flow;—
> The spousal trembling, and the 'dust to dust,'
> The prayers, the contrite struggle, and the trust
> That to the Almighty Father looks through all. (*ES*, 3.41.9–14)

The infinite scope of these small constructed spaces calls to mind the moral revelation of *The Prelude*, not that our natural impulses come down ultimately on the side of either hope or fear, but that they maintain a perpetual coursing of both, which is itself the ground of the greatest moral miracle and dignity of all, the space for the agency of "prayers, the contrite struggle, and the trust" in God through all: the choosing of hope from the endlessly presented choice between hope and fear. Spaces for the daily enactment of this faith, the great cathedrals are "Types of the spiritual Church which God hath reared" to "rouse the heart" and crucially "lead the will / By a bright ladder to the world above" (*ES*, 3.42.2, 9–10). The course of this holy river of willed faith and self-shaping recalls the concerns of *Lyrical Ballads* and opens out into its widest waters in the sonnet, "Inside of King's College Chapel, Cambridge." This agency and "glorious work of fine intelligence" is opposed to the utilitarian calculus of cost and productivity:

> ... high Heaven rejects the lore
> Of nicely-calculated less or more;
> So deemed the man who fashioned for the sense
> These lofty pillars, spread that branching roof
> Self-poised, and scooped into ten thousand cells,
> Where light and shade repose, where music dwells
> Lingering—and wandering on as loth to die;
> Like thoughts whose very sweetness yieldeth proof
> That they were born for immortality. (*ES*, 3.43.6–14)

Here the perception of sweetness and proof is the product of music sung in a constructed space, and the connection between the carefully constructed chapel and the human mind suggests that ultimately it is the self that is constructed—in uncertainty, agency, and faith—to "channel . . . the Flood / Of sacred truth," a place built with great art with the purpose of seeing light coming in from outside, to full advantage.

This culminating sonnet cannot help but echo the language used to describe Dorothy's mind in "Tintern Abbey": "thy mind / Shall be a mansion for all lovely forms, / Thy memory be as a dwelling-place / For all sweet sounds and harmonies" (*LB*, 140–43). *The Prelude* speaks of the gradual transformation of the mind as well, in cooperation with God who, in spite of the poet's youthful "trite reflections of morality," "corrected my desires" (*P* 1805, 11.373, 375). Wordsworth's future song—perhaps the never-completed *Recluse*, but also, from the viewpoint of 1805, major works like *Ecclesiastical Sonnets*—shall be of this self and its corrected desires, explicitly conceived of as a constructed edifice in which an inner liturgy of "high service" is performed:

> Here calling up to mind what then I saw
> A youthful traveller, and see daily now
> Before me in my rural neighbourhood—
> Here might I pause, and bend in reverence
> To Nature, and the power of human minds,
> To men as they are men within themselves.
> How oft high service is performed within
> When all the external man is rude in shew,
> Not like a temple rich with pomp and gold,
> But a mere mountain-chapel such as shields
> Its simple worshippers from sun and shower.
> "Of these," said I, "shall be my Song . . ." (*P* 1805, 12.220–31)

Evading History, Evading Faith

In 1805 Wordsworth might still have envisioned *The Recluse* as part of that song, the all-encompassing philosophical poem that Coleridge urged him to write and for which Mary and Dorothy Wordsworth held out hope for decades.[50] But by the 1820s as *Ecclesiastical Sonnets* was being revised and reprinted, that looked less hopeful. The moral truths at which the Wordsworth canon arrived were in the end very different from what Wordsworth had imagined in *Lyrical Ballads*, but they took their departure there nonetheless. In frequently quoted lines from the end of the 1805 manuscript of *The Prelude*, Wordsworth described his future song as the sighting of a new world:

> ... and I remember well
> That in life's everyday appearances
> I seemed about this period to have sight
> Of a new world—a world, too, that was fit
> To be transmitted and made visible
> To other eyes, as having for its base
> That whence our dignity originates,
> That which both gives it being, and maintains
> A balance, an ennobling interchange
> Of action from within and without:
> The excellence, pure spirit, and best power,
> Both of the object seen, and eye that sees. (*P* 1805, 12.368–79)

By 1850, the famous final lines of this passage remained, but the middle portion describing that "new world" had changed significantly, to read—

> ... —a world, too, that was fit
> To be transmitted, and to other eyes
> Made visible; as ruled by those fixed laws
> Whence spiritual dignity originates, ... (*P* 1850, 13.370–73)

Wordsworth's reinvocation of a Newtonian moral rhetoric here in the late works is provocative. With *The Recluse* long out of sight, and in the context of the moral-religious trajectories this chapter traces, these "laws" are not like Bunyan's rules for prayer, Hutcheson's mathematical equations, or Shaftesbury's self-imposed "Regimen." Rather, the "fixed laws / Whence spiritual dignity originates" are those of the endless flux of emotions and moral impulses that are the ground against which the agency involved in choosing hope, love, and gentleness, again and again, is possible and has meaning. This vision of the spiritual world is not a facile optimism based in man's inevitable progress or inherent goodness, but a sober understanding of human subjects as divided and radically free, creating themselves and their responses in cooperation with Nature and God, within the realities of the world and the givenness of their contrary sentiments and desires.

That Wordsworth's pervasive language of ritual and church building encouraged chief actors in the Oxford Movement to appropriate his poetry is certainly understandable. In 1843 he cooperated, when asked, with the publication of a pamphlet by Samuel Wilkinson titled *Contributions of William Wordsworth to the Revival of Catholic Truths*. Stephen Gill has documented a host of such attempts to coopt Wordsworth for Tractarianism, which as he puts it were not the "result of a conspiracy or as part of some strategic plan master-minded from Oxford," but which suggested themselves, "simply because much of his poetry, and his living presence, offered support."[51] But given the extended reading offered here of the particular significance that the recovery of ritual and liturgy held for Wordsworth, we can also understand why he consistently stood a bit to the side of the Tractarians who made that revival into a movement. Once that movement bowed to Rome for institutional sign and seal, it would have seemed to Wordsworth to have come under the sway of "abject sympathies with power" that, "of all glory disinherited," abdicated the freedom at the heart of self-transformative ritual as Wordsworth understood it.[52]

This space of freedom within form also accounts for, what has seemed to some, Wordsworth's ambivalence toward institutional religion, but which is in reality a more complex position.[53] Wordsworth values religion and ritual in the terms with which Danièle Hervieu-Léger describes premodernized or presecularized religion, as a "chain of memory," a set of practices linking us with a meaningful past. Yet he often does so within the rhetoric of a divinized Nature that shrouds religion in what Graham Ward might identify as universalized transcendentalisms. We may see this as owing to a modern commodification of religion, except that there is also something about it consonant with the rest of Wordsworth's work and his insistence that "high Heaven rejects the lore / Of nicely-calculated less or more." However grand his hopes for the inspirational office of the poet, Wordsworth does not preach or evangelize in quite the way Bunyan or Shaftesbury did. His poems make no commands for programmatic religious action, because he understands such agency and action as proper to the individual. If we read Wordsworth's religious poems alongside his ostensibly secular poetry, as he published and republished it, we see that this is not ambivalence at all, but an articulate refusal to claim his faith as institutionally preapproved rational knowledge, and an insistence on human freedom made possible by uncertainty and exercised first as hope and faith. The latest changes in the final lines of *The Prelude* reflect precisely this point: "solace in the knowledge which we have" in 1805 becomes by 1850 "solace—*knowing what we have learnt to know*," and "A lasting inspiration, sanctified / By reason and by truth" becomes "A lasting inspiration, sanctified / By reason, *blest by faith*."[54] Wordsworth's most effusive moments, from "Tintern Abbey" to the ending of *The Prelude*, are tempered by this insistence on faith as faith, on belief that owns up to its locality, contingency, and fragility.

Besides countering the assumed bifurcation between the young and old poet, this reading makes a gesture toward bridging the most pressing impasse in Wordsworth studies, the tension between the New Historicist desire for genuinely political criticism and societal change, and its inability, due in part to sweeping notions of historical determinism, and in part to its criticism of the capitalist notion of the autonomous subject, to account for individual agency. Steven Cole, in his important essay, "Evading Politics: The Poverty of Historicizing Romanticism," has articulated a focused critique of Romantic scholarship that operates with the "unargued assumption that the canonical accounts of romanticism as a denial or an evasion of historical and social contingency are accurate."[55] His charge is that New Historicism cannot produce a politics because it will not engage in difficult, pragmatic discussions of the ethics that is part of its impetus: "what historicism wants," Cole claims, "is evaluation without values."[56] But the failure to account for agency is an even larger difficulty for criticism that asserts Wordsworth's "evasion" of history. "We still know very little about how to assess the politics of romanticism," Cole claims, "in large part because our own political understanding is so warped by the unreal opposition of the capitalist defense of the autonomous subject and the Marxist retreat to what [Marjorie] Levinson calls a 'transhistorical causality.' The politics of romanticism is located somewhere else, and as yet historicism has done nothing to indicate where that somewhere else might be."[57]

By examining the paths between Wordsworthian spontaneity and ritual, this chapter enables us to locate Wordsworth's sense of both agency and politics "somewhere else" than either complete autonomy or determinism. It reveals one of the underwriting concerns of the Wordsworth canon to be a description of human ethical engagement with the world, an engagement that eschews both passivity and the revolutionary violence of an ultimately egocentric fantasy of "totality" and complete solution.[58] After a century of writing that wrestled to produce a notion of virtue in a world governed by immutable laws of Nature or of a distant Deity, Wordsworth shaped an understanding of the world in which there is room for others, and God, to act. The violence of the egocentric self is the rock that Wordsworth's political idealism crashes against time and again in *The Prelude* and in *Ecclesiastical Sonnets*, and in this linkage of the political with personal psychology he seems almost to adumbrate the melding of ideology critique with psychoanalysis that has proven so compelling in theoretical circles since the demise of the Soviet Union. This chapter shows that the agency that most concerns Wordsworth is exercised not so much in singular revolutionary moments but in the subtle psychological self-shaping that sets the arc of one's private and political behavior, a shaping that happens not in dramatic one time decisions or conversions, but in repeatedly chosen, adjusted, and re-chosen patterns of engaging the world, and in rituals of everyday life.[59] The loving, nonviolent self, Wordsworth believes, is the only workable basis for a just and nonviolent politics.

Ultimately, this reading of *Ecclesiastical Sonnets* within the larger Wordsworth corpus illumines the way that the picture of Wordsworth evading history, politics, and responsibility is produced specifically by evading his religious poetry, or the religiousness of his poetry in general, because Wordsworth's explorations of religious faith excavate the site of indeterminacy in language where the positive construction of belief-investment must take place. Alan Liu's massive *Wordsworth: The Sense of History*, for instance, includes in its index not a single reference either to the religious poem Wordsworth considered to be his highest work of imagination, *The White Doe of Rylstone*, or, more scandalously, to *Ecclesiastical Sonnets*, the most programmatically historical cycle of poems Wordsworth wrote.[60] The operating assumption of the rare pieces of New Historicist scholarship that address these poems is that religion is not a part of history, except as a blinding mechanism of the conservative ideology Wordsworth is assumed to have embraced. On the contrary, these explicitly religious works, read together with the rest of the Wordsworth canon, directly counter readings like Levinson's, which contend that Wordsworth's poetry works to "establish him as a free agent: a nonideological subject in an ideologized world."[61] I contend that we find a much more complex exploration of agency and the limitations of nature and context in the Wordsworth canon, one that faces up to the difficulty of acting in the world with limited, contingent knowledge, and the inevitability—and possibilities—of belief. For Cole the difficulty with New Historicist accounts of Wordsworth is precisely that by privileging historicism and refusing to engage with poststructuralist theories of language, the writers of these accounts find it "virtually impossible to characterize *what a belief might be*"—or, I would add, how belief can be at once personal, historical, political, and ethical.[62] History *is* religious for Wordsworth, because the "belief" that so centrally concerns "Tintern Abbey" and the other poems is not an avoidable option but a condition of living in the world as a subject whose knowledge is never objective but always mediated by language and a result of the beliefs that determine one's approach to it. The history that came to concern Wordsworth most is the history of individual efforts within community to restrain violence and to cultivate love: the uneven history of human agents, simultaneously political, ethical, and religious, who in the fabric of their lives and psyches have attempted to "weave / A crown for Hope" rather than for violence and despotism. The personal, spiritual, and quotidian are for Wordsworth the inevitable source of the political. More demanding even than framing a constitution or a declaration of the rights of man is the self-shaping of a person who would not subvert them out of his own sympathy with power.

This reading enables us to understand why the "spontaneous overflow" of *Lyrical Ballads* and the "high service within" of *The Prelude* and *Ecclesiastical Sonnets* likely sounded more harmonies than dissonances in the ear of the poet who continued over his long career to write, revise, and publish them alongside each other. To continue arguing for Wordsworth's vision of the inner life, especially in his later years, as an evasion of history or for his religion as an extension of conservative ideology is to miss its larger point. The question which Wordsworth's poems should raise, and which is more relevant at the start of the twenty-first century even than the nineteenth, is the extent to which spiritual practice in the formation of persons and identities might be the basis not necessarily of escapism (though it may be that) but of a constructive politics and of a powerful yet vulnerable, nonviolent resistance to coercive societal and economic forces that cater to the subject's desire either for mastery or to identify with and submit to power. In this sense, religion and spiritual practice may be political in the most egalitarian, feminist, or anticapitalist of senses, without being reduced to functions of these terms. We may argue that various particular spiritualities do, or do not, provide a basis for such a politics, but we have first to understand that this and not the evasion of history is the end of the religiousness Wordsworth proposes. His poetry prompts us to consider not just the politics of particular religions, spiritualities, and the subjectivities that their practices produce (a pressing question in itself), but the disavowed religiousness—the status as beliefs for which we are responsible rather than as certain knowledge—of our own political values and orthodoxies, their anthropologies and subjectivities. The evasion of faith and all its potentially intellectual and existential rigor, in which our scholarship has too long indulged, is something that, in our current historical moment, our histories and our politics can ill afford.

Conclusion
On the Religiousness of Criticism

Criticism of religion is the premise of all criticism.

—Karl Marx, "Introduction," *Contribution to the Critique of Hegel's Philosophy of Right* (1844)[1]

To God we have become unaccustomed; of God we have become unaccustomed to speak, even to think, especially to write. If we slip and find ourselves thinking, speaking, even writing of God, it seems embarrassing, horribly embarrassing—even when our inquiry is critical. All of this God stuff was supposed to have been over a long time ago.

—Mark Taylor, *About Religion* (1999)[2]

In spite of the persistent evasion of faith in many disciplines and subspecialties, and in a turn that only two decades ago would have seemed almost unthinkable, we are witnessing what is being hailed and even invited in some quarters as the "return of religion" to literary theory and critical discourse. In her Presidential Address to the Modern Language Association in December 2003, Mary Louise Pratt proclaimed the urgency of the interdisciplinary study of religion in our literature departments. "Who can doubt today," she asked, "the need to study secularism and religiosity from every viewpoint we can muster?"[3] Shortly after Jacques Derrida's death in 2004, Stanley Fish prophesied in *The Chronicle of Higher Education* that religion will "succeed high theory and the triumvirate of race, gender, and class as the center of intellectual energy in the academy."[4]

Continental philosophy has perhaps been leading us back in the direction of religious rumination for some time now. From Heidegger we have heard about the God (or gods) before whom we can sing and dance; from Lévinas, about God beyond Being, and most recently from Jean-Luc Marion about the God without Being. As John Caputo puts it, "Even contemporary French philosophers like Jacques Derrida, who writes of 'my religion,' and Luce Irigaray, who writes of 'becoming divine,' thinkers who would be counted out as cold hard-hearted atheists by conventional confessional standards, cannot stop talking about God."[5] Citing recent works of Derrida, Irigaray, Slavoj Žižek, and Jean Baudrillard, Graham Ward notes a particular "production of the religious" in academic conversation that is "re-enchanting our understanding of the world."[6] But his word "production" is carefully chosen. Nina Pelikan Straus has more wryly suggested that the return of "religious longing" in academia is a "cultural symptom," marking a certain "boredom with a narrow subversiveness and with the ethical evasions of Grand Theory." Nonetheless, this turn does not represent to her mind a break from theory; rather, the late work of Derrida points toward the "reembrace of religious themes in literature" not as a "shredding of the Linguistic Turn, but its circumcision," its sacred coming of age.[7]

Perhaps the most important thing about this new incarnation of the religious in critical discourse is what it least resembles, that is, what has come since the eighteenth century in the Western world to pass for theology or the philosophy of religion. As Caputo so wittily has it in "Who Comes After the God of Metaphysics?":

> The talk about God and religion in contemporary continental philosophy bears almost no resemblance to what passes for traditional "philosophy of religion." The latter has typically concerned itself with offering proofs for the immortality of the soul and for the existence of God, and with identifying and analyzing the divine attributes. This tradition, which goes back to the scholastic debates of the high middle ages, is largely perpetuated in the works of contemporary Anglo-American philosophers, who offer the old wine of metaphysical theology in the new bottles of analytic philosophy. Richard Swinburne alone can fill a blackboard with the symbolic logic of his proofs. All over Anglo-America, logicians and epistemologists, from the Dutch Reformed to the Roman Catholic confessions, hasten to stretch a net of argumentation under faith in the divine being, lest the leap of faith end up falling to the floor in a great crash.[8]

It is this safety net of proofs and argumentation, Derrida argues in "Faith and Knowlege," that is actually inimical to *faith*. However inadvertently, Kant's "reflecting faith" guarantees a radical dissociation between God and the moral self, who, in Kant's scheme, by virtue of pure practical reason must ultimately act not in personal relation to God, hoping for reward (or relation), but precisely as though God does not exist. Deconstructing this faith produced by the logics of law and the mechanism of abstraction, Derrida shows that rational religion, which "determines absolute knowledge as the truth of religion" and ends in ontotheology, is "distinct from faith, from prayer, or from sacrifice" per se and, in his words, "destroys religion."[9] It is ontotheology that leads to Nietzschean pronouncements and the "death of God theology" that emerged in the United States in the 1960s with the works of Thomas J. J. Altizer. But, to lean on Caputo's wit once again, "It is clearly not God who is dead, an illusion entertained mostly by academics, but metaphysics's God, the God of metaphysical theology; it is speculative ruminations on God's nature and causal arguments demonstrating God's existence whose health has been recently declining."[10]

In the late twentieth century, forms of western Christianity that had invested heavily in this rationalization of God very predictably decried the rise of high theory, particularly of deconstruction, as the death of meaning and a sort of Nietzschean nihilism redivivus. Such attacks on reason and the foundations of human knowledge amounted to no less, they thought, than attacks on God and the possibility of religion and morals. But it should perhaps come as less of a surprise than it does that, after high theory itself seemed to decline in the early 1990s in the wake of the Paul de Man scandal, it has found its most thoughtful and reflective home in departments of theology, religious studies, and philosophical theology. Indeed, writers well versed in the Christian tradition such as a/theologian Mark C. Taylor and even those who proclaim some form of Christian faith, from Caputo and Ward to Merold Westphal, have turned out to be among our best readers of Derrida. For these writers, to see deconstruction as the destruction of meaning or grounds for nihilism is a misreading, because, as Derrida's later readings continually affirmed, deconstruction does not put an end to responsibility but calls for an increase of it, by revealing the constructed nature of our systems of law and understanding. Derrida's later writings, especially "Faith and Knowledge," critique systems that come to understand the truth of religion as knowledge, and they open up a space where, beyond what he calls rational "outbidding" in the quest for knowledge, the paradoxes inherent in notions of law, agency, and knowledge might surface, and belief and the experience of sacredness or alterity might take place.[11] This place of abstraction beyond abstraction, what Derrida calls "the desert in the desert," may, he admits, resemble "desertification"—a destitution of the possibility of goodness, truth, or ethics metaphysically conceived—but it can also "render possible precisely what it appears to threaten." As he put it in "*Mes Chances*," "it is the principle of indeterminism" that in one way of thinking, "makes the conscious freedom of man fathomable."[12]

In other words, what the linguistic turn of philosophy has made possible for some thinkers is the chance for religion to own up to the *faith* of faith: to rethink religion not as knowledge but as belief, and to explore the sense in which we might speak of the need for faith not as the shame but as the substance of religion and the ground of thought. This newly religious postmodernity has begun to look more to Kierkegaard than to Nietzsche, and in rereading categories like the singular, the absolute, and the religious, has begun to consider exactly how epistemological indeterminacy may be the basis of a genuinely creative human freedom and responsibility.[13] Perhaps the most promising thing about this return to religion is that for many thinkers it is also a return to *religions*. That is, while taking some far-reaching element of linguistic uncertainty into account, it has become wary of the seventeenth-century turn of thought that Ward traces to Herbert's *De Veritate*, of attempting to extract from all world religions "religion" in the abstract. Just as an honest scholarship cannot evade faith, it cannot ignore the particularities of faiths in history. For Asad, Caputo, Derrida, Lévinas, Ward, Westphal, and Žižek, this has meant a rigorous pursuit of the implications of poststructuralism in the particular contexts of Islam, Judaism, and Christianity, and of particular sects within those faiths. In so doing, these writers push us to the realization that even the most adamant secularism must acknowledge its historical embeddedness as a singular product of a rationalistic, Protestant-Catholic dialectic in Western modernity. This new analysis of religion and secularism demands entering into those histories in careful and comparative detail, attentive to the finer points of their differences and evolutions; Christianity as we see it in eighteenth-century Britain or twenty-first-century America is not Christianity as it has always been, and the more fundamental changes may not be those that the received history of religion narrates. The cultural formations of western Christianity, growing as they do in good part from binary, Protestant-Catholic debates, can be thrown into stark relief, for instance, when studied in comparison to that much neglected third term in Christendom: the Eastern Orthodox churches from which Rome severed itself nearly half a millennium before the Reformation, charting a course for Western Christianity wed to rationalism and enamored of individual authority, whether papal or personal.

Begun in the ludic and difficult *Prayers and Tears of Jacques Derrida* and continued in books of greater degrees of accessibility, John Caputo's rethinking of religion in terms that are as thoroughly Derridean as they are specifically Christian—and yet startling to members of both parties—is, to my mind, a fine and promising example of such a critical grappling with faith and faiths after the linguistic turn. Caputo's aim is to insist unabashedly on the inescapability of faith in the most universalizing human sense. The religious, he contends, "is a very basic structure of our lives," "tied up with having a future," even "the very thing that most constitutes human experience as such." "Religion may be found with or without religion," he writes, "that is my thesis."[14] Indeed, he seems to be arguing that religion is to be found whether we like it or not; his work amounts to a deconstruction of the very notion of a secular space untainted by belief. This religious sense of life is occasioned for Caputo precisely by the uncertainty inherent in language. Echoing writers from Kierkegaard to Derrida, Caputo writes that "Non-knowing is the inescapable element in which decisions are reached. . . . We are required to act, but our decisions are covered by a thin film, a quiet and uneasy sense, of unknowing."[15] The gay science that the truth of our uncertainty brings for Caputo is the recognition that "we can only and indeed must *believe*, and indeed that we must believe *something*," and that "we" are not preexistent, given objects operating by determined laws, but rather that, in enacting belief, we are continually "called upon to invent and reinvent ourselves or—since I am talking about the sort of thing over which we do not have mastery—to let ourselves be reinvented."[16] Refusals of this vulnerability of belief are wrapped up, he claims, in trying to maintain a sense of oneself as a self-contained subject of knowledge: "Those who refuse the religious," he claims, "want to retain their own self-possession, their own power, their own will."[17]

But the inevitability of faith is not just that we must believe, but that "we must believe *something*," and Caputo embodies this by reading the meaning of faith and uncertainty in terms so full-heartedly Christian that most of what passes for Christianity in American culture, for instance, would be challenged by them. For Caputo, the necessity of faith calls for vigorous reason as much as for humility and responsibility for the beliefs one holds. "My advice is to attach a coefficient of uncertainty to what we say," but "let there be no misunderstanding," he proclaims: "I am not recommending a life of ignorance or fence-sitting, of the comfort of finding the spot that precedes the 'either/or,' the fictitious peace of a space that somehow eludes the pull of competing forces, without siding or deciding one way or the other. . . . I do not recommend ignorance and I am not saying that there is no truth, but I am arguing that the best way to think about truth is to call it the best interpretation that anybody has come up with yet while conceding that no one knows what is coming next."[18] This is an uncomfortable position, and yet one he finds authentically Christian:

> Faith is not safe. Faith is not faith all the way down, so that all the gaps and crevices of faith are filled with more faith and it all makes for a

> perfect, continuous and well-rounded whole. Faith is always—and this is its condition—faith without faith, faith that needs to be sustained from moment to moment, from decision to decision, by the renewal, reinvention, and repetition of faith which is—if I may say so—continually exposed to discontinuity. Faith is always inhabited by unfaith, which is why the prayer in the New Testament makes such perfect sense, "Lord, I do believe, help my unbelief" (Mark 9:24). For my faith cannot be insulated from unbelief; it is co-constituted by unbelief, which is why faith is faith and not knowledge.[19]

For Caputo, faith becomes unavoidable in moments of need, desire, and recognition of lack. And so the same self who must believe is a self that is a question to herself and to others: "We do not know who we are—that is who we are. '*Quaestio mihi factus sum*' . . . is the way Augustine put it: 'I have been made a question unto myself,' echoing St. Paul (Rom. 7:15). Who am I? I am one who finds his life a question, which is what gives life its salt."[20] And personhood as inherently interrelational is for Caputo a characteristic of the Christian Trinity as well. "Jesus is not The Answer," Caputo makes bold to say, "but the place of the question,"[21] inasmuch as in the Christian conception he is the Word of God who, in becoming flesh, has put himself in personal, interpretive relation to human beings and asks, as he does Peter in the Gospels, "Who do you say that I am?"[22] Faith is the unsettling mark of our mutual construction in language and in imperfect knowledge, and this uncertainty is the grounds for an open though circumscribed human freedom and for personal relations organized in other than deterministic ways. Where Hegel's abstraction of Christian theology into his "Philosophy of Spirit" ultimately negates all that is particular about Christianity, Caputo's steering into the linguistic turn sets all wheels of Christian theology and praxis spinning—Trinity, incarnation, faith—while consciously directing them away from fundamentalism. However uncomfortable his swerving between deconstruction and Christianity makes us, this is, it seems to me, the sort of philosophically rigorous and religiously specific trip we need to be making.

The difference, however, between recent philosophical and theoretical reconsiderations of faith, like Caputo's, and the treatment of religion in most arts and humanities departments could not be more vast. As Taylor writes, God-talk is an embarrassment, and "To be done with God" is "a solution every bit as reassuring" as a comfortable certainty about "God's abiding presence."[23] And there are many methods for being done with God, particularly that of making God the subject of various critical orthodoxies. Marx's assumption that criticism of religion—of unreasoned belief, superstition, and ignorance—is the premise of all criticism seems alive and well, above all in social science approaches to religion and their aspirations toward objectivity. Things seem not to have changed too much since 1956 when Gabriel Le Bras banished "religious sociology" from the French academy and declared in the first number of *Archives de Sciences Sociales des Religions* a brave new world of scientific discovery of religion: "Private feelings have no relevance here," he declared; "This journal serves no doctrine, sectarian or non-sectarian, its single concern being to serve science."[24]

The fervor of Le Bras's comments hints how establishing a science of religious study becomes, in a very real way, the crucial confession of our collective certainty about rationalism. "Western science defines itself in terms of its historical rift with religion," Hervieu-Léger writes, "and this is the abiding context in which the sociology of religion is obliged to define its own aspirations." As a result of having to separate itself from the church and from pastoral theology, the sociology of religion has seemed "trapped in an empirical positivism which other branches of sociology . . . have long ago left behind." This bind occurs, Hervieu-Léger asserts, because the need for epistemological vigilance is felt to be doubly present in this field; the close study of religion continually poses the threat of opening up an avenue to religious belief which, "readily ascribed to the abdication of reason," presumably would "invalidate sociology itself."[25] And yet, the results of maintaining this narrative of the triumph of objectivity have been of no small detriment. As political scientist Alan Wolfe narrates it, operating on the assumption that the world is becoming increasingly secular, "social scientists from the 1960s until the 1980s treated religion as marginal to their concerns. Combined with the conviction on the part of many natural scientists that religion was hostile to their enterprise, . . . that left American academics outside of divinity schools unready for the religious revival that seemed to take on new life in the 1990s," particularly the decline of mainline religions and the rise of evangelical and fundamentalist ones. This raises the serious question for Wolfe of whether our current social science scholarship on religion "is up to the task of offering Americans insights on the controversies that surround them."[26]

In this climate, the outspoken Chapel Hill professor Christian Smith appears something like the John Caputo of sociology. In his most recent book, Smith challenges naturalistic and deterministic descriptions of human beings with the notion of persons as "moral, believing animals," meaning that faith assumptions undergird all of our attempts to know, including the radically empirical approaches to knowledge. We cannot function in thinking or living without prior assumptions, he argues, and thus, we will never fully understand human nature without an examination of human beliefs. Yet,

> Ironically, the implausible nature of the believing animals thesis to us is itself the most powerful substantiation of the very thesis itself. For most of us are such committed and trusting believers in the basic assumptions that constitute our liberal democratic capitalist world that we cannot even recognize our own believing as such. The world we bring into being through believing has for us become fixed, unified, total. We are thus not in the end very different in this condition than the medieval peasant from whom the Enlightenment promised to raise and deliver us. We are finally the very same kind of animal, lacking solid foundations, and so building up our lives as firmly as we can on trust and faith.[27]

Evidence for human persons as moral and religious agents, Smith argues, calls for new research that will move beyond the radically behavioral and sociobiological theories that have dominated twentieth-century sociology. It remains to be seen whether his discipline will follow his lead.

American a/theologian Mark C. Taylor gives an even more grave account of the disavowal of religiousness in religious studies. This disavowal is greatest in what its practitioners generally imagine as the dramatic postwar split between theology and religious studies, its post-Christian, posttheological turn, and the turn to theory. In an effort to overcome the impasse created by privileging theology and Christianity in the past, many students of religion turned, in Taylor's telling, to social-science methodologies. "Claiming to have freed themselves from the limitations imposed by religious interpretations of religion," he writes, "analysts enthusiastically embraced social scientific methods," but "all too often, however, these interpreters failed to assess their newfound theories with the same critical rigor they directed toward the methods they had left behind. Thus they remained blind to the philosophical, theological, and political implications of the positions they developed. In this way, belief and ideology were not left behind but merely changed their names."[28] For Taylor the disturbing upshot of this is that "the theories that still inform leading interpretations of religion are grounded in the tenets of modernism," and that therefore "the political consequences of these theories might be more problematic than their proponents are willing to admit."[29] When understood in this way, the shift from theology to theory does not, as many contemporary theorists think, "escape God" as Taylor puts it, but merely "exchanges overt faith for covert belief in the One in and through which all is understood."[30] Secularism and secular rationality, as Asad points out, have the distinction of operating as the academy's disavowed cult of the one truth.

It might be argued that no field of studies remains as grounded in what Taylor calls the tenets of modernism as the field addressed to the origin and emergence of modernity, eighteenth-century studies, and to the detriment of its understanding of religion and secularism in the period of their most profound mutual transformation. In Robert Sullivan's words, it has long been a well-established convention among historians of the European eighteenth century to condescend toward Christianity in their period, a tendency to which he himself confesses. "Even when deemed inoffensive," he writes, Christianity "was often represented as a history of mere vestiges, of a slippery slope, or of generalized change and decay," and when it was judged to be somehow offensive, he claims (citing E. P. Thomson's *The Making of the English Working Class*), "condescension sometimes became massive, even abusive." Despite the last twenty years in which this story has been slowly disaggregating and in which, Sullivan points out, the most recently published books suggest that "the cultural role of eighteenth-century Christianity was as various as it was central," difficulties remain.[31] In her fascinating work on the "spectacular failure" of the Philadelphian Society led by Protestant mystic Jane Lead (1623–1704), Paula McDowell has come to argue that the late-seventeenth- and early-eighteenth-century reaction against certain kinds of speech, writing, and intellectual inquiry associated with religious "enthusiasm" continues to affect what now counts as the object of English literary study:

> Despite postmodernist critiques of Enlightenment claims and frames, dominant interpretive frameworks in current eighteenth-century literary and cultural studies remain rooted in those epistemes—with significant implications for literary historiography. . . . While revisionist historians increasingly argue for the continuing centrality of religion as a social and cultural force, literary studies and cultural criticism remain strikingly unaffected by these developments. Despite a few promising signs, religious writing remains marginalized in our literary histories and cultural studies models, its place in our field of vision directly inverse to its actual importance in the period we study.[32]

McDowell goes on to say that this is not due to anachronistic models of fine literature or to a conspiracy of silence, but it is rather "a matter of how we as a discipline deal with works that do not fit dominant critical models of intelligibility and value."[33] Perhaps another way of phrasing this is that our secular models of intelligibility and value continue to silence and erase the truly innumerable religious references, subtle and overt, in the texts we study, allowing them, to paraphrase Irlam from another context, "to become unheard by passing over them," like much in mid-eighteenth-century poetry, "without comment."[34]

Like McDowell, I believe that these rituals of ignoring religious references in texts, these disavowals of faith in so many registers and disciplines, are driven by no grand conspiracies. Rather, to return us to the discussion toward the end of the introduction, these disavowals are connected by the academic subjectivies they make possible. Kathy Rudy has pointed out the centrality of a narrative of loss of faith both in academic inquiry and in the thriving genre of memoir. In many of the stories we tell, she writes, "coherence becomes fixed on the narrating/narrated subject itself; the loss of belief (and/or the assessment of the damages incurred as a result of that belief) becomes the glue that holds the subject together."[35] Writing about *Blue Windows*, Barbara Wilson's memoir of her Christian Science upbringing, Rudy claims that even though loss of faith is a gradual process, "for marketing purposes [Wilson] has to declare herself as a unified person who stands in a different place than self-identified Christian Scientists, much the same that I had to declare myself to you here today as having 'lost my faith.'"[36] In plain terms, familiar narratives of the loss of faith constitute subjects who can say "I" have lost my faith; they invite us into secular ideologies that hold open a space not for the divided, uncertain person who says, "Lord I believe, help my unbelief," but for a more coherent subject-without-belief.[37] To write otherwise about faith would be to implicate oneself in it.

But what, then, would scholarship look like that did not make this ideological investment: that acknowledged its thin film of uncertainty; that enacted a return to the religious that was the result of more than boredom, more than nostalgia, more than a passing academic fashion; that lived up to the insights of deconstruction, psychoanalysis, ideology critique, and the New Historicism; that truly "traversed the fantasy" of the subject of mastery, the subject-without-belief? In the course of writing this book, I have become convinced that this is the sort of scholarship that our times call for: neither the smug orthodoxies of grand theory, nor those of a militant historicism that nonetheless, when confronted with philosophy after the linguistic turn, buries its head in the sand—and certainly not scholarship of anemic half-affirmations or silence. To borrow again from Caputo's bold style:

> I insist that the "post-secular" style should arise by way of a certain *iteration* of the Enlightenment, a continuation of the Enlightenment by another means, the production of a New Enlightenment, one that is enlightened about the limits of the old one. The "post-" in "post-secular" should not be understood to mean "over and done with" but rather *after having passed through* modernity, so that there is no danger of the emergence of an irrational relativistic left, on the one hand, or of a lapsing back into a conservative pre-modernism masquerading under the guise of post-modern, on the other. . . . A more enlightened Enlightenment is no longer taken in by the dream of Pure Objectivity, even as it deploys a new idea of reason that is no longer taken in by the illusion of Pure Reason. It has a post-critical sense of

critique that is critical of the idea that we can establish air-tight borders around neatly discriminated spheres or regions like knowledge, ethics, art, and religion.[38]

For scholarship no longer taken in by the dream of objectivity, faith will be neither ignored nor peripheral, but central and of abiding interest. As I asserted in the introduction, a troubling of the neat boundaries between the secular and the religious would upset both secular and religious self-conceptions borne of modernist ideologies. Through the scholarly inquiries I imagine, religion as well as secularism undoubtedly will be made strange. On one hand, the sometimes defensive posture of scholars working on religion, to some extent understandable and quite justified, will have to be abandoned in favor of a more vulnerable self-critique, for the religious—particularly Christian religiousness in modernity—will often be shown to be compromised by an investment in a modernism which is at odds with the very meaning of faith. And on the other hand, secularism will continue to be shown to possess its own disavowed belief investments and to propel a variety of critical arguments with an epistemological bad faith that is often antireligious. This has in some sense been Derrida's point about Marxism for some time: he refers to the "messianic mark" of Marx's legacy and reminds us that "the religious also informs . . . that 'spirit' of emancipatory Marxism, whose injunction we are reaffirming here."[39]

The scholarship I imagine will own up to the religiousness of all intellectual endeavor, to the way that a belief, even the basic belief in language, is the predicate of all knowledge production. And it will embrace this not simply as a burden but as a positive possibility; that is, the "post" in post-Enlightenment may likely bring a perpetual bit of melancholy longing with it, but can also inspire celebration and a sober sort of playfulness. This scholarship will have a theological cast, in the sense that belief will be shown to inhabit and enliven every discipline. In different disciplinary registers, such scholarship would echo Ward's exhortation that theology must embrace the linguistic turn and the paradoxes of representation as its enabling ground: "the paradox of representation [idol/icon] is the crisis which theology reads, by faith, as God's Word to us," and theology, like (we might argue) all the other inherited disciplines, is the commanded paradoxical commentary on what has been received, "recognizing the inadequacy of all human language" and admitting that all "resolution either way is an act of faith."[40]

In "Lacan and Theology," Charles Winquist has similarly suggested that theology cannot be kept outside a hermetically sealed study of religion and that "theology in the wake of Lacan will be a theology of desire," known by its form rather than its content and, implicitly, by its concern with the desire and subjectivity of the one writing theology.[41] Such work, I argue, would have a full-bodied intellectual sharpness and historical vigor that would nevertheless not be about dominance, violence, and mastery, but that would have something of what, following Drucilla Cornell, we might call epistemological humility and even compassion about it.[42] Certainly this would bring a change of tone as well as content for much of our scholarship. At a recent regional meeting of the American Society for Eighteenth-Century Studies, one of the most vibrant, interdisciplinary, and theoretically diverse organizations in the humanities, the keynote lecture provided a prime example. In a strident tone the speaker struck down, one after another, the various approaches to literary study available today, until the only one left standing was his own, based primarily on having read every extant text in genre x between years y and z (itself no unworthy ideal) and thereby becoming the final authority on pronouncements about that literature. Asked in the question-and-answer session if he saw any room for theoretically inflected conversations about questions of value or meaning, the speaker rolled his eyes, ran his fingers through his hair and said, well yes, one could engage in questions of interpretation, but the establishment of literary history would be the only "timeless" or lasting scholarship. As audience members meekly filed down the steps of the auditorium, I happened to catch the eye of the fellow who had been sitting behind me. He shrugged his shoulders and laughed sheepishly, as though he had been watching someone play a video game, "It was kind of fun to watch him demolish all those other scholars like that."

The ground of the sort of humility I imagine about a lively and engaged scholarship is not just the recognition of the limitations of our knowledge, but the recognition that, in Smart's words, in our scholarship we are "speaking ourselves" from the crown of our head to the sole of our feet: that the disavowal of belief and the claim to rational certainty in modernity has been the basis of all manner of fundamentalisms and violences, of the mass murders and reeducation camps of materialist regimes in the century preceding our own, and in this one, of gross militarism in the name of religions that have forgotten they are faiths.[43] "At the core of fundamentalism," Caputo maintains, "there lies a repressed fear that faith is only faith and as such a risk with no guarantee of anything, which is the truth about religion to which it testifies in the mode of repressing it."[44] Surfacing this repressed lack of guarantee might be the basis not only of a scholarship which is able to hear whispers about religious and secular pasts that have been passed over in silence and of a scholarship that is not about demolition, but of one that is constructive in the most nonviolent and enlivening of ways. A humbler sort of scholarly subjectivity would recognize that the question is not whether but how to believe, and therefore could undertake the task of reimagining both faith and knowledge as something other than justifications for violence and acquisition in the world. We might do well to revise Marx and say, rather, that *religion* is the basis of all *criticism*, of criticism enacted with Caputo's coefficient of uncertainty and that, in Derrida's words, would never authorize any silence about the mistreatment of any other.[45] And in this sense, we might imagine scholarship and criticism as radical acts of construction, and even acts of love, for those whose works we read, and for those for whom we write and teach.

In his recent work on Christianity and *agape*, Slavoj Žižek describes love not as an inner contemplative stance, but as the *work* of love. "As every true Christian knows," he writes,

> love is the *work* of love—the hard and arduous work of repeated "uncoupling" in which, again and again, we have to disengage ourselves from the inertia that constrains us to identify with the particular order we were born into. Through the Christian work of compassionate love, we discern in what was hitherto a disturbing foreign body, tolerated and even modestly supported by us so that we were not too bothered by it, a subject, with its crushed dreams and desires—it is *this* Christian heritage of "uncoupling" that is threatened by today's "fundamentalisms," especially when they proclaim themselves Christian.[46]

The work of love is, in part, an uncoupling of oneself from the fantasy *of oneself* that is part of desire: the basic point of Christianity proper, for Žižek, is "precisely to *break out* of the vicious superego cycle of the Law and its transgression, via Love."[47] The impetus of love is not the thrill of transgression or the desire for the other's desire (i.e., the desire to be seen from a certain position within her), but finding the point from which to love the other within the other herself: in love, I "love the beloved one *for itself*, finding *in it* the very point *from which* I find it worthy of love."[48] Žižek's notion of *faith* is rooted in finitude and this constant spiritual work of love—of uncoupling oneself from ideological fantasy, and experiencing subjective destitution. And above all it is not an escape from the material world and everyday life, but rather in Žižek's mind it elevates "finitude to its transcendental a priori dignity." The greatness of Kierkegaard, according to Žižek, is to "show that our only access to eternity is through temporality," because the "terrain of the divine is contact with other humans."[49] "Only for a finite being do you have this infinite work," he insists, "in Christian terms, this trinity of faith, hope, love. Faith that the event did take place, hope in the final state . . . and love as work, as what is between the two, fidelity to the event." The gap between event and reality—that is, the gap that erupts because no event dictates how we must respond to it, the gap that is necessarily spanned by belief, because the present moment or interpretation is only related to any past moment or mark by faith—is for Žižek precisely "that which is covered up by totalitarianism" in its sundry forms.[50]

Scholarship that is a work of love would at some level testify to this gap within society and within the self. For we cannot properly speak of the *subject* of love, or in this sense of the "religious subject," because one who loves, for Žižek, is one who, through this process of repeated uncoupling from fantasies of the subject, undergoes subjective destitution, enabling him to see the other in all her strange difference and to love her, without appropriation or violence. In his reading of 1 Corinthians 13, Žižek writes that St. Paul's point "is not simply that *with* love, I am 'something,'" but rather that, "in love, *I am also nothing*, but, as it were, a Nothing humbly aware of itself, a Nothing paradoxically made rich through the very awareness of its lack."[51]

> Only a lacking, vulnerable being is capable of love: the ultimate mystery of love, therefore, is that incompleteness is, in a way, higher than completion. On the one hand, only an imperfect, lacking being loves: we love because we do *not* know all. On the other hand, even if we were to know everything, love would, inexplicably, still be higher than completed knowledge. Perhaps the true achievement of Christianity is to elevate a loving (imperfect) Being to the place of God, that is, of ultimate perfection. That is the kernel of the Christian experience. In the previous pagan attitude, imperfect earthly phenomena can serve as signs of the unattainable divine perfection. In Christianity, on the contrary, it is physical (or mental) perfection itself that is the sign of the imperfection (finitude, vulnerability, uncertainty) of you as the absolute person. Your physical beauty itself becomes a sign of this spiritual dimension—not the sign of your "higher" spiritual perfection, but the sign of *you* as a finite, vulnerable person. Only in this way do we really break out of idolatry.[52]

Perhaps it will not be taken as so much irrational enthusiasm to say that I hold out hope for a scholarly identity that breaks out of idolatry, that sees its critical consciousness as constructed by its approach to the other, as this "Nothing humbly aware of itself, a Nothing paradoxically made rich through the very awareness of its lack," made rich by its ability to love "in word and in deed" the other whom she looks upon, without designs of mastery or possession. It has been quite some time since we had a literary scholarship that spoke of loving a text or a writer. And this is likely as it should have been, inasmuch as we have not been able to think of critique as loving, or of critique as self-critique—as, to paraphrase Wordsworth, simultaneously suspecting and revering the selves we encounter in literature and create in criticism. I would hope for a scholarship which in all its critical rigor expresses love, and the "joyful-sorrow" that comes from critique always cutting with a second edge of *metanoia*, directed at the self and one's ongoing project of "change of mind." Such a scholarship would be critically—but, more importantly, openly—listening, and somehow gentle; it would not know deterministic answers which can be manufactured in advance, though it might sometimes guess at a strangeness it comes to expect. It would have room genuinely to be surprised by the other's voice in the text, approaching it as something sacred, always partly revealed yet partly unknown, whether in our own words, another's, or God's. In fine books, essays, and the most scintillating exchanges at conferences, I think this is precisely what we see. This, too, has been my effort in writing this book, with many failures and hopefully some successes. I say hopefully, because it is most important to me that I try to find a way to live in and look at the world as an integrated, intersubjective person—a researcher, thinker, writer, teacher, lover, and believer—without denying one of those identities to create a falsely whole one. If my scholarship can be a way of my putting off this "old self," then it may also enable me to see texts, others, and myself in a way that might be true, or at least not predicated on a fantasy of subjectivity and its desires.

To return us to the topic of this book, if there is any authentic spontaneity, any non-mechanistically determined experience or communion of genuine alterities across difference, we glimpse it, I believe, through beliefs and practices that shape a self of love, not through the shoring up of the subject of mastery. As Hervieu-Léger suggests, the social processes that lead to the formation of self are in this sense fundamentally religious—pertaining to rites and shaped collective memory; in anthropologist Thomas Luckmann's words, "Pushed to an extreme, everything in humanity which lies outside biological survival taken in its most narrowly material sense has to do with religion."[53] To read is, in some sense, to be religious. It is to situate oneself in the realm of language, which is a realm of uncertainty, of doubt, and of belief. It is in owning up to our work as acts of faith and to our self-construction in it that it makes sense to meditate on rituals of spontaneity: both the ones from which we would like to free ourselves, and the ones which we have yet to create.

Notes

INTRODUCTION

1. Edward Young, *Young's Night Thoughts, with Life, Critical Dissertation, and Explanatory Notes by the Rev. George Gilfillan* (Edinburgh, 1853), 3. The "Preface" appears here in its entirety.
2. George Gilfillan relates this anecdote of Monsieur and Madame Klopstock in his *Life*, prefaced to Young, *Night Thoughts*, xviii.
3. For the legacy of spontaneity in twentieth-century American arts from bebop to the beat poets, see Daniel Belgrad, *The Culture of Spontaneity: Improvisation and the Arts in Postwar America* (Chicago: University of Chicago Press, 1998). Belgrad's is an optimistic account of spontaneity's "powerful impact" as a critique of postwar industrial capitalism that is nonetheless aware of the limitations of the spontaneous aesthetic (namely, its difficulty to sustain) and its seemingly inevitable counterreaction (247, 260).
4. Leon Guilhamet, *The Sincere Ideal: Studies on Sincerity in Eighteenth-Century English Literature* (Montreal: McGill-Queen's University Press, 1974), 24.
5. Lawrence E. Klein and Anthony J. La Vopa, introduction to *Enthusiasm and Enlightenment in Europe, 1650–1850*, ed. Lawrence E. Klein and Anthony J. La Vopa (San Marino, Calif.: Huntington Library Press, 1998), 3.
6. Shaun Irlam, *Elations: The Poetics of Enthusiasm in Eighteenth-Century Britain* (Stanford: Stanford University Press, 1999), 28.
7. Irlam, *Elations*, 17. On this point Irlam also references J. G. A. Pocock, *The Machiavellian Moment: Florentine Political Thought and the Atlantic Republican Tradition* (Princeton: Princeton University Press, 1975); Marjorie Hope Nicolson, *The Breaking of the Circle: Studies in the Effect of the "New Science"*

upon Seventeenth-Century Poetry (Evanston, Ill.: Northwestern University Press, 1950); Alexandre Koyré, *From the Closed World to the Infinite Universe* (1957; repr., Baltimore: The Johns Hopkins University Press, 1968); Don Cameron Allen, *Mysteriously Meant: The Rediscovery of Pagan Symbolism and Allegorical Interpretation in the Renaissance* (Baltimore: The Johns Hopkins University Press, 1970).

8. On the negative portrayal of ritual by Puritans and Dissenters, see chap. 1 below.
9. The secularization thesis describes a long-standing research program and explanatory model that asserts that the social significance of religion diminishes in response to three crucial aspects of modernity: social differentiation (the increasing specialization of societal institutions that gradually take over functions once performed by religion), societalization (the process by which life gradually becomes more societally or nationally, rather than locally, oriented), and rationalization (changes in human thought and action linked to developing technology and the declining necessity of faith in the functioning of everyday life). A clear and helpful starting place is Roy Wallis and Steve Bruce, "Secularization: The Orthodox Model," in *Religion and Modernization: Sociologists and Historians Debate the Secularization Thesis*, ed. Steve Bruce, 8–30 (Oxford: Clarendon, 1992). The literature supporting and challenging the secularization is far too vast to be summarized here. America's status as the most religious and simultaneously most wealthy, technologically advanced Western nation, as well as the spread of religious movements and fundamentalisms worldwide, are clearly the chief (and some would say crippling) obstacles to the thesis's explanatory force and predictive validity.
10. J. G. A. Pocock, "Enthusiasm: The Antiself of Enlightenment," in Klein and La Vopa, *Enthusiasm and Enlightenment in Europe*, 7–28, here 12.
11. Danièle Hervieu-Léger, *Religion as a Chain of Memory*, trans. Simon Lee (New Brunswick, N.J.: Rutgers University Press, 2001), 2.
12. Talal Asad, *Formations of the Secular: Christianity, Islam, Modernity* (Stanford: Stanford University Press, 2003), 200, 201.
13. Hervieu-Léger, *Chain of Memory*, 35, 83, 88, 123. While Hervieu-Léger would like to affirm modern forms of religion as being "as fully religious as are traditional religions" (71), I side more with Graham Ward in his assessment that—stripped of living ritual, the embodiment of community, and the connection to specific religious history and belief—religion in modernity most often becomes simply the transcendent "special effect" of the commodity form, less a "chain of memory" (the heart of Hervieu-Léger's definition of religion) than a ritual of forgetting. See Graham Ward, *True Religion* (Oxford: Blackwell, 2003), 114–53.
14. Slavoj Žižek, *The Sublime Object of Ideology* (London: Verso, 1989), 34.
15. *Oxford English Dictionary*, 2nd ed., s.vv. "spontaneous" and "spontaneity."
16. Asad, *Formations of the Secular*, 13–14.
17. We also must recognize the particularity of this critique and discussion to a western European and American context, where secularism and religion have long been opposed in a binary debate. Recent discussions of secularism

on the Indian subcontinent, for example, acknowledge the ubiquity and diversity of religion; rather than a choice between religion and secularism, they pose the question of what sort of political secularism will best allow for the freedom and peaceful coexistence of different religious groups. I thank my colleague Priya Kumar for this insight, drawn from her forthcoming book, *At Home with the "Stranger": Secularism and the Ethics of Coexistence in Indian Fiction.*

18. Terry Eagleton, *The Ideology of the Aesthetic* (Oxford: Blackwell, 1990), 34.
19. My findings here support Scott Paul Gordon's assertion that secularization increases the sense of paralysis associated with moral feeling; Scott Paul Gordon, *The Power of the Passive Self in English Literature, 1640–1770* (Cambridge: Cambridge University Press, 2002), 52–53.
20. Jacques Derrida, "My Chances/*Mes Chances:* A Rendezvous with Some Epicurean Stereophonies," in *Taking Chances: Derrida, Psychoanalysis, and Literature*, ed. J. H. Smith and William Kerrigan, 1–32 (Baltimore: The Johns Hopkins University Press, 1984), here 8.
21. John Caputo, *On Religion* (London: Routledge, 2001), 33–34.
22. R. S. Crane, "Suggestions toward a Genealogy of the 'Man of Feeling,'" *ELH* 1 (1934): 230.
23. Greene argued that Church of England divines (and more importantly their liturgy) had remained Augustinian and therefore could not account for the rise of sensibility's optimism about human nature; Donald Greene, "Latitudinarianism and Sensibility: The Genealogy of the 'Man of Feeling' Reconsidered," *Modern Philology* 75 (1977): 159–83. Other useful studies in the history-of-ideas tradition include Louis I. Bredvold, *The Natural History of Sensibility* (Detroit: Wayne State University Press, 1962) and John K. Sheriff, *The Good-Natured Man: The Evolution of a Moral Ideal, 1660–1800* (Tuscaloosa: University of Alabama Press, 1982).
24. R. F. Brissenden, *Virtue in Distress: Studies in the Novel of Sentiment from Richardson to Sade* (New York: Barnes & Noble, 1974); Janet M. Todd, *Sensibility: An Introduction* (London: Methuen, 1986); Robert Markley, "Sentimentality as Performance: Shaftesbury, Sterne, and the Theatrics of Virtue," in *The New Eighteenth Century: Theory, Politics, English Literature*, ed. Felicity Nussbaum and Laura Brown, 210–30 (New York: Routledge, 1987); Carol Kay, *Political Constructions: Defoe, Richardson, and Sterne in Relation to Hobbes, Hume, and Burke* (Ithaca: Cornell University Press, 1988); and John Mullan, *Sentiment and Sociability: The Language of Feeling in the Eighteenth Century* (New York: Oxford University Press, 1988).
25. G. J. Barker-Benfield, *The Culture of Sensibility: Sex and Society in Eighteenth-Century Britain* (Chicago: University of Chicago Press, 1992).
26. Robert Jones, "Ruled Passions: Re-reading the Culture of Sensibility," *Eighteenth-Century Studies* 32 (1999): 395–96.
27. Claudia L. Johnson, *Equivocal Beings: Politics, Gender, and Sentimentality in the 1790s: Wollstonecraft, Radcliffe, Burney, Austen* (Chicago: University of Chicago Press, 1995), 12. My account of scholarship on sentiment evolving from an earlier history-of-ideas framework toward more self-consciously political critiques draws from Johnson's. Barbara Benedict's work from about

the same time handles sentiment's relation to gender differently. In *Framing Feeling*, Benedict argued that sentimental literature participated in an emergent discourse concerned with controlling emotion and integrating the individual into society; sensibility is best understood, she contended, not as a cultural norm but as a set of anxiety-inducing problems around epistemology, sexuality, morality, and bodily sensation. Barbara Benedict, *Framing Feeling: Sentiment and Style in English Prose Fiction, 1745–1800* (New York: AMS Press, 1994).

28. In sentimental novels, Skinner argues, we see an "unexpected but nevertheless crucial conjunction" of the "apparently inimical discourses" of feeling and finance in the "sentimental fantasy" of a hero who is explicitly "above economy." Skinner, like Mullan, identifies *The Man of Feeling* as "the crisis" of the genre, illustrating only concerned paralysis before real economic problems and consumer practices. Gillian Skinner, *Sensibility and Economics in the Novel, 1740–1800: The Price of a Tear* (London: Macmillan, 1999), 10, 92.

29. Markman Ellis, *The Politics of Sensibility: Race, Gender and Commerce in the Sentimental Novel* (Cambridge: Cambridge University Press, 1996), 17. On the interrelation between economics and sentimentality, see also John Morillo, *Uneasy Feelings: Literature, the Passions, and Class from Neoclassicism to Romanticism* (New York: AMS Press, 2001), which argues that delimited passions made it possible to think class as opposed to rank. In a related vein, J. G. A. Pocock and scholars following him have proposed politeness as a new ideology of "virtue" that accommodated commercial society in a way older notions of civic virtue could not; see Pocock, *Machiavellian Moment*, 467–88, and his *Virtue, Commerce and History: Essays on Political Thought and History, Chiefly in the Eighteenth Century* (Cambridge: Cambridge University Press, 1985), 37–50. See also Emma Rothschild, *Economic Sentiments: Adam Smith, Condorcet, and the Enlightenment* (Cambridge, Mass.: Harvard University Press, 2001).

30. Deidre Shauna Lynch, *The Economy of Character: Novels, Market Culture, and the Business of Inner Meaning* (Chicago: University of Chicago Press, 1998), 126.

31. Julie Ellison, *Cato's Tears and the Making of Anglo-American Emotion* (Chicago: University of Chicago Press, 1999), 22, 7.

32. Ann Jessie Van Sant, *Eighteenth-Century Sensibility and the Novel: The Senses in Social Context* (Cambridge: Cambridge University Press, 1993); Robert A. Erickson, *The Language of the Heart, 1600–1750* (Philadelphia: University of Pennsylvania Press, 1997); and Geoffrey M. Sill, *The Cure of the Passions and the Origins of the English Novel* (Cambridge: Cambridge University Press, 2001).

33. William Donoghue, *Enlightenment Fiction in England, France, and America* (Gainesville: University Press of Florida, 2002), 2.

34. Adela Pinch, *Strange Fits of Passion: Epistemologies of Emotion, Hume to Austen* (Stanford: Stanford University Press, 1996), 4, 7.

35. Wendy Motooka, *The Age of Reasons: Quixotism, Sentimentalism, and Political Economy in Eighteenth-Century Britain* (London: Routledge, 1998), 1, 6. In a less skeptical analysis, John Alfred Dwyer's *The Age of the Passions: An*

Interpretation of Adam Smith and Scottish Enlightenment Culture (East Linton, Scotland: Tuckwell Press, 1998) expresses a sort of nostalgia for what he sees as the much needed social and ethical work performed by the concept of moral sentiment.

36. Gordon, *Power of the Passive Self*, 5, 10, 11.
37. Gordon, *Power of the Passive Self*, 1, 13, 5. For his purposes Gordon distinguishes passivity from spontaneity as a later Romantic notion meaning "generated from within," whereas passivity locates the source for actions outside. I would argue that the key element of sentiment is its evidentiary status as mediating the two: the mechanistic sensation and spontaneous internal registering of (ostensibly) objective states like salvation or the morality of a given action.
38. Barker-Benfield, *Culture of Sensibility*, xvii, xix; 65–77, emphasis added.
39. Asad points out that though "the terms 'secularism' and 'secularist' were introduced into English by freethinkers in the middle of the nineteenth century in order to avoid the charge of their being 'atheists' and 'infidels,'" the concept of the secular is constituted in the preceding century and early modernity through a web of related oppositions such as belief and knowledge, reason and imagination: "the representation of the Christian God as being sited quite apart in 'the supernatural' world signals the construction of a secular space that begins to emerge in early modernity." "The concept of 'the secular' today," Asad asserts, "is part of a doctrine called secularism," and the genealogy of secularism must be traced through the concept of the secular "in part to the Renaissance doctrine of humanism, in part to the Enlightenment concept of nature, and in part to Hegel's philosophy of history." Asad, *Formations of the Secular*, 23–25, 27, 191–92.
40. See Michael McKeon, *The Origins of the English Novel, 1600–1740* (Baltimore: The Johns Hopkins University Press, 1987), 20–22.
41. Hervieu-Léger, *Chain of Memory*, 23, 29.
42. Jean-François Lyotard, *The Differend: Phrases in Dispute*, trans. Georges Van Den Abbeele (Minneapolis: University of Minnesota Press, 1988), xii and passim (emphasis added). The genre of dialogue, for instance, links an ostentation (a phrase of showing) or a definition (a phrase of describing) onto a question, with the goal of two parties coming to an agreement about the sense of a referent.
43. Lyotard, *Differend*, xi.
44. Lyotard, *Differend*, xiii. The careful articulation of differends and witnessing to the real injuries and injustices which genres of discourse are used to inflict is, Lyotard affirms, the very task of philosophy; it is the way to a genuinely "philosophical politics" and nothing short of a paradigm for ethics within a declining faith in our ability to arrive at universal doctrines via rationalism or empiricism: an epilogue to modernity and a prologue to "an honorable postmodernity."
45. What we may refer to as the rationalization of religion in the West certainly began much earlier, a point discussed at length below.
46. Dipesh Chakrabarty, "The Time of History and the Times of Gods," in *The Politics of Culture in the Shadow of Capital*, ed. Lisa Lowe and David Lloyd, 35–60 (Durham, N.C.: Duke University Press, 1997), 35, qtd. in Kathy

Rudy, "Subjectivity and Belief," *Literature and Theology* 15 (2001): 227; second quotation from Rudy, "Subjectivity and Belief," 228.
47. Conrad Brunström, *William Cowper: Religion, Satire, Society* (Lewisburg, Pa.: Bucknell University Press, 2004), 169, 168.
48. Pocock, "Enthusiasm," 23.
49. Discussions that treat religion as part of an ancien régime that has either passed away or is still in place are vulnerable to the binary thinking about religion and secularism that I suggest we challenge, even as they are necessary, given the distortions of scholarship that (equally polarizing) would have a completely secular and modern eighteenth century; cf. J. C. D. Clark, *English Society, 1660–1832: Religion, Ideology and Politics During the Ancien Regime*, 2nd ed. (Cambridge: Cambridge University Press, 2000).
50. Robert Markley, "Objectivity as Ideology: Boyle, Newton, and the Languages of Science," *Genre* 16 (1983): 355; Thomas Sprat, *The History of the Royal Society of London, for the Improving of Natural Knowledge, Second edition, Corrected* (1667; London, 1702), 112.
51. Ernst Cassirer, *The Philosophy of Enlightenment* (1932; repr., Princeton: Princeton University Press, 1951).
52. See for instance Pocock, "Enthusiasm," 8, 10; Dorinda Outram, *The Enlightenment*, New Approaches to European History 7 (Cambridge: Cambridge University Press, 1995), 39; and Ward, *True Religion*, 7–8, 52–65.
53. This body of scholarship is in itself quite troublesome, mainly due to lack of precision about what constitutes secularism or secularization. B. J. Gibbons, for instance, decries what he sees as the "secularization" of Richard Overton and other Interregnum radicals by "secular minded historians" who ignore their religious professions; Gibbons cannot condone any notion of a confessing believer engaging in secularizing modes of thought within or alongside his religious beliefs. T. B. Tomlinson is more nuanced in ascribing to pious Puritans of the 1640s–1660s "an instinctive trust in *this* world" that may be more subtly secularizing. B. J. Gibbons, "Richard Overton and the Secularism of the Interregnum Radicals," *Seventeenth Century* 10 (1995): 71; T. B. Tomlinson, "The Secular Spirit of Milton's England: 1640s–1660s," *Literature and History* 10 (1984): 223.
54. William Bouwsma, "The Secularization of Society in the Seventeenth Century," chap. 4 of *A Usable Past: Essays in European Cultural History* (Berkeley: University of California Press, 1990), 112–28.
55. Raymond D. Tumbleson, *Catholicism in the English Protestant Imagination: Nationalism, Religion, and Literature 1660–1745* (Cambridge: Cambridge University Press, 1998), 204; Knud Haakonssen, ed., *Enlightenment and Religion: Rational Dissent in Eighteenth-Century Britain* (Cambridge: Cambridge University Press, 1996).
56. Markley, "Objectivity as Ideology"; Patrick Collinson, *The Birthpangs of Protestant England: Religious and Cultural Change in the Sixteenth and Seventeenth Centuries* (New York: St. Martin's Press, 1988), 147; Patrick Collinson, *The Puritan Character: Polemics and Polarities in Early Seventeenth-Century English Culture* (Los Angeles: William Andrews Clark Memorial Library, 1989), 25.

57. Bouwsma, "Secularization of Society," 121.
58. Bouwsma, "Anxiety and the Formation of Early Modern Culture," chap. 6 of *A Usable Past*, 157–89, here 171.
59. Max Horkheimer and Theodor W. Adorno, *The Dialectic of Enlightenment*, trans. John Cumming (New York: Continuum, 1972), 7. See also Jürgen Habermas, *The Philosophical Discourse of Modernity: Twelve Lectures*, trans. Frederick Lawrence (Cambridge, Mass.: MIT Press, 1987); and Michael McKeon, "The Origins of Interdisciplinary Studies," *Eighteenth-Century Studies* 28 (1994): 17–28. McKeon notes secularization (the cordoning off of religious knowledge) among these divisions of knowledge, together with historicizing knowledge, the empirical project, and the emergence of the aesthetic as a sphere untainted by interest.
60. Carlos M. N. Eire, *War Against the Idols: The Reformation of Worship from Erasmus to Calvin* (Cambridge: Cambridge University Press, 1986), 312, 3; Thomas H. Luxon, *Literal Figures: Puritan Allegory and the Reformation Crisis in Representation* (Chicago: University of Chicago Press, 1995), 4, 211 n. 14.
61. Ward, *True Religion*, 54.
62. Ward, *True Religion*, 52, 54, 55.
63. Ward, *True Religion*, 58–59.
64. I would argue that Western Christendom embarked on a simultaneously rationalizing and secularizing path with the monumental changes it inaugurated at the beginning of the second millennium: the Great Schism in 1054 reflected shifts that had been in motion for some time and severed the West from the Eastern churches and their conciliar patriarchates and resulted in the evolution of the papacy as an increasingly political and economic agent, culminating, in some senses, in the sale of indulgences. Other crucial developments included Anselm of Canterbury's rationalization of the atonement and incarnation, and even more importantly, scholasticism's replacement of ascetic notions of spiritual praxis, synergia, and hesychasm with more strictly intellectual endeavor, understood as a self-contained pathway to God and already distinctive for its Aristotelian idea of the natural, so well articulated in the life and works of Hugh de St. Victor.
65. For Marx's collected works on religion, see Karl Marx and Friedrich Engels, *On Religion*, intro. by Reinhold Niebuhr (New York: Schocken Books, 1964).
66. Max Weber, *The Protestant Ethic and the Spirit of Capitalism*, trans. Stephen Kalberg (1904; repr., Chicago: Fitzroy Dearborn, 2001). Weber further thought that the laity's need for assurances of salvation led to the modification of orthodox Calvinism known as "covenant theology," which in turn encouraged believers to seek for behavioral evidences of salvation.
67. R. H. Tawney, *Religion and the Rise of Capitalism: A Historical Study* (1922; repr., Gloucester, Mass.: Peter Smith, 1962). See also Christopher Hill, *Economic Problems of the Church, from Archbishop Whitgift to the Long Parliament* (Oxford: Clarendon, 1968), and *Society and Puritanism in Pre-Revolutionary England* (New York: Schocken Books, 1964).
68. David Zaret, *The Heavenly Contract: Ideology and Organization in Pre-Revolutionary Puritanism* (Chicago: University of Chicago Press, 1985), 165–66.

69. Zaret, *Heavenly Contract*, 167, 201. Zaret's study counters J. G. A. Pocock's and Joyce Appleby's arguments against the Tawney-Hill thesis, that the classical bourgeois ideology and market theory of personality had not yet emerged in the late seventeenth century; according to Zaret, it clearly had. See Zaret, *Heavenly Contract*, 202–3.
70. Zaret, *Heavenly Contract*, 10, 175.
71. Karl Polanyi, *The Great Transformation* (New York: Farrar & Rinehard, 1944).
72. Kurt Heinzelman, *The Economics of the Imagination* (Amherst: University of Massachusetts Press, 1980), xi.
73. Marc Shell, *Money, Language, and Thought: Literary and Philosophical Economies from the Medieval to the Modern Era* (Berkeley: University of California Press, 1982), 4.
74. Shell, *Money, Language, and Thought*, 40, 180.
75. Lyotard, *Differend*, xiii.
76. Lyotard, *Differend*, xv.
77. Gilles Deleuze, *Difference and Repetition*, trans. Paul Patton (New York: Columbia University Press, 1994); Jacques Derrida, "Force of Law: The 'Mystical Foundation of Authority,'" in *Deconstruction and the Possibility of Justice*, ed. Drucilla Cornell, Michael Rosenfeld, and David Gray Carlson, 3–67 (New York: Routledge, 1992). Deleuze's work and, as I have shown elsewhere, that of Derrida and Lyotard, points toward two sorts of repetition: the market-driven reductionism and "repetitions of the same" that are the object of their ethical critiques, and the practices of rereading and reflecting that economic life and consumer mentality make more difficult but which would be the basis for ethical, nonreductive approaches to the other. See my essay, "The Benefit of Doubt: The Ethics of Rereading," in *Critical Ethics: Text, Theory, and Responsibility*, ed. Dominic Rainsford and Tim Woods, 187–202 (New York: Macmillan, 1999).
78. Marc Shell, *The Economy of Literature* (Baltimore: The Johns Hopkins University Press, 1978), 10; Shell, *Money, Language, and Thought*, 185.
79. Graham Ward, "The Commodification of Religion, or The Consummation of Capitalism," in *Theology and the Political: The New Debate*, ed. Creston Davis, John Milbank, and Slavoj Žižek, intro. Rowan Williams, 327–39 (Durham, N.C.: Duke University Press, 2005), 338.
80. Žižek, *Sublime Object of Ideology*, 4–5.
81. Žižek, *Sublime Object of Ideology*, passim.
82. Gen 3:5, 4, paraphrase; cf. the Authorized Version (AV) and the New Revised Standard Version (NRSV).
83. Gen 3:16 (NRSV).
84. Matt 6:24, paraphrase: in the AV, "Ye cannot serve God and mammon," and in the NRSV, "You cannot serve God and wealth."
85. Hervieu-Léger, *Chain of Memory*, 74.
86. I develop this concept at length in the conclusion. The pattern of disavowal and reavowal I describe here, what Derrida calls the "outbidding structure" of reason, is visible in the long historical trajectory of this sort of subject and its secularism. The cult of biblical literalism confirmed by enthusiasm needs

the demonized superstition and papistry it supplants, an antagonism that helps distract it from its own uncertainties—which erupt nonetheless, as did Bunyan's involuntary lashing out at God and the entire theology of buying and selling, created in the subject's image. As Shaftesbury's journals likewise demonstrate, the space guaranteeing the possibility of total knowledge is posited first as the God position, but is ultimately a space from which the subject must displace God, to occupy himself; see chap. 3.
87. Asad, *Formations of the Secular*, 124.
88. Ward, *True Religion*, 126.
89. Asad, *Formations of the Secular*, 200. Similarly Hervieu-Léger points out "the affinity that modernity has retained with a set of religious themes to do with fulfillment and salvation, but from which it continually seeks to distance itself in order to exist as such" (*Chain of Memory*, 3).
90. Qtd. in Hervieu-Léger, *Chain of Memory*, 3 (emphasis added).
91. Caputo, *On Religion*, 59.
92. Caputo, *On Religion*, 100.
93. Caputo, *On Religion*, 124.
94. Jacques Derrida, "Faith and Knowledge: Two Sources of Religion at the Limits of Reason Alone," in *Religion*, ed. Jacques Derrida and Gianni Vattimo, 1–78 (Stanford: Stanford University Press, 1998), 2.
95. Ward, *True Religion*, 66.
96. Ward, *True Religion*, 67 (emphasis added).
97. Hervieu-Léger, *Chain of Memory*, 2.

CHAPTER 1

1. Ronald Hutton, *The Rise and Fall of Merry England: The Ritual Year 1400–1700* (Oxford: Oxford University Press, 1994), 68. For additional histories of ritual and liturgy in the British isles before and during the Reformation, see Eamon Duffy, *The Stripping of the Altars: Traditional Religion in England, 1400–1580* (New Haven: Yale University Press, 1992); David Cressy, *Birth, Marriage, and Death: Ritual, Religion, and the Life-Cycle in Tudor and Stuart England* (Oxford: Oxford University Press, 1997); Dom Gregory Dix, *The Shape of the Liturgy* (1945; repr., London: Dacre, 1978); Cheslyn Jones et al., eds., *The Study of Liturgy*, rev. ed. (London: SPCK, 1992). In *Transformations of the Word: Spenser, Herbert, Vaughan* (Athens: University of Georgia Press, 1989), John Wall argues that living English Church ritual and the Common Prayer are the key contexts for understanding the poems of Spenser, Herbert, and Vaughan: not primarily "intellectual assent to a specific doctrinal position but the entering in to something done" (11). For a more general treatment of carnival and the eventual "triumph of lent" 1500–1800, see Peter Burke, *Popular Culture in Early Modern Europe*, rev. ed. (Hants, UK: Scolar Press, 1994), 178–243.
2. Thomas M. Greene, introduction to *Ceremony and Text in the Renaissance*, ed. Douglas F. Rutledge, 11–18 (Newark: University of Delaware Press, 1996), 12–13. On the crisis of representation and reformed religion, and also the subsequent shift from visual images to words as vehicles of meaning, see

Eire, *War Against the Idols*, 315; Luxon, *Literal Figures*, 5ff.; Robert Markley, *Fallen Languages: Crises of Representation in Newtonian England, 1660–1740* (Ithaca: Cornell University Press, 1993). For a brilliant argument for religious discourse *as* crisis of representation, see Graham Ward, "Theology and the Crisis of Representation," in *Literature and Theology at Century's End*, ed. Gregory Salyer and Robert Detweiler, AAR Studies in Religion 72, 131–58 (Atlanta: Scholar's Press, 1995).

3. Andrew Barnes, "Religious Reform and the War Against Ritual," *Journal of Ritual Studies* 4 (1990): 132. John Bossy traces the effacement of ritual to two main factors, the influence of Erasmus and the rise of books and print; see his *Christianity in the West, 1400–1700* (Oxford: Oxford University Press, 1985), 98, 103. For the earliest critiques of liturgy in England, see Horton Davies, *From Cranmer to Hooker, 1534–1603*, vol. 1, *Worship and Theology in England* (Princeton: Princeton University Press, 1970), 255–93.

4. Luxon, *Literal Figures*, 8.

5. What Edmund Morgan has called a "morphology of conversion" emerged in sixteenth- and seventeenth-century Puritanism; see his *Visible Saints: The History of a Puritan Idea* (Ithaca: Cornell University Press, 1963), 90–91. Eugene White provides a succinct account of the standard Puritan conception of conversion, stemming from the understanding of reason as the central aspect of the human person, in *Puritan Rhetoric: The Issue of Emotion in Religion* (Carbondale: Southern Illinois University Press, 1972), 11–12. For extended descriptions and analyses of the dramatic, onetime conversion experience, see Charles Lloyd Cohen, *God's Caress: The Psychology of Puritan Religious Experience* (New York: Oxford University Press, 1986); and Michael McGiffert, ed., *God's Plot: Puritan Spirituality in Thomas Shepard's Cambridge*, rev. ed. (Amherst: University of Massachusetts Press, 1994), especially the introduction and 42–48. John Sitter has argued for the importance of the conversion plot to literature on into the eighteenth century in *Literary Loneliness in Mid-Eighteenth-Century England* (Ithaca: Cornell University Press, 1982).

6. See for instance Francis Barker, *The Tremulous Private Body: Essays on Subjection* (Ann Arbor: University of Michigan Press, 1995); and Luxon, *Literal Figures*, 6. Some recent scholarship has stressed ritual aspects of Puritan devotion; cf. Charles Hambrick-Stowe, *The Practice of Piety: Puritan Devotional Disciplines in Seventeenth-Century New England* (Chapel Hill: University of North Carolina Press, 1982).

7. Collinson, *Birthpangs of Protestant England*, 141.

8. The definition of Puritanism has been the subject of exhaustive and exhausting debate. For a helpful account of and response to this debate, see Collinson's *Puritan Character*. For helpful recent treatments of Puritanism, see John Spurr, *English Puritanism, 1603–1689* (London: Macmillan, 1998); and Christopher Durston and Jacqueline Eales's "The Puritan Ethos, 1560–1700," in *The Culture of English Puritanism, 1560–1700*, ed. Christopher Durston and Jacqueline Eales, 1–31 (New York: St. Martin's Press, 1996). Kristen Poole gives a helpful account not only of definitional debates but ways that contemporary culture and scholarship continue to use

the term problematically as a marker for a repressive past and "antithesis to [all] which is generally valued by literary critics"; Kristen Poole, *Radical Religion from Shakespeare to Milton: Figures of Nonconformity in Early Modern England* (Cambridge: Cambridge University Press, 2000), 9, 182.

9. Hutton, *Rise and Fall*, 79. Margaret Aston describes how rood-lofts and churchyard crosses were still turning up to be burnt all during Elizabeth's reign, indicating resistance to the Henrican reforms; see Margaret Aston, "Puritans and Iconoclasm, 1560–1700," in Durston and Eales, *Culture of English Puritanism*, 92–121, here 97. For responses to the Henrican reformations, see Eamon Duffy, "Continuity and Divergence in Tudor Religion," in *Unity and Diversity in the Church*, ed. R. N. Swanson, 171–205 (Oxford: Blackwell, 1996); and for primary texts, W. H. Frere and C. E. Douglas, eds., *Puritan Manifestoes: A Study of the Origins of the Puritan Revolt, with a Reprint of the Admonition to the Parliament and Kindred Documents, 1572* (London: SPCK, 1907). Peter Iver Kaufman provides a compelling account of the "prayer wars of the 1590s" in "Much in Prayer," chap. 1 of *Prayer, Despair, and Drama: Elizabethan Introspection* (Urbana: University of Illinois Press, 1996), 15–40. For a wonderful treatment of early champions of spontaneity and defenders of liturgical prayer, see Ramie Targoff, *Common Prayer: The Language of Public Devotion in Early Modern England* (Chicago: University of Chicago Press, 2001), particularly chap. 2, "Reading Prayer: Spontaneity and Conformity," 36–56.

10. Royal Injunctions, qtd. in Aston, "Puritans and Iconoclasm," 94.

11. Hutton, *Rise and Fall*, 109–10.

12. Puritans limited true worship to six biblical "ordinances": prayer, praise (primarily singing psalms), preaching the word, the "gospel sacraments" of baptism and the Lord's Supper, catechizing, and ecclesiastical censure. They parted company with Calvin by rejecting all feast days but Sunday, elevating the sermon over communion in worship, abandoning the practice of taking communion to the sick, and coming to treat marriage and burial as strictly civil ceremonies. The fullest accounts of sixteenth- and seventeenth-century Puritan worship are by Horton Davies; see his *The Worship of the English Puritans* (Westminster: Dacre Press, 1948); *From Cranmer to Hooker; From Andrewes to Baxter and Fox, 1603–1690*, vol. 2 of *Worship and Theology in England* (Princeton: Princeton University Press, 1975). A shorter account is found in chap. 2 of A. E. Peaston's *The Prayer Book Tradition in the Free Churches* (London: James Clarke, 1964). For the comparative case of England and Scotland in the seventeenth century, see Bryan D. Spinks, *Sacraments, Ceremonies and the Stuart Divines: Sacramental Theology and Liturgy in England and Scotland, 1603–1662* (Hants, UK: Ashgate, 2002), esp. chaps. 4 and 5.

13. Christopher Durston, "Puritan Rule and the Failure of Cultural Revolution, 1645–1660," chap. 7 of Durston and Eales, *Culture of English Puritanism*, 210–33, here 218.

14. Durston, "Puritan Rule," 231, 232. While Patrick Collinson defends the popular nature of these seventeenth-century reforms and the role the Laudian "anti-Calvinist innovations of the 1630s" played in (re)turning

people into Puritans (*Birthpangs of Protestant England*, 107; *Puritan Character*, 14), many studies continue to highlight popular resistance to them. In *Ritual, Myth and Magic in Early Modern Europe* (Athens: Ohio University Press, 1983), William Monter argues that in most locales, the direction worship reforms took was often tied to the predilection of local bureaucrats. In "'By this Book': Parishioners, the Prayer Book and the Established Church," Judith Maltby provides a fascinating account of the many instances of laypeople, from a variety of socioeconomic positions, who upheld use of the Common Prayer and aided in prosecuting Puritan ministers who did not obey its rubrics or perform services in their entirety. Peter Lake's "The Laudian Style: Order, Uniformity, and the Pursuit of the Beauty of Holiness in the 1630s" delineates a contemporary Laudian ethos and its grounds for affirming Anglican ritual. Maltby's and Lake's essays appear in *The Early Stuart Church, 1603–1642*, ed. Kenneth Fincham (Stanford: Stanford University Press, 1993), 115–37 and 161–85, respectively.
15. Wall, *Transformations of the Word*, 372.
16. These small groups of extreme Separatists included Barrowists, Brownists, and some Independents; Peter King, "The Reasons for the Abolition of the Book of Common Prayer in 1645," *Journal of Ecclesiastical History* 21 (1970): 331. *The Character of an Old English Puritane or Non-Conformist* (1646), for instance, related that though a Puritan much preferred free prayer, "where, by the gift of God, expressions were varied according to present wants and occasions," he might occasionally use set forms from the less corrupt parts of the Book of Common Prayer as he felt the need (qtd. in Durston and Eales, "Puritan Ethos," 15).
17. "Whilst [the English Puritans] claimed to be true heirs of the Reformed Churches, in actual fact they had proceeded with a more radical reformation than their continental mentors. The impetus in this revolution, as well as the apparent unawareness of the radical nature of the changes, it is claimed, are the direct result of the doctrine and practice of Separatist worship, mediated by the Independents" (Davies, *Worship of the English Puritans*, 48). Michael Watts's *The Dissenters* echoes this view and, moreover, consistently downplays free prayer as part of Dissenting identity; on the Ejection and the role of the Separatists and Puritans in shaping Dissenting worship, see Watts, *The Dissenters*, 2 vols. (Oxford: Oxford University Press, 1978), 1:215–20, 1:303–4. For a more three-dimensional account of the interest these groups shared and the differences that remained between them, see John Spurr, "From Puritanism to Dissent, 1660–1700," in Durston and Eales, *Culture of English Puritanism*, 234–65. In addition to Congregationalists and conformists, Spurr stresses the existence of "neutralists," people of puritan tendency who after the Restoration attended both church and conventicle, and he points out that Presbyterians and other groups cannot be said to have resigned themselves to permanent dissent until after the Toleration Act of 1689 (244, 247).
18. The logic of spontaneity extended beyond free-praying Dissenters; by midcentury, Anglicans would try to defend liturgy in the terms of emotional freshness originally used by free-prayer supporters, and by the end of the

century, some Unitarian clergy advocated liturgies in nearly free-prayer logic, proposing to keep them current and up-to-date. See, respectively, Thomas Newton, *Of forms of prayer & particularly those of the Church of England, A Sermon Preach'd in the Parish Church of St. Mary-le-Bow, According to the last will Of Mr. John Hutchins Citizen & Goldsmith, On St. Mark's day, 1745, When there was a collection for the Charity Children. Three Sermons* (London: J. & R. Tonson and S. Draper, 1745); and Theophilus Lindsey, *A Discourse addressed to the Congregation at the Chapel in Essex Street, Strand, on resigning the pastoral office among them* (London: J. Johnson, 1793).

19. For Baxter's conciliatory view toward liturgy, see his *Five Disputations of Church-Government, and Worship* (London, 1659); *The Grand Debate Between The Most Reverend the Bishops and The Presbyterian Divines, Appointed By His Sacred Majesty, As Commissioners for The Review and Alteration of the Book of Common Prayer, &c. Being An Exact Account of their whole Proceedings* (London, 1661); *To the Kings Most Excellent Majesty. The Due Account and Humble Petition of the Ministers of the Gospel, Lately Commissioned for the Review and Alteration of the Liturgy* (London, 1661); *The English Nonconformity, As under King Charles II and King James Ist. Truly Stated and Argued* (London, 1689).

20. Precision in using religious terms in this period is as important as it is challenging. Though according to the *OED* "Dissenter" is occasionally used to include Roman Catholics or to make a fine distinction between those who disagree with the established church as it is (Nonconformists) and those who disagree with the principle of state churches altogether, in the context of the Restoration period, I am using Dissenter as synonymous with Nonconformist, referring mainly to former Puritans who separated themselves from the Church of England (or Scotland) after the 1661 Act of Uniformity. From the late sixteenth century, the term "Independent" referred to English sectarians who, unlike Puritans who wished to reform the existing church, were for congregational autonomy; these included Baptists, Congregationalists, and eventually Friends. After the Act of Uniformity, these Independents and the formerly Puritan Dissenters increasingly found common ground, especially as their comprehension within the Church of England grew less likely. For the evolution of "enthusiasm" mainly as a term of abuse, see Klein and La Vopa, *Enthusiasm and Enlightenment in Europe*; Michael Heyd, *"Be Sober and Reasonable": The Critique of Enthusiasm in the Seventeenth and Early Eighteenth Centuries* (Leiden: E. J. Brill, 1995); Shaun Irlam, "Enthusiasm in the Seventeenth Century: The Vicissitudes of an Image," chap. 1 in Irlam, *Elations*, 31–52; George Williamson, "The Restoration Revolt against Enthusiasm," *Studies in Philology* 30 (1933): 571–603; Ann Taves, *Fits, Trances, and Visions: Experiencing Religion and Explaining Experience from Wesley to James* (Princeton: Princeton University Press, 1999), 17–20.

21. Histories of English liturgy abound, but scholarly treatments of free prayer in seventeenth- and eighteenth-century English worship are few. Nigel Smith notes in *Perfection Proclaimed: Language and Literature in English Radical Religion, 1640–1660* (Oxford: Clarendon, 1989) that "the expression of extremes of emotion as a supernatural encounter" was "the characteristic

feature of mid-seventeenth-century radical religious prose" (74), and mentions scriptural disputations in Baptist and separatist churches as leading to both prophesying and "spontaneous outpouring" of speech in "extreme sectarian utterances and styles" (5). See also Davies, *From Cranmer to Hooker*, 255, 268–73, *From Andrewes to Baxter and Fox*, 187–214, 329–62, and *From Watts and Wesley to Maurice, 1690–1850*, vol. 3 of *Worship and Theology in England* (Princeton: Princeton University Press, 1961), 106–7, 193–94; Patrick Collinson, "Towards a Broader Understanding of the Early Dissenting Tradition," in *The Dissenting Tradition: Essays for Leland H. Carlson*, ed. C. Robert Cole and Michael E. Moody, 13–19 (Athens: Ohio University Press, 1975); Stephen Brachlow, *The Communion of Saints: Radical Puritan and Separatist Ecclesiology, 1570–1625* (Oxford: Oxford University Press, 1988), 160–64, 175; Peaston, *Prayer Book Tradition*; King, "Reasons for the Abolition of the Common Prayer"; John Skoglund, "Free Prayer," *Studia Liturgica* 10 (1974): 151–66; Alan L. Hayes, "Spirit and Structure in Elizabethan Public Prayer," in *Spirit Within Structure: Essays in Honor of George Johnston on the Occasion of His Seventieth Birthday*, ed. E. J. Furcha, 117–32 (Allison Park, Pa.: Pickwick Publications, 1983). Kristen Poole briefly discusses the 1641 free-prayer tract *A Humble Remonstrance* by "Smectymnuus" in *Radical Religion*, 137–38. For an interesting treatment of the eroticism of private prayer in seventeenth-century English Protestant prayer guides, see Richard Rambuss, "The Prayer Closet," chap. 3 of *Closet Devotions* (Durham, N.C.: Duke University Press, 1998), 103–35. On pamphlet wars during the civil wars in general, see Nigel Smith, *Literature and Revolution in England, 1640–1660* (New Haven: Yale University Press, 1994), 21–53.

22. Chap. 3 returns to the theme of rational embarrassment over enthusiasm and examines its secular recuperation in the works of the third Earl of Shaftesbury.

23. For mercantile capitalism, commercialization, and the modern political economy of the British isles in the seventeenth and eighteenth centuries, see Zaret, *Heavenly Contract*, 163–98; Pocock, *Machiavellian Moment*, 423; Christopher Hill, "The Rich, the Poor, and the Middling Sort," chap. 1.2 in *A Turbulent, Seditious, and Factious People: John Bunyan and His Church, 1628–1688* (Oxford: Clarendon, 1988), 16–27; Neil McKendrick, John Brewer, and J. H. Plumb, *The Birth of a Consumer Society: The Commercialization of Eighteenth-Century England* (Bloomington: Indiana University Press, 1982). Chap. 2 of the present study brings Zaret's analysis of the "heavenly contract" in seventeenth-century English covenant theology to bear on the economic inflection of the traumatic spiritual life of John Bunyan.

24. Irlam, *Elations*, 18. For what Michel Foucault calls the shifting "conditions of the possibility of knowledge" in the early modern period, see *The Order of Things: An Archaeology of the Human Sciences* (New York: Vintage, 1994), xxii and passim; the opening chapters of McKeon's *Origins of the English Novel*; and the introduction, pp. 22–25 above. For the late-seventeenth- and early-eighteenth-century emergence of the new Newtonian science, and for the Restoration as a crucial period in the development of the scientific ideal of objectivity, see Markley, "Objectivity as Ideology," 355–72.

25. *Everyman*, intro. Simon Trussler (London: Nick Hern Books, 1996), lines 136, 134; Simon Trussler, introduction to *Everyman*, v–xxxv, here x.
26. Zaret, *Heavenly Contract*, 166. Zaret describes the way an emerging market economy shaped a "contractarian world view" and how "from 1500 to 1640, notions of reason and reasonableness increasingly referred to a market rationality." For the overlap between the logic and discourses of economics and of knowledge (e.g., possession, grasping, law, contract) and the propensity for economic discourse to achieve hegemony over all other discourses, see Shell, *Money, Language, and Thought*, 3–4, 131–55, 180–81; Lyotard, *Differend*; Emmanuel Lévinas, "Ethics as First Philosophy," trans. Seán Hand and Michael Temple, in *The Lévinas Reader*, ed. Seán Hand (Oxford: Blackwell, 1999), 75–87. See also the discussion of Gustaf Aulén, the atonement, and covenant theology in chap. 2.
27. Bouwsma, "Anxiety," 157–89.
28. Margreta de Grazia, "The Secularization of Language in the Seventeenth Century," *Journal of the History of Ideas* 41 (1980): 319–29.
29. Qtd. in N. Smith, *Perfection Proclaimed*, 27. The experiential basis of Puritanism has led to its being called experimental Calvinism; what has been called "experimental" theology emerged as Puritans related their experiences as progressions from sin and unbelief to faith and grace (*Perfection Proclaimed*, 5). See also Peter Lake, "Calvinism and the English Church, 1570–1635," *Past and Present* 114 (1987): 75; and R. T. Kendall, *Calvin and English Calvinism to 1649* (Oxford: Oxford University Press, 1979), 8–9, 80. Norman Pettit rightly points out that it is hard to say whether Calvinistic covenant theology lays the groundwork for experiential religion or whether an experiential worldview expresses itself in covenant theology. I lean toward the latter view, though Pettit surmises, "Probably both were true." See Norman Pettit, *The Heart Prepared: Grace and Conversion in Puritan Spiritual Life* (New Haven: Yale University Press, 1966), 11.
30. In preparing this chapter I studied approximately one hundred pamphlets, tracts, and sermons, defenses of and attacks on both liturgy and free prayer (roughly one-quarter of which are represented here), at the Lilly Library, Indiana University, and at the Bodleian and Duke Humfrey's libraries, Oxford, and am immensely grateful to librarians in both locations for their assistance. The material texts themselves testify to the pervasive cultural controversy this debate was perceived to be; a collection of tracts will sometimes be carefully arranged in argument/ rebuttal/counter-response order and handsomely bound. Not a few extant tracts also bear copious handwritten marginalia, including refutations or additional supporting scripture.
31. John Ley, *A Debate concerning the English Liturgy, Both As Established in & As Abolished out of the Worship of GOD. Drawn out in Two English and two Latine Epistles, Written betwixt Edward Hyde Doctor in Divinity, and John Ley Rector of the Church of Solyhull in Warwick-shire* (London: Printed by A.M., for Edward Brewster, 1656), 24.
32. *A Directory for The Publique Worship of God, Throughout the Three Kingdoms of England, Scotland, and Ireland Together with an Ordinance of Parliament for the taking away of the Book of Common-Prayer* (London, 1644), 53; hereafter cited parenthetically as *DPW*.

33. Vavasor Powell's *Common-Prayer-Book No Divine Service: A Small Curb to the Bishops Careere: or, Imposed Liturgies Tried, The Common-prayer-book Anatomized, and Diocesan-Bishops Questioned* (London: Printed for Livewell Chapman, 1660) is representative of the genre in its attacks on liturgy. Powell's main heads argue that set forms are "vain worship" (i.e., not "in spirit and in truth"), idolatrous and therefore unlawful (against the second commandment), unnecessary, that they thwart ministers' gifts as well as promote an unhealthy spirit of conformity, that they are unedifying, offend the "weaker brother," are popish and superstitious, and full of vain repetitions and tautologies. Another useful summation of free-prayer views is Baxter's *Grand Debate*. John Scott's *Certain Cases of Conscience Resolved, Concerning the Lawfulness of Joyning with Forms of Prayer in Publick Worship* (London, 1683) also summarizes the main free-prayer objections before responding to them. For the recurrent contention of the "dryness" of the Prayer Book, see Spurr, "From Puritanism to Dissent," 243. Quaker worship presented perhaps the limit case of rejection of forms. T. L. Underwood's *Primitivism, Radicalism, and the Lamb's War: The Baptist-Quaker Conflict in Seventeenth-Century England* (New York: Oxford University Press, 1997) tells how Friends rejected human actions that might interfere with "immediate experience," and accused Baptists of that of which Baptists accused "Papists" and Anglicans: using forms that stinted the spirit (94–95).
34. *The Common Prayer Book Unmasked, wherein is declared the Unlawfulnesse and Sinfulnesse of it, by Several Undeniable Arguments, Viz. From the Name of it, From the Original of it. From the Matter contained in it. The ridiculous Manner of using it. The Evil Effects it hath upon Ministers, People, and Ordinances.... Published by divers Ministers of Gods Word, and formerly printed and dedicated to the Lords and Commons Assembled in Parliament. Now newly reprinted* (N.p., 1660), 68; hereafter parenthetically cited as *CPU*. The title page gave "DWALPHINTRAMIS" as the author, whom Early English Books Online identifies as a pseudonym of John Barnard, i.e., Richard Barnard (1568–1641); cf. C. A. Stonehill, *Anonyma and Pseudonyma* (New York: R. R. Bowker, 1927).
35. John Bunyan, *I Will Pray with the Spirit, and I will Pray with the Understanding also: Or, A Discourse Touching Prayer, From I Cor. 14.15.*, 2d ed. (London: Printed for the Author, 1663), 4–5; hereafter cited parenthetically in the text as *IWP*.
36. Pro-liturgy writers would also claim the sincerity case: Scott's *Certain Cases of Conscience Resolved* claimed that emotional response to liturgical prayer is more genuine because it is not a response to novelty; 53. For the concept and value of sincerity in eighteenth-century England and its origins in Puritanism, see Guilhamet, *Sincere Ideal*, esp. chap. 2, and Lionel Trilling, *Sincerity and Authenticity* (Cambridge, Mass.: Harvard University Press, 1972).
37. Contemporaries regarded such anxieties as a central feature of the Puritan mentality, and much work on Puritan spirituality stresses the complex connections between anguish, anxiety, the quest for certainty, and self-scrutiny for evidence of conversion. See for instance William Bouwsma, *John Calvin:*

A Sixteenth-Century Portrait (New York: Oxford University Press, 1988), 184–85; David Leverenz, *The Language of Puritan Feeling: An Exploration in Literature, Psychology, and Social History* (New Brunswick, N.J.: Rutgers University Press, 1980), 9, 13; Collinson, *Puritan Character*, 11; Kaufman, *Prayer, Despair, and Drama*, 6–7; McGiffert, *God's Plot*, 10, 25; White, *Puritan Rhetoric*, 13; Perry Miller, *The New England Mind: From Colony to Province* (Cambridge, Mass.: Harvard University Press, 1967), 440. On the broadest level, there is no consensus about the relationship between religion and anxiety. Jean Deprun, for instance, argues in *La philosophie de l'inquietude en France au XVIIIe siècle* (Paris: J. Vrin, 1979) that anxiety is the fabric of religion, while Bouwsma implies in "Anxiety and the Formation of Early Modern Culture" that religion assuages anxiety by providing reliable knowledge of boundaries and reality.

38. For the legacy of this religious concern for emotional correctness later in the eighteenth century, see Brunström, *William Cowper*.
39. Matthew Henry, *A Method for Prayer, with Scripture Expressions Proper to be Us'd under each Head*, 2nd ed., with additions (London: Printed for Nath. Cliff and Daniel Jackson, 1710), [3]; hereafter parenthetically cited in the text as *MP*. Pages in square brackets are not enumerated in the original.
40. Isaac Watts, *A Guide to Prayer. Or, A Free and Rational Account of the Gift, Grace and Spirit of Prayer, With Plain Directions how every Christian may attain them* (London: Printed for Emmanuel Matthews, 1715), 44, 49; hereafter cited parenthetically in the text as *GP*.
41. Liturgy also registers semantically as an imposition against believers' freedom and liberty in John Owen's *A Discourse Concerning Liturgies, and Their Imposition* (London, 1662).
42. Milton, *Eikonoklastes*, ed. Merritt Y. Hughes, vol. 3, *Complete Prose Works*, ed. Don M. Wolfes (New Haven: Yale University Press, 1962), 505.
43. "*Forms* of prayer . . . tend to *damp* and *deaden* Devotion . . . being so well known and commonly repeated. . . . it is very certain a Man may subscribe a Set of *Articles* or read over a *Set of Prayers*, and not believe the Doctrines or Principles they contain. How far such a Conduct is consistent with sincerity ought to be considered; to me it appears to be totally subversive of it"; John Phelps, *A Vindication of Free and Unprescribed Prayer: In Some Remarks upon Dr. Newton's Sermon on the Liturgy of the Church of England, according to the Will of Mr. Hutchins. Inscribed to the Trustees of Mr. Hutchins's Charity* (London: M. Cooper, 1746), 18, 49–50; hereafter cited parenthetically in the text as *VF*.
44. Unfortunately there is no *DNB* entry for Henry Dawbeny.
45. The *OED* confirms the legal and economic valences of "interest" in this period, "having a right or title to, a claim upon, or share in," especially "in right or title to property, or to some of the uses or benefits pertaining to property."
46. [Henry Dawbeny], *A Sober and Temperate Discourse, Concerning the Interest of Words in Prayer. The just Antiquity and Pedigree of Liturgies, or Forms of Prayer in Churches: With a View of the State of the Church, when they were first composed, or imposed* (London, 1661), 1–2; hereafter cited parenthetically as *ST*.

47. The *OED* also confirms seventeenth-century usages of the word "performance" both in the broad sense of an action accomplished and in the more specific sense of an "action of performing a ceremony, play, part in a play, piece of music, etc.; formal or set execution." In Dawbeny's repetition of the word, the continual slippage back and forth between its two meanings becomes clear.
48. For abstraction, alienation, and reification, see Marx's classic analysis of money and exchange in the first volume of *Capital*, as well as Georg Lukács's standard explication of reification and alienation in Georg Lukács, "Reification and the Consciousness of the Proletariat," chap. 4 of *History and Class Consciousness: Studies in Marxist Dialectics*, trans. Rodney Livingstone (London: Merlin Press, 1971), 83–222. See chap. 2 for Bunyan's alienation and anxiety based on relating to God in terms of commodity and exchange.
49. The Puritan and Dissenting understanding of effective/affective language can be traced back to Ramus and his profound affect on Calvinism. Ramus's influence came largely through William Perkins's *The Arte of Prophesying* (London, 1592) and later Alexander Richardson's *Logician's School-Master* (London, 1657). Perkins described an "affective language which combined the proper interpretation of scriptural texts with a profound moving of the individual towards a sense of salvation"; see Smith, *Perfection Proclaimed*, 308.
50. In *Imagined Communities*, Benedict Anderson describes the ways modern nations imagine themselves as communities moving in a "homogenous, empty time" out of an immemorial past into a limitless future in a simultaneity imaginable across space through clocks, calendars, and especially the print commodities of newspapers and novels; Benedict Anderson, *Imagined Communities: Reflections on the Origin and Spread of Nationalism* (London: Verso, 1991), 9–36. One might argue that in the free-prayer tradition and its heirs, where bodily signs of sincerity remain so important, it is not in the print commodity but eventually in mass revivals, late-twentieth-century megachurches and televangelism that Protestantism finds what Anderson calls "that remarkable confidence of community in anonymity" that is the hallmark of ways modern communities imagine themselves.
51. Sam[uel] Wotton, *A View of the Face Unmasked, or, an Answer to A Scandalous Pamphlet, published by divers Ministers, and Entituled [sic], The Common Prayer-Book Unmasked* (London: Thomas Newcomb, 1661), 49.
52. For clothing metaphors and the trope of seduction in Puritan logic, see John Charles Adams, "Linguistic Values and Religious Experience: An Analysis of the Clothing Metaphors in Alexander Richardson's Ramist-Puritan Lectures on Speech: 'Speech is a Garment to Cloath Our Reason,'" *Quarterly Journal of Speech* 9 (1990): 58–68. Clothing and fashion metaphors haunt all the discourses of spontaneity in this study, marking a site where writers are quasi-cognizant of their performativity and constructedness. While the earlier work of Marjorie Garber and Judith Butler emphasized the transgressive and transformative potential of costume and cross-dressing, recent analyses of performativity and clothing point to the lack of real subversiveness and transgression in many aspects of consumer culture. See Jessica Munns and Penny Richards, eds., *The Clothes that Wear Us: Essays on Dressing and*

Transgressing in Eighteenth-Century Culture (Newark: University of Delaware Press, 1999), 14–15.
53. Alan Clifford, "The Westminster Directory of Public Worship (1645)," in *The Reformation of Worship: Papers Read at the 1989 Westminster Conference*, no editor given, 53–75 (Colchester: Westminster Conference, 1989), 55. The *Directory* still appears at the end of most British editions of *The Confession of Faith*, which along with the *Shorter Catechism* are the most influential products of the Westminster Assembly, still in use by several Presbyterian and Reformed churches. It is also available in a recent edition with a brief introduction by editor Ian Breward, as *The Westminster Directory, being A Directory for the Publique Worship of God in the Three Kingdomes* (Bramcote, UK: Grove Books, 1980); the original is still preferable since reprinted editions do not maintain the variable size of type face (though Breward's edition does adhere to the alternation between roman and italic type). The best overview of the *Directory* is Iain H. Murray, "The Directory for Public Worship," in *To Glorify and Enjoy God: A Commemoration of the 350th Anniversary of the Westminster Assembly*, ed. John L. Carson and David W. Hall, 169–91 (Edinburgh: Banner of Truth Trust, 1994), and the entire collection of which it is a part provides an authoritative introduction to the work of the Westminster Assembly. See also King, "Abolition," 336–38; Hutton, *Rise and Fall*, 208–26; Durston, "Puritan Rule," 211–13 and 215–16, 226–29, for public distaste for its pared-down marriage and baptismal rites.
54. Syntactical freedom stopped short, though, of the words of institution at communion and the pronouncements at marriage and baptism. At these three moments the words of the minister were directly dictated, as if to express discomfort with trusting legal union with Christ, the church or a spouse to free, unregulated speech. These are also the three moments in Puritan worship in which actual material objects were directly involved or exchanged: in water baptism, consuming the elements, or becoming "one flesh" with one's spouse. When the material and bodily emerges undeniably into the constitution of the modern religious subject, so it seems do ritual and ritualized speech.
55. Related to the logic that positions free prayer as the divine gift to God's appointed male minister is a repeated logic in the pamphlets that figures set forms as crutches for infants and invalids; "parties in their infancy or ignorance, may use *formes* of *prayer*, well and wholesomely set, for helps and props of their imbecility" (*CPU*, 68). Similarly, Giles Firmin's *The Liturgical Considerator Considered* (London: Printed for Ralph Smith, 1661) calls set forms "*convenient Crutches for Ministers of weak abilities*," 7.
56. See n. 37 above.
57. Spurr, "From Puritanism to Dissent," 259.
58. Watts (1674–1748) was an Independent with a large Dissenting readership, best known as the writer of hymns, and whose philosophical and religious books, especially his *Logic*, were standard works into the nineteenth century.
59. Henry (1662–1714) was a Nonconformist minister and author of a popular Bible commentary that is still in print.
60. This notion of the collection of scripture phrases as storehouse of prayer material from which it is hoped scripturally correct prayer will sponta-

neously emerge stands in interesting contrast to the active art and "theater" of memory which declined in the seventeenth century after having emerged in ancient Greece and Rome and having flourished in the Middle Ages. See Frances A. Yates, *The Art of Memory* (Chicago: University of Chicago Press, 1966).

61. Bouwsma, *John Calvin*, 180.
62. Ward, *True Religion*, 52–65.
63. Zaret, *Heavenly Contract*, 10. In taking this position I join historians and critics skeptical of accounts that reduce historical phenomena to purely economic and social determinants. In *Rise and Fall*, for instance, Hutton describes reading all extant English parish records from 1450–1700 expecting to find that the decline of the ritual year was explicable in terms of economic decline; sources convinced him that in this period people clearly had changed their ritual practices based on distinctly religious and philosophical ideas. Patrick Collinson also criticizes the tendency he sees in the work of Christopher Hill and David Underwood (and behind them Marx, Weber, and Durkheim) to turn "explaining religion" into "explaining religion away," that is, turning religion into a confluence of economic or ideological forces that is not registered in its distinctive religiousness. See Collinson, *Birthpangs*, 152–54.
64. Contemporary theories of religion increasingly dissociate religious faith from the binaries rationality/irrationality and knowledge/superstition, understanding these as Enlightenment paradigms that confined religious experience either to "rational religion" (morality) or irrational "mysticism." Religion or religiousness is instead becoming associated with the realm of interpersonal relations, ethics, and faith that is both made possible and necessitated by the epistemological indeterminacy that has been the concern of much postmodern philosophy. See for example Derrida, "Faith and Knowledge" and several works by John Caputo: *On Religion*; *The Prayers and Tears of Jacques Derrida: Religion Without Religion* (Bloomington: Indiana University Press, 1997); and "Who Comes after the God of Metaphysics?" introduction to *The Religious*, ed. John Caputo, 1–19 (Oxford: Blackwell, 2002). On the construction of "mysticism" in *Enlightenment*, see Leigh Eric Schmidt, "The Making of Modern 'Mysticism,'" *Journal of the American Academy of Religion* 71 (2003): 273–302.
65. For instance, over and against the passivity associated with spontaneity, Ramie Targoff has argued for early-modern English willingness to believe in the power of ritual prayer to transform the self. For Nigel Smith, the search for spiritual perfection in the Interregnum led to claims of a subjectivity merged with the godhead. Peter Iver Kaufman argues that sixteenth-century Puritan self-interrogation was as much about recomposition as it is about decomposition and erasure, and his interest in free prayer of the 1590s stems from what he sees as its self-fashioning. Anticipating the changes I find in Restoration spirituality, Debora Kuller Shuger provides a fascinating account of the way that a specifically Protestant form of Christian selfhood emerges in the Renaissance, one "gripped by intense, contradictory emo-

tions and an ineradicable tension between its natural inclinations and religious obligations," driven by the need for self-control and filled with revulsion at its passivity, leading her to argue in her final chapter that female desire is the structure of religious subjectivity. See Targoff, *Common Prayer*; Smith, *Perfection Proclaimed*, 10, 18; Kaufman, *Prayer, Despair, and Drama*, 9, 17; Debora K. Shuger, *The Renaissance Bible: Scholarship, Sacrifice, and Subjectivity* (Berkeley: University of California Press, 1994), 7, 191.

66. Because of what Saussure calls the differential logic of language, reason is binary and othering, tending toward a transcendentalism that removes meaning to an ever higher realm in a movement that has been called, more positively by Hegel, sublimation, or more negatively by Derrida, the mechanistic structure of "outbidding"; see Derrida, "Faith and Knowledge," 21, 33.

67. The possibility of human agency and of a religious faith beyond that invoked by reason are both themes in recent works by Derrida. In "Faith and Knowledge," he points to the possibility of a religious faith as one that would resist the comforts of abstraction and the mechanisms of the law by going through them without stopping at false certainty or abstraction, to what he calls the "desert in the desert": where, beyond the rational outbidding in the quest for knowledge, the aporias of law and knowledge appear, and belief and the experience of the sacredness of the other might take place; 33, 17. This desert in the desert may indeed, he admits, resemble "desertification" or a destitution of the possibility of goodness, truth, or ethics, but it can also "render possible precisely what it appears to threaten" (Derrida, "Faith and Knowledge," 17)—or, as he has put it in "My Chances/*Mes Chances*," it is "the principle of indeterminism" that, in one way of thinking, "makes the conscious freedom of man fathomable" (8).

68. Asad, *Formations of the Secular*, 191–92. For related understandings of secularization, see Ward, *True Religion*, esp. chaps. 1 and 2, and the introduction of this book. Similarly, Bouwsma describes secularization as a process of the separation of politics, economic life, and culture from religious legal control that was well advanced at the beginning of the seventeenth century and that flourished alongside seventeenth-century Catholicism, Protestantism, and Puritanism; see Bouwsma, "Secularization of Society." For Calvin's transcendentalizing, secularizing rationality see Luxon, *Literal Figures*, 4, 211 n. 14, and Eire, *War Against the Idols*, 3, 312.

CHAPTER 2

1. Bunyan, *IWP*, 33.
2. For the transvaluation of enthusiasm as a secular term in English moral philosophy, particularly by the third Earl of Shaftesbury, see chap. 3 of this study as well as Lawrence Klein, "Sociability, Solitude, and Enthusiasm," in Klein and La Vopa, *Enthusiasm and Enlightenment in Europe*, 168.
3. Robert Markley, "Objectivity as Ideology." For Bunyan's literalist approach to Scripture, see Graham Ward, "To Be a Reader: Bunyan's Struggle with

the Language of Scripture in *Grace Abounding to the Chief of Sinners*," *Journal of Literature and Theology* 4 (1990): 29–49.
4. Kevin Cope, "The Propositions of Faith: The Ideology of the Royal Society and Bunyan's Academy of Maxims," *Publications of the Mississippi Philological Association* 7 (1988): 31, 38, 28.
5. Hill, *Turbulent*, 171. For Bunyan's covenant theology, see also Richard L. Greaves, *John Bunyan* (Abingdon: Sutton Courtenay Press, 1969), 97–121.
6. John Bunyan, *The Doctrine of the Law and Grace Unfolded*, ed. Richard L. Greaves, vol. 2, *The Miscellaneous Works of John Bunyan*, ed. Roger Sharrock (Oxford: Clarendon, 1976), 90, 95.
7. Gustaf Aulén, *Christus Victor: An Historical Study of the Three Main Types of the Idea of Atonement*, trans. A. G. Herbert, fore. Jaroslav Pelikan (1931; repr., New York: Macmillan, 1969), 93.
8. Aulén, *Christus Victor*, 128–29. For a more recent consideration of the role of rationalism in shaping the interpretation of the three central metaphors of atonement—victory, justice, and sacrifice—see Colin E. Gunton, *The Actuality of Atonement: A Study of Metaphor, Rationality and the Christian Tradition* (Edinburgh: T&T Clark, 1988). For critical, historical contextualization of changes in Christian doctrine more broadly, see the work of Yale historical theologian Jaroslav Pelikan, particularly *Historical Theology: Continuity and Change in Christian Doctrine* (Philadelphia: Westminster Press, 1971) and *The Christian Tradition: A History of the Development of Doctrine*, 5 vols. (Chicago: University of Chicago Press, 1971–1989).
9. Zaret, *Heavenly Contract*, 165. See also Hill, *Turbulent*, 16–27.
10. Qtd. in Zaret, *Heavenly Contract*, 167.
11. Zaret, *Heavenly Contract*, 16, 175.
12. John Bunyan, *Israel's Hope Encouraged* and *The Saints Privilege and Profit*, ed. W. R. Owens, vol. 13, *The Miscellaneous Works of John Bunyan*, ed. Roger Sharrock (Oxford: Clarendon, 1994), 3–95, 163–252.
13. See Bunyan, *IWP*, 63, 8; and pp. 76–78 below.
14. Most scholarship has followed Roger Sharrock in affirming the important connection between *Grace Abounding* and *The Pilgrim's Progress*, articulated primarily as "creative reworking." See Roger Sharrock, *John Bunyan* (London: Macmillan, 1968), 157; Hill, *Turbulent*, 206–7; Kathleen M. Swaim, *Pilgrim's Progress, Puritan Progress: Discourses and Contexts* (Urbana: University of Illinois Press, 1993), 14.
15. Shell, *Money, Language, and Thought*, 40. Scholarship has shown the discourse of commodities and advertising to be present and opposed to religious value as early as the Middle Ages; see Andrew Cowell, "Advertising, Rhetoric, and Literature: A Medieval Response to Contemporary Theory," *Poetics Today* 22 (2001): 795–827. Jean-François Lyotard has persuasively argued that the problem with economic discourse, as with academic discourses of mastery, is the facility with which it is used for hegemonic ends, reducing everything to a final meaning or "bottom line" and refusing to allow for elements of experience inarticulable in its terms of efficiency, profit, possession, equivalence, and exchange. See Lyotard, *Differend*.
16. For the notion of the religious fetish and commodities, see Ward, *True Religion*, esp. the last chapter, "True Religion as Special Effect," 114–53.

17. Vincent Newey, "'With the Eyes of My Understanding': Bunyan, Experience, and Acts of Interpretation," in Keeble, *John Bunyan*, 189–216, here 190–91. In the 1650s Bunyan joined a congregation of Particular Open-Communion Baptists. Paralleling controversy about the definition of Puritanism, there has been debate as to whether Bunyan can be classified as a Puritan. Gordon Campbell has argued that Bunyan was more properly a sectarian or separatist, but most biographers and critics agree that doctrinally, and as an itinerant craftsman preacher and a moderate enthusiast, Bunyan expresses the breadth and depth of the Puritan worldview and religious experience. See Gordon Campbell, "Fishing in Other Men's Waters: Bunyan and the Theologians," in Keeble, *John Bunyan*, 137–51, here 150–51; for a full discussion of the term *Puritan* and its applicability to Bunyan, see Swaim, *Pilgrim's Progress*, 7–13. For Bunyan's place in the spectrum of nonconformity, see Isabel Rivers, "The Religion of Grace: Baxter, Bunyan, and the Nonconformist Reaction," chap. 3 of *Reason, Grace, and Sentiment: A Study of the Language of Religion and Ethics in England, 1660–1780*, 2 vols., Cambridge Studies in Eighteenth-Century English Literature 8, 37 (Cambridge: Cambridge University Press, 1991), 89–163.
18. John Bunyan, *Grace Abounding to the Chief of Sinners*, ed. Roger Sharrock (Oxford: Clarendon, 1962), ¶37:14, hereafter cited parenthetically in the text as *GA*. Citations are to paragraph and page number.
19. For details of Bunyan's early life, see the standard biography, Sharrock's *John Bunyan*; Hill, *Turbulent*; and, more recently, Michael Mullett, *John Bunyan in Context* (Pittsburgh: Duquesne University Press, 1997). For a brief account, see the introduction to Greaves's study of Bunyan's theology, *John Bunyan*.
20. His queries were answered in "a kind of vision" which confirmed the importance of emotional sincerity in faith and which showed him "that none could enter into life but those that were in down-right earnest" (*GA*, ¶55:20).
21. For the Puritan conversion experience, see chap. 1, n. 5.
22. Zaret, *Heavenly Contract*, 17, 186, 192; Hill, *Turbulent*, 16–27.
23. Peter Carlton has famously diagnosed this structure in Bunyan as his "disclaiming locutions"; Peter Carlton, "Bunyan: Language, Convention, Authority," *ELH* 51 (1984): 17–32. The assignation of all inner experience to the agency of the self reduces the profound ambiguities that haunt all accounts of consciousness and which Bunyan grapples with more subtlely than Carlton seems to allow. More provocatively, Scott Paul Gordon has suggested that claiming this sort of passivity is a "counter-tradition" to the "thoroughly centered self, integral and consistent," one that "resists 'autonomy' and defers agency from the individual to external nature"; see *Power of the Passive Self*, 5. I argue that it is the pressure for certainty itself, when brought to bear on the self and moral qualities, that produces a sort of paralysis and passivity that is psychologically harrowing. Eugene White connects the logic of binary thinking to this anxious paralysis when he notes "man's terrifying helplessness" before the "terrifyingly total" Reformed God: "completely powerful, utterly inscrutable, implacably unforgiving, perfectly merciful," whom "only the devout could bring themselves to love" and before whom "man was absolutely without power either to promote or to impede his salvation"; see White, *Puritan Rhetoric*, 7–8.

24. The event closest to a conversion experience, though still not declared as such, is described briefly and without flair in the next two paragraphs (*GA*, ¶114–15:36).
25. Roger Pooley notes in "*Grace Abounding* and the New Sense of the Self," in *John Bunyan and His England, 1628–1688*, ed. Anne Laurence, W. R. Owens, and Stuart Sim, 105–14 (London: Hambledon Press, 1990), that *Grace Abounding* "notoriously does not present a single moment of conversion" (109), a fact which not a few critics have been happy to overlook in favor of identifying such a moment. After many months, Bunyan's anxieties about conversion are only partly allayed when certain verses from the Bible encourage him "that if I were not already, yet time might come [when] I might be in truth converted to Christ" (*GA*, ¶76:25). He says he continued "for some years together" in a state of despair that he could ever be converted into a state of grace (*GA*, ¶84:27), and though he makes reference to the time in his life "before conversion" (*GA*, ¶83:27), never in the book does he explicitly point to a moment he will name as conversion. Anne Hawkins has argued in "The Double Conversion in Bunyan's *Grace Abounding*," *Philological Quarterly* 61 (1982): 259–76, that Bunyan experiences a gradual conversion unlike the dramatic Pauline conversion favored in Puritan culture.
26. Newton was among the first to proclaim, in the third edition of the *Opticks*, empiricism's promise for "enlarging" the certainty of moral philosophy. That empirical method always leaves room for doubt and brings (in the eighteenth century, Humean) skepticism is a philosophical commonplace. See for instance William Donoghue's work on skepticism and the novel in *Enlightenment Fiction*, 11. Isaac Newton, *Opticks: or, A Treatise of the Reflections, Refractions, Inflections and Colours of Light* (London, 1717/18).
27. Shell, *Money, Language, and Thought*, 1–4, 40, 180, 184–86.
28. For the notion of objective certainty as definitive of notions of science in the Restoration period, see Markley, "Objectivity as Ideology," 355–72. My account differs most from interpretations of Bunyan that paint him as deliberately challenging rationality or the possibility of knowledge; see for example Stanley Fish, "Progress in *The Pilgrim's Progress*," chap. 4 of *Self-Consuming Artifacts: The Experience of Seventeenth-Century Literature* (Berkeley: University of California Press, 1972), 224–64; Adam Sills, "Mr. Bunyan's Neighborhood and the Geography of Dissent," *ELH* 70 (2003): 67–87; and Michael Davies, "Bunyan's Exceeding Maze: *Grace Abounding* and the Labyrinth of Predestination," in *Awakening Words: John Bunyan and the Language of Community*, ed. David Gay, James G. Randall, and Arlette Zinck, 97–112 (Newark: University of Delaware Press, 2000).
29. For the perceived irrationality of enthusiasm in the period and in contemporary criticism, see Pocock, "Enthusiasm," in Klein and La Vopa, *Enthusiasm and Enlightenment in Europe*; Heyd, *"Be Sober and Reasonable"*; Williamson, "Restoration Revolt." Both Pocock and Heyd note that enlightened antienthusiasts were aware that materialism, rationalism, and atheism could become their own sorts of fanatical enthusiasm (ergo reason meant a balanced reason and control of the passions), and that various national and

disciplinary enlightenments (theological, medical, experimental) constructed themselves against an enthusiasm that served as their needed other. To my mind, neither sufficiently recognizes the full extent to which enthusiasm is enlightened and enlightenment enthusiastic, sharing key epistemological attitudes and subjective positions.

30. For the notion that ideologies and the subjectivities into which they call individuals produce their own resistances, see Shell, *Money, Language, and Thought*, and also Paul Smith, *Discerning the Subject* (Minneapolis: University of Minnesota Press, 1988), esp. 38–40 and "Resistance," 56–69.

31. Most treatments of the "Sell him" episode follow Sharrock in his concern for its status as the "sin against the Holy Ghost"; Newey for example refers to it as "the election episode." David Seed treats the incident as an example of the workings of Bunyan's conscience externalized as speech. For Carlton, Bunyan's attributing "Sell him" to another voice is an example of his characteristically Puritan disclaiming locutions. Felicity Nussbaum notes the incident's economic aspect in passing but reads it as "toying with" disobedience and the "notion of losing God's love." Hill reads Bunyan's sin expressly as the sin of Esau to which Bunyan later compares it, selling his birthright. Sharrock, *John Bunyan*, 63–64; Newey, "'With the Eyes of My Understanding,'" in Keeble, *John Bunyan*, 198; Seed, "Dialogue and Debate in *The Pilgrim's Progress*," in The Pilgrim's Progress: *Critical and Historical Views*, ed. Vincent Newey, 69–90 (Totowa, N.J.: Barnes & Noble, 1980), 72–73; Carlton, "Bunyan: Language, Convention, Authority," 22; Nussbaum, "'By These Words I was Sustained': Bunyan's *Grace Abounding*," *ELH* 49 (1982): 24; Hill, *Turbulent*, 69–70.

Two interpretations of the economic valence of Bunyan's temptation were presented at the Third Triennial Meeting of the International John Bunyan Society, in Cleveland, 10–14 October 2001: a version of this chapter, and David Hawkes's "The Concept of the Hireling in Bunyan's Theology." Hawkes argued that the essential context for Bunyan's equation of "sell him" with the "sin against the Holy Ghost" is the seventeenth-century shift from seeing tithes and priestcraft as part of a gift economy to seeing them as part of an alienating market economy in which pastoral care becomes mere labor for wages. To my mind, explicit connection of this concern to *Grace Abounding* is lacking, and the hireling debate does not account for the epic proportions of the "Sell him" trauma in Bunyan's life, particularly before he is called to preaching.

32. Jacques Lacan, *The Four Fundamental Concepts of Psychoanalysis*, ed. Jacques-Alain Miller, trans. Alan Sheridan (New York: Norton, 1981), 55–56, hereafter cited parenthetically in the text as *FF*. For the symptom as a perpetually resutured wound caused by the eruption of the inassimilable real, see also Žižek, *Sublime Object of Ideology*, 11–53. For Lacan, there are three psychical processes or dimensions of psychological existence: the imaginary, the symbolic, and the real. The ego takes in images of the world and reality, and so the imaginary and ego-formation are associated with the prelinguistic state in the mirror image and relation to the body of the mother. The subject as we know it comes into being in relation to signifiers, a symbolic order that

stands in for other things and is continually being used to try to control those things, their value and possession. The real is that which is neither imaginary nor symbolic, that which is outside analytic experience or articulation in speech.

33. This distinction is also that between the "subject" produced as an effect of language and the symbolic order, and the person or human agent in any broader sense; for this difference in terminology, a helpful source is again Smith's *Discerning the Subject*. On the repeated "unplugging" or "uncoupling" from socio-symbolic structures necessary to love the other as a unique person and thus break out of the cycle of law and transgressive object-desire, see Slavoj Žižek, *The Fragile Absolute—Or, Why Is the Christian Legacy Worth Fighting For?* (London: Verso, 2001), 123–30.

34. Nussbaum is the first to observe that the period of Bunyan's great "Sell him" temptation, sometime in 1650, coincided with the birth of his first child, Mary, who was born blind; "'By These Words,'" 33 n. 8.

35. Newey, "'With the Eyes of My Understanding,'" 201; Peter Goldman, "Living Words: Iconoclasm and Beyond in John Bunyan's *Grace Abounding*," *New Literary History* 33 (2002): 478; Leopold Damrosch Jr., *God's Plot and Man's Stories: Studies in the Fictional Imagination from Milton to Fielding* (Chicago: University of Chicago Press, 1985), 126.

36. For Bunyan's literalist hermeneutic, see Ward, "To Be a Reader," 29–49.

37. For Žižek, this is precisely the moment when an ideology truly works, when even experience resisting the ideology is co-opted to support it; *Sublime Object of Ideology*, 47–49.

38. Shuger, *Renaissance Bible*, 189, 106.

39. Goldman observes that Bunyan's main metaphors for reception of the scriptural word in *Grace Abounding* are violence and destruction. Thomas Luxon also underscores the importance of violence for Bunyan in yielding knowledge; knowledge of Scripture is attained by "unutterable revelations," Bunyan's favorite allegorical model for which is "physical violence, often imagined as painful." Isabel Rivers points out that Bunyan's contemporary Richard Baxter shared the view that the sinner must be "bruised" to be converted. See Goldman, "Living Words," 477–78; Luxon, *Literal Figures*, 142; Rivers, "Religion of Grace," 154.

40. See "other of the Lord's dealings with me" and "A Brief Account of the Author's Imprisonment" (*GA*, ¶253–339, 78–101).

41. In the context of seventeenth-century English Puritanism, evangelization was conceived of as "awakening" the elect to the realization that they were saved, an understanding consonant with the empirical satisfaction I describe; Hill, *Turbulent*, 172.

42. A massive body of scholarship concerns the status of *The Pilgrim's Progress* as allegory; the most substantial studies are by Maureen Quilligan, Kathleen Swaim, and Thomas Luxon. Treatments vary in terms of Bunyan's adherences to and innovations in allegorical conventions and their political ramifications. Sharon Achinstein has argued that Bunyan's allegorical "riddling" is itself an act of political resistance. Both Brian Nellist and Thomas Luxon see Bunyan's use of allegory as ultimately conservative. For Nellist, though

Bunyan toys with allegorical conventions, the damnation of Ignorance keeps him within the allegorical tradition's elevation of knowledge. Luxon reads *Grace Abounding* and *The Pilgrim's Progress* as "culminating moments in the Reformation crisis of representation": "at once practicing and denying allegory, Bunyan preaches an anti-hermeneutics of 'experience' available only to those who have been spiritually parted from this world and reborn in the next." For Luxon, allegory preserves Bunyan from the chiliastic moment he desires and resists; he argues that *The Pilgrim's Progress* is an allegory because "reformed Christianity, for all of its insistence on literalism, remains profoundly committed to an allegorical ontology." David Mills on the other hand stresses that Bunyan uses the dream-frame to overcome the potential restrictions of the allegorical mode, and stresses its irony. Stanley Fish has famously argued that Bunyan's allegory undoes itself and that *The Pilgrim's Progress* is no progress at all and is the ultimate self-consuming artifact. To my mind the shortcoming of Fish's argument is that it is unable to help us understand either the appeal and cultural work of this extremely popular text—inasmuch as that appeal lies in the compelling idea of progress and not in its undoing—or its relation to Bunyan's experiences and articulation of them in *Grace Abounding*. See Maureen Quilligan, *The Language of Allegory: Defining the Genre* (Ithaca: Cornell University Press, 1979), 121–31; Swaim, *Pilgrim's Progress*, 18–41; Sharon Achinstein, "Honey from the Lion's Carcass: Bunyan, Allegory, and the Samsonian Moment," in Gay, Randall, and Zinck, *Awakening Words*, 68–80, here 70; Brian Nellist, "The Pilgrim's Progress and Allegory," in Newey, Pilgrim's Progress, 132–52; Luxon, *Literal Figures*, 32, 180; David Mills, "The Dreams of Bunyan and Langland," in Newey, Pilgrim's Progress, 154–81; Fish, "Progress in *The Pilgrim's Progress*."

43. John Bunyan, *The Pilgrim's Progress*, ed., intro., and notes by Roger Sharrock (New York: Penguin, 1987), 5; hereafter cited parenthetically in the text as *PP*.
44. See Michael McKeon's wonderful treatment of *The Pilgrim's Progress* and the novel as the Protestant fetishization of allegory, and the "deforming secularization" of its commodification and claim to "an utter self-sufficiency of meaning," in *Origins of the English Novel*, 311–12. *The Pilgrim's Progress* might rightly be considered the first great landmark in what R. Laurence Moore has described as the commodification of Protestant religion; see R. Laurence Moore, *Selling God: American Religion in the Marketplace of Culture* (New York: Oxford University Press, 1994), 5–10.
45. My reading here supports Wolfgang Iser's assertion that the implied reader of *The Pilgrim's Progress* is motivated by intense anxiety regarding predestination and therefore eager for assurances of salvation. See Wolgang Iser, "Bunyan's *Pilgrim's Progress:* The Doctrine of Predestination and the Shaping of the Novel," chap. 1 of *The Implied Reader: Patterns of Communication in Prose Fiction from Bunyan to Beckett* (Baltimore: The Johns Hopkins University Press, 1974), 1–28.
46. Critics generally agree that implicit in the Slough of Despond as well as other scenes is the idea that despair is avoidable or in some sense the fault of

the pilgrim. See Swaim, *Pilgrim's Progress*, 29–30; McKeon, *Origins of the English Novel*, 309; Luxon, *Literal Figures*, 187–88; Damrosch, *God's Plot*, 164. These readings and my own run counter to that of Adam Sills, who argues that Bunyan invokes maps and spatial metaphors in the context of his contemporaries' surveying and mapping of Dissenting communities "only to expose the flaws in thinking religious community in terms of map and survey," claiming that *The Pilgrim's Progress* "redistribute[s] space in particular ways that perhaps contradict or resist a hegemonic Cartesian logic"; see Sills, "Mr. Bunyan's Neighborhood," 71, 84. My readings of *Grace Abounding* and *The Pilgrim's Progress* suggest that Bunyan intensely inhabits this sort of Cartesian logic and that his resistances to it are symptomatic and often masked. Sills's reading seems particularly strained when he attempts, in a footnote, to read Bunyan's famous *Mapp Shewing the Order & Causes of Salvation & Damnation* as *undermining* the logic of map and system.

47. Hill, *Turbulent*, 198; McKeon, *Origins of the English Novel*, 308. Vincent Newey implies that the roll is the mark of predestination to being elect; Vincent Newey, "Bunyan and the Confines of the Mind," chap. 2 of Pilgrim's Progress, 21–48, here 43. In *Language of Allegory*, 124–26, Maureen Quilligan mistakenly equates the roll with Scripture, when the roll is clearly distinct from the Bible, the book Christian is reading at the beginning of the tale.

48. Ignorance has generated the widest variety of identifications of any character in the book. Richard Hardin identifies him as a Quaker; John Draper as a disciple of natural religion; William York Tindall and Henri Talon as a Latitudinarian; Christopher Hill as simply "the man who thought he knew he was saved"; Vincent Newey, as one who was predestined to hell; Kathleen Swaim as the blindness or refusal of vision; James F. Forrest, not as representative of a sect, but of pride. For Brian Nellist, Ignorance is a parody of Christian, ignorant of terror; for Leopold Damrosch, the allegory is in a general way the overcoming of Ignorance or lack of knowledge. In a Fishian vein, Stuart Sim argues that we must "allow for the possibility of the text undermining itself in unwittingly promoting sympathy for the unfortunate Ignorance." Thomas Luxon contends that Ignorance personifies the inability to keep hold of ecstatic experiences as experiences and that he is damned because he never believed sufficiently in "invisible things." For Roger Sharrock, Ignorance's condemnation to hell makes for an "anti-novelist Bunyan" who avoids "the too-easy ending with a celestial choir" in favor of "the necessary continuation of the imperfect human struggle." See Richard Hardin, "Bunyan, Mr. Ignorance, and the Quakers," *Studies in Philology* 69 (1972): 496–508; John Draper, "Bunyan's Mr. Ignorance," *MLR* 22 (1927): 15–21; William York Tindall, *John Bunyan: Mechanick Preacher* (New York: Russell & Russell, 1964), 62–63; Henri Talon, *John Bunyan: The Man and His Works*, trans. Barbara Wall (Cambridge, Mass.: Harvard University Press, 1951), 212; Christopher Hill, "Bunyan's Contemporary Reputation," in Lawrence, Owens, and Sim, *John Bunyan and His England*, 3–15, here 13; Newey, "Confines of the Mind," 43; Swaim, *Pilgrim's Progress*, 38–39; James F. Forrest, "Bunyan's Ignorance and The Flatterer: A Study in the Literary

Art of Damnation," *Studies in Philology* 60 (1963): 12–22; Nellist, *"Pilgrim's Progress* and Allegory," 149; Damrosch, *God's Plot*, 157; Stuart Sim, *Negotiations with Paradox: Narrative Practice and Narrative Form in Bunyan and Defoe* (Savage, Md.: Barnes & Noble, 1990), 51; Luxon, *Literal Figures*, 182–90; Roger Sharrock, "Life and Story in *The Pilgrim's Progress*," in Newey, Pilgrim's Progress, 49–68, here 67.

49. Peter Stallybrass and Allon White identify Sturbridge Fair in Cambridge as Bunyan's model for Vanity Fair; see their *The Politics and Poetics of Transgression* (Ithaca: Cornell University Press, 1986), 36.
50. Criticism has generally yielded a straightforward reading of the Vanity Fair scene as critical of capitalism, overlooking the deeper implications of "We buy the truth," partly because both Marxist and religious critics have preferred to read Bunyan as a political and socioeconomic radical; see for instance David Herreshoff, "Marxist Perspectives on Bunyan," in *Bunyan in Our Time*, ed. Robert G. Collmer, 161–85 (Kent, Ohio: Kent State University Press, 1989), and particularly Christopher Hill's work on "Satire and Vanity Fair" in *Turbulent*, 223–26. Hill notes that the allegory's attacks on monied power were "too pointed to be taken seriously" and that adults who came to terms with the market economy let their children enjoy *The Pilgrim's Progress* and *Gulliver's Travels* as fairy stories (Hill, *Turbulent*, 226). Though McKeon points out key ways in which *The Pilgrim's Progress* is embedded in both feudal and early capitalist economic structures, he sees the text as a "castigation of aristocratic luxury and corruption." James Turner views the scene as repudiating collusion between this world and the next, and Newey takes Faithful and Christian at their accusers' word when they are reputed to have said that the fair is "diametrically opposed" to Christianity and that "we buy the truth." Brean Hammond does point out, however, that Bunyan's satire of Vanity is ultimately conservative because it sees worldly commitment and social reform as secondary to spiritual concerns. See McKeon, *Origins of the English Novel*, 307–9; James Turner, "Bunyan's Sense of Place," in Newey, Pilgrims Progress, 91–110, here 102; Newey, "Confines of the Mind," 30; Brean Hammond, *"The Pilgrim's Progress:* Satire and Social Comment," in Newey, Pilgrim's Progress, 118–31, here 126.
51. Žižek, *Sublime Object of Ideology*, 45.
52. See chap. 2, n. 15.
53. Žižek, *Sublime Object of Ideology*, passim.
54. Hill, *Turbulent*, 210; Campbell, "Fishing in Other Men's Waters," 150.
55. Sir Charles Firth, qtd. in Sharrock, *Bunyan:* The Pilgrim's Progress; *A Casebook*, ed. Roger Sharrock (London: Macmillan, 1976), 102; Samuel Taylor Coleridge, *Coleridge on the Seventeenth Century*, ed. Roberta F. Brinkley (Durham: Duke University Press, 1955), 476; [Isaac] Disraeli and Thomas Adams, qtd. in Lynn Veach Sadler, *John Bunyan* (Boston: G. K. Hall, 1979), 135; James F. Forrest and Richard L. Greaves, *John Bunyan: A Reference Guide* (Boston: G. K. Hall, 1982), 31; J. A. Froude, qtd. in Donald Davie, *A Gathered Church: The Literature of the English Dissenting Interest, 1700–1930* (New York: Oxford University Press, 1978), 77. I am indebted here to

Swaim's account of Bunyan's popularity in *Pilgrim's Progress*, 1–2. See also Richard Greaves, "Bunyan through the Centuries: Some Reflections," *English Studies* 64 (1983): 113–21; C. Stephen Finley, "Bunyan among the Victorians: Macaulay, Froude, Ruskin," *Journal of Literature and Theology* 3 (1989): 77–94; N. H. Keeble, "'Of him thousands daily Sing and talk': Bunyan and His Reputation," in Keeble, *John Bunyan*, 241–63.

56. Contemporary theories of religion increasingly dissociate religious faith from the binaries rationality/irrationality and knowledge/superstition: Enlightenment paradigms that confined religious experience either to "rational religion" (morality) or irrational "mysticism." See chap. 1, n. 64.
57. This secularizing rationality is not limited in Christianity to Protestantism but adheres to much of medieval scholasticism as well. For the Reformation and Puritanism as secularizing forces, see the introduction, 22–29.
58. For the ethico-religious as that which exists outside knowledge, calculation, and quantification, see Derrida, "Faith and Knowledge"; Ward, "Theology and the Crisis of Representation"; and Branch, "Benefit of Doubt." In terms of psychoanalysis, religious experience and practice often take place at the cusp of the symbolic and the real, and are charged with constantly negotiating the demands of both and the slippage between them. Žižek has made a similar point, correlating Lacan's imaginary, symbolic, and real with Kierkegaard's three modes of existence (the aesthetic, ethical, and religious) and identifying art's continual revisiting of the "either/or" between the aesthetic and the ethical or the ethical and the religious; see Žižek's "Why Is Every Act a Repetition?" chap. 3 of *Enjoy Your Symptom! Jacques Lacan in Hollywood and Out* (New York: Routledge, 1992), 69–110.
59. From the Geneva Bible. The AV reads, "Thou hast given us like sheep appointed for meat; and hast scattered us among the heathen. Thou sellest thy people for nought, and dost not increase thy wealth by their price." Gordon Campbell has asserted that in his early works Bunyan used a sixteenth-century English translation, probably the Geneva Bible, deviations from which come from memory, alternate versions, and even the AV, which he would have heard in church; Campbell believes that in the later works Bunyan turns more to the AV because "sectarian misgivings about the Authorized Version were receding, and the new enemy was the *Book of Common Prayer*"; Campbell, "Fishing in Other Men's Waters," 138–39.
60. McGiffert, introduction to *God's Plot*, 18. The sort of self-scrutiny this emphasis on sincerity brings about is perhaps best exemplified by seventeenth-century Puritan Nehemiah Wallington, who wrote 20,000 pages in at least 50 volumes between 1618 and 1654, "glorify[ing] God by self-examination and judgement of myself"; see Paul Seaver, *Wallington's World: A Puritan Artisan in Seventeenth-Century London* (Stanford: Stanford University Press, 1985), 26.

CHAPTER 3

1. Anthony Ashley Cooper, third Earl of Shaftesbury, Ασκηματα, p. 360; hereafter cited parenthetically in the text as *A*. All references to the Ασκηματα

or *Exercises* refer to page numbers in the two manuscript volumes, located in the Public Record Office of the National Archives, Kew, Surrey, UK, document number PRO 30/24/27/10, parts 1 and 2. Pages of the *Exercises* are numbered consecutively by Shaftesbury, with the exception that the first volume ends with p. 201 as the last used, and the second volume begins with p. 187; thus page numbers 187–201 are duplicated. A volume number will be indicated only for those pages for which the volume is in question. I am extremely grateful to the University of Iowa for a generous Arts and Humanities Initiative Grant that allowed me to spend a wonderful month studying the Shaftesbury Papers at the National Archives.

Unless otherwise noted, translations from the Greek and French are mine. I am grateful to Jonathan Clark of Iowa City for the translations from Latin.

2. A more balanced view gives Britain a key role in a larger phenomenon. While contending that the development of aesthetic morality in the eighteenth century was "a collective enterprise carried out by the entire European Enlightenment," Richard Norton, for instance, entitles the first chapter of his study "The Advent of Modern Ethics in Britain and the Emergence of the Idea of Moral Beauty," claiming that "it had been in Britain that the modern science devoted to improving the 'moral constitution' of humanity had first gained a sizable following as an independent field of philosophical endeavor"; Richard E. Norton, *The Beautiful Soul: Aesthetic Morality in the Eighteenth Century* (Ithaca: Cornell University Press, 1995), 6, 10. Norton also criticizes the longstanding consideration of Shaftesbury's aesthetic ideas independent of his moral ones, when for him they were inseparable (28). On the connection of Shaftesbury's ethics and aesthetics, see for instance Preben Mortensen, "Shaftesbury and the Morality of Art Appreciation," *Journal of the History of Ideas* 55 (1994): 631–50.

3. Though Anthony, Lord Ashley does not become the third Earl of Shaftesbury until his father's death in November 1699, for convenience's sake I refer to him as Shaftesbury throughout. J. B. Schneewind notes that Shaftesbury was not the first to suggest that a special sense enables us to make moral distinctions, but rather it was Thomas Burnet, in his *Remarks* on Locke (1697), whose work Shaftesbury may have read before writing the *Inquiry*. Nevertheless, Shaftesbury comes down to us, as to his eighteenth-century readers via Francis Hutcheson, as the inventor of the moral sense. See J. B. Schneewind, *The Invention of Autonomy: A History of Modern Moral Philosophy* (Cambridge: Cambridge University Press, 1998), 301–2.

4. *The Life, Unpublished Letters, and Philosophical Regimen of Anthony, Earl of Shaftesbury*, ed. Benjamin Rand (London: Swan Sonnenschein, 1900), 403–4. For a helpful account of Hobbes's view of morality and the decades of responses it elicited, see Norton, *Beautiful Soul*, 10–14ff.

5. The first edition of the *Inquiry* was published without Shaftesbury's permission in 1699. It was later revised and its title expanded to "An Inquiry Concerning Virtue and Merit."

6. Eagleton, *Ideology of the Aesthetic*, 34. For similar accounts of the moral sense, see Schneewind, *Invention of Autonomy*, 295–309; Gordon, *Power of the*

Passive Self, 17–18; D. D. Raphael, *The Moral Sense* (London: Oxford University Press, 1947); Robert Voitle, "Shaftesbury's Moral Sense," *Studies in Philology* 52 (1955): 17–38; Stephen Darwall, *The British Moralists and the Internal 'Ought,' 1640–1740* (Cambridge: Cambridge University Press, 1995); Stanley Grean, *Shaftesbury's Philosophy of Religion and Ethics: A Study in Enthusiasm* (Athens: Ohio University Press, 1967); Norton, *Beautiful Soul*, 32–33, 40–42.

7. Shaftesbury, "An Inquiry concerning Virtue and Merit," in *Characteristicks of Men, Manners, Opinions, Times*, ed. Philip Ayres, 2 vols. (Oxford: Clarendon, 1999), 1.193–274, here 1:202; Schneewind, *Invention of Autonomy*, 302, 304.
8. Norton, *Beautiful Soul*, 32–33, 44–45. This caricature stems back at least to Berkeley's 1732 parody of Shaftesbury in *Alciphron*, a work that inaugurated a fallacy of the false dilemma—morality as based either in the head or the heart, in reason or sentiment—debated for most of the eighteenth century.
9. *The Sociable Enthusiast*, qtd. in Robert Voitle, *The Third Earl of Shaftesbury, 1671–1713* (Baton Rouge: Louisiana State University Press, 1984), 322. *The Sociable Enthusiast* was published either in 1703 or 1704 and later substantially revised, appearing in *Characteristicks* as *The Moralists, A Philosophical Rhapsody*.
10. Robert Markley, "Sentimentality as Performance."
11. Eagleton, *Ideology of the Aesthetic*, 51, 37. For the appeal of an ideology of universal aesthetic, literary, and moral value in the works of Adam Smith and the context of post-Union Scotland's "internal colonialism" within Great Britain, see Lori Branch, "Plain Style, or The High Fashion of Empire: Colonialism, Resistance, and Assimilation in Adam Smith's *Lectures on Rhetoric and Belles Lettres*," *Studies in Scottish Literature* 33 (2002): 435–53.
12. Shaftesbury, "Preface," 1698, in *Characteristicks of Men, Manners, Opinions, Times, Etc. To Which is Prefixed the Preface to the Select Sermons of Dr. Whichcote*, ed. John M. Robertson (1900; repr., Bristol: Thoemmes Press, 1995), [8].
13. Shaftesbury, *An Inquiry Concerning Virtue, in Two Discourses* (1699; facsimile, Delmar, N.Y.: Scholars' Facsimiles & Reprints, 1991), 3–4, emphasis added. This wording was considerably toned down when Shaftesbury revised the *Inquiry* for the *Characteristicks*.
14. Shaftesbury, "A Letter Concerning Enthusiasm," in Ayres, *Characteristicks*, 1:7–33, here 1:9, 11–13, 15, 27, 29. The "Letter" encourages a misleading overhistoricization of Shaftesbury's concern with enthusiasm, linking it too directly to the arrival of the "French Prophets" in England in the winter of 1706; see for instance Voitle, *Third Earl*, 324–25; Grean, *Shaftesbury's Philosophy*, chap. 2; and Ronald A. Knox, *Enthusiasm: A Chapter in the History of Religion with Special Reference to the Seventeenth and Eighteenth Centuries* (New York: Galaxy, 1961), 368. Shaftesbury's notebooks show enthusiasm to be a major category in his thought as early as 1699, as in the following: "Why fear *Enthousiasme*? why shun the Name? where should I be extasied but here? where enamoured but here? Is my Subject true, or is It Fiction? . . . shall I be ashamed of this Diviner Love, & of an Object of Love so far excelling all those other Objects, in Dignity, Majesty, Grace Beauty & Amiableness? Is this *Enthousiasme*? Be it: and so may I be ever an Enthousiast. Happy Me, if I

can grow in this Enthousiasme, so as to loose all those Enthousiasms of every other kind, and be whole towards *this*" (*A*, 153).
15. Klein, "Sociability, Solitude, and Enthusiasm," 168.
16. This pointedly secular rationality purports both to guard against superstitious, mistaken religion and to discern and define the nature of Deity itself, decreeing "that there is nothing in GOD but what is *Godlike;* and that He is either *not at all*, or *truly and perfectly Good*"; Shaftesbury, "Letter Concerning Enthusiasm," 17, 22. In his great schema of moral thought before Kant, Schneewind also positions Shaftesbury among the secular theorists of morality, stretching from Gassendi through the British moralists to Sade, who succeeded the natural law and perfectionist traditions; Schneewind, *Invention of Autonomy*.
17. Norton, *Beautiful Soul*, 38.
18. Bernard Mandeville attacked Shaftesbury's optimistic view of innate moral virtue in *The Grumbling Hive* (1705) and *The Fable of the Bees* (1714). Before Shaftesbury's death his legacy had forked, with the mainstream following the moral sense trajectory via Hutcheson, but with another path followed by Deists, (a group that he privately ridiculed), who took up his "Letter Concerning Enthusiasm" as a touchstone for wry balance and objectivity: see Heyd, *"Be Sober and Reasonable,"* 228.
19. Hutcheson's first two treatises appeared in London in 1725 as *An Inquiry into the Original of Our Ideas of Beauty and Virtue . . . In Which the Principles of the Late Earl of Shaftesbury are explain'd and defended . . . With an Attempt to introduce a Mathematical Calculation in Subjects of Morality . . . in Two Treatises. I. Concerning Beauty, Order, Harmony, Design. II. Concerning Moral Good and Evil*. Subsequent citations will refer to these treatises as *Inquiry* 1 and 2, though they were and continue to be published in the same volume. These he followed in London in 1728 by *An Essay on the Nature and Conduct of the Passions and Affections and Illustrations upon the Moral Sense*. See n. 21 in this chapter for modern publication information.
20. Ian Simpson Ross, *The Life of Adam Smith* (Oxford: Clarendon, 1995), 51.
21. Hutcheson, "Preface," *An Inquiry into the Original of Our Ideas of Beauty and Virtue . . . In Which the Principles of the Late Earl of Shaftesbury are explain'd and defended . . . With an Attempt to introduce a Mathematical Calculation in Subjects of Morality . . . in Two Treatises. I. Concerning Beauty, Order, Harmony, Design. II. Concerning Moral Good and Evil*, 2nd ed. (London, 1726; facsimile, New York: Garland Publishing, 1971), xxi.
22. "We see therefore . . . that the whole Sum of Interest lies upon the Side of *Virtue, Publick-spirit*, and *Honour*[;] that to *forfeit* these Pleasures . . . is the most foolish Bargain; and . . . to secure them with the *Sacrifice* of all others, is the *truest* Gain"; Hutcheson, *An Essay on the Nature and Conduct of the Passions and Affections* [with] *Illustrations upon the Moral Sense*, 2nd ed. (Dublin, 1728; facsimile, New York: Garland Publishing, 1971), 165 (from the *Essay*). Subsequent citations to the *Illustrations* reference this edition. Quotation in the text from Hutcheson, *Inquiry*, 1:106.
23. Hutcheson, *Illustrations*, 304.
24. Hutcheson, *Illustrations*, 333.

25. Hume to Adam Smith, Leicester Fields, 12 April 1759, in David Hume, *New Letters of David Hume*, ed. Raymond Klibansky and Ernest C. Mossner (Oxford: Clarendon, 1954), 51–55.
26. Adam Smith, *The Theory of Moral Sentiments*, ed. D. D. Raphael and A. L. Macfie (Indianapolis: Liberty Fund, 1984), 265–342. Smith's first category is that of Epicurean morality, in which virtue consists in prudence or wisely providing for one's physical needs. He excludes "Licentious Systems" (such as Mandeville's) which he claims make no real distinction between virtue and vice.
27. A. Smith, *Theory of Moral Sentiments*, 25.
28. A. Smith concurs with Hutcheson that only a thorough conviction of the existence of a "great, benevolent, and all-wise Being" brings a solid happiness, and that "on the contrary, the very suspicion of a fatherless world, must be the most melancholy of all reflections" (*Theory of Moral Sentiments*, 235). The lengthening shadow of that fatherless world on Smith's thought was glimpsed by his readers in his moving and finally removing the famous "atonement passage" from the *Theory of Moral Sentiments*. For its strange history, see A. Smith, *Theory of Moral Sentiments*, app. 2, 383–401.
29. Hutcheson, *Inquiry*, 177. Bentham did not use the term *utilitarianism* and used what would become his most famous phrase, "the greatest happiness for the greatest number," only in his first published work and late in his career, then with some reservation; see Schneewind, *Invention*, 419–21. Bentham's is yet another case in the history of British moral philosophy illustrating that the economic logics of these systems have a life and trajectory of their own, outside the ways individual thinkers would mediate and circumscribe them.
30. Edmund Burke, "On Taste," in *A Philosophical Enquiry into the Origin of Our Ideas of the Sublime and Beautiful*, ed. James T. Boulton (Notre Dame: University of Notre Dame Press, 1968), 11–27, here 26. The first edition of Burke's *Enquiry* appeared in 1757; he added "On Taste" as an introduction to the second edition in 1759. Burke was a careful reader of Hutcheson, and Burke's debt to him is clear in both the title and conception of the *Enquiry*.
31. The classic essay connecting the moral philosophy and its discourse of objectivity to its libidinal structures is Jacques Lacan's "Kant *avec* Sade," trans. James B. Swenson Jr., *October* 51 (1990): 55–75. See also chap. 3, n. 81.
32. For the centrality of religion to Sade's erotics, see n. 79 in this chapter and pp. 117–18 below.
33. Victor Stater, review of *Shaftesbury and the Culture of Politeness*, by Lawrence E. Klein, *Albion* 27 (1995): 127.
34. Laurent Jaffro, "Présentation" to *Exercises*, by Shaftesbury, trans. from the English, intro., and notes by Laurent Jaffro, 7–35 (Paris: Aubier, 1993), here 32–33.
35. Voitle, *Third Earl*, 160.
36. Though Voitle occasionally oversimplifies issues relevant to the notebooks (e.g., seeing Shaftesbury's sexuality as an either/or between hetero- and homosexuality), his biography of Shaftesbury goes further than other sources in allowing lengthy, startling passages from them to appear in their

full strangeness. There has yet to be a book-length study of the Ασκηματα in English. Friedrich Uehlein's German-language study *Kosmos und Subjectivität: Lord Shaftesbury's Philosophical Regimen* (Freiburg: K. Alber, 1976) draws on the Rand edition.
37. Grean, *Shaftesbury's Philosophy*, xviii, 34, 36, 163.
38. Lawrence E. Klein, *Shaftesbury and the Culture of Politeness: Moral Discourse and Cultural Politics in Early Eighteenth-Century England* (Cambridge: Cambridge University Press, 1994), 2, 7, 17–18, and chaps. 3 and 4, 71–90. Klein's reading of the Ασκηματα is puzzling on several accounts, particularly because he locates the "kernel of politeness" as the "art of pleasing in company" (3), something for which Shaftesbury constantly upbraids himself in the notebooks. He also claims that the opening entry is "typical of the notebooks as a whole" (71), where my reading documents important shifts over the seven years that the notebooks represent. Klein's approach also brackets the notebooks as written during a hiatus from public writing, eliding the way passages from the notebooks make their way wholesale into the essays of the *Characteristicks*. Laurent Jaffro, however, agrees with my assessment that the public and private writings are profoundly connected, going so far as to call "Soliloquy" the "published theory of the private *Exercises*"; Jaffro, "Présentation," 24. Michael Prince is similarly critical of Klein's flattening of Shaftesbury; see Michael Prince, *Philosophical Dialogue in the British Enlightenment: Theology, Aesthetics and the Novel* (Cambridge: Cambridge University Press, 1996), 25–28.
39. Derrida, "Faith and Knowledge," 2.
40. Shaftesbury dated his philosophical awakening to this period of worldly initiation. In an entry of 1703/4, he refers to being in his 33rd year, "the 10th at least since Conviction" (*A*, 2:197), which would put his awakening in 1693–94, around age 22–23.
41. *A*, 1:196. For details of Shaftesbury's life in this period, see Voitle, *Third Earl*, 52–53, 72–78.
42. PRO 30/24/27/11, marked "Holland 1704 Coming away and on Shipboard."
43. "Wouldst thou willingly be perjur'd, wouldst thou be fals, wouldst thou lye, flatter, be debauch'd & dissolute to serve it? But if I think to serve it as I now am bid, all this will necessarily follow. for I must prostitute my mind: I must grow corrupt, interessed, fals. and where will then be the service I shall render to my Country?" (*A*, 70). And again, ". . . remember only w^t thou hadst been, without such a G^d father to lay the Foundation of thy Education? without such times as made Thee awake, & early sensible of publick Good? . . . without thy happy Breaking from Courts, by being broken first with the Court in Holland, & afterwards with King William's & the Court-Whiggs? in fine, without thy first & second Retreat & Studdy in Holland & all the providentiall Deliverances inward & outward? ((!.) ω. χ. ↓,) early Family-Troubles, & later; wch with those in the Publick, however injuriouse to *outward* Health, good for *inward*" (*A*, 1:196). Shaftesbury's grandfather, the first earl, had overseen his grandson's education, bringing him to live with him and appointing John Locke as his private tutor ("thy good Friend & Ruler

of thy youth"), initiating a friendship that lasted until Locke's death, notwithstanding their eventual philosophical differences. The first earl fell out of favor with the court of Charles II and died in political shame in 1683, when Shaftesbury was 12. Shaftesbury suffered ill-treatment from his grandfather's enemies as a youth. This passage also references Shaftesbury's growing distance from and distaste for court life, ca. 1698–1708 (the latter being the date of the entry), in spite of periodic attempts to reinvolve him, and an earlier contentious rift between his parents which left him caught as mediator between them ("early family troubles"). The cryptographic symbols are treated later in this chapter.

44. At one point Shaftesbury chastises himself when he "com'st to [his] Work heavily & with regret, hardly parting with other matters, & quitting other pursuits" (*A*, 94).

45. Each entry in the notebooks bears a specific heading, and Shaftesbury at some point compiled an index of the topics treated in the exercises. In the first volume for instance he records fourteen headings: "Natural Affections," "Deity," "The End," "Good & Ill," "Shame," "Human affaires," "Self," "Simplicity," "Passions," "Life," "Philosophy," "Ideas" (Visa), "Φαντασιαι" (fancies or fantasies), and "Δοξαριον" (mere opinion or belief).

46. Edited by Rand and published as "The Philosophical Regimen," in *Life, Unpublished Letters, and Philosophical Regimen*, 1–272. Following older scholarly practices and his own sense of decorum, Rand sorted the entries by topic, often rearranging not just the topics themselves but the chronology of paragraphs within the topics, mistranscribing letters (giving for instance "Fly-traps" instead of "Eye-traps" for beautiful women), and, most problematically of all, whitewashing by omitting key words and eliding entire unsettling paragraphs.

47. The Shaftesbury Standard Edition, published in Stuttgart by Friedrich Frommann Verlag–Günther Holzboog, will eventually include the complete works of Shaftesbury, parallel in English and German, in approximately twenty-one volumes, eight of which are available at this writing. The Ασκηματα have been transcribed by the SSE team, are being translated into German, and will be published as the *Askēmata*, vols. 2:5 and 2:6, in 2006 or 2007. In an extraordinary act of academic generosity, Dr. Friedrich Uehlein of the SSE editorial team shared the English transcription of the Ασκηματα with me as a searchable computer document after my having spent a month studying the manuscripts at the PRO. Being able to check my notes against their transcription is a luxury for which I am immensely grateful. While their transcription is highly precise, including Shaftesbury's indications of place and date, strike-throughs and marginalia, the manuscript order has inevitably posed a challenge. They also have collated the entries under Shaftesbury's topics, with bracketed page numbers indicating the manuscript pages—a subtle trail of breadcrumbs by which one might retrace the original order of spliced entries, though with great effort. Reproducing the manuscript in its exact order would certainly pose its own problems, and so one hopes the SSE will include as an appendix a "Table of Contents" based on the strict ordering of pages and entries and the manuscripts.

48. In this chapter, I use "god" in reference to Shaftesbury's "Deity," which is distinctly not the Christian "God" or Trinity in the sense that any other writer in this study uses the word. I thank Carey Newman for suggesting this distinction.
49. *A*, 17, 20, 227, 232, 348.
50. For the grudging favorable comparison of Christianity to druidism, see *A*, 121; for references to Marcus and Epictetus as the "Divine Men," see *A*, 128, 100, 283, 374. In the parchments, Shaftesbury also directs prayers toward the "Divine Man" in a regimen of morning and evening self-examination.
51. "Consider how it had been with Thee in former days, if, according to the Idea then conceived of Deity, a Voice had been heard; an Angell or Messenger appear'd. what an immediate chang? how suddain a renouncing of all other things?" (*A*, 103).
52. On Shaftesbury's vexed sexual relationships, see pp. 109–15 and n. 56 below.
53. Asad, *Formations of the Secular*, 124, 109.
54. *A*, 2:190.
55. See chap. 2, pp. 74–75 and 77–78, and Lacan, *Four Fundamental Concepts*, 55–56, 49, 69.
56. "Remember what thou cunyest in thy Breast: remember those former inflammations & how suddainly all takes fire again, when once a spark is got in. remember the **Fuell** within, & those unextinguish'd Passions wch lye but as in the Embers. think of that Impetuouse, furiouse, impotent Temper, & what trust is to be given to it. This too remember, that as in certain Machines that are fast'ned by many Wedges, tho' they be made ever so compact & firm by this means, yet if one Wedg be loosen'd, the whole Frame shakes; so with respect to the Mind, it is not meerly in *one* Passion that the mischeif is receiv'd, but in *all*: it is not *one* String that looses its accord, but *all*—" (A, 65). "Deceive not thy self. There is no Relaxation, no Remission, no Un-bending, no relieving, resting, recreating reposing. deceitfull Names! . . . wch have no place as to the Work within; wch will ever be carrying on either in the right or wrong Way, ever advancing. & pressing on, even when most unseen: growing imperceptibly, ripening & coming to a head either as good Fruit, or as the Fungus's" (*A*, 205). The last sentence includes a characteristic Shaftesburian pun and reference to sexual arousal.
57. Jaffro also stresses the intimate connection between "Soliloquy" and the Ασκηματα: "In a curious reversal, that which was a real practice of Shaftesbury is presented, ten years later, as a fiction"; Jaffro, "Présentation," 31.
58. Shaftesbury also mentions another technique or art, though much less frequently than the other two: "reduction," that is, identifying a particular desire as part of a general category, the more quickly to dismiss it (*A*, 354–55). These methods are drawn from Shaftesbury's deep reading in Stoic authors, particularly Marcus Aurelius and Epictetus. For a reading of the Ασκηματα as Stoic texts in the tradition of Marcus Aurelius's *Meditations* and Epictetus's *Encheiridion*, see Esther A. Tiffany, "Shaftesbury as Stoic," *PMLA* 38 (1923): 642–84, and Voitle, *Third Earl*, 135–63. Rather than tracing the influence of Stoicism on Shaftesbury—itself a problematic task because of

his selective use and transformation of Stoic ideas—I am seeking here to understand precisely how and to what effect Shaftesbury employs them and makes these concepts his own.

59. This art of inversion he deems higher than all the other arts: "I had rather this," he tells himself, "than the Cubilo of Michel Angelo: I had rather this than the Philippicks of Demosthenes or Cicero: rather than to have wrote like Homer, or fought like Alexander" (*A*, 129); it is complete in itself, needing no external materials or spectators, and "itself is Happiness & Prosperity" (*A*, 130). On Shaftesbury's inversion and inner discourse as a method of "re-educating" the self, see Klein, *Culture of Politeness*, 86–90; see also Voitle, *Third Earl*, 153.

60. In one fascinating instance of inversion, Shaftesbury attempts to divorce his notion of self from nationality and parentage, asserting that he is first a man of the world and not an Englishman, deriding himself for national sympathy and desire to "gain esteem to England" (*A*, 134). Continually asking himself "Who am I?" he finally answers, "Thou art **a Man**. Dos this signify anything or nothing? . . . What therefore is *Man* but Reason & Humanity, Faith, Friendship, Justice, Integrity?" (*A*, 135). In the space of two pages he inverts his ideas of caring what others think, reduces their esteem to monstrous "deceit," and then, faced with this blankness of a completely insular self, arrives at wholly emptied and abstracted notions of "Man, Humanity, Faith, Friendship, Justice, Integrity."

61. The injunction to see the "viler but truer side of things" is also distilled into Shaftesbury's "Appendix" of core principles, inserted in the opening pages of the first notebook, probably in 1700, after this entry, written between December 1699 and January 1700 (*A*, 3).

62. The notebooks indicate that Shaftesbury seems to have had early affairs with women, men, and boys, something which was apparently disconcerting to Rand, who regularly elided such references in his edition of the text. Voitle does not treat Shaftesbury's sexuality in depth, but operates with an implicit, binary heterosexual/homosexual framework, seeing Shaftesbury as most likely homosexual, having married reluctantly at the very end of his life to produce an heir. The sexual references in the Ασκηματα to women, men, and boys would seem to invoke a broader spectrum of sexual desires. The most conflicted passages seem to refer to homosexual involvement as an adult, in the context of intense friendships and society, most likely (based on the timeframe) in London life surrounding Parliament.

63. Asad, *Formations of the Secular*, 124.

64. Jaffro interprets the symbols as mnemonic devices. We agree in thinking that in particular series of symbols Shaftesbury is concerned to identify the pattern by which specific "mistakes" and "falls" characteristically lead to greater problems that concern him; Jaffro, "Présentation," 29; and "Note sur le Texte," in Jaffro, *Exercices*, by Shaftesbury, 36–37.

65. Žižek, *Sublime Object of Ideology*, 44–47.

66. See for instance Žižek, *Sublime Object of Ideology*, 47–49. In a related passage in which Shaftesbury tries to curtail his desire for intimacy, he recites a grotesque litany of the body's porous appetitiveness: "What are we? . . .

Guts. Tails. Pallats. Warm Flesh with feelings, Itches, Aches, Appetites. The Puppet-Play of Fancyes . . . . . Dreams. Hobby-horses. Houses of Cards. . . . The Kitching-Pomp: the Copulating-Pomp: the Carcass-Pomp. Shews: Spectacles: Rites: Formalitys: Processions. . . . The Gowns! Habits! Robes! . . . . . How underneath? How in the Night-Caps, between the Curtains & Sheets? How anon in the Family with Wife, Servants Children, or where even none of these must see? Private Pleasures, other Privacyes? the Closet, Back-Room & Bed chamber? Parlours, Dining-Rooms, Dressing-Rooms, & other Rooms? in Sickness, in lazy Hours, in Wine, in Leachery? Taking in; letting out? . . . . O, the August Assembly! Each of You such as You are apart!" (*A*, 219). The long ellipses in this passage, as elsewhere, are Shaftesbury's.

67. This reading corresponds with the Lacanian idea that "what was foreclosed from the Symbolic returns in the Real" of the symptom and of desire; see Žižek, *Sublime Object of Ideology*, 21, 71–75. The sexualized fantasy-symptom of rational violence and "penetration" into others' psyches that we see in the next section likewise resonates with Lacan's notion of the subject as *sinthome*, as constituted *by* his symptom; paradoxically, that which seems to present the barrier to one's subjectivity actually provides the consistency of one's being. Žižek would likely read the externalization of disgust as bodily wound and disease as an indication that the trauma here is not about the body but about the "symbolic network in which the body is caught"; the rottenness points to a corruption in Shaftesbury's moral ideology or the symbolic order itself, and is a "materialization of moral-symbolic decay" (78).

68. The purification of the self eventually becomes, in Shaftesbury's rhetoric, a mystery religion which it would be sacrilege to expose: "Silence ab^t the Θεωρηματα [principles] & all belonging [to them]. . . . If *then;* how much more *now*? now that the Whole is a Mistery & unknown? a Madness a Meer Blasphemy . . . . . And would not this indeed be madness & Blasphemy thus to expose wt is this sacred? . . . How sacred shou'd this Reserve & Silence be, above all other, not to expose, reveal betray . . . . Detestable Prostitution!" (*A*, 371).

69. "As how then *not a Child?* how *least like Woman?* how *far from Beast?* how remov'd from any thing of this kind? How properly *a Man?* . . . *A Man.* & not a Woman; effeminate, soft, delicate, supine: impotent in Pleasure, in Anger, Talk: pusillanimouse, light, changeable &c: but the contrary to this in each particular . . . . . *A Man* & not a Beast: not Gluttonouse as a Hogg: not leacherouse as a Goat: not savage as a Lyon: but sociable as the creatures that live in society & have a Publick . . . . *A Man* & not a Child: not taken with Trifles, not admiring Shews: not playing crying taking on: angry, & pleas'd again: forward pettish: in humour out of humour: Wanton & cross: Stomach: the Belly Play-thing: Mama: Nurs. . . . . **The Contraryes.** *Manhood. Manlyness. Humanity* . . . . *Manly, Humane Masculine*" (*A*, 334).

70. "To be dissolved in debauchery, pleasures, idleness."

71. The appeal of the other's "secret & hidden mistery" resonates with Žižek's explication of Lacanian desire and the simultaneous attraction and repulsion expressed in the formula "I love something in you more than you, therefore

I destroy you." See Žižek, *The Puppet and the Dwarf: The Perverse Core of Christianity* (Cambridge, Mass.: MIT Press, 2003), 150–51.
72. Henry George Liddell and Robert Scott, *A Lexicon Abridged from Liddell and Scott's Greek-English Lexicon* (Oxford: Clarendon, 2002), 751. See also F. E. Peters, *Greek Philosophical Terms: A Historical Lexicon* (New York: New York University Press, 1967), 156. Φαντασια (singular; plural φαντασιαι), like its usual Latin correlate *Visa* (which Shaftesbury usually uses in the plural; singular *visum*), can be translated as "image" or "imagination," which, given our post-Romantic notions of the word, can be more confusing than helpful. For Shaftesbury, Fancy is clearly somewhere between sensation and reflection, and seems constantly to suggest desires to him. He generally uses Φαντασια to denote the faculty and *visa* to indicate the images, thoughts, and desires it suggests.
73. The following is representative: "Fancy has spoke. 'Tis now my turn. '.... Good! is this all? have You any more to say? Let us hear all out; and then answer. But speak out: speak plain, high up, aloud: no muttering: no half-Words: no Whispering, dumb Signs, nodding, winking, & those other misteriouse sly Ways. away with this. 'Tis not to be endur'd........ If Thou has ought to say (Fancy!) say it: let us hear patiently. but if from one Thing to another, I interrupt: *To the Point (Fancy!) to the Point!* Is not this what you advanc'd just now; tho' you have since past to other things, & so to other, heaping, mixing confounding? But to bring Things to an Issue; that we may fix somewhere; Let us take it up here: Let us hear distinctly. Was not this the Suggestion? these the Words? as thus, or thus? ..... Sayd yee not so, or so? ...... These were the **Words** .... Repeat 'em. ... Once again .... Again a Third time—Tis Well. By your Leave then; a Word ere you depart. I must talk a little in my Turn, & be familiar, very familiar: as well I may. for Thy Turn (Fancy!) has been long enough. **Ohe, jam satis est!**'" (*A*, 274).
74. "*Responsare cupidinibus*" appears in Horace, *Satires* 2.7.85, where the sense of *responsare* is "to resist." I thank Jonathan Clark for this insight.
75. Acts 17:28. *A*, 309.
76. Shaftesbury's change from a posture of (feminine) submission towards God to one of masculine affront bears a striking resemblance to John Donne's unstable gender position before an increasingly masculinized God as described by Stanley Fish and Michael Schoenfelt. Fish notes how Donne casts himself in a female role but betrays an inability to maintain it in the face of his fierce desire to be master of himself. Building on Fish's work, Schoenfeldt shows how the God of Reformation Protestantism became progressively masculinized, forcing men either to assume a female persona or embrace a discourse of same-sex desire. Fish, "Masculine Persuasive Force: Donne and Verbal Power," in *Soliciting Interpretation: Literary Theory and Seventeenth-Century English Poetry*, ed. Elizabeth D. Harvey and Katharine Eisaman Maus, 223–52 (Chicago: University of Chicago Press, 1990), cited in Michael Schoenfeldt, "The Gender of Religious Devotion: Amelia Lanyer and John Donne," in *Religion and Culture in Renaissance England*, ed. Claire McEachern and Debora Shuger, 209–33 (Cambridge: Cambridge University Press, 1997), 211, 242.

77. See for example Paula McDowell, "Enlightenment Enthusiasms and the Spectacular Failure of the Philadelphian Society," *Eighteenth-Century Studies* 35 (2002): 515–33, and Pocock, "Enthusiasm." Derrida also addresses reason's vexed reinvocation of a form of religion it has itself constructed in "Faith and Knowledge."
78. Donatien Alphonse François Sade, "Déposition de Jeanne Testard," in *Oeuvres completes du marquis de Sade*, ed. Gilbert Lely, 16 vols. (Paris: Cercle du Livre Précieux, 1966–1967) 12:645. Here I have used the eloquent translation by Neil Schaeffer in his *The Marquis de Sade: A Life* (New York: Knopf, 1999), 56.
79. Schaeffer, *Marquis de Sade*, 136. It is unclear whether Sade actually committed this particular sacrilege, but, as Schaeffer notes, his writings return again and again to "the communion wafer, toward which so many of [his] fantasies had run" (297). Similarly, according to the deposition given by beggar and possible prostitute Rose Kailair (or Keller) on Easter Sunday, 3 April 1767, Sade picked her up after mass that morning on the pretense of hiring her for housecleaning, bound her naked to a bed, beat her in parody of the scourging of Christ, then masturbated, bringing himself to orgasm by shouting blasphemies; see Sade, "Déclaration de Rose Kailair," in *L'affaire Kailair*, vol. 4 of *Correspondances du marquis de Sade et de ses proches, enrichies du documents, notes et commentaires*, ed. Alice M. Laborde, 27 vols. to date, 26–30 (Paris-Genève: Champion-Slatkine, 1991). Schaeffer also links blasphemy and sexualized aggression toward God with Sade's craving for certainty about metaphysical matters and frustration at its impossibility; see Schaeffer, *Marquis de Sade*, 316–17, 374, 456. For the sadomasochistic appeal of Christ and the cross, see Rambuss, *Closet Devotions*, 20, 99.
80. Hume to Henry Home, London, 2 December 1737, in Hume, *New Letters of David Hume*, 1–3.
81. In addition to Lacan's "Kant *avec* Sade," for a more accessible treatment explaining the developmental difficulties that lead to the sadomasochistic erotics of (masculinized) domination and (feminized) submission, see Jessica Benjamin's *Bonds of Love*. G. J. Barker-Benfield documents this logic of domination as Shaftesbury's "anti-effeminacy" in *Culture of Sensibility*. My account differs most from that of John Barrell, who treats Shaftesbury's masculinity in terms of the inherent tension between the masculinity of abstinence and the masculinity of virility, without considering the way male abstinence such as Shaftesbury's is already explicitly, psychologically sexualized. For treatments of masculinity in eighteenth-century British aesthetic and moral philosophy, see for instance Mary Poovey and Julie Ellison. Poovey demonstrates that an ideology of gender and sexualized desire is central to the eighteenth-century discourses of aesthetics and political economics, both of which attempted to reconcile virtue and commerce. Ellison argues that later female sentimental authors only make sense in the context of the prestige of male tenderheartedness, but that male sentimental display and the sort of masculine emotional reserve we see in Shaftesbury are mutually legitimating for masculine identity. Claudia L. Johnson argues that the gradual masculinization of sentiment in the later eighteenth century left women the positions of the "equivocal or the hyperfeminine." Jessica

Benjamin, *The Bonds of Love: Psychoanalysis, Feminism, and the Problem of Domination* (New York: Pantheon, 1988), esp. 51–84; Barker-Benfield, *Culture of Sensibility*, 105–19; John Barrell, "'The Dangerous Goddess': Masculinity, Prestige, and the Aesthetic in Early Eighteenth-Century Britain," *Cultural Critique* 12 (1989): 101–31; Mary Poovey, "Aesthetics and Political Economy in the Eighteenth Century: The Place of Gender in the Social Constitution of Knowledge," in *Aesthetics and Ideology*, ed. George Levine (New Brunswick, N.J.: Rutgers University Press, 1994), 79–105; Ellison, *Cato's Tears*, 9; Johnson, *Equivocal Beings*, 12.

82. Markley, "Objectivity as Ideology," 369.
83. Žižek, *Sublime Object of Ideology*, 30–33, 43–49, 66–69, 114, 124–28.
84. In several places the Ασκηματα rails against atheism, but in light of the following paragraphs, it is unjustified to equate this raillery with an increase of religious faith (cf. Voitle, *Third Earl*, 347).
85. An epigraph inserted on the opening page of volume 2, as well as a page of citations at the end of volume 1, are inscribed "St. G[iles]: 1707/8." These are the latest dated entries in the notebooks.
86. Jaffro reads the connection more straightforwardly, considering that the years between the Ασκηματα and the publication of the *Characteristicks* allowed Shaftesbury time to practice the method he had formulated and to prepare to have something to say; Jaffro, "Présentation," 31. The final entry and the general tone of unraveling in the second volume weigh heavier in my reading.
87. Shaftesbury, *Second Characters* (PRO 30/24/27/15), 93. The passage goes on in like manner to complain of representations of Joseph, the husband of the Virgin Mary, as an old man. An index then points from the "Wretched model" passage back across to 92V, where Shaftesbury continues to rail about paintings of the Trinity, angels, and "mixed forms" in language that evokes the "monstrous copulations" of the Ασκηματα: The problem for Shaftesbury is that Christianity is decidedly not Hellenistic or classical. He continues, revealing that his contention is not only with enthusiasm but with high church devotion to an unmanly Christ and a weak God the Father:

> Mem^d here the general subject. vizt God the Father a Broken, wrapt up, nurs'd, old Man: consumptive-Look, haggard, with Carcass in Lap, a Dead X^t held forth in Winding Sheet: a Pigeon in Bosom, and a lubberly *Hobende boy* or two, of an Angel (Hermaphroditical Forms half-Man, half Woman, in Petticoats & Grand flopping Wings) with a Douzen or score of Peepers, raw callow Heads (like gaping birds out of a Nest) stuck in unnaturally between a pair of wings without a Body, & call'd Cherubs.
>
> From hence (as taking Ground from a high station) thunder & rant (but comically stil & in a good Humour) ag^t common prayer-book-cult, Glass Window & Tapestry-Figures of High Church & Chappel. Better the perfect in the kind, & statuary introducd Altar a true altar, & Image &c as becoming. And justify this by Queen Elizabeth's rant cited by an ingenious Author . . . in *Priest Craft in Perfection*. (*Second Characters*, 92V; folio #100)

Again, late passages like these caution against generalizing from the published writings about what some have noted as Shaftesbury's eventual

"marked toning down of the wit directed at religion"; Richard B. Wolf, "Shaftesbury's Just Measure of Irony," *SEL* 33 (1993): 582.
88. Voitle, *Third Earl*, 366; for an overview of Shaftesbury's views of the great masters in *Second Characters*, see *Third Earl*, 361–66.
89. On the figure of the Jew as ideologically loathed fantasy-supplement, see for instance Žižek, *Sublime Object of Ideology*, 124–28.
90. This is explicitly the weight of Hutcheson's *Essay*.
91. Shaftesbury recoils from Christ in exactly the bodily, excremental terms that Bishop Warbarton used to blast William Law's mysticism as a spiritual carpophagia: in Leigh Eric Schmidt's terms, as "one more excremental waste in the making of an enlightened, reasonable religion"; Schmidt, "Making of Modern 'Mysticism,'" 279. The shared registers of disgust point to just how much Latitudinarian religion had in common with Shaftesburian rationality.
92. Derrida, "Faith and Knowledge," 12–13.

Coda to Chapter 3

1. Prince, *Philosophical Dialogue*, 25. Based on the overall inconsistency of Shaftesbury's oeuvre rather than the Ασκηματα, Prince nevertheless reaches conclusions about Shaftesbury's self-splitting similar to mine. "Like the female in the frontispiece to his *An Inquiry concerning Virtue, or Merit*," he writes, "Shaftesbury is a split figure, torn between emancipation and control, transformation and stasis, the Cumean Sibyl dispersing fragments and a just Prometheus forging wholes.... Unwilling to bank on a philosophically suspect concept of politeness, Shaftesbury attempted to heal his split identity in two ways, both decisive for the subsequent philosophical and literary history of the eighteenth century": a distinctive vocabulary of aesthetics, and a renovation of philosophical dialogue that would both represent and reconcile his divided allegiances, and provide "one blueprint for the emerging novel" (Prince, *Philosophical Dialogue*, 28, 43). Prince focuses strictly on dialogue in Shaftesbury's philosophical works rather than the inner dialogue described in chap. 3.
2. Felix Paknadel, "Shaftesbury's Illustrations of *Characteristics*," *Journal of the Warburg and Courtland Institute* 37 (1974): 291.
3. Wind goes on to add that Shaftesbury "himself invented the programme and pattern of all the works of art produced to his order"; Edgar Wind, "Shaftesbury as a Patron of Art," *Journal of the Warburg and Courtland Institute* 2 (1938): 185.
4. Paknadel, "Shaftesbury's Illustrations," 294.
5. Marcus Brainard concurs that "Soliloquy" is "the central essay of the collection ... [T]he aim of *Soliloquy* pervades the whole of the *Characteristicks*"; Brainard, "Minding One's Manners: On the 'Moral Architecture' of Shaftesbury's *Characteristics*," *Bochumer Philosophisches Jarhbuch Antike und Mittelalter* 6 (2001): 226 n. 30. In the following sentences, Shaftesbury's instructions for the engravings are taken from Paknadel.
6. Shaftesbury, "Soliloquy: Or Advice to an Author," in Ayres, *Characteristicks*, 1:83–186, here 1:93.

7. Shaftesbury, "Soliloquy," 1:105.
8. Shaftesbury, "Soliloquy," 1:101.
9. Paknadel, "Shaftesbury's Illustrations," 307.
10. Brainard, "Minding One's Manners," 225–26. Brainard also reads the flowing garment as a toga (223).
11. I am grateful to Lady Shaftesbury for permission to use a color copy of this portrait, and to Matthew Bailey at the National Portrait Gallery for his kind correspondence and providing the image. I am likewise indebted to my colleagues, art historians Dorothy Johnson and Wallace Tomasini, for their conversations with me about this portrait, Shaftesbury's notebooks, and my theory about the unidentified figure. Their expertise and knowledge of the portraiture of the period have been invaluable to me.

    As mentioned in the text below, Wind documents the "amanuensis" relationship between Shaftesbury and Closterman spanning a decade. In Wind's view, the portrait of Shaftesbury clearly shows Shaftesbury's invention with its emblematic elements, particularly in the arrangement of the books. However, Wind makes no mention of the second figure in the painted portrait, and there is no specific evidence in the article that he saw Closterman's painting; rather he may have viewed only the engraving, which indicates that it is made from the painting by Closterman. Wind, "Shaftesbury as a Patron of Art," 186–87. For Closterman's life and that of his brother, John Baptist Closterman, see Malcolm Rogers, "John and John Baptist Closterman: A Catalogue of Their Works," in *The Forty-Ninth Volume of the Walpole Society*, 224–76 (London: Pitman, 1983), here 224–36.
12. I am grateful to art historian Wallace Tomasini for this insight.
13. Voitle, *Third Earl*, xii; David Leatherbarrow, "Character, Geometry and Perspective: the Third Earl of Shaftesbury's Principals of Garden Design," *Journal of Garden History* 4 (1984): 339. The previous dating of 1700–1701 and the view of the present earl appeared in the catalog for the NPG exhibition; Malcolm Rogers, *John Closterman: Master of the English Baroque, 1660–1711* (exhibit catalogue, London: National Portrait Gallery, 1981), 15–16.
14. For the clearly subservient position of servants in other Closterman portraits, see Rogers, "John and John Baptist Closterman," plates 35, 44, 54, and 58.
15. The scar is also visible in two other portraits of Maurice by Closterman; see Rogers, "John and John Baptist Closterman," plates 58 and 60.
16. This possibility was suggested to me by art historian Dorothy Johnson.
17. A negative interpretation of the first earl would not in itself explain the figure being unidentified; such a moral lesson would have fit with Shaftesbury's didacticism, instructing his descendants to follow the path of philosophy, not politics.
18. Voitle has suggested that the unidentified volumes may include the *Meditations* of Marcus Aurelius; Voitle, *Third Earl*, 344.
19. John Barrell, *The Political Theory of Painting from Reynolds to Hazlitt: "The Body of the Public"* (New Haven: Yale University Press, 1986), qtd. in Alison Conway, *Private Interests: Women, Portraiture, and the Visual Culture of the*

English Novel, 1709–1791 (Toronto: University of Toronto Press, 2001), 16–20.
20. Conway, *Private Interests*, 16.
21. Wind, "Shaftesbury as a Patron of Art," 186–87.
22. Shaftesbury, *Second Characters*, 68.
23. Cynthia Marshall, *The Shattering of the Self: Violence, Subjectivity, and Early Modern Texts* (Baltimore: The Johns Hopkins University Press, 2002), 12.
24. If Shaftesbury did intend the second figure to be his grandfather, Closterman would appear to have painted his likeness by projecting backwards, so to speak, from Shaftesbury's features, aging them slightly and adding his grandfather's blond hair, rather than having copied the rather flat portraits that existed of the first earl; see for instance, after John Greenhill, Anthony Ashley Cooper, First Earl of Shaftesbury, oil on canvas, 50 x 39 ¼ inches, National Portrait Gallery, London, NPG 3893. As I suggest, the two readings of the portrait entertained here are not necessarily mutually exclusive; if the second figure is meant on one level to be his grandfather, the "painting backwards" from Shaftesbury's appearance makes the painting reflect the profound division both between self and other and within the self as well.
25. The primary reason given for previously dating the Shaftesbury portrait 1700–1701 was because little is known of Closterman's life between 1702 and his death in 1711; Rogers, *John Closterman*, 3. What is certain is that Closterman continued to work for Shaftesbury during this period, both as painter and collector; one of Closterman's drawings for Shaftesbury, *The Triumph of Liberty*, is based on the fifth treatise of the *Characteristicks*, *The Moralists*, the first version of which was written in 1705, so Closterman was working closely with Shaftesbury on emblematic work at or after this time (Paknadel, "Shaftesbury's Illustrations," 291). In a letter of 1699, now lost, Shaftesbury proposed a "family picture" to Closterman, but a close reading of Closterman's reply makes almost certain that the painting he refers to is the one of Ashley and Maurice. Closterman writes: "I am extremely glad to hear of your thoughts for a family picture, and that I shall perform it as soon as I come home . . . I promise your Lordship so for that nobody shall prevent me till *your pictures* are done [emphasis added], and to go in to the country is better still, th[e]n we shall have wholly our thought together" (qtd. in Wind, "Shaftesbury as a Patron of Art," 187). The double portrait of the brothers bears the date 1702, was painted outdoors in a wooded setting, and with its stunningly elaborate background very much suggests the work of two hands. Both John Closterman and his brother John Baptist Closterman are recorded as having stayed at Shaftesbury's home on 23 July 1700 (Rogers, *John Closterman*, 4). The likeliest scenario, then, is that they worked together on the brothers' double portrait, which might have been finished as late as 1702.

Since the Closterman exhibit at the National Portrait Gallery in 1981, Malcolm Rogers has changed his mind about the dating of the Shaftesbury portrait, now placing it later, around 1701–1702, marking "the transition to Closterman's later style" (Rogers, "John and John Baptist Closterman,"

231–32). The tablet marked "1702" may be a later speculation based on the inscription on the double portrait. Given Shaftesbury's ongoing relationship with Closterman, there seems no reason not to date it later still. The portrait in toga suggests the work of only one hand (Rogers, *John Closterman*, 15), is rougher and less finished, and seems austere and of a different cloth compared to the more elegant, refined Closterman portraits of 1700–1702 (plates following Rogers, "John and John Baptist Closterman"). In fact, its color scheme corresponds exactly to what Rogers describes as predominant greys and soft blues—the "grey uncertain colors" George Vertue complained of in Closterman's later work—that characterize what appear to be Closterman's latest portraits, completed 1702–1706. My own inclination would be to date it at some point after Shaftesbury's second Holland retreat, perhaps 1704–1706.

26. Voitle, *Third Earl*, 344.
27. See chap. 3 above.
28. Benjamin, *Bonds of Love*, 60–62, 65. Benjamin also points out that the masculine, dominating subject generally carries out his activities under the gaze of an even greater figure of mastery, "more rational, calculating, and self-controlled . . . more fully independent," in whose eyes he wishes to be recognized (58–59). To my mind, the abstraction of the literary market and literary-philosophical fame comes to replace the Deity in presenting for Shaftesbury a gaze before which to display his mastery and achieve recognition, but one in the face of which he can have more control, in the form of his painstakingly revised (and later illustrated) essays.
29. In his final months, Shaftesbury obsessed about the reception of the first edition of the *Characteristicks* and spoke of it as his "offspring" and only "allay of pain." Sir John Cropley reproved Shaftesbury for speaking about his writings "more often and with more affection" than he spoke of his only son, then in Cropley's care; see Paknadel, "Shaftesbury's Illustrations," 290. In his final months Shaftesbury also left detailed instructions for a deathbed painting of himself (which was never completed), obviously with his image before a reading public in mind; see J. E. Sweetman, "Shaftesbury's Last Commission," *Journal of the Warburg and Courtland Institute* 19 (1956): 110–16.
30. Markley, "Objectivity as Ideology," 366. Resonant with the case of Shaftesbury, Markley shows how the notion of objectivity is both psychologically and ideologically imbedded in the lives and works of Boyle and Newton. Both never married and led existences that "verged on compulsive asceticism." Markley contends that this is because physical reality was for them both "the work of a divine intelligence" and, as post-Reformation Protestants, "fallen and irrevocably corrupt"; "the evil traditionally associated with the body is both repressed and projected onto a world that becomes filthy, corrupt, and frankly excremental." He continues, "Asceticism and extreme piety become their defenses against contamination by the diabolic realm of experience[, and] both, in this respect, are preconditions for their scientific studies" (364–65).

Chapter 4

1. Barker-Benfield, *Culture of Sensibility*, 262.
2. In mid-eighteenth-century Britain, "sentiment" and "sensibility," as Janet Todd explains, were used almost synonymously, with "sentiment" highlighting the moral element of emotional sensation. Todd, *Sensibility*, 7.
3. Samuel Richardson, *Selected Letters of Samuel Richardson*, ed. and intro. John Carroll (Oxford: Clarendon, 1964), 91–92. The poem is Herbert's "The Church Porch" [letter dated 6 October 1748].
4. Richardson, *Selected Letters*, 73, 144; Barker-Benfield, *Culture of Sensibility*, 259.
5. Florian Stuber, "Clarissa: A Religious Novel?" *Studies in the Literary Imagination* 28 (1995): 120, 122.
6. Samuel Richardson, *The Correspondence of Samuel Richardson*, ed. Anna Laetitia Barbauld, 6 vols. (London, 1804), 5:60 [letter dated 22 September 1755].
7. Because sensitivity was so prized as the source of the poetic faculty, "spontaneity in creation became a necessary quality of poetry," Todd explains; "the figure of the Aeolian harp which sings God-given music spontaneously was deployed for the artist's function and it became commonplace as a metaphor for the responsive sentimental poet in the work of Thomson, Akenside, Gray, Collins and Macpherson." The purpose of such spontaneous art is, naturally enough, spontaneous reading: "readers are taught by the poet's stance within the poem how to surrender to the work." Todd, *Sensibility*, 54.
8. Ian Watt, *The Rise of the Novel: Studies in Defoe, Richardson and Fielding*, afterword W. B. Carnochan (1957; repr. Berkeley: University of California Press, 2001), 173.
9. William B. Warner, *Licensing Entertainment: The Elevation of Novel Reading in Britain, 1684–1750* (Berkeley: University of California Press, 1998), 6–7, 249.
10. Ellison, *Cato's Tears*, 22.
11. Ward, *True Religion*, 114–53.
12. Charles Welsh, *A Bookseller of the Last Century: Being Some Account of the Life of John Newbery, and of the Books he published, with a Notice of the later Newberys* (London: Griffith, Farran, Okeden & Welsh, 1885), 72.
13. Oliver Goldsmith, *The Vicar of Wakefield*, vol. 4 of *Collected Works of Oliver Goldsmith*, ed. Arthur Friedman (Oxford: Clarendon, 1966), 94; hereafter cited parenthetically in the text as *VW*.
14. Samuel Johnson, *The Idler, by the Author of The Rambler, in Two Volumes*, 3rd ed. (London, 1767), no. 19, 1:103, 104, 106. Welsh recounts that Newbery took Johnson's caricaturing him with good nature and threatened to return the compliment in a subsequent number; Welsh, *Bookseller*, 73.
15. Paula McDowell, *The Women of Grub Street: Press, Politics, and Gender in the London Literary Marketplace, 1678–1730* (Oxford: Clarendon, 1998), 4–5, 10–11.
16. Pat Rogers, *Grub Street: Studies in a Subculture* (London: Methuen, 1972). Rogers differentiates between Grub Street and the function of the "Grub Street Myth" in literary history, and provides a "Lexical History" of the term

and its decline from specificity into generality; Rogers, *Grub Street*, 397–404. Where Rogers is more sympathetic to the sharp distinction between Grubeans and non-Grubeans on which writers like Swift and Pope (and Smart) insisted—the line between their enemies' dullness and their own wit—I follow McDowell in using Grub Street as shorthand for the more general world of hack writing that Goldsmith and Smart experienced working for Newbery and others alongside their duller contemporaries, a shared experience dominated by economic concerns and market pressures imposed by the publishers and booksellers and, as McDowell also notes, dominated by religious, moral and didactic titles; McDowell, *Women of Grub Street*, 122.
17. Welsh, *Bookseller*, 5–9, 14–15.
18. Qtd. in Welsh, *Bookseller*, 12.
19. Qtd. in Welsh, *Bookseller*, 14–15.
20. The Newbery titles are taken from the catalog of his works in Welsh, *Bookseller*, 168–347. My account of Newbery's titles and those by Smart and Goldsmith is not exhaustive but highlights the major themes of the output and the most important and popular works.
21. The cleverness of publishing this title is evident when viewed against the backdrop of the huge number of printed works which it indexed. According to Paula McDowell, "Religious and religio-political works formed by far the largest category of printed materials available to seventeenth- and early eighteenth-century British readers, and religious, religio-political, and didactic works formed the bulk of British men and women's literary productions as well. At a time when the number of separately published items appearing in Britain averaged about 600 items annually, more than 200 religious works were published every year"; *Women of Grub Street*, 122. On the number and importance of religious works in the eighteenth century, see Terry Belanger, "Publishers and Writers in Eighteenth-Century England" and Thomas R. Preston, "Biblical Criticism, Literature, and the Eighteenth-Century Reader," both in *Books and Their Readers in Eighteenth-Century England*, ed. Isabel Rivers, 5–25 and 97–126 (Leicester: Leicester University Press, 1982). On the annual output of sermons and other religious works, see Preston, "Biblical Criticism," 98–99.
22. *The History of Little Goody Two-Shoes; otherwise called, Mrs. Margery Two-Shoes* (1766; repr. York, 1800), 10; "Blossoms of Morality," qtd. in Welsh, *Bookseller*, 110.
23. Welsh, *Bookseller*, 23; Arthur Sherbo, *Christopher Smart: Scholar of the University* (East Lansing: Michigan State University Press, 1967), 59.
24. Welsh, *Bookseller*, 30; Christopher Devlin, *Poor Kit Smart* (Carbondale: Southern Illinois University Press, 1961), 60; Sherbo, *Christopher Smart*, 59–61.
25. Sherbo, *Christopher Smart*, 62.
26. Sherbo, *Christopher Smart*, 67. Sherbo explains that the Seatonian prize money was drawn from the rents on the Seaton estate, which was small, and once the cost of publishing 500 copies of each poem and taxes were subtracted, Smart received only nine or ten pounds for each poem, not the amount of thirty or forty pounds that has sometimes been quoted.

27. Sherbo, *Christopher Smart*, 68–69; Welsh, *Bookseller*, 30–31, 34. Chris Mounsey's provocative, original biography, *Christopher Smart: Clown of God* (Lewisburg, Pa.: Bucknell University Press, 2001), asserts that while the many personae Smart used in *The Midwife* seemed innocuous, "together, they produced a clear critique of the government led by the Pelham brothers" (Mounsey, *Christopher Smart*, 100ff). Mounsey speculates that the magazine got Smart into political hot water that, together with his sexual dalliances, led "his ruthless father-in-law [Newbery], acting either alone or in concert with unknown political figures, [to] spread rumors about Smart's alcoholism, sexuality, and insanity after having had him locked away in one of the private prisons of the eminent physician, William Battie" (17). Mounsey's reading is suggestive at several points, especially in its reading of *The Midwife* and *Pretty Poems for the Amusement of Children Six Foot High* and in calling Newbery's reputation for sheer benevolence to his writers into question, and we are in agreement with other scholars including Clement Hawes and Thomas Keymer in denying that Smart was "mad." But Mounsey admits that his interpretation of the role of politics, sexuality, and his employer in Smart's incarceration, developed over chapters 5 and 6 of his study, is highly speculative and largely conjecture. Though some of my differences with this interpretation will become clear in this chapter, my main caveats are that Mounsey's interpretation of Newbery takes the most negative possible direction at every turn, distorting even humorous and positive accounts of Newbery like Johnson's *Idler* piece (Mounsey, *Christopher Smart*, 146–50), and that this reading virtually passes over in silence the reason that all of Smart's contemporaries and, in *Jubilate Agno*, Smart himself, gave for his incarceration in the madhouse: a diagnosis of "religious mania," the main symptom of which was spontaneous public prayer, and which was followed by a completely religious output following his release. Even so, Mounsey's biography has been a wonderful heuristic tool for me, sharpening my research on Newbery, Smart, and Goldsmith, and I thank him for his positive feedback when I presented an earlier version of this chapter at St. John's College, Oxford, and for generously sharing the galleys of his book, and his delight in Smart, with me.
28. Sherbo, *Christopher Smart*, 75, 77, 81; Welsh, *Bookseller*, 31.
29. Even after he had moved to London, friends had helped Smart to stay on the roster at Pembroke so he could continue to compete for the Seatonian prize.
30. Sherbo, *Christopher Smart*, 75, 81–88.
31. Sherbo, *Christopher Smart*, 86.
32. Devlin, *Poor Kit Smart*, 52; Mounsey, *Christopher Smart*, 149–50. On Mounsey's reading, see chap. 4, n. 27.
33. Ralph M. Wardle, *Oliver Goldsmith* (Lawrence: University of Kansas Press, 1957; repr. Hamden, Conn.: Archon Books, 1969), 151; Mounsey, *Christopher Smart*, 150.
34. Devlin, *Poor Kit Smart*, 52.
35. For Griffiths and for Thomas Davies and William Griffin, for whom Goldsmith wrote before and after Newbery respectively, see Elizabeth Eaton Kent, *Goldsmith and His Booksellers* (Ithaca: Cornell University Press, 1933), 10–32, 81–112, here 94 (emphasis added).

36. Sherbo, *Christopher Smart*, 93–94, 98.
37. Sherbo, *Christopher Smart*, 102.
38. Sherbo, *Christopher Smart*, 103–4.
39. Sherbo, *Christopher Smart*, 104–11.
40. Devlin, *Poor Kit Smart*, 103. Devlin writes that by 1759, Smart's "place as Newbery's chief writer had been taken by Oliver Goldsmith . . . [who] had much the same attitude towards money and business; he found Newbery a fussy and exacting employer, but honest, friendly and appreciative—a very pleasant change from Griffiths."
41. The year of Goldsmith's birth remains uncertain, but most sources estimate 1730. For Goldsmith's early life, see Wardle, *Oliver Goldsmith*, 14–107. The classic early biographies of Goldsmith are Bp. Thomas Percy, *The Life of Dr. Oliver Goldsmith*, in *The Miscellaneous Works of Oliver Goldsmith, M.B., . . . in Four Volumes, to which is prefixed, Some Account of His Life and Works*, 4 vols. (London, 1801); James Prior, *The Life of Oliver Goldsmith, M.B.* (London: J. Murray, 1837); and John Forster, *The Life and Times of Oliver Goldsmith*, 2 vols. (London: Chapman & Hall, 1871).
42. Welsh, *Bookseller*, 35–36. Goldsmith's biographer Prior thought that Goldsmith's first piece for Newbery appeared in January 1758, but the nineteenth-century editor of his works, J. M. W. Gibbs, thinks it may have been a month or two earlier; see Welsh's appendix to *Bookseller*, 348–50. Modern biographies are only less exact on this detail. Wardle says that the exact condition of Goldsmith's introduction to Newbery is unknown and places it around 1760. It must be earlier, because Goldsmith begins writing *Chinese Letters* in the *Public Ledger* in January of that year for a guinea a letter, a substantial commitment on both sides.
43. Kent, *Goldsmith and His Booksellers*, 64. Welsh claims that the exact date of Goldsmith's lodging at Canonbury House cannot be determined, but he moved on to the Temple in 1764 (Welsh, *Bookseller*, 46, 48, 54). Wardle dates the move at 1762, after Goldsmith's arrest for rent troubles when Newbery apparently would not advance him any more money and Johnson rescued him by selling his manuscript of *The Vicar of Wakefield* (to either Newbery or his nephew or son) for sixty pounds; Wardle, *Oliver Goldsmith*, 139. Newbery had provided a way for his stepdaughter Anna Maria to support herself during Smart's incarceration; she ran a shop at "Mr. McMahon's in Cape Street Dublin," for two years, 1759–1761, which sold, among other things, Dr. James's Fever Powders, while leaving her two children with her mother and stepfather at Canonbury. She moved to Reading in late 1761 or early 1762 to edit the *Reading Mercury* which Newbery also made available for her livelihood, which she managed capably and for many years (Sherbo 126–27, 243). Sherbo writes that in 1763, Newbery and Goldsmith were both occupied in helping Smart: "Newbery continued his kindness towards his son-in-law, setting apart for his benefit the profits from the *Martial Review, or General History of the Late War*, a publication in which Goldsmith had a hand and which was announced as published in the *Gentleman's Magazine* for September. At about this time or a little later Goldsmith was also doing something on his own for Smart, for among his 'papers at his death was found

a copy of an appeal to the public for poor Kit Smart, who had married Newbery's stepdaughter ten years before, and had since, with his eccentricities and imprudences, wearied out all his friends but Goldsmith and Johnson.' This appeal was to have been printed and circulated, for Bishop Percy describes it as a 'Paper, which [Goldsmith] wrote to set about a subscription for poor Smart the mad poet: (I believe this last was never printed.)'" (189–90; internal quotation from Forster, *Life of Goldsmith*, 2:167–68).
44. Wardle, *Oliver Goldsmith*, 139, 150.
45. For the date of the composition of *The Vicar of Wakefield*, see Welsh, *Bookseller*, 58–59; Wardle, *Oliver Goldsmith*, 137–39; Stephen Coote, "Text and Publication History," in Oliver Goldsmith, *The Vicar of Wakefield*, ed., intro., and notes Stephen Coote (New York: Penguin, 1986), 25.
46. Qtd. in Wardle, *Oliver Goldsmith*, 160.
47. Wardle, *Oliver Goldsmith*, 169–72.
48. Wardle, *Oliver Goldsmith*, 230; Kent, *Goldsmith and His Booksellers*, 94.
49. "Copy of the Will of John Newbery, 1763," in Welsh, *Bookseller*, 160.
50. See chap. 4, n. 27 above. In *Oliver Goldsmith: A Biography*, Irving wrote that Newbery "coined the brains of authors in the times of their exigency, and made them pay dear for the plank put out to keep them from drowning" (qtd. in Welsh, *Bookseller*, 79).
51. Skinner, *Sensibility and Economics*, 190.
52. For prominent readings of *The Vicar of Wakefield* as ironic, see Ricardo Quintana, *Oliver Goldsmith: A Georgian Study* (New York: Macmillan, 1967), and Robert Hopkins, *The True Genius of Oliver Goldsmith* (Baltimore: The Johns Hopkins University Press, 1969).
53. Goldsmith, "An Essay on the Theatre; or, A Comparison between Laughing and Sentimental Comedy," in *Collected Works of Oliver Goldsmith*, ed. Arthur Friedman, 5 vols., 209–13 (Oxford: Clarendon, 1966), here 3:212.
54. Goldsmith, *The Citizen of the World*, "Letter LXXV," in Friedman, *Collected Works of Oliver Goldsmith*, 2:310–14, here 2:313.
55. John Bender, "Prison Reform and the Sentence of Narration in The Vicar of Wakefield," in Nussbaum and Brown, *The New Eighteenth Century*, 168–88, here 170–71. Timothy Dykstal and Jonathan Lamb have also noted the novel's reformist intent, even if it is a conservative sort of reform; see Timothy Dykstal, "The Story of O: Politics and Pleasure in The Vicar of Wakefield," *ELH* 62 (1995): 329–46, and Jonathan Lamb, *The Rhetoric of Suffering: Reading the Book of Job in the Eighteenth Century* (Oxford: Clarendon, 1995), 144–49.
56. Bender, "Prison Reform," 178.
57. On the dating of the composition of *The Vicar of Wakefield*, see chap. 4, n. 45.
58. Frank Donoghue, *The Fame Machine: Book Reviewing and Eighteenth-Century Literary Careers* (Stanford: Stanford University Press, 1996), 86–124.
59. The term *social gospel* refers to a late-nineteenth- and twentieth-century-Christian movement that emphasizes social justice and addresses the ills of industrialized society. It is sometimes faulted for losing touch with its particularly Christian basis. For a history of the social gospel movement in America, see Ronald C. White, *The Social Gospel: Religion and Reform in Changing America* (Philadelphia: Temple University Press, 1976). For the

social gospel in the contemporary United States, see for instance Susan Curtis, *A Consuming Faith: The Social Gospel and Modern American Culture* (Baltimore: The Johns Hopkins University Press, 1991).

60. In an argument that in some ways parallels mine, Maureen Harkin contends that Goldsmith puts forth the figure of the author as the hope for reform in the novel, with literature "as a possible replacement for religion, and the author as a substitute for the priest, an attempt about which the novel expresses ambivalence and which ultimately does not succeed." My reading focuses more on the extent to which it is religion itself that Goldsmith puts forth as a method of reform, through the medium of the novel. Maureen Harkin, "Goldsmith on Authorship in *The Vicar of Wakefield*," *Eighteenth-Century Fiction* 14 (2002): 328.
61. Harkin, "Goldsmith on Authorship," 326–27.
62. Dykstal, "The Story of O," 336.
63. On the Whistonean controversy, see Eric Rothstein and Howard D. Weinbrot, "*The Vicar of Wakefield*, Mr. Wilmot, and the 'Whistonean Controversy,'" *Philological Quarterly* 55 (1976): 225–40.
64. Ward, *True Religion*, 115, ix.
65. Laurence Sterne, *A Sentimental Journey through France and Italy By Mr. Yorick, with The Journal to Eliza and A Political Romance*, ed. Ian Jack (Oxford: Oxford University Press, 1998), 112.
66. Sterne, *Sentimental Journey*, 119–20.
67. Brissenden, *Virtue in Distress*, 248, 249.
68. Jonathan Lamb, *Sterne's Fiction and the Double Principle* (Cambridge: Cambridge University Press, 1989), 31.
69. On the "abrupt transition" to Sir William's rescue of the family, see Harkin, "Goldsmith on Authorship," 342; Marshall Brown, *Preromanticism* (Stanford: Stanford University Press, 1991), 113, 141–42; and several of the essays in *Goldsmith: The Critical Heritage*, ed. G. S. Rousseau (London: Routledge, 1974).
70. Lamb, *Sterne's Fiction*, 31.
71. Brissenden, *Virtue in Distress*, 250. Barbara Benedict also reads *The Vicar of Wakefield* as indicting a sensibility Goldsmith saw as false and superficial; Benedict, *Framing Feeling*.
72. Smart's major illnesses were reported in various literary magazines as well; see Sherbo, *Christopher Smart*, 110.
73. Smart, dedicatory letter to Dr. Robert James, in *The Annotated Letters of Christopher Smart*, ed. Betty Rizzo and Robert Mahony (Carbondale: Southern Illinois University Press, 1991), 67–68, here 67.
74. Smart, "Hymn to the Supreme Being, on Recovery from a dangerous Fit of Illness," in *The Poetical Works of Christopher Smart*, ed. Karina Williamson, 6 vols. (Oxford: Clarendon, 1980–1996), 4:319–23, lines 47–48.
75. Smart, "Hymn," lines 78, 98, 105–9.
76. Devlin, *Poor Kit Smart*, 79.
77. Hester Lynch Thrale Piozzi, *British Synonymy; or, An Attempt at Regulating the Choice of Words in Familiar Conversation*, 2 vols. (London: G. G. and J. Robinson, 1794), 2:4.
78. Piozzi, *British Synonymy*, 2:4.

79. Hester Lynch Thrale Piozzi, *Thraliana: The Diary of Mrs. Hester Lynch Thrale (later Mrs. Piozzi)*, ed. Katherine C. Balderston, 2nd ed., 2 vols. (Oxford: Clarendon, 1951), 2:728.
80. James Boswell, *Boswell's Life of Johnson*, intro. Chauncey Brewster Tinker, 2 vols. (London: Oxford University Press, 1933), 1:265.
81. Major studies that challenge the notion that Smart was insane include Clement Hawes, *Mania and Literary Style: The Rhetoric of Enthusiasm from the Ranters to Christopher Smart* (Cambridge: Cambridge University Press, 1996); Mounsey, *Christopher Smart*; and Thomas Keymer's delightful "Johnson, Madness and Smart," in *Christopher Smart and the Enlightenment*, ed. Clement Hawes, 177–94 (New York: St. Martin's Press, 1999). Russell Brain has argued that Smart may have been cyclomythic; *Some Reflections on Genius and Other Essays* (Philadelphia: Lippincott, 1960), 113–22.
82. Christopher Smart, *Jubilate Agno*, vol. 1 of Williamson, *Poetical Works of Christopher Smart*, 89. Cited parenthetically in the text as *JA* by fragment and line number.
83. Hawes, *Mania and Literary Style*; Devlin, *Poor Kit Smart*, 81.
84. Qtd. in Devlin, *Poor Kit Smart*, 81.
85. Keymer, "Johnson, Madness and Smart," 188.
86. Devlin, *Poor Kit Smart*, 82.
87. Devlin, *Poor Kit Smart*, 83. Christopher Hunter, Smart's nephew and first biographer, claimed that Smart yielded completely to "these temporary alienations of mind" and that if these "alienations" were opposed, they "were at last attended by paroxysms so violent and continued as to render confinement necessary." This leads Devlin to speak of three separate phenomena related to Smart's illness: the urge to pray, the alienations of mind that led to praying in public, and the violent paroxysms "when he was right out of his wits." Devlin reveals a startling rationalistic bias when he claims that Smart's conversion was "certainly from God" but that his urge to pray was just as certainly "not from God." Christopher Hunter, "The Life of Christopher Smart," in *The Poems of the Late Christopher Smart*, ed. Christopher Hunter, v–xlii (Reading, 1791), xx; qtd. in Devlin, *Poor Kit Smart*, 83.
88. Smart and Young shared several friends, and Young was among the subscribers to Smart's translation of Psalms after his release; Sherbo, *Christopher Smart*, 202.
89. Brean Hammond, *Professional Imaginative Writing in England, 1670–1740: 'Hackney for Bread'* (Oxford: Clarendon, 1997), 8–9. On the buying, selling, and otherwise circulating of sentimental objects, see Deidre Lynch, "Personal Effects and Sentimental Fictions," *Eighteenth-Century Fiction* 12 (2000): 345–68.
90. On the religious form of *Jubilate Agno*, see for instance Jeanne Murray Walker, "*Jubilate Agno* as Psalm," *Studies in English Literature* 20 (1980): 449–59. The significances of many of the more specific references in the poem have been incorporated into Karina Williamson's notes to the Oxford edition of *Jubilate Agno*.
91. Patricia Meyer Spacks, *The Poetry of Vision: Five Eighteenth-Century Poets* (Cambridge, Mass.: Harvard University Press, 1967); Geoffrey Hartman,

"Christopher Smart's Magnificat: Toward a Theory of Representation," *ELH* 41 (1974): 429–54. See also Allan J. Gedalof, "Smart's Poetics in *Jubilate Agno*," *English Studies in Canada* 5 (1979): 262–74 and, more recently, Dennis Costa, "Language in Smart's *Jubilate Agno*," *Essays in Criticism* 52 (2002): 295–313. Gedalof's reading of Smart's "subjective reaction" to the world around him resonates somewhat with my own, though he attributes Smart's freedom to the influence of Berkeley's philosophy.

92. Harriet Guest, *A Form of Sound Words: The Religious Poetry of Christopher Smart* (Oxford: Clarendon, 1989); Hawes, *Mania and Literary Style*.
93. Smart was institutionalized in May 1757, and manuscript evidence indicates that he began the *Jubilate Agno* sometime between June 1758 and April 1759; see Karina Williamson, introduction to *Jubilate Agno*, vol. 1 of *The Poetical Works of Christopher Smart*, xxiii–xxiv (Oxford: Clarendon, 1980–1986), xxiv.
94. Smart, "Hymn III. Epiphany," in Williamson, *The Poetical Works of Christopher Smart*, 2:37–39, lines 9–12.
95. I thank Chris Mounsey for pointing this out to me. Moira Dearnley writes that though Smart makes no direct reference to Nelson, his influence is everywhere visible in Smart's *Hymns and Spiritual Songs*; Moira Dearnley, *The Poetry of Christopher Smart* (New York: Barnes & Noble, 1969), 249–63.
96. On the dating of the various folios of *Jubilate Agno*, see Williamson, introduction to *Jubilate Agno*, vol. 1 of *The Poetical Works of Christopher Smart*, xxiii–xxiv.
97. Williamson explains in her note to this passage that the shawm was actually a reed instrument, but that it became associated with stringed instruments in the seventeenth century; Smart, *Jubilate Agno*, 54.
98. See the introduction to this chapter and n. 7.
99. For the concept of *theosis* or deification in the history of Christian theology, see Timothy Ware, *The Orthodox Church*, rev. ed. (New York: Penguin, 1993), 231–38.
100. The concept and terminology of *synergia* (Greek, συνεργια; literally, "with-energy"; the energies of God and human beings working together in communion) are found as early as St. Paul, as in "We are fellow-workers (συνεργοι) with God" (1 Cor 3:9). For a brief account of the concept in Eastern as opposed to Western Christian theology, see Ware, *Orthodox Church*, 221–22, 224.
101. Clement Hawes, "The Utopian Public Sphere: Intersubjectivity in *Jubilate Agno*," in Hawes, *Christopher Smart and the Enlightenment*, 195–212, here 208.
102. And perhaps it is also due to the fact that one of the few activities he was allowed in the madhouse, by Samuel Johnson's account, was gardening; Keymer, "Johnson, Madness and Smart," 191 n. 7. On this passage, see Costa, "Language in Smart's *Jubilate Agno*," 305–9.
103. Smart was likely familiar with titles such as John Hall-Stevenson's *A Nosegay and a Simile for Reviewers* (1760), as well as *The Virgin's Nosegay* (1744) and *The Craftsman's Nosegay* (1729). As it happens, an undated volume is listed in the Newbery catalogs between 1740–1800, titled *The Florist, or Poetical*

Nosegay and Drawing Book. Walsh dates it to "c. 1800," but it is interesting to speculate that if it were published earlier it might have been known to Smart, or even have been his own work.

104. On Smart and Newton, see for instance Karina Williamson's appendix to *Jubilate Agno,* "Smart and the Hutchisonians," in *Poetical Works of Christopher Smart,* 1:131–32, and Costa, "Language in Smart's *Jubilate Agno,*" 302.
105. Intersubjectivity may also be grounds for arguing that Smart's view of the self and of God challenges the masculinist subject positions we saw in Shaftesbury's rationalism in chap. 3. The issue of gender in *Jubilate Agno* is vexed and complex, not least because of Smart's bitterness about what he felt as his wife's public abandonment of him, and something that this already lengthy chapter cannot adequately address.
106. Keymer, "Johnson, Madness and Smart," 181.
107. Sherbo and Mounsey both agree that Smart must have been working on *A Song to David*—and likely also his translation of the Psalms as well—in the asylum because of how quickly this intricate poem came out after his release; Sherbo, *Christopher Smart,* 168, and Mounsey, *Christopher Smart,* 239.
108. Sherbo, *Christopher Smart,* 243.
109. Sherbo, *Christopher Smart,* 255–56, 265.
110. Bender, "Prison Reform," 177–78.
111. McKeon, *Origins of the English Novel,* 20–22.

CHAPTER 5

1. William Wordsworth, "The Tables Turned," in *Lyrical Ballads, 1798,* ed. W. J. B. Owen, 2d ed. (Oxford: Oxford University Press, 1969), lines 13–24. Poems from *Lyrical Ballads* are hereafter referenced parenthetically as *LB* followed by line numbers of the appropriate poem.
2. William Wordsworth, "Preface" to the 1800 edition of *Lyrical Ballads,* in Owen, *Lyrical Ballads,* 153–79, here 173; hereafter cited parenthetically in the text as "Preface." The Owen/Oxford edition provides a collation of the Prefaces of 1800 and 1802, noting the 1802 additions and changes in the footnotes.
3. M. H. Abrams, *The Mirror and the Lamp* (New York: Norton, 1958), 102, 105, 111, 113, and passim.
4. Shelley and Keats qtd. in Paul Magnuson, "Wordsworth and Spontaneity," in *The Evidence of the Imagination: Studies of Interactions between Life and Art in English Romantic Literature,* ed. Donald H. Reiman et al., 101–18 (New York: New York University Press, 1978), 102. The Keats passage is from a letter to John Taylor, 27 February 1818.
5. Wordsworth, *Ecclesiastical Sonnets,* in *Poetical Works,* ed. Thomas Hutchinson, rev. Ernest de Selincourt (Oxford: Oxford University Press, 1999), 329–55 (this quotation is from 2.37.11–12); hereafter cited parenthetically in the text as *ES* by section, sonnet, and line numbers. I have also consulted Abbie Findlay Potts's *The Ecclesiastical Sonnets of William Wordsworth: A Critical Edition* (New Haven: Yale University Press, 1922), whose notes are extremely helpful.

6. Wordsworth allowed this note to be printed as his own, but it was actually written by his young friend Frederick Faber. It is reprinted in Wordsworth, *Poetical Works*, 708.
7. Stephen Gill, *Wordsworth and the Victorians* (Oxford: Clarendon, 1998), 80. For Wordsworth's relationship with key figures of the Oxford Movement, see B. W. Martin, "Wordsworth, Faber, and Keble: Commentary on a Triangular Relationship," *Review of English Studies* 26 (1975): 436–42; Stephen Gill, "Wordsworth and the 'Catholic Truth': The Role of Frederick William Faber," *Review of English Studies* 45 (1994): 204–20 (reprinted in *Wordsworth and the Victorians*); and Peter Manning, "Wordsworth at St. Bee's: Scandals, Sisterhoods, and Wordsworth's Later Poetry," *ELH* 52 (1985): 33–58.
8. Major studies that stress the discontinuity between the early and late Wordsworths offer different accounts of that transition. Ian Scott rehearses the now commonplace and somewhat moderate narrative of British Romantic poets, including Wordsworth, moving through three stages of gradually more conservative political views in response to the French Revolution and Napoleonic wars: initial enthusiasm for rational philosophy, radical change, and a Rousseauist state of Nature, 1789–1794; faith in republicanism tempered by counterrevolutionary critique in the wake of the Terror and the Burkean idea that the natural state of man was to live in society with all its customs, institutions, and moral duties, 1795–1802; and finally, more conservative nationalism, in which war with France and the rising esteem of Burkean philosophy encouraged most writers to blend their humanitarian, popular concerns with Tory sentiments, 1803–1815. See Ian Scott, "'Things As They Are': The Literary Response to the French Revolution 1789–1815," in *Britain and the French Revolution 1789–1815*, ed. H. T. Dickinson, 229–49 (London: Macmillan, 1989).

   Jerome McGann might serve as the most radical example of the "discontinuity" thesis: "Between 1793 and 1798 Wordsworth lost the world merely to gain his immortal soul. . . . If Wordsworth's poetry elides history, we observe in this 'escapist' or 'reactionary' move its own self-revelation. . . . The idea that poetry, or even consciousness, can set one free of the ruins of history and culture is the grand illusion of every Romantic poet"; Jerome McGann, *The Romantic Ideology: A Critical Investigation* (Chicago: University of Chicago Press, 1985), 88, 91. To my mind, this view represents a misreading of Wordsworth, as this chapter shows, however accurately it might speak to ways his works were read and used in the nineteenth and twentieth centuries. My point is to stress the continuity of concern between Wordsworth's earlier political radicalism and rationalism and his later views, and to deny that it represents an "escape" from history. Other major studies that emphasize disjunction between the early and late Wordsworths include but certainly are not limited to: Geoffrey Hartman, *Wordsworth's Poetry, 1787–1814* (New Haven: Yale University Press, 1964) and *The Unremarkable Wordsworth* (London: Methuen, 1987); Kenneth R. Johnston, *The Hidden Wordsworth* (New York: Norton, 2000); Marjorie Levinson, *Wordsworth's Great Period Poems: Four Essays* (New York: Cambridge University Press, 1986); Alan Liu,

Wordsworth: The Sense of History (Stanford: Stanford University Press, 1989); David Simpson, *Wordsworth's Historical Imagination: The Poetry of Displacement* (New York: Methuen, 1987).

9. Recent studies stressing the continuities across the Wordsworth canon are generally also more attentive to his middle and late works and less dismissive of his evolving religious beliefs. These include but, again, are not limited to: Richard Gravil, *Wordsworth's Bardic Vocation, 1787–1842* (New York: Palgrave, 2003); Robert M. Ryan, *The Romantic Reformation: Religious Politics in English Literature 1789–1824* (Cambridge: Cambridge University Press, 1997); William A. Ulmer, *The Christian Wordsworth, 1798–1805* (Albany: State University of New York Press, 2001), the conclusion of which is particularly lucid and helpful.
10. For the connected philosophical and scientific desire for perfection expressed in the French Revolution, see Marie-Hélène Huet, *Mourning Glory: The Will of the French Revolution* (Philadelphia: University of Pennsylvania Press, 1997), 1–32.
11. Wordsworth, Advertisement to the 1798 and 1799 editions, *Lyrical Ballads*, 3.
12. Ellis, *Politics of Sensibility*, 17; see also introduction, 15–17.
13. Shaftesbury, "Soliloquy," in Ayres, *Characteristicks*, 1:93.
14. Wordsworth, Advertisement, *Lyrical Ballads*, 3. For the dismissal of the connection between the prefaces and *Lyrical Ballads*, see Kenneth R. Johnston, "The Triumphs of Failure: Wordsworth's Lyrical Ballads of 1798," chap. 7 of *The Age of Wordsworth: Critical Essays of the Romantic Tradition*, ed. Kenneth R. Johnston and Gene W. Ruoff, 133–59 (New Brunswick: Rutgers University Press, 1987).
15. *The Monthly Mirror*, October 1798, and *The New London Review*, January 1799, in *The Romantics Reviewed: Contemporary Reviews of British Romantic Writers. Part A: The Lake Poets*, ed. Donald Reiman, 2 vols. (New York: Garland Publishing, 1972), 685, 792–93. In this and subsequent notes, identities of the reviewers are given when provided in Reiman; otherwise, the reviewer is uncertain.
16. Robert Southey, *The Critical Review*, October 1798, in Reiman, *Romantics Reviewed*, 310.
17. John Stoddart, *The British Critic*, February 1801, in Reiman, *Romantics Reviewed*, 131–33.
18. John Herman Merivale, *The Monthly Review*, February 1815, in Reiman, *Romantics Reviewed*, 729; *Monthly Magazine*, January 1815, in Reiman, *Romantics Reviewed*, 665.
19. James Montgomery, *The Eclectic Review*, January 1815, in Reiman, *Romantics Reviewed*, 353–54.
20. *The British Critic*, 2nd series, May 1815, in Reiman, *Romantics Reviewed*, 139.
21. See for instance *The Monthly Review*'s October 1820 piece on *The River Duddon*, in Reiman, *Romantics Reviewed*, 766–71; and the May 1819 review of Peter Bell in *Blackwood's Edinburgh Magazine*, in Reiman, *Romantics Reviewed*, 766, 90–96.
22. See *The British Critic*, June and November 1819, in Reiman, *Romantics Reviewed*, 165–75, 175–83; *The Monthly Magazine*, June and July 1819, in

Reiman, *Romantics Reviewed*, 682–83; and *The Gentleman's Magazine*, August 1819 and October 1820, in Reiman, *Romantics Reviewed*, 558–59, 560–61.

23. *Blackwood's Edinburgh Magazine*, May 1819, in Reiman, *Romantics Reviewed*, 91.
24. *The Monthly Review*, October 1820, in Reiman, *Romantics Reviewed*, 769; and *Blackwood's Edinburgh Magazine*, May 1820, in Reiman, *Romantics Reviewed*, 106.
25. John Wilson, *Blackwood's Edinburgh Review*, August 1822, in Reiman, *Romantics Reviewed*, 108.
26. *The Eclectic Review*, November 1842, in Reiman, *Romantics Reviewed*, 403.
27. Yu Liu, "Reevaluating Revolution and Radicalness in the *Lyrical Ballads*," *SEL* 36 (1996): 747–61, here 753, 747.
28. Burke, *Philosophical Enquiry*, 24, 26.
29. A. Liu, *Wordsworth*, 38.
30. Paul Magnuson has offered a similarly corrective view of spontaneity as expressed in the "Preface," though his concern is with Wordsworth's poetic rather than moral theory. For Wordsworth, he argues, "poetry was a result of meditation and discipline which changed life's emotions into essentially different moods, ones which overflow spontaneously into poetry"; Magnuson, "Wordsworth's Spontaneity," 115.
31. Note to "The Thorn," included in "Commentary," in Owen, *Lyrical Ballads*, 140.
32. Note to "The Thorn," in Owen, *Lyrical Ballads*, 140–41.
33. "Tintern Abbey" has in some ways been the most spectacular battlefield in the conflict over political interpretations of Wordsworth's poetry and his presumed retreat from history. My discussion of the poem here is necessarily telescoped to its place in the argument of this chapter and book, and does not engage most of this criticism explicitly. In my reading, the poem's reference of history is clear and deliberately connected to Wordsworth's moral and religious arguments. Major volleys in this conflict include: M. H. Abrams, "On Political Readings of *Lyrical Ballads*," in *Romantic Revolutions: Criticism and Theory*, ed. Kenneth R. Johnston et al., 320–49 (Bloomington: Indiana University Press, 1990); David Bromwich, "The French Revolution and 'Tintern Abbey,'" *Raritan* 10 (1991): 1–23; Kenneth R. Johnston, "The Politics of 'Tintern Abbey,'" *The Wordsworth Circle* 14 (1983): 6–14; Marjorie Levinson, "Insight and Oversight: Reading 'Tintern Abbey,'" in Levinson, *Wordsworth's Great Period Poems*, 1–57.
34. For Wordsworth's note to Isabella Fenwick on the composition of "Tintern Abbey" and evidence that has been produced ostensibly to the contrary, see Owen's "Commentary," in Owen, *Lyrical Ballads*, 149.
35. Johnston, "Triumphs of Failure," 141, 143.
36. In an 1808 letter to Coleridge, smarting from Charles Lamb's mockery of *The White Doe of Rylstone* while it was still in manuscript form, Wordsworth wrote: "If [a man of genius] . . . is to be a Dramatist, let him crowd his scene with gross and visible action; but if a narrative Poet . . . then let him see if there are no victories in the world of spirit, no changes, no commotions, no revolutions there"; in introduction to *The White Doe of Rylstone; or The Fate*

of the Nortons, by William Wordsworth, ed. and intro. Kristine Dugas, 3–65 (Ithaca: Cornell University Press, 1988), 12. The phrase "litanies of everyday life" I borrow from Michel de Certeau, *The Practice of Everyday Life*, trans. Steven Rendall (Berkeley: University of California Press, 1988).

37. Critical work on *Ecclesiastical Sonnets* is indeed scarce. The two most recent book-length studies of *Ecclesiastical Sonnets* are also its most sympathetic (and almost uncritical) readings and testify to the enduring interest of the sonnets for the reader interested in religion: Anne L. Rylstone, *Prophetic Memory in Wordsworth's* Ecclesiastical Sonnets (Carbondale: Southern Illinois University Press, 1991), and John Delli Carpini, *History, Religion and Politics in William Wordsworth's* Ecclesiastical Sonnets (Lewiston: Edwin Mellen Press, 2004). Rylstone's brief introduction supplies a helpful account of the extremes of critical estimations of *Ecclesiastical Sonnets* across the last two centuries. Helmuth Carl Poggemiller's unpublished "Wordsworth's Concept of the Imagination in the *Ecclesiastical Sonnets*" argues the coherence of Wordsworth's views of the imagination across his lifetime (Ph.D. diss., University of Toledo, 1980). The most sympathetic and genuinely critical essay on *Ecclesiastical Sonnets* is Regina Hewitt's, discussed in the text of this chapter. John Kerrigan assimilates *Ecclesiastical Sonnets* into the "inevitable" story of Wordsworth's decline and argues that in them we see Wordsworth displacing his "ideal" of building and dwelling from this world to the next. "Neither causal nor quite passive, Christianity disabled Wordsworth by allowing him to elevate the most pressing concern of his imaginative life—the question of Dwelling—but by exalting it to resolve it too"; John Kerrigan, "Wordsworth and the Sonnet: Building, Dwelling, Thinking," *Essays in Criticism* 35 (1985): 45–75, here 51. The most critical essays on the series are as extreme as the most sympathetic. For Kenneth J. Hughes, the punch line of *Ecclesiastical Sonnets* is Wordsworth as a "fully committed ideologue who publishes a most skillfully executed piece of propaganda," pitting Tory landed interests against the prospect of Catholic emancipation. "Clearly we can see in all this Hegel's cunning of reason working in the interests of a landed bourgeois class as the Idea, despite the efforts of men, works itself out in history and realizes itself"; Kenneth J. Hughes, "Troubled Tories: Theory of History and Didactic Function of Wordsworth's *Ecclesiastical Sonnets*," *CIEFL Bulletin* 15 (1979): 29–44, here 44, 43. Barbara T. Gates faults the sonnets for "distort[ing] history" and being "highly selective" rather than giving a "realistic account" of church history; "Wordsworth's Mirror of Morality: Distortions of Church History," *The Wordsworth Circle* 12.2 (1981): 129–32, here 129.
38. Regina Hewitt, "Church Building as Political Strategy in Wordsworth's *Ecclesiastical Sonnets*," *Mosaic* 25 (1992): 31–46, here 33.
39. John 7:37-39: "On the last day of the festival, the great day, while Jesus was standing there, he cried out, 'Let anyone who is thirsty come to me, and let the one who believes in me drink. As the scripture has said, "Out of the believer's heart shall flow rivers of living water."' Now he said this about the Spirit, which believers in him were to receive" (NRSV). The AV also uses the locution "rivers of living water." The language of living water also recalls Jesus' encounter with the Samaritan woman at the well: "Jesus said to her,

'Everyone who drinks of this water will be thirsty again, but those who drink of the water that I will give them will never be thirsty. The water that I will give will become in them a spring of water gushing up to eternal life'" (John 4:13-14, NRSV). Cf. Hewitt, "Church Building," 37, and the last sonnet of *Ecclesiastical Sonnets*.

40. Wordsworth's note to the first edition supports this reading, situating the sequence against parliamentary debates on "the Catholic question." The note and the sonnets indicate that Wordsworth opposed Catholic suffrage because of the threat to English liberty. The note also makes a claim for the profound relationship between the "pictures" offered in each sonnet: they "are often so closely connected as to have jointly the effect of passages of a poem in a form of stanza"; Wordsworth, notes to *Ecclesiastical Sonnets*, in Wordsworth, *Poetical Works*, 721.

41. Wordsworth, *The Prelude: 1799, 1805, 1850*, ed. Jonathan Wordsworth, M. H. Abrams, and Stephen Gill (New York: Norton, 1979), 1805, 3.575–78 and 1805, 6.90–100; hereafter cited parenthetically in the text as *P* 1805 or *P* 1850. Without access to the manuscripts of *The Prelude* between 1805 and 1850, particularly around the early 1820s, in this chapter I lean toward using the 1805 version as perhaps closer to the state of *The Prelude* when Wordsworth was writing *Ecclesiastical Sonnets*. I compare the 1805 with the 1850 version, usually in footnotes, when differences are significant and yield a deeper understanding of the evolution of his reflections on morality and sentiment.

42. Linda Palumbo calls Bede "the spiritual father of the *Ecclesiastical Sketches*" and points out that Bede's having written his *Ecclesiastical History of the English People* late in life and for the benefit of the nation was a parallel Wordsworth wished to highlight; Linda J. Palumbo, "The Later Wordsworth and the Romantic Ego: Bede and the Recreant Soul," *The Wordsworth Circle* 17 (1986): 181–84, here 181.

43. Despite a degree of pacifism that made his works popular with Quakers, Wordsworth throughout *Ecclesiastical Sonnets* allows somewhat problematically for the notion of a just war, particularly of defense, and no doubt with the Napoleonic Wars in mind.

44. Wordsworth here followed Foxe's *Acts and Monuments*, which echoed other historical sources in recording as fact Pope Alexander III "treading on the neck of Emperor Frederick" in the year 1164. In Wordsworth's note on *Ecclesiastical Sonnets*, dictated to Isabella Fenwick, he explained this error, but did not correct it in the poem: "The sonnets were written long before ecclesiastical history and points of doctrine had excited the interest with which they have been recently enquired into and discussed. The former particular is mentioned as an excuse for my having fallen into error in respect to [this incident]. . . . Though this is related as a fact in history, I am told it is a mere legend of no authority. Substitute for it an undeniable truth not less fitted for my purpose, namely the penance inflicted by Gregory the Seventh upon the Emperor Henry the Fourth." Qtd. in Potts, *Critical Edition*, 245.

45. In the 1850 published edition of *The Prelude*, this sympathy with power is contrasted more explicitly with religious faith, speaking of "This last oppro-

brium, when we see a people, / That once looked up in faith, as if to Heaven / For manna, take a lesson from the dog / Returning to his vomit" (*P* 1850, 11.360–63).
46. The moral disorientation and inconclusive evidence of moral sentiment to which Wordsworth points in this passage are, I argue, more profound than is generally recognized. The 1850 version makes the contradictory evidence more plain:

> . . . amid the awe
> Of unintelligible chastisement
> Not only acquiescences of faith
> Survived, but daring sympathies with power,
> Motions not treacherous or profane, else why
> Within the folds of no ungentle breast
> Their dread vibration to this hour prolonged?
> Wild blasts of music thus could find their way
> Into the midst of turbulent events;
> So that worst tempests might be listened to. (*P* 1850, 10.454–63)

The additional lines here, "Motions not treacherous or profane, else why / Within the folds of no ungentle breast / Their dread vibration to this hour prolonged?" represent not straight questioning but the way Wordsworth reasoned about his "sympathies with power" in 1793–1794, rationalizing them in a way he later finds questionable and darkly revelatory.
47. "Sympathy" is the key category of moral sentiment in the most influential work of moral sense philosophy in the eighteenth century, Adam Smith's *Theory of Moral Sentiments*. Wordsworth shows throughout his poems a familiarity with and suspicion of Smith's moral and economic writings.
48. Wordsworth added the phrase "troubled human heart" to this passage by 1850; *P* 1850, 10.439.
49. The 1850 edition of *The Prelude* stresses in this passage even more Wordsworth's intellectual arrogance and this despair's relation to "the wounds / Of mortified presumption" that "nought could heal" (*P* 1850, 10.215–16).
50. Ken Johnston notes that Wordsworth "continued to talk about [*The Recluse*] as a lively possibility—or onerous duty—until the last decade of his life," though this was "counterpointed by realistic comments from friends and relatives who doubted that it would ever be done," and "the storm of critical abuse provoked by *The Excursion* [1814–1815] . . . effectively halted his efforts to finish" it; Kenneth Johnston, *Wordsworth and* The Recluse (New Haven: Yale University Press, 1984), xii, 333. The case could well be made for the way *The Excursion* supports the moral trajectory I trace here, but that project is outside the scope of this chapter. Sally Bushell, for instance, has argued that, far from a straightforwardly didactic work, *The Excursion* uses dramatic, dialogic form to teach readers to think for themselves and to form moral habits and mental constructs by which to learn; Sally Bushell, *Re-Reading* The Excursion (Aldershot: Ashgate, 2002).
51. Stephen Gill, "Wordsworth and 'Catholic Truth,'" 209.
52. Wordsworth, *ES*, 1.38.8; cf. *P* 1805, 10.938.

53. As Gill puts it, "in the early Victorian period few people doubted that Wordsworth could be best characterized as a religious poet. What was in dispute was the exact nature of his teaching" ("Wordsworth and 'Catholic Truth,'" 204). The literally incredible range of interpretations of Wordsworth's religious beliefs is typified by the contrast between two recent works, Martin Priestman's *Romantic Atheism: Poetry and Freethought, 1780–1830* (Cambridge: Cambridge University Press, 1999) and Ryan's *The Romantic Reformation*. Priestman views Wordsworth's conspicuously omitted signs of straightforward orthodoxies as evidence for his incipient atheism, while Ryan sees Wordsworth's crisis of 1794–1795 as a brief episode of apostasy from orthodoxy into natural religion. It is important to note that both works recognize, in Eric Nye's words, that "religion was an agency of social change" and reform, "not social stability"; Eric Nye, "The Most Perfect Protestant: Romantic Politics and Religion," review of *Romantic Atheism*, by Martin Priestman, and *The Romantic Reformation*, by Robert Ryan, *Eighteenth-Century Studies* 35 (2002): 323. The classic account of the secularizing trajectory of Wordsworth's poetry is M. H. Abrams, *Natural Supernaturalism: Tradition and Revolution in Romantic Literature* (New York: Norton, 1971). This has been countered in the work of Stephen Prickett, whose contributions highlight the religiousness we see in Wordsworth's poems and its historical afterlife; see Stephen Prickett, *Romanticism and Religion: The Tradition of Coleridge and Wordsworth in the Victorian Church* (Cambridge: Cambridge University Press, 1976) and *Words and* The Word: *Language, Poetics and Biblical Interpretation* (Cambridge: Cambridge University Press, 1986). Helpful accounts of Wordsworth's religiousness and use of the Bible and Christian traditions include Edith Batho's detailed chapter on the poet's religion in *The Later Wordsworth* (Cambridge: Cambridge University Press, 1933; repr., New York: Russell & Russell, 1963); Deeanne Westbrook, *Wordsworth's Biblical Ghosts* (New York: Palgrave, 2001).
54. *P* 1805, 13.436, *P* 1850, 14.440; *P* 1805, 13.443–44, *P* 1850, 14.447–48, emphasis added.
55. Steven E. Cole, "Evading Politics: The Poverty of Historicizing Romanticism," *Studies in Romanticism* 34 (1995): 29–49, here 30.
56. Cole, "Evading Politics," 48.
57. Cole, "Evading Politics," 49.
58. For the revolutionary substitution of a longing for totality for pragmatic ethical wrangling, see Cole, "Evading Politics," 48, and Bernard Yack, *The Longing for Total Revolution: Philosophical Sources of Social Discontent from Rousseau to Marx and Nietzsche* (Princeton: Princeton University Press, 1986).
59. Kenneth Johnston's biography highlights the role of self-fashioning in Wordsworth's poetry; Johnston, *Hidden Wordsworth*, 7–8. For the limited yet profound sorts of agency and resistance available in practices of everyday life—its "litanies" and repetitive belief mechanisms—see Certeau, *Practice of Everyday Life*, 177–89.
60. A. Liu has himself critiqued New Historicist presumptions to objectivity that make New Historicism another formalism and not a historicism at all. His insistence that the "'acknowledgment' of non-objectivity must become .

". . . a serviceable critical tool" resonates with my insistence that we come to grips with the meaning of the epistemological indeterminacies that language continually presents and the inevitability of belief investment in the production of knowledge; Alan Liu, "The Power of Formalism: The New Historicism," *ELH* 56 (1989): 721–71, here 753. For New Historicist treatments of *The White Doe*, see Marlon Ross, "Romancing the Nation State: The Poetics of Romantic Nationalism," in *Macropolitics of Nineteenth-Century Literature: Nationalism, Exoticism, Imperialism*, ed. Jonathan Arac and Harriet Ritvo, 56–85 (Philadelphia: University of Pennsylvania Press, 1991); and Nicola Watson, "Footnoting the Romantic: Forms of History and *The White Doe of Rylstone*," *The Wordsworth Circle* 24 (1993): 141–43.

61. Marjorie Levinson, "The New Historicism: Back to the Future," in *Rethinking Historicism: Critical Readings in Romantic History*, ed. Marjorie Levinson, Marilyn Butler, Jerome McGann, and Paul Hamilton, 18–63 (Oxford: Basil Blackwell, 1989), 50.
62. Cole, "Evading Politics," 31, emphasis added.

CONCLUSION

1. Karl Marx, introduction to *Contribution to the Critique of Hegel's Philosophy of Right* (Deutsch-Französische Jarbücher, 1844), in *On Religion*, by Karl Marx and Friedrich Engels, intro. Reinhold Niebuhr (New York: Schocken Books, 1964), 41–58, here 41.
2. Mark Taylor, "Denegating God," chap. 2 of *About Religion: Economies of Faith in Virtual Culture* (Chicago: University of Chicago Press, 1999), 29–47, here 30. Originally published in *Critical Inquiry* 20 (1994): 592–610.
3. Mary Louise Pratt, "Presidential Address 2003: Language, Liberties, Waves, and Webs—Engaging the Present," *PMLA* 119 (2004): 427.
4. Stanley Fish, "One University Under God?" *The Chronicle of Higher Education* 51.18, 7 January 2005, C1.
5. Caputo, "Who Comes After?" 2.
6. Ward, *True Religion*, 131.
7. Nina Pelikan Straus, "Dostoevsky's Derrida," *Common Knowledge* 8 (2002): 559.
8. Caputo, "Who Comes After?" 2.
9. Derrida, "Faith and Knowledge," 10, 15.
10. Caputo, "Who Comes After?" 2.
11. Derrida, "Faith and Knowledge," 21, 33.
12. Derrida, "Faith and Knowledge," 17; Derrida, "My Chances/*Mes Chances*," 8.
13. See for instance the wonderful volume *Kierkegaard in Post/Modernity*, ed. Merold Westphal and Martin Matuštík (Indianapolis: Indiana University Press, 1995).
14. Caputo, *On Religion*, 8, 9, 3.
15. Caputo, *On Religion*, 19.
16. Caputo, *On Religion*, 23–24.
17. Caputo, *On Religion*, 29.

18. Caputo, *On Religion*, 19, 21.
19. Caputo, *On Religion*, 33–34.
20. Caputo, *On Religion*, 18.
21. Caputo, *On Religion*, 35.
22. All three synoptic gospels record this question: cf. Matt 16:15, Mark 8:29, and Luke 9:20.
23. Taylor, *About Religion*, 46–47.
24. Qtd. in Hervieu-Léger, *Chain of Memory*, 10.
25. Hervieu-Léger, *Chain of Memory*, 17, 28.
26. Alan Wolfe, "Scholars Infuse Religion with Cultural Light," *Chronicle of Higher Education* 51.9: 22 October 22 2004, B6.
27. Christian Smith, *Moral, Believing Animals: Human Personhood and Culture* (Oxford: Oxford University Press, 2003), 60–61.
28. Taylor, *About Religion*, 52.
29. Taylor, *About Religion*, 54.
30. Taylor, *About Religion*, 76.
31. Robert Sullivan, "Rethinking Christianity in Enlightened Europe," *Eighteenth-Century Studies* 34 (2001): 305.
32. McDowell, "Enlightenment Enthusiasms," 517–18.
33. McDowell, "Enlightenment Enthusiasms," 518.
34. Irlam, *Elations*, 20.
35. Rudy, "Subjectivity and Belief," 228.
36. Rudy, "Subjectivity and Belief," 232. She continues, dissatisfied with this conundrum: "What I need is a theory of subjectivity that would allow me to be two contradictory things at the same time, that would allow me to say 'I believe' and 'I don't' in a way that does not require coherent explanation. I need a theory that will allow me to be fragmented, not as a temporary stop-gap measure until I figure out where I will end up, but a theory that will allow me to understand myself as divided forever. I need a model that does not obligate me to be only one, unified person, that does not rest its idea of subjectivity on Enlightenment individuality, that sees fragmentation as a natural state and not one to be worked through" (232). She finally concludes: "Maybe what I need is not a three-dimensional theory, but a community" (235).
37. It must be noted, however, that 2004 was remarkable for major, award-winning works that are narratives of faith in all its unsettledness, both from my colleagues here at the University of Iowa: Marilynne Robinson's momentous first novel since *Housekeeping*, titled *Gilead: A Novel* (New York: Farrar, Straus & Giroux, 2004) was published in late 2004 and won the Pulitzer Prize for fiction, as well as the The Grawemeyer Award in Religion for 2006; and Christopher Merrill's memoir *Things of the Hidden God: Journey to the Holy Mountain* (New York: Random House, 2005) was released in America in early 2005 after having already won international awards and garnered critical acclaim.
38. Caputo, *On Religion*, 60–61.
39. Jacques Derrida, *Specters of Marx: The State of the Debt, the Work of Mourning, and the New International*, trans. Peggy Kamuf (New York: Routledge, 1994),

166–67, qtd. in Pelikan Straus, "Dostoevsky's Derrida," 562.
40. Ward, "Crisis of Representation," 131, 137, 138.
41. Charles Winquist, "Lacan and Theology," in *Post-Secular Philosophy: Between Philosophy and Theology*, ed. Phillip Blond, 305–17 (London: Routledge, 1998), 313–14.
42. On humility, see for example Drucilla Cornell, *The Philosophy of the Limit* (London: Routledge, 1992), 70–72, 89–90.
43. A growing body of scholarship squarely asserts that religious fundamentalism is not a product of a benighted past but of enlightened modernity. As but one example, see Minoo Moallem, *Between Warrior Brother and Veiled Sister: Islamic Fundamentalism and the Politics of Patriarchy in Iran* (Berkeley: University of California Press, 2005), which shows how Islamic nationalism and fundamentalism are byproducts of secular modernity.
44. Caputo, *On Religion*, 124.
45. Jacques Derrida, "'Eating Well,' or the Calculation of the Subject: An Interview with Jacques Derrida," in *Who Comes After the Subject?* ed. Eduardo Cadava, Peter Connor, and Jean-Luc Nancy, 96–119 (London: Routledge, 1991), 118.
46. Žižek, *Fragile Absolute*, 128–29.
47. Žižek, *Fragile Absolute*, 145.
48. Žižek, *Fragile Absolute*, 21.
49. Slavoj Žižek, "An Interview with Slavoj Žižek: 'On Divine Self-Limitation and Revolutionary Love,'" *Journal of Philosophy and Scripture* 1 (2004): 3, 6.
50. Žižek, "Interview," 2.
51. Žižek, *Puppet and the Dwarf*, 115.
52. Žižek, *Puppet and the Dwarf*, 115–16.
53. Qtd. in Hervieu-Léger, *Chain of Memory*, 35.

Works Cited

Abrams, M. H. *The Mirror and the Lamp*. New York: Norton, 1958.

———. *Natural Supernaturalism: Tradition and Revolution in Romantic Literature*. New York: Norton, 1971.

———. "On Political Readings of *Lyrical Ballads*." In *Romantic Revolutions: Criticism and Theory*, edited by Kenneth R. Johnston et al., 320–49. Bloomington: Indiana University Press, 1990.

Achinstein, Sharon. "Honey from the Lion's Carcass: Bunyan, Allegory, and the Samsonian Moment." In *Awakening Words: John Bunyan and the Language of Community*, edited by David Gay, James G. Randall, and Arlette Zinck, 68–80. Newark: University of Delaware Press, 2000.

Adams, John Charles. "Linguistic Values and Religious Experience: An Analysis of the Clothing Metaphors in Alexander Richardson's Ramist-Puritan Lectures on Speech: 'Speech is a Garment to Cloath Our Reason.'" *Quarterly Journal of Speech* 9 (1990): 58–68.

Allen, Don Cameron. *Mysteriously Meant: The Rediscovery of Pagan Symbolism and Allegorical Interpretation in the Renaissance*. Baltimore: The Johns Hopkins University Press, 1970.

Anderson, Benedict. *Imagined Communities: Reflections on the Origin and Spread of Nationalism*. London: Verso, 1991.

Asad, Talal. *Formations of the Secular: Christianity, Islam, Modernity*. Stanford: Stanford University Press, 2003.

Aston, Margaret. "Puritans and Iconoclasm, 1560-1700." In *The Culture of English Puritanism, 1560–1700*, edited by Durston and Eales, 92–121.

Aulén, Gustaf. *Christus Victor: An Historical Study of the Three Main Types of the Idea of Atonement*. Translated by A. G. Herbert. Foreword by Jaroslav Pelikan. 1931. Reprint, New York: Macmillan, 1969.

Ayres, Philip, ed. *Characteristicks of Men, Manners, Opinions, Times*. Oxford: Clarendon, 1999.

Barker, Francis. *The Tremulous Private Body: Essays on Subjection*. Ann Arbor: University of Michigan Press, 1995.

Barker-Benfield, G. J. *The Culture of Sensibility: Sex and Society in Eighteenth-Century Britain*. Chicago: University of Chicago Press, 1992.

Barnes, Andrew. "Religious Reform and the War Against Ritual." *Journal of Ritual Studies* 4 (1990): 127–33.

Barrell, John. "'The Dangerous Goddess': Masculinity, Prestige, and the Aesthetic in Early Eighteenth-Century Britain." *Cultural Critique* 12 (1989): 101–31.

———. *The Political Theory of Painting from Reynolds to Hazlitt: "The Body of the Public."* New Haven: Yale University Press, 1986.

Batho, Edith. *The Later Wordsworth*. Cambridge: Cambridge University Press, 1933. Reprint, New York: Russell & Russell, 1963.

Baxter, Richard. *The English Nonconformity, As under King* Charles II *and King* James Ist. *Truly Stated and Argued*. London, 1689.

———. *Five Disputations of Church-Government, and Worship*. London, 1659.

———. *The Grand Debate Between The most Reverend the Bishops and The Presbyterian Divines, Appointed By His Sacred Majesty, As Commissioners for The Review and Alteration of the Book of Common Prayer, &c. Being An Exact Account of their whole Proceedings*. London, 1661.

———. *To the Kings Most Excellent Majesty. The Due Account and Humble Petition of the Ministers of the Gospel, Lately Commissioned for the Review and Alteration of the Liturgy*. London, 1661.

Belanger, Terry. "Publishers and Writers in Eighteenth-Century England." In *Books and Their Readers in Eighteenth-Century England*, edited by Isabel Rivers, 5–25. Leicester: Leicester University Press, 1982.

Belgrad, Daniel. *The Culture of Spontaneity: Improvisation and the Arts in Postwar America*. Chicago: University of Chicago Press, 1998.

Bender, John. "Prison Reform and the Sentence of Narration in *The Vicar of Wakefield*." In *The New Eighteenth Century: Theory, Politics, English Literature*, edited by Felicity Nussbaum and Laura Brown, 168–88. New York: Routledge, 1987.

Benedict, Barbara. *Framing Feeling: Sentiment and Style in English Prose Fiction, 1745–1800.* New York: AMS Press, 1994.

Benjamin, Jessica. *The Bonds of Love: Psychoanalysis, Feminism, and the Problem of Domination.* New York: Pantheon, 1988.

Bossy, John. *Christianity in the West, 1400–1700.* Oxford: Oxford University Press, 1985.

Boswell, James. *Boswell's Life of Johnson.* Introduction by Chauncey Brewster Tinker. 2 vols. London: Oxford University Press, 1933.

Bouwsma, William. *John Calvin: A Sixteenth-Century Portrait.* New York: Oxford University Press, 1988.

———. "The Secularization of Society in the Seventeenth Century" and "Anxiety and the Formation of Early Modern Culture." Chaps. 4 and 6 of his *A Usable Past: Essays in European Cultural History,* 112–28 and 157–89. Berkeley: University of California Press, 1990.

Brachlow, Stephen. *The Communion of Saints: Radical Puritan and Separatist Ecclesiology, 1570–1625.* Oxford: Oxford University Press, 1988.

Brain, Russell. *Some Reflections on Genius.* Philadelphia: Lippincott, 1960.

Brainard, Marcus. "Minding One's Manners: On the 'Moral Architecture' of Shaftesbury's *Characteristics.*" *Bochumer Philosophisches Jarhbuch Antike und Mittelalter* 6 (2001): 217–38.

Branch, Lori. "The Benefit of Doubt: The Ethics of Rereading." In *Critical Ethics: Text, Theory, and Responsibility,* edited by Dominic Rainsford and Tim Woods, 187–202. New York: Macmillan, 1999.

———. "Plain Style, or The High Fashion of Empire: Colonialism, Resistance, and Assimilation in Adam Smith's *Lectures on Rhetoric and Belles Lettres.*" *Studies in Scottish Literature* 33 (2002): 435–53.

———. "Wounds of Exchange and Symptoms of the Real in *Grace Abounding.*" Presented at the Third Triennial Meeting of the International John Bunyan Society. Cleveland, Ohio, 10–14 October 2001.

Bredvold, Louis I. *The Natural History of Sensibility.* Detroit: Wayne State University Press, 1962.

Breward, Ian, ed. *The Westminster Directory, being A Directory for the Publique Worship of God in the Three Kingdomes.* Bramcote, UK: Grove Books, 1980.

Brissenden, R. F. *Virtue in Distress: Studies in the Novel of Sentiment from Richardson to Sade.* New York: Barnes & Noble, 1974.

Bromwich, David. "The French Revolution and 'Tintern Abbey.'" *Raritan* 10 (1991): 1–23.

Brown, Marshall. *Preromanticism.* Stanford: Stanford University Press, 1991.

Brunström, Conrad. *William Cowper: Religion, Satire, Society*. Lewisburg, Pa.: Bucknell University Press, 2004.

Bunyan, John. *The Doctrine of the Law and Grace Unfolded*, edited by Richard L. Greaves. Vol. 2 of *The Miscellaneous Works of John Bunyan*, edited by Roger Sharrock. Oxford: Clarendon, 1976.

———. *Grace Abounding to the Chief of Sinners*, edited by Roger Sharrock. Oxford: Clarendon, 1962.

———. *Israel's Hope Encouraged and The Saints Privilege and Profit*, edited by W. R. Owens. Vol. 13 of *The Miscellaneous Works of John Bunyan*, edited by Roger Sharrock. Oxford: Clarendon, 1994.

———. *I Will Pray with the Spirit, and I will Pray with the Understanding also: Or, A Discourse Touching Prayer, From I Cor. 14.15*. 2nd ed. London: Printed for the author, 1663.

———. *Mapp Shewing the Order & Causes of Salvation & Damnation*, edited by W. R. Owens. In vol. 12 of *The Miscellaneous Works of John Bunyan*, edited by Roger Sharrock, 417–23. Oxford: Clarendon, 1994.

———. *The Pilgrim's Progress*, edited, introduction, and notes by Roger Sharrock. New York: Penguin, 1987.

Burke, Edmund. "On Taste." In *A Philosophical Enquiry into the Origin of Our Ideas of the Sublime and Beautiful*, edited by James T. Boulton, 11–27. Notre Dame: University of Notre Dame Press, 1968.

Burke, Peter. *Popular Culture in Early Modern Europe*. Revised ed. Hants, UK: Scolar Press, 1994.

Bushell, Sally. *Re-Reading* The Excursion. Adlershot: Ashgate, 2002.

Campbell, Gordon. "Fishing in Other Men's Waters: Bunyan and the Theologians." In *John Bunyan: Conventicle and Parnassus; Tercentenary Essays*, edited by Keeble, 137–51.

Caputo, John. *On Religion*. London: Routledge, 2001.

———. *The Prayers and Tears of Jacques Derrida: Religion Without Religion*. Bloomington: Indiana University Press, 1997.

———. "Who Comes after the God of Metaphysics?" Introduction to *The Religious*, edited by John Caputo, 1–19. Oxford: Blackwell, 2002.

Carlton, Peter. "Bunyan: Language, Convention, Authority." *English Literary History* 51 (1984): 17–32.

Carpini, John Delli. *History, Religion and Politics in William Wordsworth's Ecclesiastical Sonnets*. Lewiston: Edwin Mellen Press, 2004.

Cassirer, Ernst. *The Philosophy of Enlightenment*. 1932. Reprint, Princeton: Princeton University Press, 1951.

Certeau, Michel de. *The Practice of Everyday Life*. Translated by Steven Rendall. Berkeley: University of Califronia Press, 1988.

Chakrabarty, Dipesh. "The Time of History and the Times of Gods." In *The Politics of Culture in the Shadow of Capital*, edited by Lisa Lowe and David Lloyd, 35–60. Durham, N.C.: Duke University Press, 1997.

Clark, J. C. D. *English Society, 1660–1832: Religion, Ideology and Politics During the Ancien Regime*. 2nd ed. Cambridge: Cambridge University Press, 2000.

Clifford, Alan. "The Westminster Directory of Public Worship (1645)." In *The Reformation of Worship: Papers Read at the 1989 Westminster Conference*, no editor given, 53–75. Colchester: Westminster Conference, 1989.

Cohen, Charles Lloyd. *God's Caress: The Psychology of Puritan Religious Experience*. New York: Oxford University Press, 1986.

Cole, Steven E. "Evading Politics: The Poverty of Historicizing Romanticism." *Studies in Romanticism* 34 (1995): 29–49.

Coleridge, Samuel Taylor. *Coleridge on the Seventeenth Century*, edited by Roberta F. Brinkley. Durham: Duke University Press, 1955.

Collinson, Patrick. *The Birthpangs of Protestant England: Religious and Cultural Change in the Sixteenth and Seventeenth Centuries*. New York: St. Martin's Press, 1988.

———. *The Puritan Character: Polemics and Polarities in Early Seventeenth-Century English Culture*. Los Angeles: William Andrews Clark Memorial Library, 1989.

———. "Towards a Broader Understanding of the Early Dissenting Tradition." In *The Dissenting Tradition: Essays for Leland H. Carlson*, edited by C. Robert Cole and Michael E. Moody, 13–19. Athens: Ohio University Press, 1975.

The Common Prayer-Book Unmasked, wherein is declared the Unlawfulnesse and Sinfulnesse of it, by Several Undeniable Arguments, Viz. From the Name of it, From the Original of it. From the Matter contained in it. The ridiculous Manner of using it. The Evil Effects it hath upon Ministers, People, and Ordinances.... Published by divers Ministers of Gods Word, and formerly printed and dedicated to the Lords and Commons Assembled in Parliament. Now newly reprinted. N.p., 1660.

Conway, Alison. *Private Interests: Women, Portraiture, and the Visual Culture of the English Novel, 1709–1791*. Toronto: University of Toronto Press, 2001.

Coote, Stephen. "Text and Publication History." In *Oliver Goldsmith, The Vicar of Wakefield*, edited, introduction, and notes by Stephen Coote, 25. New York: Penguin, 1986.

Cope, Kevin. "The Propositions of Faith: The Ideology of the Royal Society and Bunyan's Academy of Maxims." *Publications of the Mississippi Philological Society* 7 (1988): 28–38.

Cornell, Drucilla. *The Philosophy of the Limit*. London: Routledge, 1992.

Costa, Dennis. "Language in Smart's *Jubilate Agno*." *Essays in Criticism* 52 (2002): 295–313.

Cowell, Andrew. "Advertising, Rhetoric, and Literature: A Medieval Response to Contemporary Theory." *Poetics Today* 22 (2001): 795–827.

Crane, R. S. "Suggestions toward a Genealogy of the 'Man of Feeling.'" *English Literary History* 1 (1934): 203–30.

Cressy, David. *Birth, Marriage, and Death: Ritual, Religion, and the Life-Cycle in Tudor and Stuart England*. Oxford: Oxford University Press, 1997.

Curtis, Susan. *A Consuming Faith: The Social Gospel and Modern American Culture*. Baltimore: The Johns Hopkins University Press, 1991.

Damrosch, Leopold Jr. *God's Plot and Man's Stories: Studies in the Fictional Imagination from Milton to Fielding*. Chicago: University of Chicago Press, 1985.

Darwall, Stephen. *The British Moralists and the Internal 'Ought,' 1640–1740*. Cambridge: Cambridge University Press, 1995.

Davie, Donald. *A Gathered Church: The Literature of the English Dissenting Interest, 1700–1930*. New York: Oxford University Press, 1978.

Davies, Horton. *From Cranmer to Hooker, 1534–1603; From Andrewes to Baxter and Foxe, 1603–1690;* and *From Watts and Wesley to Maurice, 1690–1850*. Worship and Theology in England 1–3. Princeton: Princeton University Press, 1961–1975.

———. *The Worship of the English Puritans*. London: Dacre Press, 1948.

Davies, Michael. "Bunyan's Exceeding Maze: *Grace Abounding* and the Labyrinth of Predestination." In *Awakening Words: John Bunyan and the Language of Community*, edited by David Gay, James G. Randall, and Arlette Zinck, 97–112. Newark: University of Delaware Press, 2000.

[Dawbeny, Henry]. *A Sober and Temperate Discourse, Concerning the Interest of Words in Prayer. The just Antiquity and Pedigree of Liturgies, or Forms of Prayer in Churches: With a View of the State of the Church, when they were first composed, or imposed*. London, 1661.

De Grazia, Margreta. "The Secularization of Language in the Seventeenth Century." *Journal of the History of Ideas* 41 (1980): 319–29.

Dearnley, Moira. *The Poetry of Christopher Smart*. New York: Barnes & Noble, 1969.

Deleuze, Gilles. *Difference and Repetition*. Translated by Paul Patton. New York: Columbia University Press, 1994.

Deprun, Jean. *La philosophie de l'inquietude en France au XVIIIe siècle*. Paris: J. Vrin, 1979.

Derrida, Jacques. "'Eating Well,' or the Calculation of the Subject: An Interview with Jacques Derrida." In *Who Comes After the Subject?* edited by Eduardo Cadava, Peter Connor, and Jean-Luc Nancy, 96–119. London: Routledge, 1991.

———. "Faith and Knowledge: Two Sources of Religion at the Limits of Reason Alone." In *Religion*, edited by Jacques Derrida and Gianni Vattimo, 1–78. Stanford: Stanford University Press, 1998.

———. "Force of Law: The 'Mystical Foundation of Authority.'" In *Deconstruction and the Possibility of Justice*, edited by Drucilla Cornell, Michael Rosenfeld, and David Gray Carlson, 3–67. New York: Routledge, 1992.

———. "My Chances/*Mes Chances:* A Rendezvous with Some Epicurean Stereophonies." In *Taking Chances: Derrida, Psychoanalysis, Literature*, edited by J. H. Smith and William Kerrigan, 1–32. Baltimore: The Johns Hopkins University Press, 1984.

———. *Specters of Marx: The State of the Debt, the Work of Mourning, and the New International*. Translated by Peggy Kamuf. New York: Routledge, 1994.

Devlin, Christopher. *Poor Kit Smart*. Carbondale: Southern Illinois University Press, 1961.

A Directory for The Publique Worship of God, Throughout the Three Kingdoms of England, Scotland, and Ireland Together with an Ordinance of Parliament for the taking away of the Book of Common-Prayer. London, 1644.

Dix, Dom Gregory. *The Shape of the Liturgy*. 1945. Reprint, London: Dacre, 1978.

Donoghue, Frank. *The Fame Machine: Book Reviewing and Eighteenth-Century Literary Careers*. Stanford: Stanford University Press, 1996.

Donoghue, William. *Enlightenment Fiction in England, France, and America*. Gainesville: University Press of Florida, 2002.

Draper, John. "Bunyan's Mr. Ignorance." *Modern Language Review* 22 (1927): 15–21.

Duffy, Eamon. "Continuity and Divergence in Tudor Religion." In *Unity and Diversity in the Church*, edited by R. N. Swanson, 171–205. Oxford: Blackwell, 1996.

———. *The Stripping of the Altars: Traditional Religion in England, 1400–1580*. New Haven: Yale University Press, 1992.

Dugas, Kristine, ed. Introduction to *The White Doe of Rylstone; or The Fate of the Nortons*, by William Wordsworth, 3–65. Ithaca: Cornell University Press, 1988.

Durston, Christopher, and Jacqueline Eales, eds. *The Culture of English Puritanism, 1560-1700.* New York: St. Martin's Press, 1996.

———. "The Puritan Ethos, 1560–1700." In his *The Culture of English Puritanism, 1500–1700,* 1–31.

———. "Puritan Rule and the Failure of Cultural Revolution, 1645–1660." In his *The Culture of English Puritanism, 1560–1700,* 210–33.

Dwyer, John Alfred. *The Age of the Passions: An Interpretation of Adam Smith and Scottish Enlightenment Culture.* East Linton, Scotland: Tuckwell Press, 1998.

Dykstal, Timothy. "The Story of O: Politics and Pleasure in *The Vicar of Wakefield.*" *English Literary History* 62 (1995): 329–46.

Eagleton, Terry. *The Ideology of the Aesthetic.* Oxford: Blackwell, 1990.

Eire, Carlos M. N. *War Against the Idols: The Reformation of Worship from Erasmus to Calvin.* Cambridge: Cambridge University Press, 1986.

Ellis, Markman. *The Politics of Sensibility: Race, Gender and Commerce in the Sentimental Novel.* Cambridge: Cambridge University Press, 1996.

Ellison, Julie. *Cato's Tears and the Making of Anglo-American Emotion.* Chicago: University of Chicago Press, 1999.

Erickson, Robert A. *The Language of the Heart, 1600–1750.* Philadelphia: University of Pennsylvania Press, 1997.

Everyman. Introduction by Simon Trussler. London: Nick Hern Books, 1996.

Fincham, Kenneth, ed. *The Early Stuart Church, 1603–1642.* Stanford: Stanford University Press, 1993.

Finley, C. Stephen. "Bunyan among the Victorians: Macaulay, Froude, Ruskin." *Journal of Literature and Theology* 3 (1989): 77–94.

Firmin, Giles. *The Liturgical Considerator Considered.* London: Printed for Ralph Smith, 1661.

Fish, Stanley. "Masculine Persuasive Force: Donne and Verbal Power." In *Soliciting Interpretation: Literary Theory and Seventeenth-Century English Poetry,* edited by Elizabeth D. Harvey and Katharine Eisaman Maus, 223–52. Chicago: University of Chicago Press, 1990.

———. "One University Under God?" *The Chronicle of Higher Education* 51.18, 7 January 2005, C1.

———. "Progress in *The Pilgrim's Progress.*" Chap. 4 of his *Self-Consuming Artifacts: The Experience of Seventeenth-Century Literature,* 224–64. Berkeley: University of California Press, 1972.

Forrest, James F. "Bunyan's Ignorance and The Flatterer: A Study in the Literary Art of Damnation." *Studies in Philology* 60 (1963): 12–22.

———, and Richard L. Greaves. *John Bunyan: A Reference Guide*. Boston: G. K. Hall, 1982.

Forster, John. *The Life and Times of Oliver Goldsmith*. 2 vols. London, 1854.

Foucault, Michel. *The Order of Things: An Archaeology of the Human Sciences*. New York: Vintage, 1994.

Frere, W. H. and C. E. Douglas, eds. *Puritan Manifestoes: A Study of the Origins of the Puritan Revolt, with a Reprint of the Admonition to the Parliament and Kindred Documents*, 1572. London: SPCK, 1907.

Gates, Barbara T. "Wordsworth's Mirror of Morality: Distortions of Church History." *The Wordsworth Circle* 12.2 (1981): 129–32.

Gedalof, Allan J. "Smart's Poetics in *Jubilate Agno*." *English Studies in Canada* 5 (1979): 262–74.

Gibbons, B. J. "Richard Overton and the Secularism of the Interregnum Radicals." *Seventeenth Century* 10 (1995): 63–75.

Gill, Stephen. "Wordsworth and 'Catholic Truth': The Role of Frederick William Faber." *Review of English Studies* 45 (1994): 204–20.

———. *Wordsworth and the Victorians*. Oxford: Clarendon, 1998.

Goldman, Peter. "Living Words: Iconoclasm and Beyond in John Bunyan's *Grace Abounding*." *New Literary History* 33 (2002): 461–89.

Goldsmith, Oliver. *The Citizen of the World*, "Letter LXXV." In *Collected Works of Oliver Goldsmith*, edited by Arthur Friedman, 2:310–14. Oxford: Clarendon, 1966.

———. "An Essay on the Theatre; or, A Comparison between Laughing and Sentimental Comedy." In *Collected Works of Oliver Goldsmith*, edited by Arthur Friedman, 209–13. Oxford: Clarendon, 1966.

———. *The Vicar of Wakefield*. Vol. 4 of *Collected Works of Oliver Goldsmith*, edited by Arthur Friedman. Oxford: Clarendon, 1966.

———. *The Vicar of Wakefield*, edited, introduction, and notes by Stephen Coote. New York: Penguin, 1986.

Gordon, Scott Paul. *The Power of the Passive Self in English Literature, 1640–1770*. Cambridge: Cambridge University Press, 2002.

Gravil, Richard. *Wordsworth's Bardic Vocation, 1787–1842*. New York: Palgrave, 2003.

Grean, Stanley. *Shaftesbury's Philosophy of Religion and Ethics: A Study in Enthusiasm*. Athens: Ohio University Press, 1967.

Greaves, Richard L. "Bunyan through the Centuries: Some Reflections." *English Studies* 64 (1983): 113–21.

———. *John Bunyan*. Abingdon: Sutton Courtenay Press, 1969.

Greene, Donald. "Latitudinarianism and Sensibility: The Genealogy of the 'Man of Feeling' Reconsidered." *Modern Philology* 75 (1977): 159–83.

Greene, Thomas, M. Introduction to *Ceremony and Text in the Renaissance*, edited by Douglas F. Rutledge, 11–18. Newark, University of Deleware Press, 1986.

Guest, Harriet. *A Form of Sound Words: The Religious Poetry of Christopher Smart*. Oxford: Clarendon, 1989.

Guilhamet, Leon. *The Sincere Ideal: Studies on Sincerity in Eighteenth-Century English Literature*. Montreal: McGill-Queen's University Press, 1974.

Gunton, Colin E. *The Actuality of Atonement: A Study of Metaphor, Rationality and the Christian Tradition*. Edinburgh: T&T Clark, 1988.

Haakonssen, Knud, ed. *Enlightenment and Religion: Rational Dissent in Eighteenth-Century Britain*. Cambridge: Cambridge University Press, 1996.

Habermas, Jürgen. *The Philosophical Discourse of Modernity: Twelve Lectures*. Translated by Frederick Lawrence. Cambridge: Mass., MIT Press, 1987.

Hambrick-Stowe, Charles. *The Practice of Piety: Puritan Devotional Disciplines in Seventeenth-Century New England*. Chapel Hill: University of North Carolina Press, 1982.

Hammond, Brean S. "*The Pilgrim's Progress:* Satire and Social Comment." In The Pilgrim's Progress: *Critical and Historical Views*, edited by Newey, 118–31.

———. *Professional Imaginative Writing in England, 1670–1740: "Hackney for Bread."* Oxford: Clarendon, 1997.

Hardin, Richard F. "Bunyan, Mr. Ignorance, and the Quakers." *Studies in Philology* 69 (1972): 496–508.

Harkin, Maureen. "Goldsmith on Authorship in *The Vicar of Wakefield*." *Eighteenth-Century Fiction* 14 (2002): 325–44.

Hartman, Geoffrey. "Christopher Smart's Magnificat: Toward a Theory of Representation." *English Literary History* 41 (1974): 429–54.

———. *The Unremarkable Wordsworth*. London: Methuen, 1987.

———. *Wordsworth's Poetry, 1787–1850*. New Haven: Yale University Press, 1964.

Hawes, Clement, ed. *Christopher Smart and the Enlightenment*. New York: St. Martins Press, 1999.

———. *Mania and Literary Style: The Rhetoric of Enthusiasm from the Ranters to Christopher Smart*. Cambridge: Cambridge University Press, 1996.

———. "The Utopian Public Sphere: Intersubjectivity in *Jubilate Agno*." Chap. 10 of his *Christopher Smart and the Enlightenment*, 195–212.

Hawkes, David. "The Concept of the 'Hireling' in Bunyan's Theology." Presented at the Third Triennial Meeting of the International John Bunyan Society, 10–14 October 2001, Cleveland, Ohio.

Hawkins, Anne. "The Double Conversion in Bunyan's *Grace Abounding*." *Philological Quarterly* 61 (1982): 259–76.

Hayes, Alan L. "Spirit and Structure in Elizabethan Public Prayer." In *Spirit Within Structure: Essays in Honor of George Johnston on the Occasion of His Seventieth Birthday*, edited by E. J. Furcha, 117–32. Allison Park, Pa.: Pickwick Publications, 1983.

Heinzelman, Kurt. *The Economics of the Imagination*. Amherst: University of Massachusetts Press, 1980.

Henry, Matthew. *A Method for Prayer, with Scripture Expressions Proper to be Us'd under each Head*. 2d ed., with additions. London: Printed for Nath. Cliff and Daniel Jackson, 1710.

Herreshoff, David. "Marxist Perspectives on Bunyan." In *Bunyan in Our Time*, edited by Robert G. Collmer, 161–85. Kent, Ohio: Kent State University Press, 1989.

Hervieu-Léger, Danièle. *Religion as a Chain of Memory*. Translated by Simon Lee. New Brunswick, N.J.: Rutgers University Press, 2001.

Hewitt, Regina. "Church Building as Political Strategy in Wordsworth's *Ecclesiastical Sonnets*." *Mosaic* 25 (1992): 31–46.

Heyd, Michael. *"Be Sober and Reasonable": The Critique of Enthusiasm in the Seventeenth and Early Eighteenth Centuries*. Leiden: E. J. Brill, 1995.

Hill, Christopher. "Bunyan's Contemporary Reputation." In *John Bunyan and His England, 1628–1688*, edited by Anne Laurence, W. R. Owens, and Stuart Sim, 3–15. London: Hambledon Press, 1990.

———. *Economic Problems of the Church, from Archbishop Whitgift to the Long Parliament*. Oxford: Clarendon, 1968.

———. "The Rich, the Poor, and the Middling Sort." Chap. 1.2 of his *A Turbulent, Seditious, and Factious People: John Bunyan and His Church, 1628–1688*, 16–27. Oxford: Clarendon, 1988.

———. *Society and Puritanism in Pre-Revolutionary England*. New York: Schocken Books, 1964.

The History of Little Goody Two-Shoe,; otherwise called, Mrs. Margery Two-shoes. 1766. Reprint, York, 1800.

Hopkins, Robert. *The True Genius of Oliver Goldsmith*. Baltimore: The Johns Hopkins University Press, 1969.

Horkheimer, Max, and Theodor W. Adorno. *The Dialectic of Enlightenment*. Translated by John Cumming. New York: Continuum, 1972.

Huet, Marie-Hélène. *Mourning Glory: The Will of the French Revolution*. Philadelphia: University of Pennsylvania Press, 1997.

Hughes, Kenneth J. "Troubled Tories: Theory of History and Didactic Function of Wordsworth's *Ecclesiastical Sonnets*." *CIEFL Bulletin* 15 (1979): 29–44.

Hume, David. *New Letters of David Hume*. Edited by Raymond Klibansky and Ernest C. Mossner. Oxford: Clarendon, 1954.

Hunter, Christopher. "The Life of Christopher Smart." In *The Poems of the Late Christopher Smart*, edited by Christopher Hunter, v–xlii. Reading, 1791.

Hutcheson, Francis. *An Essay on the Nature and Conduct of the Passions and Affections* [with] *Illustrations upon the Moral Sense*. 2nd ed. Dublin, 1728. Facsimile, New York: Garland Publishing, 1971.

———. *An Inquiry into the Original of Our Ideas of Beauty and Virtue . . . In Which the Principles of the Late Earl of Shaftesbury are explain'd and defended . . . With an Attempt to introduce a Mathematical Calculation in Subjects of Morality . . . in Two Treatises. I. Concerning Beauty, Order, Harmony, Design. II. Concerning Moral Good and Evil*. London, 1725. Facsimile, New York: Garland Publishing, 1971.

Hutton, Ronald. *The Rise and Fall of Merry England: The Ritual Year 1400–1700*. Oxford: Oxford University Press, 1994.

Irlam, Shaun. *Elations: The Poetics of Enthusiasm in Eighteenth-Century Britain*. Stanford: Stanford University Press, 1999.

———. "Enthusiasm in the Seventeenth Century: The Vicissitudes of an Image." Chap. 1 of his *Elations: The Poetics of Enthusiasm in Eighteenth-Century Britain*, 31–52.

Iser, Wolfgang. "Bunyan's *Pilgrim's Progress*: The Doctrine of Predestination and the Shaping of the Novel." Chap. 1 of his *The Implied Reader: Patterns of Communication from Bunyan to Beckett*, 1–28. Baltimore: The Johns Hopkins University Press, 1974.

Jaffro, Laurent. "Présentation" and "Note sur le Texte." In *Exercices*, by Shaftesbury. Translated from the English, introduction, and notes by Laurent Jaffro, 7–35 and 36–37. Paris: Aubier, 1993.

Johnson, Claudia L. *Equivocal Beings: Politics, Gender, and Sentimentality in the 1790s: Wollstonecraft, Radcliffe, Burney, Austen*. Chicago: University of Chicago Press, 1995.

Johnson, Samuel. *The Idler, by the Author of The Rambler, in Two Volumes*. 3rd ed. London, 1767.

Johnston, Kenneth R. *The Hidden Wordsworth*. New York: Norton, 2000.

———. "The Politics of 'Tintern Abbey.'" *The Wordsworth Circle* 14 (1983): 6–14.

———. "The Triumphs of Failure: Wordsworth's *Lyrical Ballads* of 1798." Chap. 7 of *The Age of Wordsworth: Critical Essays of the Romantic Tradition*, edited by Kenneth Johnston and Gene W. Ruoff, 133–59. New Brunswick: Rutgers University Press, 1987.

———. *Wordsworth and* The Recluse. New Haven: Yale University Press, 1984.

Jones, Cheslyn, et al. *The Study of Liturgy*. Revised edition. London: SPCK, 1992.

Jones, Robert. "Ruled Passions: Re-reading the Culture of Sensibility." *Eighteenth-Century Studies* 32 (1999): 395–402.

Kaufman, Peter Iver. "Much in Prayer." Chap. 1 of his *Prayer, Despair, and Drama: Elizabethan Introspection*, 15–40. Urbana: University of Illinois Press, 1996.

Kay, Carol. *Political Constructions: Defoe, Richardson, and Sterne in Relation to Hobbes, Hume, and Burke*. Ithaca: Cornell University Press, 1988.

Keeble, N. H., ed. *John Bunyan: Conventicle and Parnassus; Tercentenary Essays*. Oxford: Clarendon, 1988.

———. "'Of him thousands daily Sing and talk': Bunyan and His Reputation." In *John Bunyan: Conventicle and Parnassus; Tercentenary Essays*, edited by Keeble, 241–63.

Kendall, R. T. *Calvin and English Calvinism to 1649*. Oxford: Oxford University Press, 1979.

Kent, Elizabeth Eaton. *Goldsmith and His Booksellers*. Ithaca: Cornell University Press, 1933.

Kerrigan, John. "Wordsworth and the Sonnet: Building, Dwelling, Thinking." *Essays in Criticism* 35 (1985): 45–75.

Keymer, Thomas. "Johnson, Madness and Smart." In *Christopher Smart and the Enlightenment*, edited by Hawes, 177–94.

King, Peter. "The Reasons for the Abolition of the Book of Common Prayer in 1645." *Journal of Ecclesiastical History* 21 (1970): 327–39.

Klein, Lawrence E. *Shaftesbury and the Culture of Politeness: Moral Discourse and Cultural Politics in Early Eighteenth-Century England*. Cambridge: Cambridge University Press, 1994.

———. "Sociability, Solitude, and Enthusiasm." Chap. 1 of *Enthusiasm and Enlightenment in Europe, 1650–1850*, edited by Klein and La Vopa, 153–77.

Klein, Lawrence E., and Anthony J. La Vopa, eds. *Enthusiasm and Enlightenment in Europe, 1650–1850*. San Marino, Calif.: Huntington Library Press, 1998.

Knox, Ronald A. *Enthusiasm: A Chapter in the History of Religion with Special Reference to the Seventeenth and Eighteenth Centuries*. New York: Galaxy, 1961.

Koyré, Alexandre. *From the Closed World to the Infinite Universe*. 1957. Reprint, Baltimore: The Johns Hopkins University Press, 1968.

Lacan, Jacques. *The Four Fundamental Concepts of Psychoanalysis*, edited by Jacques-Alain Miller. Translated by Alan Sheridan. New York: Norton, 1981.

———. "Kant *avec* Sade." Translated by James B. Swenson Jr. *October* 51 (1990): 55–75.

Lake, Peter. "Calvinism and the English Church, 1570–1635." *Past and Present* 114 (1987): 32–76.

———. "The Laudian Style: Order, Uniformity, and the Pursuit of the Beauty of Holiness in the 1630s." In *The Early Stuart Church: 1603–1642*, edited by Fincham, 161–85

Lamb, Jonathan. *The Rhetoric of Suffering: Reading the Book of Job in the Eighteenth Century*. Oxford: Clarendon, 1995.

———. *Sterne's Fiction and the Double Principle*. Cambridge: Cambridge University Press, 1989.

Lawrence, Anne, W. R. Owens, and Stuart Sim, eds. *John Bunyan and His England, 1628–1688*. London: Hamilton Press, 1990.

Leatherbarrow, David. "Character, Geometry and Perspective: The Third Earl of Shaftesbury's Principals of Garden Design." *Journal of Garden History* 4 (1984): 332–58.

Leverenz, David. *The Language of Puritan Feeling: An Exploration in Literature, Psychology, and Social History*. New Brunswick, N.J.: Rutgers University Press, 1980.

Lévinas, Emmanuel. "Ethics as First Philosophy." Translated by Seán Hand and Michael Temple. In *The Lévinas Reader*, edited by Seán Hand, 75–87. Oxford: Blackwell, 1999.

Levinson, Marjorie. "The New Historicism: Back to the Future." In *Rethinking Historicism: Critical Readings in Romantic History*, edited by Majorie Levinson, Marilyn Butler, Jerome McGann, and Paul Hamilton, 18–63. Oxford: Basil Blackwell, 1989.

———. *Wordsworth's Great Period Poems: Four Essays*. New York: Cambridge University Press, 1986. See especially "Insight and Oversight: Reading 'Tintern Abbey,'" 1–57.

Ley, John. *A Debate concerning the English Liturgy, Both As Established in & As Abolished out of the Worship of GOD. Drawn out in Two English and two Latine Epistles, Written betwixt Edward Hyde Doctor in Divinity, and John Ley Rector of the Church of Solyhull in Warwick-shire*. London: Printed by A. M., for Edward Brewster, 1656.

Liddell, Henry George, and Robert Scott. *A Lexicon Abridged from Liddell and Scott's Greek-English Lexicon*. Oxford: Clarendon, 2002.

Lindsey, Theophilus. *A Discourse addressed to the Congregation at the Chapel in Essex Street, Strand, on resigning the pastoral office among them*. London: J. Johnson, 1793.

Liu, Alan. "The Power of Formalism: The New Historicism." *English Literary History* 56 (1989): 721–71.

———. *Wordsworth: The Sense of History*. Stanford: Stanford University Press, 1989.

Liu, Yu. "Reevaluating Revolution and Radicalness in the *Lyrical Ballads*." *Studies in English Literature* 36 (1996): 747–61.

Lukács, Georg. "Reification and the Consciousness of the Proletariat." Chap. 4 of his *History and Class Consciousness: Studies in Marxist Dialectics*. Translated by Rodney Livingstone, 83–222. London: Merlin Press, 1971.

Luxon, Thomas H. *Literal Figures: Puritan Allegory and the Reformation Crisis in Representation*. Chicago: University of Chicago Press, 1995.

Lynch, Deidre Shauna. *The Economy of Character: Novels, Market Culture, and the Business of Inner Meaning*. Chicago: University of Chicago Press, 1998.

———. "Personal Effects and Sentimental Fictions." *Eighteenth-Century Fiction* 12 (2000): 345–68.

Lyotard, Jean-François. *The Differend: Phrases in Dispute*. Translated by Georges Van Den Abbeele. Minneapolis: University of Minnesota Press, 1988.

McDowell, Paula. "Enlightenment Enthusiasms and the Spectacular Failure of the Philadelphian Society." *Eighteenth-Century Studies* 35 (2002): 515–33.

———. *The Women of Grub Street: Press, Politics, and Gender in the London Literary Marketplace, 1678–1730*. Oxford: Clarendon, 1998.

McGann, Jerome. *The Romantic Ideology: A Critical Investigation*. Chicago: University of Chicago Press, 1985.

McGiffert, Michael, ed. *God's Plot: Puritan Spirituality in Thomas Shepard's Cambridge*. Revised ed. Amherst: University of Massachusetts Press, 1994.

McKendrick, Neil, John Brewer, and J. H. Plumb. *The Birth of a Consumer Society: The Commercialization of Eighteenth-Century England*. Bloomington: Indiana University Press, 1982.

McKeon, Michael. *The Origins of the English Novel, 1600–1740*. Baltimore: The Johns Hopkins University Press, 1987.

———. "The Origins of Interdisciplinary Studies." *Eighteenth-Century Studies* 28 (1994): 17–28.

Magnuson, Paul. "Wordsworth and Spontaneity." In *The Evidence of the Imagination: Studies of Interactions between Life and Art in English Romantic Literature*, edited by Donald H. Reiman et al., 101–18. New York: New York University Press, 1978.

Maltby, Judith. "'By this Book': Parishioners, the Prayer Book and the Established Church." In *The Early Stuart Church, 1603–1642*, edited by Fincham, 115–37.

Mandeville, Bernard. *The Fable of the Bees and Other Writing*, edited, introduction, and notes by E. J. Hundert. Indianapolis: Hackett Publishing, 1997.

Manning, Peter. "Wordsworth at St. Bee's: Scandals, Sisterhoods, and Wordsworth's Later Poetry." *English Literary History* 52 (1985): 33–58.

Markley, Robert. *Fallen Languages: Crises of Representation in Newtonian England, 1660–1740*. Ithaca: Cornell University Press, 1993.

———. "Objectivity as Ideology: Boyle, Newton, and the Languages of Science." *Genre* 16 (1983): 355–72.

———. "Sentimentality as Performance: Shaftesbury, Sterne, and the Theatrics of Virtue." In *The New Eighteenth Century: Theory, Politics, English Literature*, edited by Felicity Nussbaum and Laura Brown, 210–30. New York: Routledge, 1987.

Marshall, Cynthia. *The Shattering of the Self: Violence, Subjectivity, and Early Modern Texts*. Baltimore: The Johns Hopkins University Press, 2002.

Martin, B. W. "Wordsworth, Faber, and Keble: Commentary on a Triangular Relationship." *Review of English Studies* 26 (1975): 436–42.

Marx, Karl. Introduction to *Contribution to the Critique of Hegel's Philosophy of Right*. *Deutsch-Französische Jarbücher*, 1844. In *On Religion*, by Karl Marx and Friedrich Engels. Introduction by Reinhold Niebuhr, 41–58. New York: Schocken Books, 1964.

———, and Friedrich Engels. *On Religion*. Introduction by Reinhold Niebuhr. New York: Schocken Books, 1964.

Merrill, Christopher. *Things of the Hidden God: Journey to the Holy Mountain*. New York: Random House, 2005.

Miller, Perry. *The New England Mind: From Colony to Province*. Cambridge, Mass.: Harvard University Press, 1967.

Mills, David. "The Dreams of Bunyan and Langland." In The Pilgrim's Progress: *Critical and Historical Views*, edited by Newey, 154–81.

Milton, John. *Eikonoklastes*. Vol. 3 of *Complete Prose Works*, edited by Don. M. Wolfe. New Haven: Yale University Press, 1962.

Moallem, Minoo. *Between Warrior Brother and Sister Veiled: Islamic Foundation and the Politics of Patriarchy in Iran*. Berkeley: University of California Press, 2005.

Monter, William. *Ritual, Myth and Magic in Early Modern Europe*. Athens: Ohio University Press, 1983.

Moore, R. Laurence. *Selling God: American Religion in the Marketplace of Culture*. New York: Oxford University Press, 1994.

Morgan, Edmund. *Visible Saints: The History of a Puritan Idea*. Ithaca: Cornell University Press, 1963.

Morillo, John. *Uneasy Feelings: Literature, the Passions, and Class from Neoclassicism to Romanticism*. New York: AMS Press, 2001.

Mortensen, Preben. "Shaftesbury and the Morality of Art Appreciation." *Journal of the History of Ideas* 55 (1994): 631–50.

Motooka, Wendy. *The Age of Reasons: Quixotism, Sentimentalism, and Political Economy in Eighteenth-Century Britain*. London: Routledge, 1998.

Mounsey, Chris. *Christopher Smart: Clown of God*. Lewisburg, Pa.: Bucknell University Press, 2001.

Mullan, John. *Sentiment and Sociability: The Language of Feeling in the Eighteenth Century*. New York: Oxford University Press, 1988.

Mullett, Michael. *John Bunyan in Context*. Pittsburgh: Duquesne University Press, 1997.

Munns, Jessica, and Penny Richards, eds. *The Clothes that Wear Us: Essays on Dressing and Transgressing in Eighteenth-Century Culture*. Newark: University of Delaware Press, 1999.

Murray, Iain H. "The Directory for Public Worship." In *To Glorify and Enjoy God: A Commemoration of the 350th Anniversary of the Westminster Assembly*, edited by John L. Carson and David W. Hall, 169–91. Edinburgh: Banner of Truth Trust, 1994.

Nellist, Brian. "*The Pilgrim's Progress* and Allegory." In The Pilgrim's Progress: *Critical and Historical Views*, edited by Newey, 132–52.

Newey, Vincent. "Bunyan and the Confines of the Mind." Chap. 2 of his The Pilgrims Progress: *Critical and Historical Views*, 21–48.

———, ed. The Pilgrim's Progress: *Critical and Historical Views*. Totowa, N.J.: Barnes & Noble, 1980.

———. "'With the Eyes of My Understanding': Bunyan, Experience, and Acts of Interpretation." In *John Bunyan: Conventicle and Parnassus; Tercentenary Essays*, edited by Keeble, 189–216.

Newton, Isaac. *Opticks: or, A Treatise of the Reflections, Refractions, Inflections and Colours of Light.* London, 1717/18.

Newton, Thomas. *Of forms of prayer & particularly those of the Church of England, A Sermon Preach'd in the Parish Church of St. Mary-le-Bow, According to the last-will of Mr. John Hutchins Citizen & Goldsmith, On St. Mark's day, 1745, When there was a collection for the Charity Children. Three Sermons.* London: J. & R. Tonson and S. Draper, 1745.

Nicolson, Marjorie Hope. *The Breaking of the Circle: Studies in the Effect of the "New Science" upon Seventeenth-Century Poetry.* Evanston, Ill: Northwestern University Press, 1950.

Norton, Richard E. *The Beautiful Soul: Aesthetic Morality in the Eighteenth Century.* Ithaca: Cornell University Press, 1995.

Nussbaum, Felicity. "'By These Words I was Sustained': Bunyan's *Grace Abounding*." *English Literary History* 49 (1982): 18–34.

Nye, Eric. "The Most Perfect Protestant: Romantic Politics and Religion." Review of *Romantic Atheism*, by Martin Priestman, and *The Romantic Reformation*, by Robert Ryan. *Eighteenth-Century Studies* 35 (2002): 323–25.

Outram, Dorinda. *The Enlightenment.* New Approaches to European History 7. Cambridge: Cambridge University Press, 1995.

Owen, John. *A Discourse Concerning Liturgies, and Their Imposition.* London, 1662.

Owen, W. J. B., ed. *Lyrical Ballads, 1798.* 2nd ed. Oxford: Oxford University Press, 1969.

Paknadel, Felix. "Shaftesbury's Illustrations of *Characteristics*." *Journal of the Warburg and Courtland Institute* 37 (1974): 290–312.

Palumbo, Linda J. "The Later Wordsworth and the Romantic Ego: Bede and the Recreant Soul." *The Wordsworth Circle* 17 (1986): 181–84.

Peaston, A. E. *The Prayer Book Tradition in the Free Churches.* London: James Clarke, 1964.

Pelikan, Jaroslav. *The Christian Tradition: A History of the Development of Doctrine.* 5 vols. Chicago: University of Chicago Press, 1971–1989.

———. *Historical Theology: Continuity and Change in Christian Doctrine.* Philadelphia: Westminster Press, 1971.

Percy, Thomas. *The Life of Dr. Oliver Goldsmith.* Vol. 1 of *The Miscellaneous Works of Oliver Goldsmith, M.B., . . . in Four Volumes, to which is prefixed, Some Account of His Life and Works*, 1–118. 4 vols. London, 1801.

Perkins, William. *The Arte of Prophesying.* London, 1592.

Peters, F. E. *Greek Philosophical Terms: A Historical Lexicon.* New York: New York University Press, 1967.

Pettit, Norman. *The Heart Prepared: Grace and Conversion in Puritan Spiritual Life*. New Haven: Yale University Press, 1966.

Phelps, John. *A Vindication of Free and Unprescribed Prayer: In Some Remarks upon Dr. Newton's Sermon on the Liturgy of the Church of England, according to the Will of Mr. Hutchins. Inscribed to the Trustees of Mr. Hutchins's Charity*. London: M. Cooper, 1746.

Pinch, Adela. *Strange Fits of Passion: Epistemologies of Emotion, Hume to Austen*. Stanford: Stanford University Press, 1996.

Piozzi, Hester Lynch Thrale. *British Synonymy; or, An Attempt at Regulating the Choice of Words in Familiar Conversation*. London: G. G. & J. Robinson, 1794.

———. *Thraliana: The Diary of Mrs. Hester Lynch Thrale (later Mrs. Piozzi)*, edited by Katherine C. Balderston. 2nd ed. 2 vols. Oxford: Clarendon, 1951.

Pocock, J. G. A. "Enthusiasm: The Antiself of Enlightenment." In *Enthusiasm and Enlightenment in Europe, 1650–1850*, edited by Klein and La Vopa, 7–28.

———. *The Machiavellian Moment: Florentine Political Thought and the Atlantic Republican Tradition*. Princeton: Princeton University Press, 1975.

———. *Virtue, Commerce and History: Essays on Political Thought and History, Chiefly in the Eighteenth Century*. Cambridge: Cambridge University Press, 1985.

Poggemiller, Helmuth Carl. "Wordsworth's Concept of the Imagination in the *Ecclesiastical Sonnets*." Ph.D. diss., University of Toledo, 1980.

Polanyi, Karl. *The Great Transformation*. New York: Farrar & Rinehard, 1944.

Poole, Kristen. *Radical Religion from Shakespeare to Milton: Figures of Nonconformity in Early Modern England*. Cambridge: Cambridge University Press, 2000.

Pooley, Roger. "*Grace Abounding* and the New Sense of the Self." In *John Bunyan and His England, 1628–1688*, edited by Anne Laurence, W. R. Owens, and Stuart Sim, 105–14. London: Hambledon Press, 1990.

Poovey, Mary. "Aesthetics and Political Economy in the Eighteenth Century: The Place of Gender in the Social Constitution of Knowledge." In *Aesthetics and Ideology*, edited by George Levine, 79–105. New Brunswick, N.J.: Rutgers University Press, 1994.

Potts, Abbie Findlay. *The* Ecclesiastical Sonnets *of William Wordsworth: A Critical Edition*. New Haven: Yale University Press, 1922.

Powell, Vavasor. *Common-Prayer-Book No Divine Service: A Small Curb to the Bishops Careere: or, Imposed Liturgies Tried, The Common-prayer-book Anatomized, and Diocesan-Bishops Questioned*. London: Printed for Livewell Chapman, 1660.

Pratt, Mary Louise. "Presidential Address 2003: Language, Liberties, Waves, and Webs—Engaging the Present," *PMLA* 119 (2004): 417–28.

Preston, Thomas R. "Biblical Criticism, Literature, and the Eighteenth-Century Reader." In *Books and Their Readers in Eighteenth-Century England*, edited by Isabel Rivers, 97–126. Leicester: Leicester University Press, 1982.

Prickett, Stephen. *Romanticism and Religion: The Tradition of Coleridge and Wordsworth in the Victorian Church*. Cambridge: Cambridge University Press, 1976.

———. *Words and* The Word: *Language, Poetics and Biblical Interpretation*. Cambridge: Cambridge University Press, 1986.

Priestman, Martin. *Romantic Atheism: Poetry and Freethought, 1780–1830*. Cambridge: Cambridge University Press, 1999.

Prince, Michael. *Philosophical Dialogue in the British Enlightenment: Theology, Aesthetics and the Novel*. Cambridge: Cambridge University Press, 1996.

Prior, James. *The Life of Oliver Goldsmith, M.B.* London, 1837.

Quilligan, Maureen. *The Language of Allegory: Defining the Genre*. Ithaca: Cornell University Press, 1979.

Quintana, Richard. *Oliver Goldsmith: A Georgian Study*. New York: Macmillan, 1967.

Rambuss, Richard. *Closet Devotions*. Durham, N.C.: Duke University Press, 1998.

———. "The Prayer Closet." Chap. 3 of his *Closet Devotions*, 103–35.

Rand, Benjamin, ed. *The Life, Unpublished Letters, and Philosophical Regimen of Anthony, Earl of Shaftesbury*. London: Swan Sonnenschein, 1900.

Raphael, D. D. *The Moral Sense*. London: Oxford University Press, 1947.

Reiman, Donald, ed. *The Romantics Reviewed: Contemporary Reviews of British Romantic Writers. Part A: The Lake Poets*. 2 vols. New York: Garland Publishing, 1972.

Richardson, Alexander. *Logician's School-Master*. London, 1657.

Richardson, Samuel. *Clarissa: Or The History of a Young Lady. 1747–1748*, edited, introduction, and notes by Angus Ross. New York: Penguin, 1985.

———. *The Correspondence of Samuel Richardson*, edited by Anna Laetitia Barbauld. 6 vols. London, 1804.

———. *Selected Letters of Samuel Richardson*, edited and introduction by John Carroll. Oxford: Clarendon, 1964.

Rivers, Isabel. "The Religion of Grace: Baxter, Bunyan, and the Nonconformist Reaction." Chap. 3 of her *Reason, Grace, and Sentiment: A Study of the Language of Religion and Ethics in England, 1660–1780*. 2 vols. Cambridge

Studies in Eighteenth-Century Literature 8, 37, 89–163. Cambridge: Cambridge University Press, 1991.

Robinson, Marilynne. *Gilead: A Novel.* New York: Farrar, Straus & Giroux, 2004.

Rogers, Malcolm. "John and John Baptist Closterman: A Catalogue of Their Works." In *The Forty-Ninth Volume of the Walpole Society,* 224–76 and plates 11–73. London: Pitman, 1983.

———. *John Closterman: Master of the English Baroque, 1660–1711.* Exhibit catalogue, London: National Portrait Gallery, 1981.

Rogers, Pat. *Grub Street: Studies in a Subculture.* London: Methuen, 1972.

Ross, Ian Simpson. *The Life of Adam Smith.* Oxford: Clarendon, 1995.

Ross, Marlon. "Romancing the Nation State: The Poetics of Romantic Nationalism." In *Macropolitics of Nineteenth-Century Literature: Nationalism, Exoticism, Imperialism,* edited by Jonathan Arac and Harriet Ritvo, 56–85. Philadelphia: University of Pennsylvania Press, 1991.

Rothschild, Emma. *Economic Sentiments: Adam Smith, Condorcet, and the Enlightenment.* Cambridge, Mass.: Harvard University Press, 2001.

Rothstein, Eric, and Howard D. Weinbrot, "*The Vicar of Wakefield,* Mr. Wilmot, and the 'Whistonean Controversy.'" *Philological Quarterly* 55 (1976): 225–40.

Rousseau, G. S., ed. *Goldsmith: The Critical Heritage.* London: Routledge, 1974.

Rudy, Kathy. "Subjectivity and Belief." *Literature and Theology* 15 (2001): 224–40.

Ryan, Robert M. *The Romantic Reformation: Religious Politics in English Literature 1789–1824.* Cambridge: Cambridge University Press, 1997.

Rylstone, Anne L. *Prophetic Memory in Wordsworth's* Ecclesiastical Sonnets. Carbondale: Southern Illinois University Press, 1991.

Sade, Donatien Alphonse François. "Déclaration de Rose Kailair." In *L'affaire Kailair.* Vol. 4 of *Correspondances du marquis de Sade et de ses proches, enrichies du documents, notes et commentaires,* edited by Alice M. Laborde, 27 vols. to date, 26–30. Paris-Genève: Champion-Slatkine, 1991.

———. "Déposition de Jeanne Testard." In *Oeuvres completes du marquis de Sade,* edited by Gilbert Lely, 12:644–47. Paris: Cercle du Livre Précieux, 1966–67.

Sadler, Lynn Veach. *John Bunyan.* Boston: G. K. Hall, 1979.

Schaeffer, Neil. *The Marquis de Sade: A Life.* New York: Knopf, 1999.

Schmidt, Leigh Eric. "The Making of Modern 'Mysticism.'" *Journal of the American Academy of Religion* 71 (2003): 273–302.

Schneewind, J. B. *The Invention of Autonomy: A History of Modern Moral Philosophy.* Cambridge: Cambridge University Press, 1998.

Schoenfeldt, Michael. "The Gender of Religious Devotion: Amelia Lanyer and John Donne." In *Religion and Culture in Renaissance England*, edited by Claire McEachern and Debora Shuger, 209–233. Cambridge: Cambridge University Press, 1997.

Scott, Ian. "'Things As They Are': The Literary Response to the French Revolution, 1789–1815." In *Britain and the French Revolution 1789–1815*, edited by H. T. Dickinson, 229–49. London: Macmillan, 1989.

Scott, John. *Certain Cases of Conscience Resolved, Concerning the Lawfulness of Joyning with Forms of Prayer in Publick Worship*. London, 1683.

Seaver, Paul. *Wallington's World: A Puritan Artisan in Seventeenth-Century London*. Stanford: Stanford University Press, 1985.

Seed, David. "Dialogue and Debate in *The Pilgrim's Progress*." In The Pilgrim's Progress: *Critical and Historical Views*, edited by Newey, 69–90.

Shaftesbury, Anthony Ashley Cooper, Third Earl of. *An Inquiry Concerning Virtue, in Two Discourses*. 1699. Delmar, N.Y.: Scholars' Facsimiles & Reprints, 1991.

———. "An Inquiry concerning Virtue and Merit." In *Characteristicks of Men, Manners, Opinions, Times*, edited by Ayres, 1:193–274.

———. "A Letter Concerning Enthusiasm." In *Characteristicks of Men, Manners, Opinions, Times*, edited by Ayres, 1:7–33.

———. "Preface." 1698. In *Characteristicks of Men, Manners, Opinions, Times, Etc. To Which is Prefixed the Preface to the Select Sermons of Dr. Whichcote*, edited by John M. Robertson. 1900. Reprint, Bristol: Thoemmes Press, 1995.

———. *Shaftesbury Papers*. National Archives, Kew, Surrey, UK.

———. "Soliloquy: Or Advice to an Author." In *Characteristicks of Men, Manners, Opinions, Times*, edited by Ayres, 1:83–186.

Sharrock, Roger, ed. *Bunyan:* The Pilgrim's Progress; *A Casebook*. London: Macmillan, 1976.

———. *John Bunyan*. London: Macmillan, 1968.

———. "Life and Story in *The Pilgrim's Progress*." In The Pilgrim's Progress: *Critical and Historical Views*, edited by Newey, 49–68.

Shell, Marc. *The Economy of Literature*. Baltimore: The Johns Hopkins University Press, 1978.

———. *Money, Language, and Thought: Literary and Philosophical Economies from the Medieval to the Modern Era*. Berkeley: University of California Press, 1982.

Sherbo, Arthur. *Christopher Smart: Scholar of the University*. East Lansing: Michigan State University, 1967.

Sheriff, John K. *The Good-Natured Man: The Evolution of a Moral Ideal, 1660–1800.* Tuscaloosa: University of Alabama Press, 1982

A Short Catechism, for the Instruction of Young and Old. By R. C. Philo-Presbyt. Glasgow, 1720.

Shuger, Debora Kuller. *The Renaissance Bible: Scholarship, Sacrifice, and Subjectivity.* Berkeley: University of California Press, 1994.

Sill, Geoffrey M. *The Cure of the Passions and the Origins of the English Novel.* Cambridge: Cambridge University Press, 2001.

Sills, Adam. "Mr. Bunyan's Neighborhood and the Geography of Dissent." *English Literary History* 70 (2003): 67–87.

Sim, Stuart. *Negotiations with Paradox: Narrative Practice and Narrative Form in Bunyan and Defoe.* Savage, Md.: Barnes & Noble, 1990.

Simpson, David. *Wordsworth's Historical Imagination: The Poetry of Displacement.* New York: Methuen, 1987.

Sitter, John. *Literary Loneliness in Mid-Eighteenth-Century England.* Ithaca: Cornell University Press, 1982.

Skinner, Gillian. *Sensibility and Economics in the Novel, 1740–1800: The Price of a Tear.* London: Macmillan, 1999.

Skoglund, John. "Free Prayer." *Studia Liturgica* 10 (1974): 151–66.

Smart, Christopher. *The Annotated Letters of Christopher Smart*, edited by Betty Rizzo and Robert Mahony. Carbondale: Southern Illinois University Press, 1991.

———. "Hymn to the Supreme Being, on Recovery from a dangerous Fit of Illness" and "Hymn III. Epiphany." In *The Poetical Works of Christopher Smart.* Edited by Karina Williamson. 6 vols. 4:319–23 and 2:37–39. Oxford: Clarendon, 1980–1996.

———. *Jubilate Agno.* Vol. 1 of *The Poetical Works of Christopher Smart*, edited by Karina Williamson. 6 vols. Oxford: Clarendon, 1980.

Smith, Adam. *The Theory of Moral Sentiments*, edited by D. D. Raphael and A. L. Macfie. Indianapolis: Liberty Fund, 1984.

Smith, Christian. *Moral, Believing Animals: Human Personhood and Culture.* Oxford: Oxford University Press, 2003.

Smith, Nigel. *Literature and Revolution in England, 1640–1660.* New Haven: Yale University Press, 1994.

———. *Perfection Proclaimed: Language and Literature in English Radical Religion, 1640–1660.* Oxford: Clarendon, 1989.

Smith, Paul. *Discerning the Subject.* Minneapolis: University of Minnesota Press, 1988.

Spacks, Patricia Meyer. *The Poetry of Vision: Five Eighteenth-Century Poets.* Cambridge, Mass.: Harvard University Press, 1967.

Spinks, Bryan D. *Sacraments, Ceremonies and the Stuart Divines: Sacramental Theology and Liturgy in England and Scotland, 1603–1662.* Hants, UK: Ashgate, 2002.

Sprat, Thomas. *The History of the Royal Society of London, for the Improving of Natural Knowledge, Second edition, Corrected.* 1667. Reprint, London, 1702.

Spurr, John. *English Puritanism, 1603–1689.* London: Macmillan, 1998.

———. "From Puritanism to Dissent, 1660–1700." In *The Culture of English Puritanism, 1560–1700*, edited by Durston and Eales, 234–65.

Stallybrass, Peter and Allon White. *The Politics and Poetics of Transgression.* Ithaca: Cornell University Press, 1986.

Stater, Victor. Review of *Shaftesbury and the Culture of Politeness*, by Lawrence E. Klein. *Albion* 27 (1995): 126–28.

Sterne, Laurence. *A Sentimental Journey through France and Italy By Mr. Yorick, with The Journal to Eliza and A Political Romance*, edited by Ian Jack. Oxford: Oxford University Press, 1998.

Stonehill, Charles Archibald. *Anonyma and Pseudonyma.* New York: R. R. Bowker, 1927.

Straus, Nina Pelikan. "Dostoevsky's Derrida." *Common Knowledge* 8 (2002): 555–67.

Stuber, Florian. "Clarissa: A Religious Novel?" *Studies in the Literary Imagination* 28 (1995): 105–20.

Sullivan, Robert. "Rethinking Christianity in Enlightened Europe." *Eighteenth-Century Studies* 34 (2001): 298–309.

Swaim, Kathleen M. *Pilgrim's Progress, Puritan Progress: Discourses and Contexts.* Urbana: University of Illinois Press, 1993.

Sweetman, J. E. "Shaftesbury's Last Commission." *Journal of the Warburg and Courtland Institute* 19 (1956): 110–16.

Talon, Henri. *John Bunyan: The Man and His Works.* Translated by Barbara Wall. Cambridge, Mass.: Harvard University Press, 1951.

Targoff, Ramie. *Common Prayer: The Language of Public Devotion in Early Modern England.* Chicago: University of Chicago Press, 2001. See esp. chap. 2, "Reading Prayer: Spontaneity and Conformity."

Taves, Ann. *Fits, Trances, and Visions: Experiencing Religion and Explaining Experience from Wesley to James.* Princeton: Princeton University Press, 1999.

Tawney, R. H. *Religion and the Rise of Capitalism: A Historical Study*. 1922. Reprint, Gloucester, Mass.: Peter Smith, 1962.

Taylor, Mark. "Denegating God." Chap. 2 of his *About Religion: Economies of Faith in Virtual Culture*, 29–47. Chicago: University of Chicago Press, 1999.

Tiffany, Esther A. "Shaftesbury as Stoic." *PMLA* 38 (1923): 642–84.

Tindall, William York. *John Bunyan: Mechanick Preacher*. New York: Russell & Russell, 1964.

Todd, Janet M. *Sensibility: An Introduction*. London: Methuen, 1986.

Tomlinson, T. B. "The Secular Spirit of Milton's England: 1640s–1660s." *Literature and History* 10 (1984): 218–30.

Trilling, Lionel. *Sincerity and Authenticity*. Cambridge, Mass.: Harvard University Press, 1974.

Trussler, Simon. Introduction to *Everyman*, v–xxxv. London: Nick Hern Books, 1996.

Tumbleson, Raymond D. *Catholicism in the English Protestant Imagination: Nationalism, Religion, and Literature 1660–1745*. Cambridge: Cambridge University Press, 1998.

Turner, James. "Bunyan's Sense of Place." In The Pilgrim's Progress: *Critical and Historical Views*, edited by Newey, 91–110.

Uehlein, Friedrich. *Kosmos und Subjectivität: Lord Shaftesbury's Philosophical Regimen*. Freiburg: K. Alber, 1976.

Uehlein, Friedrich, et al., ed. *Shaftesbury Standard Edition*. 8 volumes (to date). Stuttgart: Friedrich Frommann Verlang–Günther Holzboog, 1981–.

Ulmer, William A. *The Christian Wordsworth, 1798–1805*. Albany: State University of New York Press, 2001.

Underwood, T. L. *Primitivism, Radicalism, and the Lamb's War: The Baptist-Quaker Conflict in Seventeenth-Century England*. New York: Oxford University Press, 1997.

Van Sant, Ann Jessie. *Eighteenth-Century Sensibility and the Novel: The Senses in Social Context*. Cambridge: Cambridge University Press, 1993.

Voitle, Robert. "Shaftesbury's Moral Sense." *Studies in Philology* 52 (1955): 17–38.

———. *The Third Earl of Shaftesbury, 1671–1713*. Baton Rouge: Louisiana State University Press, 1984.

Walker, Jeanne Murray. "*Jubilate Agno* as Psalm." *Studies in English Literature* 20 (1980): 449–59.

Wall, John. *Transformations of the Word: Spenser, Herbert, Vaughan*. Athens: University of Georgia Press, 1989.

Wallis, Roy, and Steve Bruce. "Secularization: The Orthodox Model." In *Religion and Modernization: Sociologists and Historians Debate the Secularization Thesis*, edited by Steve Bruce, 8–30. Oxford: Clarendon, 1992.

Ward, Graham. "The Commodification of Religion, or The Consummation of Capitalism." In *Theology and the Political: The New Debate*, edited by Creston Davis, John Milbank, and Slavoj Žižek, introduction by Rowan Williams, 327–39. Durham, N.C.: Duke University Press, 2005.

———. "Theology and the Crisis of Representation." In *Literature and Theology at Century's End*, edited by Gregory Salyer and Robert Detweiler, 131–58. American Academy of Religion Studies in Religion 72. Atlanta: Scholar's Press, 1995.

———. "To Be a Reader: Bunyan's Struggle with the Language of Scripture in *Grace Abounding to the Chief of Sinners*." *Journal of Literature and Theology* 4 (1990): 29–49.

———. *True Religion*. Oxford: Blackwell, 2003.

Wardle, Ralph M. *Oliver Goldsmith*. Lawrence: University of Kansas Press, 1957. Reprint, Hamden, Conn.: Archon Books, 1969.

Ware, Timothy. *The Orthodox Church*. Revised ed. New York: Penguin, 1993.

Warner, William B. *Licensing Entertainment: The Elevation of Novel Reading in Britain, 1684–1750*. Berkeley: University of California Press, 1998.

Watson, Nicola. "Footnoting the Romantic: Forms of History and *The White Doe of Rylstone*." *The Wordsworth Circle* 24 (1993): 141–43.

Watt, Ian. *The Rise of the Novel: Studies in Defoe, Richardson and Fielding*. Afterword by W. B. Carnochan. 1957. Reprint, Berkeley: University of California Press, 2001.

Watts, Isaac. *A Guide to Prayer. Or, A Free and Rational Account of the Gift, Grace and Spirit of Prayer, With Plain Directions how every Christian may attain them*. London: Printed for Emmanuel Matthews, 1715.

Watts, Michael. *The Dissenters*. 2 vols. Oxford: Oxford University Press, 1978.

Weber, Max. *The Protestant Ethic and the Spirit of Capitalism*. Translated by Stephen Kalberg. 1904. Reprint, Chicago: Fitzroy Dearborn, 2001.

Welsh, Charles. *A Bookseller of the Last Century: Being some Account of the Life of John Newbery, and of the Books he published, with a Notice of the later Newberys*. London: Griffith, Farran, Okeden & Welsh, 1885.

Westbrook, Deeanne. *Wordsworth's Biblical Ghosts*. New York: Palgrave, 2001.

Westphal, Merold, and Martin Matuštík, eds. *Kierkegaard in Post/Modernity*. Indianapolis: Indiana University Press, 1995.

White, Eugene. *Puritan Rhetoric: The Issue of Emotion in Religion.* Carbondale: Southern Illinois University Press, 1972.

White, Ronald C. *The Social Gospel: Religion and Reform in Changing America.* Philadelphia: Temple University Press, 1976.

Williamson, George. "The Restoration Revolt against Enthusiasm." *Studies in Philology* 30 (1933): 571–603.

Williamson, Karina. Introduction and appendix to *Jubilate Agno.* In *The Poetical Works of Christopher Smart,* edited by Karina Williamson, 6 vols., 1:xxiii–xxiv and 1:131–32. Oxford: Clarendon, 1980–1996.

Wind, Edgar. "Shaftesbury as a Patron of Art." *Journal of the Warburg and Courtland Institute* 2 (1938): 185–88.

Winquist, Charles. "Lacan and Theology." In *Post-Secular Philosophy: Between Philosophy and Theology,* edited by Phillip Blond, 305–17. London: Routledge, 1998.

Wolf, Richard B. "Shaftesbury's Just Measure of Irony." *Studies in English Literature* 33 (1993): 565–85.

Wolfe, Alan. "Scholars Infuse Religion with Cultural Light." *Chronicle of Higher Education* 51.9. 22 October 2004, B6.

Wordsworth, William. *Ecclesiastical Sonnets.* In *Poetical Works,* edited by Thomas Hutchinson, revised by Ernest de Selincourt, 329–55. Oxford: Oxford University Press, 1999.

———. *Lyrical Ballads, 1798,* edited by W. J. B. Owen. 2nd ed. Oxford: Oxford University Press, 1969.

———. Preface to the 1800 edition of *Lyrical Ballads.* In *Lyrical Ballads, 1798,* edited by Owen, 153–79.

———. *The Prelude: 1799, 1805, 1850,* edited by Jonathan Wordsworth, M. H. Abrams, and Stephen Gill. New York: Norton, 1979.

———. "The Tables Turned." In *Lyrical Ballads, 1798,* edited by Owen.

———. *The White Doe of Rylstone; or, The Fate of the Nortons, by William Wordsworth,* edited and introduction by Kristine Dugas. Ithaca: Cornell University Press, 1988.

Wotton, Sam[uel]. *A View of the Face Unmasked, or, an Answer to A Scandalous Pamphlet, published by divers Ministers, and Entituled [sic], The Common Prayer-Book Unmasked.* London: Thomas Newcomb, 1661.

Yack, Bernard. *The Longing for Total Revolution: Philosophical Sources of Social Discontent from Rousseau to Marx and Nietzsche.* Princeton: Princeton University Press, 1986.

Yates, Frances A. *The Art of Memory.* Chicago: University of Chicago Press, 1966.

Young, Edward. *Conjectures on Original Composition*. 1759. Reprint, Leeds, U.K.: Scolar Press, 1966.

———. *Young's Night Thoughts, with Life, Critical Dissertation, and Explanatory Notes by the Rev. George Gilfillan*. Edinburgh, 1853.

Zaret, David. *The Heavenly Contract: Ideology and Organization in Pre-Revolutionary Puritanism*. Chicago: University of Chicago Press, 1985.

Žižek, Slavoj. *The Fragile Absolute—Or, Why Is the Christian Legacy Worth Fighting for?* London: Verso, 2001.

———. "An Interview with Slavoj Žižek: 'On Divine Self-Limitation and Revolutionary Love,'" *Journal of Philosophy and Scripture* 1 (2004): 1–7.

———. *The Puppet and the Dwarf: The Perverse Core of Christianity*. Cambridge, Mass.: MIT Press, 2003.

———. *The Sublime Object of Ideology*. London: Verso, 1989.

———. "Why Is Every Act a Repetition?" Chap. 3 of his *Enjoy Your Symptom! Jacques Lacan in Hollywood and Out*, 69–110. New York: Routledge, 1992.

Index

Abrams, M. H., 176, 178, 284n33, 288n53
abstraction, 24, 244n48, 247n67; secularization and, 246n66. *See also* sublimation; Derrida; "outbidding" as a structure of reason
academic discourse (of knowledge), 28–29, 241n26
Achinstein, Sharon, 252n42
Act of Uniformity of 1549, 38
Act of Uniformity of 1661–1662, 2, 39, 40, 239n20
Act of Union of 1707, 258n11
Acts and Monuments (Foxe), 286n44
Acts of the Apostles, 266n75
Adams, John Charles, 244n52
Adams, Thomas, 255n55
Adorno, Theodor, 24
"Advertisement" to *Lyrical Ballads* of 1798 (Wordsworth), 179–80
Aeolian harp, 136, 166
agency, 6–7, 12, 14–15, 18, 22, 59, 69–70, 71, 81, 138, 157, 163–72, 177–78, 182, 184–90, 197–204, 205, 206–9, 213–14, 247n67, 249n23, 288n59
Ainsworth, Michael, 92
Alexander III (pope), 195
Alexander, Hugh, 110 fig. 4, 132 fig. 11
alienation, 56–58, 244n48
allegory, 252n42
Allen, Don Cameron, 227n7
Allen, Edmund, 145
Althusser, Louis, 30
Altizer, Thomas J. J., 213
American Society for Eighteenth-Century Studies, 222
Anatomie of the Common Prayer-Book, 43
Anderson, Benedict, 244n50
Anglicanism and Anglican Church. *See* Church of England
Anselm of Canterbury, 65, 68, 233n64
Anthony, St., 122
anti-Semitism, 120, 269n89
anxiety, 56, 58, 59–61, 242n37
Appleby, Joyce, 234n69
Aristotle, 233n64

Arte of Prophesying (Perkins), 244n49
Asad, Talal, 5, 7, 12, 19, 31, 60, 104, 105, 108, 214, 218, 231n39
ASECS. *See* American Society for Eighteenth-Century Studies
Ashley-Cooper, Maurice (brother of 3rd earl of Shaftesbury), 127, 131, 132
Ασκηματα, or "Exercises" (Shaftesbury), 10, 32, 91, 96–122, 110 fig. 4, 124, 129, 130, 136, 162, 269n1; secular corollary to *Grace Abounding*, 97; self-splitting in, 106, 133; manuscript/textual information, 99–100, 256n1, 261nn45–47, 264n61, 268n85; relation to "Soliloquy," 263n57
Aston, Margaret, 237n9, 237n10
atheism, 102, 119, 268n84
atonement, theology of, 64–66, 248n8; classical view, 65; Latin view, 65
Augustine, St., 216
Aulén, Gustaf, 65, 241n26
Aurelius, Marcus, 102, 119, 130, 133, 263n58
author and author function, 85, 134
Authorized Version, 256n59

Bailey, Matthew, 270n11
baptism, 37, 38, 53, 237n12, 245n53, 245n54
Baptists, 239n20, 239n21, 242n33; Particular Open Communion, 249n17
Barker, Francis, 37
Barker-Benfield, G. J., 16, 18, 135, 151, 267n81, 273n4
Barnard, John (i.e., Richard Barnard; pseud. DWALPHIN-TRAMIS), 242n34
Barnes, Andrew, 236n3
Barrell, John, 130, 267n81
Barrowists, 238n16
Bastille, 187
Batho, Edith, 288n53
Baudrillard, Jean, 212
Baxter, Richard, 40, 242n33, 252n39
Be Merry and Wise, 144
Beaumont, Sir George, 191
Bede, Venerable, 193
Belanger, Terry, 274n21
Belgrad, Daniel, 227n3
belief, 5, 221, 225; disavowal of, 222; modernity and, 31; as radically exterior, 6; 184–85. *See also* faith
Bender, John, 147–48, 173
Benedict, Barbara, 229n27, 278n69
Benjamin, Jessica, 133–34, 267n81, 272n28
Bentham, Jeremy, 96
Berkeley, George, 258n8, 279n91
Bethnal Green, 159
Bible and Sun, Sign of, 135, 137, 167
Bible. *See individual books of and* Authorized Version; biblical literalism; Geneva Bible; Scripture
biblical literalism, 76, 98, 234n86; of Bunyan, 64
Blackwood's Edinburgh Magazine, 181
blood, 76–77
"Blossoms of Morality," 142
Bodleian library, 8, 241n30
Bonaparte, Napoleon, 195
book form, 133. *See also* print culture and market

Book of Common Prayer, 8, 11, 38, 39, 47, 150, 154, 199–200, 235n1, 242n33; banning of, 52; imposition of, 42; Prayer Book of 1559, 38
Book of Martyrs (Foxe). *See Acts and Monuments* (Foxe)
Borderers, The (Wordsworth), 182
Bossy, John, 236n3
Boswell, James, 174, 279n80
Bouwsma, William, 23, 24, 41, 58, 242n37, 247n68
Boyle, Robert, 64, 272n30
Brachlow, Stephen, 239n21
Bradshaigh, Lady Dorothy, 136
Brain, Russell, 279n81
Brainard, Marcus, 125–26, 269n5
Branch, Lori, 234n77, 251n31, 256n58, 258n11
Bredvold, Louis I., 229n23
Breward, Iain H., 245n53
Brewer, John, 240n23
Brissenden, R. F., 15, 155, 157
British Critic, The, 180
British National Archives. *See* Public Record Office
Britten, Benjamin, 163
Bromwich, David, 284n33
Brown, Marshall, 278n69
Browning, Robert, 174
Brownists, 238n16
Bruce, Steve, 228n9
Brunström, Conrad, 21, 243n38
Bunyan, John, 9, 22, 23, 28, 47, 51, 58, 61, 63–89, 97, 100, 103, 134, 174, 201, 205, 206, 234n86; anxiety, 71; covenant theology of, 64–65, 81–82, 248n5; conversion of, 68–69, 70, 250n24, 250n25; daughter (Mary) born blind, 252n34; disclaiming locutions of, 249n23; early life and spiritual awakening, 68; economic nature of spiritual crisis, 73, 251n31; enthusiasm of, 71; gold imagery, 69, 71–72, 80; hope for spiritual relation, 87–89; psychological resistance to rationalization, 71; Puritanism and, 249n17; rationalization and, 71; connection between *Grace Abounding* and *Pilgrim's Progress*, 67–68, 78, 248n14; self-scrutiny, 71; separatism and, 249n17; skepticism and suspicion of experiences, 70; spiritual crisis, 71–78; temptation to sell Christ, 71–78; use of Geneva Bible and Authorized Version, 256n59; chief symptom of his theology, 74; wounds and resistances of his spirituality, 76–78
Bunyan, John, works of: *Doctrine of Law and Grace Unfolded*, 65; *Grace Abounding to the Chief of Sinners*, 9, 33, 61, 66–78, 97, 100, 134; *I Will Pray with the Spirit*, 9, 43–45, 63–64, 66, 76; *Israel's Hope Encouraged*, 66; *Mapp Shewing the Order & Causes of Salvation & Damnation*, 253n46; *The Pilgrim's Progress*, 9, 32, 61, 67–68, 79–87, 133, 134, 136, 147, 152; *Saints Privilege and Profit*, 66
Burke, Edmund, 96, 183, 260n30
Burnet, Thomas, 257n3
Burney, Charles, 142, 143, 145
Burney, Frances, 174
Bushell, Sally, 287n50
Butler, Joseph (Bp.), 118
Butler, Judith, 244n52
Byzantium, 75

Calvin, John, 24, 37, 237n12; secularizing influence of, 247n68
Calvinism, 37; experimental, 241n29; violent spirituality, 77
Campbell, Gordon, 85, 249n17, 256n59
Canonbury House, Islington, 144, 145–146, 172, 276n43
capitalism and early capitalist development, 26, 29, 41, 240n23, 248n15; in sixteenth- and seventeenth-century England, 65–66; relation to covenant theology, 26–27; relation to free prayer, 66; Wordsworth's criticism of, 183, 192–93
Caputo, John, 14, 31–32, 212, 213, 214–16, 220–221, 222, 246n64
Carlton, Peter, 249n23, 251n31
Carnan, Anna Maria, 143, 144, 158, 159, 172, 276n43
Carnan, William, 140
Carpini, John Delli, 285n37
Carracci, Agostino, Annibale, and Ludovico, 121
Cassirer, Ernst, 23
Certain Cases of Conscience Resolved (J. Scott), 242n33
Certeau, Michel de, 284n36, 288n59
Chakrabarty, Dipesh, 21
Character of an Old English Puritane or Non-Conformist, 238n16
Characteristicks (Shaftesbury), 10, 97, 98, 120, 201, 258n9; illustrations of, 10, 122, 123–34, 271n25, 272n29
charity. *See* love
Charles I, 46
Charles II, 23, 261n43

Cherbury. *See* Herbert of Cherbury, Lord.
Chinese Letters (Goldsmith), republished as *The Citizen of the World*, 146, 276n42
Christ. *See* Jesus Christ. *See also* God; Trinity
Christian (protagonist of *Pilgrim's Progress*), 68, 81–85
Christian doctrine, historical development of, 248n8
Christian's New Year's Gift, The, 142
Christianity, 102, 119, 215–16, 219, 221, 223–24, 268n87. *See also* Christian doctrine; Eastern Orthodox Christianity; Protestantism; Roman Catholicism; Western Christianity
Christmas, 36, 200
Church Building Act of 1818, 190–91
Church of England, 191; use of logic of free prayer/spontaneity, 238n18
church year, English, 36; decline of, 36–43, 246n63; in Smart, 163; in Wordsworth, 199
Citizen of the World, The (Goldsmith), 146, 147
Clarissa (S. Richardson), 117, 136, 156
Clark, J. C. D., 232n49
Clark, Jonathan, 256n1, 266n74
class, economic, 101–3, 115, 120. *See also* economics and economic rationality
Clifford, Alan, 52
Closterman, John Baptist (brother of John), 270n11, 271n25
Closterman, John, 10, 126, 126 fig. 7, 127, 129 figs. 8–9, 131,

132, 132 fig. 10, 133, 270n11, 270n14, 271nn24–25; amanuensis relationship with 3rd Earl of Shaftesbury, 123, 270n11
clothing metaphors, 51–52, 244n52
Cohen, Charles Lloyd, 236n5
Cole, Stephen, 207, 208, 288n58
Coleridge, Samuel Taylor, 202, 255n55, 284n36
Collection of Pretty Poems for the Amusement of Children Six Foot High (Smart), 144, 275n27
Collection of Pretty Poems for the Amusement of Children Three Feet High (Smart), 144
Collinson, Patrick, 23–24, 37, 236n8, 237n14, 239n21, 242n37, 246n63
commodity fetishism, 248n16
Common Prayer. *See* Book of Common Prayer
Common Prayer-Book Unmasked (Barnard), 43, 46, 242n34, 245n55
Common-Prayer-Book No Divine Service (Powell), 242n33
communion. *See* Eucharist; Lord's Supper
Companion to the Festivals and Fasts of the Church of England (Nelson), 163
Compendium of Biography (Goldsmith), 146
Congregationalists, 239n20
Conjectures on Original Composition (Young), 1, 160
contracts and contractarian world view, 81–82, 241n26
Contributions of William Wordsworth to the Revival of Catholic Truths (Wilkinson), 206
conversion, 37; in Bunyan, 68–69, 70, 81–82, 250n24, 250n25; Puritan morphology of, 236n5
Conway, Allison, 130–31, 270n19
Cooper, Anthony Ashley. *See* Shaftesbury, 3rd Earl of (Anthony Ashley Cooper)
Coote, Stephen, 277n45
Cope, Kevin, 248n4
Cornell, Drucilla, 222
Costa, Dennis, 279n91, 280n102, 281n104
covenant theology, 26–27, 41, 64–66, 81; Bunyan's, 64–65, 76, 81–82, 248n5
Cowell, Andrew, 248n15
Craftsman's Nosegay, The, 280n103
Crane, R. S., 15
Cressy, David, 235n1
crisis of representation. *See* representation, early modern crisis of
Critical, The, 146
criticism, literary: religiousness of, 211–25; "return of religion" to, 211–16, 220–25; high theory, 213; secular assumptions of, 18; binary view of religion and secularism, 232n49. *See also* scholarship
Cropley, Sir John, 272n29
Cur Deus Homo? (Anselm), 65, 68
Curtis, Susan, 277n55

Damrosch, Leopold, Jr., 252n35, 253n46, 254n48
Darwall, Stephen, 257n6
Davie, Donald, 255n55
Davies, Horton, 40, 236n3, 237n12, 238n17, 239n21
Davies, Michael, 250n28
Davies, Thomas, 144, 146
DaVinci, Leonardo. *See* Leonardo da Vinci

326 Index

Dawbeny, Henry, 48–52, 243n44
De Religione Gentilium (Herbert of Cherbury), 25
De Sacra Poesi Hebraeorum (Lowth), 161
De Veritate (Herbert of Cherbury), 25
Dearnley, Moira, 280n95
"death of God" theology, 213
Debate Concerning the English Liturgy (Ley), 35–36, 40–41, 43
deconstruction, 220
Defence of Poetry (Shelley), 176
Defoe, Daniel, 32, 152
Deists, 259n18
Deity, Shaftesbury's, 101–4, 116–20, 121, 134, 207, 263n48, 272n28. *See also* God
Deleuze, Gilles, 28
Deprun, Jean, 242n37
Derrida, Jacques, 14, 28, 32, 98, 211, 212–14, 215, 221, 234n86, 246n64, 247n67, 256n58, 267n77; "outbidding" as a mechanistic structure of reason, 121, 247n66, 269n92
Deserted Village, The (Goldsmith), 147, 151, 157
desire, 87–89, 109–13
Devlin, Christopher, 159–60, 274n24, 275n32, 275n34, 276n40, 278n72, 279nn83–84, 279nn86–87
Directory for the Publique Worship of God, 39, 43, 46, 52–56, 54 fig. 1; anxiety and, 56; as help and furniture, 55–56; material objects and, 245n54; public distaste for, 245n53; regulation of spontaneity, 53–55; relation to contemporary Protestant worship, 52, 245n53; relation to previous prayer books, 53; understanding of language in, 55; doubt of the praying subject, 55
Discourse addressed to the Congregation at the Chapel in Essex Street (Lindsey), 238n18
Discourse Concerning Liturgies, and Their Imposition (Owens), 243n41
disembodiment, 109–113
Disraeli, Isaac, 255n55
Dissent and Dissenters, 40, 238n17; and economic rationality, 26–29; as rationalizing and secularizing, 23, 25, 232n53; definition, 239n20; guides to free prayer, 56–58; Lord's Prayer as used by, 58. *See also* Nonconformists
Dix, Dom Gregory, 235n1
Doctrine of Law and Grace Unfolded (Bunyan), 65
Donne, John, 266n76
Donoghue, Frank, 277n58
Donoghue, William, 17, 250n26
doubt, benefit of, 33, 234n77, 256n58
Douglas, C. E., 237n9
Dr. James's Fever Powders, 142, 157, 276n43
Draper, John, 254n48
dreams, 85, 86 fig. 2, 109–13, 110 fig. 4, 134
Duffy, Eamon, 235n1, 237n9
Dugas, Kristine, 284n36
Duke Humfrey's library, 8, 241n30
Durkheim, Emile, 246n63
Durston, Christopher, 39, 236n8, 238n16, 245n53
DWALPHINTRAMIS. *See* Barnard, John
Dwyer, John Alfred, 230n35
Dykstal, Timothy, 152, 277n55

Eagleton, Terry, 10, 93, 257n6
Eales, Jacqueline, 236n8, 238n16
Easter, 36
Eastern Christianity. *See* Eastern Orthodox Christianity
Eastern churches. *See* Eastern Orthodox Christianity
Eastern Orthodox Christianity, 65, 214, 233n64
Ecclesiastical Sketches (Wordsworth), 176, 181, 191. *See also* Ecclesiastical Sonnets
Ecclesiastical Sonnets (Wordsworth), 13, 177, 190–209; Book of Common Prayer, 199–200; church building and self-construction, 197–204; church year, 199; faith, 202–4; hope, 200–201; liturgy and ritual, 197–204; love, 197–204; monasticism, 194, 202–3; music and song, 197–98; notes to, 286n40; prayer, 192; recuperation of labor, 192–93; resistance to violence, 192; threat of power, 194; sympathy with power, 195–96
Echlin, Lady Elizabeth, 136
Eclectic Review, The, 181
economic development. *See* capitalism and early capitalist development
economic discourse, 28–29, 241n26
economics and economic rationality, 4, 5, 8, 9, 12, 14–15, 16–17, 20–21, 23, 24, 26–29, 31, 32, 40–42, 47–52, 57–60, 64–68, 68–78, 79–89, 106, 124, 129, 134, 135, 136–139, 146–147, 151, 152–157, 161–163, 169–174, 194, 204, 209; covenant theology and, 26–27, 65–66; development in sixteenth- and seventeenth-century England, 65–66; in *Grace Abounding*, 68–71; Newbery's enterprise, 139–147; spontaneity, free prayer and, 48–52; faith and, 26–29; relationship to epistemology, 48–52; religious resistance to, 173. *See also* class, economic; economic discourse
Eden, 30
Edinburgh Review, The, 180
Edward VI, 38
effeminacy and anti-effeminacy, 114, 116, 267n81
ego (Lacanian), 251n32
Eikon Basilike (Charles I), 46
Eikonoklastes (Milton), 46
Eire, Carlos, 24, 236n2, 247n68
Elizabeth I, 38
Ellis, Markman, 16, 20, 283n12
Ellison, Julie, 16, 20, 136–37, 267n81
emotional correctness, 21, 45, 243n38
empiricism and empirical reasoning, 2, 4, 5, 6, 8, 12, 17, 20, 21, 22, 24, 27, 29, 41, 42, 47, 50, 56, 59, 64, 66, 70, 78, 79, 85, 88, 92, 94, 96, 98, 119, 160, 171, 173, 177, 179, 180, 182, 184, 185, 196, 201, 217, 231n44, 233n59, 250n26, 252n41
English Civil Wars, 239n21
English Protestantism. *See* Protestantism
Enlightenment: accelerating systematization and, 24; as itself enthusiastic, 250n29; construction of mysticism, 246n64; attempts to preserve enchantment, 4; enthusiasm and, 3–4;

rationality and, 23; fantasy of secular space, 22
Enlightenment, Scottish, 93
enthusiasm, 9, 59, 134, 194, 234n86; and Enlightenment, 3–4; as a term of abuse, 239n20; connection to rationalization and enlightenment, 71, 250n29; revolt against, 91; secular transvaluation of, 247n2; Shaftesbury's "true enthusiasm," 93–94, 98, 133, 152
Epictetus, 102, 119, 130, 263n58
Erasmus, Desiderius, 37, 236n3
Erickson, Robert A., 17
Esau, 73, 75, 81
Essay on the nature and Conduct of the Passions and Affections (Hutcheson), 259n19, 259n22
"Essay on the Theatre, An" (Goldsmith), 147
Eucharist, 165. *See also* Lord's Supper
Evangelical History of our Lord Jesus Christ, The, 141
evangelism, 79–81, 134, 152, 199; Puritan view, 252n41. *See also* proselytism
Everyman, 41
Excursion, The (Wordsworth), 180, 190, 287n50
"Exercises" (Shaftesbury). See Ασκηματα; Shaftesbury, 3rd Earl of (Anthony Ashley Cooper), works of
experiment, 41, 241n29
experimental theology, 68
"Expostulation and Reply" (Wordsworth), 179, 182

Faber, Frederick William, 177, 282n6
Fable of the Bees (Mandeville), 259n18

faith, 5, 14, 167–68, 212–16, 217–18, 225; Derridean, 247n67; economic rationality and, 26–29; indeterminism and, 247n67; linguistic turn and, 7; Wordsworth's sense of, 178, 197. *See also* belief
Fancy, 115–17, 119, 266n72
fantasy, 118–119; fantasy-supplement, 121, 269n89
Female Quixote, The (Lennox), 17
feminine, the, 98
Fenwick, Isabella, 187
Fielding, Henry, 152
Finley, C. Stephen, 255n55
Firmin, Giles, 245n55
Firth, Sir Charles, 255n55
Fish, Stanley, 211, 250n28, 252n42, 266n76
Florist, or Poetical Nosegay and Drawing Book, The, 280n103
forms of prayer. *See* liturgy
Forrest, James F., 254n48, 255n55
Forster, John, 276n41, 276n43
Foucault, Michel de, 19, 134, 240n24
Foxe, John, 286n44
Frederick Barbarossa, Emperor, 195
freedom. *See* agency
Freemasons and Freemasonry, 3, 161
free-prayer, 2, 8, 34–61, 63–64, 133, 176, 201, 238n16, 239n21; alienation and, 51–52; anxiety and, 52, 58, 59–61; as basis of religious community, 49–50; as blood from a wound, 76–77; as clothing or costume, 51–52, 244n52; as culmination of crisis of representation, 8; as "evidence of the Spirit," 43–48; connection to secular, commercial culture, 59; discourses of

Index 329

evidence, exchange, and emotional experience and, 8, 42, 43–48; economic discourse and, 48–52, 243n45; economic rationality of, 66; freedom/liberty of, 46, 64; guidebooks to, 56–58; logic of spontaneity and, 42; lesson of, 27; makes private into public prayer, 50; misery, 45; moral sense similarities to, 92; pamphlets and tracts about, 241n30; resulting in skepticism, 61; Wordsworth's use of, 176. *See also* prayer, spontaneous prayer
French Revolution, 177, 178, 182, 187, 196, 201
Frere, W. H., 237n9
Friends, Society of, 239n20, 242n33, 286n43
Froude, J. A., 255n55
fundamentalism, 5, 222, 291n43; secularism and, 32, 222
Furly, Benjamin, 99

Galilei, Galileo. *See* Galileo
Galileo, 41, 92
Garber, Marjorie, 244n52
Gardner, Thomas, 145
Garrick, David, 145
Gassendi, Pierre, 259n16
Gates, Barbara T., 285n37
Gedalof, Allan J., 279n91
Genesis, book of, 30, 234n82
Geneva Bible, 256n59
Gentleman Tradesman's and Traveller's Pocket Library, The, 171
Gibbons, B. J., 232n53
Gibbs, J. M. W., 276n42
Gilfillan, George, 227n2
Gill, Stephen, 206, 282n7, 288n53
God (Christian Trinity), 21, 29, 30, 31, 32, 44, 57, 58, 60, 61, 63, 69, 72, 75, 76, 78, 83, 95, 101–4, 121, 156, 170, 207, 225, 263n48, 268n87; beyond exchange, 87–89; extravagant generosity and love of, 170, 171; "having God," 47–48; intersubjectivity of, 167; love of, 77, 170; Reformed God, 249n23, 266n76; violation of God, 116–20. *See also* Deity, Shaftesbury's; Trinity
god. *See* Deity, Shaftesbury's
gold, 69, 71–72, 80
Goldman, Peter, 252n35, 252n39
Goldsmith, Oliver, 11, 137–139, 144, 147–57, 183; death, 172; debt, 172; early life, 145; lodging at Canonbury House, 145–46; work for John Newbery, 145–46
Goldsmith, Oliver, works of: *Chinese Letters*, republished as *The Citizen of the World*, 146, 276n42; *The Citizen of the World*, 146, 147; *Compendium of Biography*, 146; *The Deserted Village*, 147, 151, 157; "An Essay on the Theatre," 147; *The Good Natur'd Man*, 147; *History of England, A*, 146; *Life of Christ, The*, 146; *Life of the Fathers*, 146; *Millennium Hall* (Scott), edited by Goldsmith, 146; *The Traveller*, 146, 151, 157; *She Stoops to Conquer*, 147; *Vicar of Wakefield*, 7, 11, 12, 137–39, 146, 147–57, 183
Good Natur'd Man, The (Goldsmith), 147
Gordon, Scott Paul, 18, 19, 22, 229n19, 231n37, 249n23, 257n6
Grace Abounding to the Chief of Sinners (Bunyan), 9, 33, 61,

66–78, 97, 100, 134; blood imagery, 77; crisis after spiritual evidence, 71–72; disclaiming locutions in, 249n23; economic nature of spiritual crisis, 73, 251n31; Esau, 73, 75; God, 69, 72, 75, 76, 77, 78, 88–89; gold, 69, 71–72; knowledge and exchange, 68–71; Jesus Christ, 74–76, 77, 88–89; love, 69–70, 73, 75; relation to covenant theology, 69, 76; relation to *Pilgrim's Progress*, 67–68, 78, 79–87, 248n14; temptation to sell Christ, 71–78; search for tokens of godliness, 68–71, 82
Grand Debate (Baxter), 242n33
Gravil, Richard, 283n9
Grazia, Margreta de, 41
Grean, Stanley, 97, 257n6, 258n14
Great Ejection of 1662, 40
Great Fire of London of 1666, 91
Great Schism of 1054, 233n64
Great Transformation, 27
Greaves, Richard L., 248n5, 249n19, 255n55
Greenblatt, Stephen, 131
Greene, Donald, 15, 229n23
Greene, Thomas M., 235n2
Greenhill, John, 271n24
Gregory VII (pope), 286n44
Gribelin, Simon, 125, 126, 134
Griffin, William, 144, 146
Griffiths, Ralph, 144
Grub Street, 140, 157, 160, 161
Grumbling Hive (Mandeville), 259n18
Guest, Harriet, 161
Guide to Prayer (I. Watts), 45–47, 56
Guilhamet, Leon, 3, 242n36
Gunton, Colin E., 248n8
Guthrie, William, 142

Haakonssen, Knud, 23
Habermas, Jürgen, 233n59
Hades, 75
Hall-Stevenson, John, 280n103
Hambrick-Stowe, Charles, 236n6
Hammond, Brean, 161, 255n50
Hardin, Richard, 254n48
Harkin, Maureen, 152, 157, 278n60, 278n69
Hartman, Geoffrey, 161, 282n8
Hawes, Clement, 159, 161, 167, 279n81, 279n83
Hawkes, David, 251n31
Hawkins, Anne, 250n25
Hayes, Alan L., 239n21
Hegel, Georg Wilhelm Friedrich, 29–30, 216, 247n66
Heidegger, Martin, 212
Heinzelman, Kurt, 27–28
hell, 83
Henrican Reformation of 1529–1537, 38, 237n9
Henry IV (HRE), 286n44
Henry, Matthew, 33, 45, 56–58, 61, 171, 245n59
Herbert of Cherbury, Lord, 25, 32, 214
Herbert, George, 136, 235n1
Herreshoff, David, 255n50
Hervieu-Léger, Danièle, 5, 6, 14, 19, 31, 33, 206, 217, 225, 235n89, 290n24
hesychasm, 233n64
Hewitt, Regina, 190–191
Heyd, 239n20, 250n29, 259n18
Hill, Christopher, 64–65, 81, 85, 233n67, 240n23, 246n63, 248n14, 249n19, 249n22, 251n31, 252n41, 254n48, 255n50
Hill, John, 143
"Hilliad, The" (Smart), 144
History of England, A (Goldsmith), 146

History of Little Goody Two-Shoes, 142
history, 208
Hobbes, Thomas, 9, 15, 18, 26, 91, 96, 196, 257n4
Holy Ghost. *See* Holy Spirit
Holy Spirit, 50; rivers of living water, 191, 285n39; sin against, 251n31
Holy Week, 36
Home, Henry, Lord Kames, 118
Hooke, Robert, 41
Hooker, Richard, 38, 200
hope, 87–89, 200–201
Hopkins, Robert, 277n52
Horace, 143
Horkheimer, Max, 24
House of Commons, 99
House of Lords, 99
Huet, Marie-Hélène, 178
Hugh de St. Victor, 233n64
Hughes, Kenneth J., 285n37
Humble Remonstrance, 239n21
Hume, David, 10, 94, 95, 98, 118, 120, 177
Humphrey Clinker (Smollett), 156
Hunter, Christopher, 279n87
Huntington Library, 86 fig. 2
Hutcheson, Francis, 48, 92, 94–95, 96, 121, 135, 179, 196, 205, 257n3, 259n18, 259n19, 260n30
Hutcheson, Francis, works of: *Inquiry into the Original of Our Ideas of Beauty and Virtue ... in Two Treatises*, 94, *Inquiry into the Original of Our Ideas of Beauty and Virtue ... Treatise II: An Inquiry Concerning Moral Good and Evil*, 95 fig. 3; *An Essay on the nature and Conduct of the Passions and Affections*, 259n19, 259n22; *Illustrations upon the Moral Sense*, 259n19, 259n22
Hutton, Ronald, 36, 237n9, 245n53; criticism of materialistic determinism, 246n63
"Hymn to the Supreme Being, On recovery from a dangerous fit of illness" (Smart), 157–158
Hymns and Spiritual Songs (Smart), 171–72
hypocrisy, in prayer, 44

I Will Pray with the Spirit (Bunyan), 9, 43–45, 63–64, 66, 76
ideology critique, 220
ideology of objectivity, 23, 42, 119, 272n30
ideology of spontaneity, 6, 11, 42; and love, 14; and prayer, 14. *See also* spontaneity
ideology, 30, 85
Idler, The, 140, 275n27
Ignorance (character in *Pilgrim's Progress*), 82–83, 84–85, 254n48
Illustrations upon the Moral Sense (Hutcheson), 259n19, 259n22
imaginary, the (Lacanian), 251n32
impossible kernel. *See* kernel, impossible
Incarnation, 121
Independents, 238n16; definition of, 239n20
indeterminacy and indeterminacies of language, 12, 14, 214, 215; occasion for faith and freedom, 247n67. *See also* linguistic turn
Index to the Sermons published since the Restoration, 141
Inquiry Concerning Virtue (Shaftesbury), 92, 93, 258n13; revised as "An Inquiry Concerning Virtue and Merit," 257n5

"Inquiry Concerning Virtue and Merit" (Shaftesbury), 258n7, 269n1. *See also Inquiry Concerning Virtue*
Inquiry into the Original of Our Ideas of Beauty and Virtue ... in Two Treatises (Hutcheson), 94
Inquiry into the Original of Our Ideas of Beauty and Virtue ... Treatise II: An Inquiry Concerning Moral Good and Evil (Hutcheson), 95 fig. 3
insincerity, 63–64. *See also* hypocrisy
Interregnum, 91
Irenaeus, St., 167
Irigaray, Luce, 212
Irlam, Shaun, 4, 219, 239n20, 240n24
Irving, Washington, 146, 277n50
Iser, Wolfgang, 253n45
Israel's Hope Encouraged (Bunyan), 66

Jaffro, Laurent, 97, 261n38, 263n57, 264n64, 268n86
Jeffrey, Francis, 180
Jesus Christ, 24, 25, 30, 50, 57–58, 64–65, 74, 75–76, 77, 88–89, 100, 117–18, 120–22, 165, 167, 168–69, 171, 191, 199, 216, 245n54, 267n79, 285n39
Jews. *See* anti-Semitism
John, Gospel according to St., 193, 285n39
Johnson, Claudia, 16, 229n27, 267n81
Johnson, Dorothy, 270n11, 270n16
Johnson, Samuel, 11, 138, 140, 142, 145, 146, 158–59, 174, 275n27, 276n43, 280n102

Johnston, Kenneth, 187, 190, 282n8, 283n14, 284n33, 287n50, 288n59
Jones, Cheslyn, 235n1
Jones, Griffith and Giles, 142
Jones, Robert, 229n26
Joseph, St. (the Betrothed), 268n87
joyful-sorrow, 224–25
Jubilate Agno (Smart), 3, 12, 138–39, 161–73; celebration of resistance, 162; echo, 165; faith, 167–68; flowers, 168–69; God's communication in, 167, 170; gender, 281n105; intersubjectivity, 167, 281n105; Jesus Christ, 165, 167, 168–169; knowledge, 167; liturgical spontaneity of, 163; as ritual/liturgy, 162–63; liturgy, 166, 167, 169; love, 169; God's love as non-economic, 170; madness in, 169; prayer as self-construction, 164; prayer as illumination, 167; prayer opposed to market values, 169–70; recovery of agency and prayer, 163, 164; reconfiguring relation of piety and sentiment, 169; resistance to empirical pressures, 170–71; resistance to economic pressures, 170–71; resistance to politeness, 163; voice, 164–70

Kailair, Rose, 267n79
Kames, Lord. *See* Home, Henry, Lord Kames
Kant, Immanuel, 212–13, 259n16
Kaufman, Peter Iver, 237n9, 242n37, 246n65
Kay, Carol, 15, 16

Keats, John, 176
Keble, John, 177
Keeble, N. H., 255n55
Keller, Rose. *See* Kailair, Rose
Kelly, Hugh, 142
Kendall, R. T., 241n29
Kent, Elizabeth Eaton, 146, 275n35
kernel, impossible, 78
Kerrigan, John, 285n37
Keymer, Thomas, 159, 171, 279n81, 280n102
Kierkegaard, Søren, 214, 215, 256n58
King, Peter, 238n16, 239n21, 245n53
Klein, Lawrence, 3–4, 93–94, 97–98, 239n20, 247n2, 261n38, 264n59
Klopstock, Friedrich Gottlieb, Monsieur and Madame, 227n2
Knox, Ronald A., 258n14
Koyré, Alexandre, 227n7
Kumar, Priya, 228n17

La Vopa, Anthony, 3–4, 239n20
Lacan, Jacques, 30, 74, 77–78, 105, 109, 119, 221, 251n32, 256n58, 260n31, 265n67, 265n71, 267n81
Lake, Peter, 237n14, 241n29
Lamb, Charles, 284n36
Lamb, Jonathan, 156, 277n55
language, differential logic of, 246n66. *See also* indeterminacy; linguistic turn
Latitudinarians, 15, 269n91
Laud, William (Abp.), 200, 237n14
Law, William, 269n91
Le Bras, Gabriel, 217
Lead, Jane, 219
Leatherbarrow, David, 127

Lennox, Charlotte; *The Female Quixote*, 17
Lent, 36
Leonardo da Vinci, 121
"Letter Concerning Enthusiasm" (Shaftesbury), 93, 147, 258n14
Leverenz, David, 242n37
Lévinas, Emmanuel, 212, 214, 241n26
Levinson, Marjorie, 207, 208, 282n8, 284n33
Ley, John, 35–36, 40–41, 43
Lidell, Henry George, 266n72
Life and Opinions of Tristram Shandy (Sterne), 154
Life of Christ, The (Goldsmith), 146
Life of the Fathers (Goldsmith), 146
Lilliputian Magazine, The, 143
Lilly library (Bloomington, Ind.), 8, 54 fig. 1, 241n30
"Lines left upon a Seat in a Yew-Tree" (Wordsworth), 182, 197
"Lines Written a Few Miles above Tintern Abbey" (Wordsworth), 187–89, 192, 204, 208
"Lines Written at a Small Distance from My House" (Wordsworth), 176
"Lines Written in Early Spring" (Wordsworth), 184–85, 186, 187
Lindsey, Theophilus, 238n18
linguistic turn, 20, 212–13, 216, 221; and faith, 7
literalism. *See* biblical literalism
Literary Magazine, 145
literary market. *See* print culture and market
literary criticism and theory. *See* criticism, literary
Liturgical Considerator Considered (Firmin), 245n55

liturgy: as crutches for infants and invalids, 245n54; as resistance to violence, 197; as self–construction, 197–204; as "the work of the people," 50; community and, 60, 197; critique of, 2; defense of sincerity of, 242n36; hope and, 13; imposition against believers' liberty, 243n41; popular support of, 237n14; rejection of, 34–61; Smart's view of, 162. *See also* ritual
Liu, Alan, 208, 282n8, 284n29
Liu, Yu, 181–82
living water (John 7:37-39). *See* Holy Spirit
loathing, 103–4
Locke, John, 9, 17, 92, 99, 119, 257n3, 261n43
Logic (I. Watts), 245n58
Logician's School-Master, 244n49
Lord's Prayer, 57–58, 63–64, 82, 89, 104, 116, 119
Lord's Supper, 38, 53, 237n12, 245n54. *See also* Eucharist
love, 14–15, 29, 69–70, 75, 77, 89, 94–95, 95–96, 98, 100–101, 158, 169, 171, 197, 223–24, 225; breaking out of idolatry, 224; faith and, 224; Hutchesonian equation for, 94–95; in ideology of spontaneity, 14; seeking proof of, 73; self-construction and, 197–204, 223–24, 225
Lowth, Robert, 161
Luckmann, Thomas, 224
Lukács, Georg, 244n48
Luke, Gospel according to St., 290n22
Luxon, Thomas, 37, 236n2, 236n6, 247n68, 252n39, 252n42, 253n46, 254n48

Lynch, Deidre, 16, 279n89
Lyotard, Jean-François, 19–20, 28–29, 85, 231n42, 231n44, 241n26, 248n15
Lyrical Ballads (Wordsworth), 175–77, 178–82, 182–90, 195, 205. *See also* Prefaces to *Lyrical Ballads*

Mackenzie, Henry, 182
Magnuson, Paul, 281n4, 284n30
Maltby, Judith, 237n14
Man of Feeling, The (Mackenzie), 182
Man, Paul de, 213
Mandeville, Bernard de, 18, 94, 96, 196, 259n18
Manning, Peter, 282n7
Mapp Shewing the Order & Causes of Salvation & Damnation (Bunyan), 253n46
Marcus Aurelius. *See* Aurelius, Marcus
Marion, Jean-Luc, 212
Mark, Gospel according to St., 290n22
market rationality. *See* economic rationality
Markley, Robert, 15, 23, 42, 64, 93, 118, 134, 236n2, 240n24, 250n28
marriage, rite of, 53, 245n53, 245n54
Marshall, Cynthia, 131
Martin, B. W., 282n7
Martin, Benjamin, 142
Marx, Karl, 26, 59, 211, 216, 221, 233n65, 244n48, 246n63
Mary Tudor, 38
Mary, Virgin, 117, 268n87
masculinity, 98, 109, 114–20, 266n76, 267n81, 272n28, 281n105
materialism, 222

mathematics and mathematical reasoning, 24, 41
Matthew, Gospel according to St., 30, 234n84, 290n22
Matuštík, Martin, 289n13
McDowell, Paula, 140, 219, 267n77, 273n15, 273n16, 274n21
McGann, Jerome, 282n8
McGiffert, Michael, 89, 236n5, 242n37
McKendrick, Neil, 240n23
McKeon, Michael, 19, 81, 173, 233n59, 240n24, 253n44, 253n46, 255n50
Meditations (Aurelius), 133
megachurches, 3, 244n50
Memorials of a Tour (Wordsworth), 181
memory, theater of, 245n60
Merchant Adventurers, 66
Merivale, John Herman, 180
Merrill, Christopher, 290n37
Method for Prayer (M. Henry), 33, 56–58
Methodism, 159
Methodism, 40
Michelangelo di Lodovico Buonarroti, 121
Midwife, or The Old Woman's Magazine, The, 143, 144, 275n27
Millennium Hall (S. Scott), edited by Goldsmith, 146
Miller, Perry, 242n37
Mills, David, 252n42
Milton, John, 4, 46, 165; *Paradise Lost*, 4
mirror stage (Lacanian), 251n32
misogyny, 120–21
Moallem, Minoo, 291n43
modern and early modern religious subject/subjectivity, 37, 44, 49, 58, 59–61, 220, 224; as object, 75; Bunyan's, 75, 85; isolation of, 60–61; result of evidentiary, economic theology, 67; reimagined by Smart, 167–68, 173, 174; reimagined by Wordsworth, 197–204, 205–6, 208–9
Modern Language Association, 211
modern secular subject, 8, 97, 174, 220; academic, 219; book form, 133; self–splitting, 98, 123–134; disintegration, 122, 201; print culture, 133; religion in, 133; suturing in images, 122, 121–134
modernity: and belief, 31; and spontaneity, 7; as a set of ideals, 7; fundamentalism and, 291n43; religious products of, 33
monasticism, 194, 202–3
Monter, William, 237n14
Montgomery, James, 283n19
Monthly Magazine, The, 180
Monthly Review, 143
Monthly Review, The, 180, 181
Monthly, The, 146
Moore, R. Laurence, 253n44
moral philosophy, modern: 91–96; British origins, 257n2; context of French Revolution, 178. See also moral sense
moral sense, 9, 10, 60, 92, 257n3; context of French Revolution, 178; scientism of, 96. See also moral philosophy, modern
Moralists, A Philosophical Rhapsody, The (Shaftesbury), 258n9, 271n25
morality: as rationalized religion, 178, 246n64
Morgan, Edward, 236n5

Morillo, John, 230n29
Mortensen, Preben, 257n2
Motooka, Wendy, 17, 18, 22
Mounsey, Chris, 144, 146, 170, 275n27, 275n33, 279n81, 280n95, 281n107
Mullan, John, 15, 16, 20, 230n28
Mullett, Michael, 249n19
Munns, Jessica, 244n52
Muses Banquet, The, 144
music, 197–98
"Musings Near Aquapedente, April, 1837" (Wordsworth), 176
mysticism, 76; Enlightenment construction of, 246n64

Napoleon Bonaparte. *See* Bonaparte, Napoleon
Napoleonic Wars, 177, 286n43
National Archives, British. *See* Public Record Office
National Portrait Gallery, 126 fig. 7, 127, 270n11, 270n13, 271n24–25
Nellist, Brian, 252n42, 254n48
Nelson, Robert, 163
New Historicism, 220, 288n60
New Science, 23, 41, 64, 70, 91
Newberry Library, 95 fig. 3
Newbery Award and Medal, 146, 174
Newbery, Francis, 138–39
Newbery, John, 11, 137, 139–47, 148, 151, 153, 156, 161, 167, 170–71, 172, 275n27, 276n43, 280n103; catalog, 141–42; connection between money and morality, 147; early life and business, 140–47; move to London, 141; others' impressions of, 139–40; tour of England, 140–41; shop at the Sign of the Bible and Sun, 141–42; work with Christopher Smart, 142–45, 157–58; work with Oliver Goldsmith, 145–46, 157
Newey, Vincent, 68, 251n31, 252n35, 254n47, 254n48, 255n50
Newman, Carey, 263n48
Newman, John Henry, 3, 177
newspapers, 162
Newton, Sir Isaac, 17, 41, 64, 92, 170–71, 205, 240n24, 250n26, 272n30
Newton, Thomas, 238n18
Nicolson, Marjorie Hope, 227n7
Nietzsche, Friedrich, 214
Night Thoughts (Young), 1–2
Nonconformists, 39–40; definition, 239n20
Northington, Lord Chancellor (Robert Henley), 159
Norton, Richard E., 92, 257n2, 257n4, 257n6
Nosegay and a Simile for Reviewers, A, 280n103
notebooks (Shaftesbury). *See* Ασκηματα, Second Characters
novel, origin of English, 78
novelty, 4, 64, 80
Nussbaum, Felicity, 251n31, 252n34
Nye, Eric, 288n53

objectivity. *See* ideology of objectivity
Of forms of Prayer (T. Newton), 238n18
Of the Laws of Ecclesiastical Polity (Hooker), 38
On the Eternity of the Supreme Being (Smart), 143
120 Days of Sodom (Sade), 118
ontotheology, 213
Opticks (I. Newton), 250n26
Our Father. *See* Lord's Prayer

Index 337

outbidding, as a mechanistic structure of reason, 121, 247n66, 269n92
Outram, Dorinda, 232n52
Overton, Richard, 232n53
Owens, John, 243n41
Oxford Movement, 3, 7, 13, 200, 206

Paknadel, Felix, 123–24, 269n2, 269nn4–5, 270n9, 271n25, 272n29
Palumbo, Linda, 286n42
Pamela (S. Richardson), 136
pamphlet wars, during English Civil Wars, 239n21
papacy, 194–95
Paradise Lost (Milton), 4
paradise, 30
Parchments (Shaftesbury), 99, 132
Pascal, Blaise, 99
Paul, St., 116, 119, 200, 216, 224, 280n100
Peaston, A. E., 237n12, 239n21
Pelikan, Jaroslav, 248n8
Pepys, Samuel, 2
Percy, Thomas (Bp.), 276n41, 276n43
Perkins, William, 244n49
Peter Bell (Wordsworth), 181
Peter, St., 216
Peters, F. E., 266n72
Pettit, Norman, 241n29
Phelps, John, 47, 56–57
Philadelphian Society, 219
Philo-Presbyt., R. C. (pseudonym), 35, 40
Philosophical Enquiry into the Origin of Our Ideas of the Sublime and Beautiful (Burke), 96, 183
Philosophy in the Bedroom (Sade), 118

philosophy of religion. *See* religion, philosophy of
Pilgrim's Progress, The (Bunyan), 9, 32, 61, 67–68, 79–87, 133, 134, 136, 147, 152; as allegory, 252n42; as dream commodity, 80–81; buying truth, 84; Christian, 68, 81–85; conversion in, 81–82, 83; evangelistic aim of, 79–81; fantasy of rational religion, 78, 85; fantasy of the subject, 85; frontispiece, 85, 86 fig. 2; God, 83, 84, 85; Ignorance, 82–83, 84–85, 254n48; origin of English novel, 78; relation to *Grace Abounding*, 67–68, 78, 79–87, 248n14; roll or certificate, 81–82, 133, 254n47; salvation of commodity culture, 84–87; secularizing trajectory, 68, 85; Slough of Despond, 81; Vanity Fair, 83–84
Pinch, Adela, 17, 18
Piozzi, Hester Thrale, 158, 174
Plague Year of 1665, 91
Plato, 125, 130
Plumb, J. H., 240n23
Pocock, J. G. A., 5, 22, 97, 161, 227n7, 230n29, 232n52, 234n69, 240n23, 250n29
Poems in Two Volumes (Wordsworth), 180
Poems on Several Occasions (Smart), 143
Poggemiller, Helmuth Carl, 285n37
Polanyi, Karl, 27
politeness, culture of, 97, 157; role in Smart's incarceration, 157–63
Poole, Kristen, 236n8, 239n21
Pooley, Roger, 250n25

338 Index

Poovey, Mary, 267n81
Pope, Alexander, 146
Potter's Asylum, Mr., 159, 172
Potts, Abbie Findlay, 281n5, 286n44
Poussin, Nicolas, 121
Powell, Vavasor, 41–42, 242n33
Pratt, Mary Louise, 211
Prayer Book of 1559, 38. *See also* Book of Common Prayer
prayer, 11–12, 14–15, 237n12; as blood from a wound, 76; as illumination, 167; as paid labor, 49, 51–52, 243n45; as performance, 48–49, 51–52, 244n47; as rational prerogative, 192; as resistance to violence, 197; as self-construction, 164–70; as workshop, 166; eroticism of private, 239n21; hypocrisy and insincerity in, 44–45, 63–64; misery in, 64; off-stage in *Vicar of Wakefield*, 149–51, 154–57; opposed to market values, 169–70; Shaftesbury's, 103–4; Smart's, 158–61; storehouse of materials for, 56–58, 245n60; without ceasing, 158; Wordsworth's, 189. *See also* free prayer; liturgy; Lord's Prayer
Preface, *Select Sermons of Dr. Whichcote* (Shaftesbury), 93, 119
Prefaces to *Lyrical Ballads* (Wordsworth), 3, 175, 178–79, 183, 186, 189
Prelude, The (Wordsworth), 177, 190, 192, 193, 195–96, 198, 201–2, 206–7
Presbyterians, 245n53
Preston, Thomas R., 274n21
Pretty Little Pocket-Book, A, 141
Prickett, Stephen, 288n53
Priestman, Martin, 288n53

Prince, Michael, 123, 261n38, 269n1
print culture and market, 4; decline of ritual effected by, 236n3; relation to God, 272n28; role in modern subjectivity, 133–34
Prior, James, 276n41, 276n42
proselytism, 33. *See also* evangelism
Protestantism and English Protestantism: and economic rationality, 26–29; as self-secularizing, 21, 23, 25, 232n53; commodification of, 253n44; critique of liturgy, 2; declining importance of Christ in, 25; God in, 266n76; intensification of medieval atonement theology, 65; violent spirituality in, 77
Psalms, Book of, 88, 161, 171; verse setting by Smart, 171–72
psychoanalysis, 78, 220
Public Ledger, 146, 276n42
Public Record Office (PRO), British National Archives, 110 fig. 4, 132 fig. 11, 256n1, 262n47
Puritans and Puritanism (English), 37, 38, 40, 133, 171, 192: affective language and, 244n49; anxiety connected with, 242n37; Bunyan as, 249n17; covenant theology of, 64–66; critique of ritual, 35–42, 200; economic rationality of, 26–29; as "experimental Calvinism," 241n29; as rationalizing and secularizing, 23, 25, 232n53; definition of, 236n8, 239n20; graphomania, 97; origins of sincerity, 242n36; reciprocal relation to economic

life, 27, 59, 246n63; relation to Separatists, 238n17; resistance to their ritual reforms, 237n14; ritual aspects of their worship, 236n6; six biblical "ordinances" of their worship, 237n12; view of conversion, 236n5; view of evangelism, 252n41
Puseyism. *See* Oxford Movement

Quakers. *See* Friends, Society of
Quilligan, Maureen, 252n42, 254n47
Quintana, Ricardo, 277n52

Rambuss, Richard, 239n21, 267n79
Ramus, Petrus, 244n49
Rand, Benjamin, 100, 262n46, 264n62
Raphael (Raffaello Sanzio, painter and architect), 120, 121, 133
Raphael, D. D., 257n6
rationalization, 8, 21, 24, 26, 41, 46, 61, 71, 96, 213, 228n9
real, the (Lacanian), 74, 77–78, 251n32; religious aspect, 77
Recluse, The (Wordsworth), 190, 205
Reformation religious subject. *See* modern and early modern religious subject
Reformation: and economic rationality, 26–29; and critique of ritual, 36–42; as rationalizing and secularizing, 23, 25, 232n53; God in, 266n76; power in, 195. *See also* Dissent, God, Protestantism, Puritanism
Reformed churches, 245n53
Regimen. *See* under Shaftesbury, 3rd Earl of (Anthony Ashley Cooper)

reification, 244n48
Reiman, Donald, 283nn15–22, 284nn23–26
religion: anxiety and, 242n37; academic subjectivities and, 219–20; binary thinking about secularism and, 232n49; contemporary theories of, 246n64, 256n56, 256n58; criticism and, 211–25; in eighteenth-century studies, 218–19; in humanities study, 216; in religious studies, 218; in sociology, 216–18; made strange, 221; misunderstanding itself in modernity, 87; persistence in modernity, 22; philosophy of, 212, 213; rationalization of, 24–25; rationalized as morality, 246n64; reading and, 225; secularization of, 26–29; sentimentalized, 157; tendency to explain away, 246n63; without religion, 215. *See also* religion, modern; religion, traditional
religion, modern, 33: as self-secularizing, 21; as "special effect" in commodity culture, 12; declining importance of Christ in, 25. *See also* Protestantism
religion, traditional: adaptation of, 5; forms of believing and self-formation, 6
religious discourse: as crisis of representation, 236n2
religious studies, 213
religious subjectivity, female desire as structure of, 246n65. *See also* modern and early modern religious subject
representation, early modern crisis of, 8, 36–42; basis of critique of ritual, 8, 36–42, 60; in reformed religion, 236n2

resistance and resistances, 6, 87
Restoration, the (1660), 23, 25, 27, 39, 240n24
Revolutionary War, American, 200
Richards, Penny, 244n52
Richardson, Alexander, 244n49
Richardson, Samuel, 10, 96, 98, 117, 120, 136, 152
ritual year. *See* Church year, English
ritual: and community, 2; and crisis of representation, 8; and hope, 13; early modern critique of, 36–42; Erasmus and critique of, 236n3; material objects linked to, 245n54; popular support of, 237n14; print culture and critique of, 236n3; devaluation of, 4; pre– and early–modern belief in, 3; nostalgia for, 3; as self-construction, 197–204; as resistance to violence, 197. *See also* liturgy
rituals of spontaneity, 6–7, 31, 225; composition of *Jubilate Agno* as, 12; Closterman's portrait of Shaftesbury as, 130; Wordsworth's, 183
River Duddon, The (Wordsworth), 181, 191, 197
rivers of living water (John 7:37–39). *See* Holy Spirit
Rivers, Isabel, 249n17, 252n39
Robinson Crusoe (Defoe), 32, 152
Robinson, Henry Crabb, 177
Robinson, Marilynne, 290n37
Rogers, Malcolm, 270n11, 270n13–14, 271n25
Rogers, Pat, 140, 273n16
Roman Catholicism, 3, 159, 177, 206, 286
Romans, Epistle of St. Paul to the, 216

Romantic poetry and Romanticism, 61; politics of, 207
Ross, Ian Simpson, 259n20
Ross, Marlon, 288n60
Rothschild, Emma, 230n29
Rothstein, Eric, 278n63
Rousseau, G. S., 278n69
Rousseau, Jean-Jacques, 96
Royal Injunctions of Elizabeth I, 38
Royal Society for the Improving of Natural Knowledge, 23, 64, 91
Rudy, Kathy, 220, 231n46, 290n36
Ryan, Robert M., 283n9, 288n53
Rylstone, Anne L., 285n37

Sade, Donatien Alphonse François, Marquis de, 10, 96, 98, 117–18, 120, 177, 259n16
Sadler, Lynn Veach, 255n55
sadomasochism, 133–34
Saints Privilege and Profit (Bunyan), 66
Saussure, Ferdinand de, 246n66
Savoy Liturgy (Baxter), 40
Schaeffer, Neil, 118, 267n78–79
Schmidt, Leigh Eric, 246n64, 269n91
Schneewind, J. B., 257n3, 257n6, 258n7, 259n16, 260n29
Schoenfelt, Michael, 266n76
scholarship: as demolition, 222; as metanoia (repentance), 224–25; as religion, 223; as self-construction, 222, 225; as a work of love, 223–25; humility of, 222; problems of determinism in, 246n63; tendency to explain away religion, 246n63. *See also* criticism, literary
scholasticism, medieval: 24, 25, 233n64; as secularizing, 256n56

Scotland, 258n11
Scott, Ian, 282n8
Scott, John, 242n33
Scott, Robert, 266n72
Scott, Sarah, 146
scriptural literalism. *See* biblical literalism
Scripture, 37, 42, 57, 61, 79, 133, 187, 237n12. *See also* biblical literalism
Seatonian prize, 143, 274n26, 275n29
Seaver, Paul, 256n60
Second Characters (Shaftesbury), 131
secular subject. *See* modern secular subject
secularism, 5, 7, 8, 10, 11, 12, 19, 22–25, 31–33, 60, 97, 98, 104, 119, 133, 136, 174, 178, 211; academic, 218; academic subjectivities and, 219–20; and spontaneity, 29–33; and subjectivity, 29–33; as Enlightenment fantasy, 22; as fundamentalism, 32; as support of modern subjectivity, 8; historical embeddedness, 214; in eighteenth-century studies, 218–19; in humanities study, 216; in religious studies, 218; in sociology, 216–18; made strange, 221; old and new narratives of, 22–25; on the Indian subcontinent, 228n17
secularization thesis, 228n9; binary concepts of religion and secularism, 232n49; critique of, 5; persistence of religion in spite of, 22
secularization, 4, 6, 14, 18, 19, 21, 22, 23, 25, 31, 41, 60, 105, 118, 247n68; as abstraction from the world, 60; as rhetorical process, 5; as process of rationalization, 8; as process of separation of religion/indeterminacy from politics, economics and culture, 87, 247n68; problems solved by separating religious from secular, 87; old and new narratives of, 22–25; within Western Christianity, 25; of/within religion/religious discourse, 5, 8, 21, 26–29
Seed, David, 251n31
self-fashioning, 59, 197–204; early modern willingness to believe in, 246n65
self-scrutiny, 256n60
self-splitting, 98, 106, 123–134
sensibility, culture of, 135–137
sentiment, critical history of, 15–22
Sentimental Journey (Sterne), 154–55, 162
sentimentality and sentimental literature, 11, 61, 96, 135–37, 147, 201; agency in, 18; belief and, 18; connection between money and morality, 16, 147; context of French Revolution, 178; and religious and secular discourses, 19, 135–37; connection to science, 17; piety and, 169; political criticism of, 15; prayer in, 156–57; sentimentalized religion, 157; skepticism and, 17, 18; Wordsworth's criticism of, 183
Separatists, 40, 238n16, 239n21; Bunyan and, 249n17
service books, 53
set forms. *See* liturgy
sexuality. *See* under Shaftesbury, 3rd earl of (Anthony Ashley Cooper)
Shaftesbury Standard Edition, 100, 262n47

Shaftesbury, 10th Earl of (Anthony Ashley Cooper), 127
Shaftesbury, 1st Earl of (Anthony Ashley Cooper), 98, 128–29, 261n43, 271n24
Shaftesbury, 3rd Earl of (Anthony Ashley Cooper), 10, 19, 28, 48, 91–134, 135, 156, 169, 171, 174, 177, 178, 179, 196, 199, 201, 205, 206, 234n86, 257n3; amanuensis relationship with Closterman, 123, 270n11; anti-Semitism, 120; asthma, 99, 122; atheism, 102, 119, 268n84; Christianity, 102, 119, 268n87; cryptographic symbols, 109, 261n43, 264n64; disgust at Christ, 10, 120–22, 268n87; disgust at "vulgar" devotion, 102; dreams, 109–13, 110 fig. 4; effeminacy and anti-effeminacy, 114, 116, 267n81; Fancy, 115–17, 119; isolation, 108; learning to be natural, 105; life and politics, 98–100, 120, 128; loathing of the body, 10, 98, 264n66; masculinity, 109, 114–20, 266n76, 267n81; mastery of the body, 109–13; misogyny, 120–21; notebooks (see Ασκηματα; *Second Characters*); paralysis, 98; philosophical awakening, 261n40; portraits/engravings of, 125–34; portraiture, views of, 130–31; prayer, 103–4; national identity, 264n60; quest for love and natural affection, 98; quest for self-identity/ wholeness, 105; vis-à-vis reading audience, 134; Regimen, 10, 98, 104–8, 205; relation of art/aesthetics to moral philosophy, 123, 257n2; retreats, 99; secular subject, 97, 98, 108; self-splitting, 98, 106, 113, 124–25, 129–30, 132–33, 269n1; sexuality 10, 104, 107, 111–13, 113–20, 260n36, 263n56, 264n62, 264n66; sexualization of philosophy, 10, 98, 265n67; techniques for controlling desire, 106–7, 263n58; "true enthusiasm," 93–94; "true Religion," 105; self–mastery, 106; unraveling, 111, 268n86; violation of God, 10, 98, 116–20. *See also* Deity, Shaftesbury's; moral philosophy; moral sense; *see* under enthusiasm

Shaftesbury, 3rd Earl of (Anthony Ashley Cooper), works of: Ασκηματα or "Exercises," 10, 32, 91, 96–122, 110 fig. 4, 124, 129, 130, 136, 162, 263n57, 269n1; *Characteristicks*, 10, 97, 98, 120, 123–126, 201, 258n9, 271n25; *Inquiry Concerning Virtue*, 92, 93, 257n5, 258n13; "Inquiry Concerning Virtue and Merit," 258n7, 269n1; "Letter Concerning Enthusiasm," 93, 147, 258n14; *The Moralists, A Philosophical Rhapsody*, 258n9, 271n25; Parchments, 99, 132; Preface, *Select Sermons of Dr. Whichcote*, 93, 119; *Second Characters* (notebook), 131; *Sociable Enthusiast*, 93, 105, 258n9; "Soliloquy: Or Advice to an Author," 124–25, 126, 130, 263n57

Shaftesbury, Lady. 126 fig. 7, 270n11

Shaftesbury, Maurice. *See* Ashley-Cooper, Maurice

Sharrock, Roger, 248n14, 249n19, 251n31, 254n48
She Stoops to Conquer (Goldsmith), 147
Shell, Marc, 28, 29, 70, 241n26, 251n30
Shelley, Percy Bysshe, 176
Sherbo, Arthur, 143, 274nn23–26, 275nn27–28, 275nn30–31, 276nn36–39, 276n43, 278n72, 279n88, 281nn107–9
Sheriff, John K., 229n23
Short Catechism, for the Instruction of Young and Old, 35, 40
Shuger, Debora Kuller, 77, 246n65
Sign of the Bible and Sun. *See* Bible and Sun, Sign of
Sill, Geoffrey M., 17
Sills, Adam, 250n28, 253n46
Sim, Stuart, 254n48
sin against the Holy Ghost. *See* Holy Spirit, sin against
sincerity, 44, 63–64, 242n36, 249n20
Sitter, John, 236n5
Sixpennyworth of Wit, A, 171
Skinner, Gillian, 16, 20, 147, 230n28
Skoglund, John, 239n21
Slough of Despond, 81, 253n46
Smart, Anna Maria. *See* Carnan, Anna Maria
Smart, Christopher, 3, 7, 11–12, 14, 28, 137, 137–39, 157–74; death, 172; debt, 172; diagnosis of madness, 159–60; ghost of, 172–73; incarceration, 145, 159, 162; life and career, 142–45; liturgical spontaneity, 163; liturgy, 162; lodging at Canonbury House, 144; marriage to Anna Maria Carnan, 143; religious beliefs, 160; rupture of his career, 161; Seatonian prizes, 143, 274n26, 275n29; spontaneous public prayer, 158–61; work for John Newbery, 143–45

Smart, Christopher, works of: *Collection of Pretty Poems for the Amusement of Children Six Foot High*, 144, 275n27; *Collection of Pretty Poems for the Amusement of Children Three Feet High*, 144; "The Hilliad," 144; "Hymn to the Supreme Being, On recovery from a dangerous fit of illness," 157–58; *Hymns and Spiritual Songs*, 171–72; *Jubilate Agno*, 3, 12, 138–39, 161–73; *On the Eternity of the Supreme Being*, 143; *Poems on Several Occasions*, 143; Psalms, 171–72; *A Song to David*, 171, 281n107; *Works of Horace*, 145, 172

Smectymnuus (pseudonymn), 239n21
Smith, Adam, 17, 48, 94, 95–96, 103, 150, 196, 258n11; "atonement passage," 260n28
Smith, Christian, 217–18
Smith, Nigel, 239n21, 241n29, 244n49, 246n65
Smith, Paul, 251n30, 252n33
Smollett, Tobias, 156
Sober and Temperate Discourse, Concerning the Interest of Words in Prayer (Dawbeny), 48–52
Sociable Enthusiast (Shaftesbury), 93, 105; revised as *The Moralists, A Philosophical Rhapsody*, 258n9
social gospel, 150, 277n59

sociology of religion, 216–18
"Soliloquy: Or Advice to An Author" (Shaftesbury), 263n57; emblem for, 124–25, 126, 130
Song to David, A (Smart), 171, 281n107
song, 197–98
Southey, Robert, 180
Spacks, Patricia Meyer, 161
Spenser, Edmund, 235n1
Spinks, Bryan D., 237n12
spiritual praxis, 209, 233n64
spirituality of spontaneity, 76–77, 87
spontaneity, 20; alienation and, 51–52, 56–58; anxiety and, 8–9, 11, 27–28; as epistemological-economic proof of religious-moral value, 9; as evidence and economic value, 4; as secularizing, 5–6, 11; as support of modern subjectivity, 8; at odds with religiousness, 9; connection to ritual, 7; authentic, 225; clothing metaphors for, 51–52, 244n52; early modern backgrounds of, 36–42; etymology, 7; free prayer and, 42; history of sentiment and, 15–22; ideology of, 6, 8, 11; imperative/obligation for, 6, 8, 42; in the moral sense, 9; limited acceptance of, 138; link to morality, 176; masking ritual and belief, 6; material objects and, 245n54; modernity and, 7; moral and aesthetic valuation of, 3; passivity/paralysis and, 7, 11, 249n23; regulation of, 52–56; religious and secular discourses and, 19; resistances to, 20, 29; ritual's decline and, 4; secularism and, 29–33; shared logic of religious and secular forms, 20; subjectivity and, 29–33; tensions of, 7; tyrannies of, 29; uncertainty and, 21. *See also* ideology of spontaneity; spontaneous subject; spontaneous prayer
spontaneous overflow of powerful feelings. *See* under Wordsworth, William
spontaneous prayer, 8, 11–12; Smart's, 158–61. *See also* free prayer
spontaneous subject, 6, 29–33
Sprat, Thomas, 23, 41
Spurr, John, 56, 236n8, 238n17, 242n33
St. Luke's Hospital for the Curably Insane, 145, 159, 161
St. Paul's Cathedral, 92
St. Victor, Hugh de. *See* Hugh de St. Victor
Stallybrass, Peter, 255n49
Stater, Victor, 260n33
Sterne, Laurence, 154–155, 162
Stoddart, John, 180
stoics and stoicism, 97, 102, 104, 263n58
Stonehill, C. A., 242n34
Straus, Nina Pelikan, 212
Stuber, Florian, 136
Student, The, 143
Sturbridge Fair, 255n49
subaltern studies, 21
subject, the: as object, 75; distinguished from person or agent, 252n33; of love, 224. *See also* modern and early modern religious subject; modern secular subject; spontaneous subject; subject without belief; subjective destitution; subjectivity
subject without belief, 31, 220, 234n86

subjective destitution, 122, 224
subjectivity, resistances produced by, 251n30; secularism and, 29–33, 219–20; spontaneity and, 29–33; ideal of self-transparency, 44. *See also* spontaneous subject; modern and early modern religious subject; modern secular subject; subject without belief
sublimation, 247n66
Sullivan, Robert, 219
superstition, 4, 38, 59, 234n86, 246n64
Swaim, Kathleen M., 248n14, 249n17, 252n42, 253n46, 254n48, 255n55
Sweetman, J. E., 272n29
symbolic and symbolic order, the (Lacanian), 251n32
sympathy, 287n47; "abject sympathies with power" (Wordsworth), 195–196
symptom, 87, 88; repetitive, 74, 78
synergia, 167, 233n64, 280n100

"Tables Turned, The" (Wordsworth), 175, 179
Talon, Henri, 254n48
Targoff, Ramie, 237n9, 246n65
Taves, Ann, 239n20
Tawney, R. H., 26
Tawney-Hill thesis, 234n69
Taylor, Mark C., 211, 213, 216, 218
televangelism, 3, 244n50
Terror, The. *See* French Revolution
Testard, Jeanne, 117
"Thanksgiving Ode" (Wordsworth), 13
Theory of Moral Sentiments (A. Smith), 95–96, 150, 260n28

theosis, 167, 280n99
Thomson, E. P., 219
"Thorn, The" (Wordsworth), note to, 187
Tindall, William York, 254n48
Todd, Janet, 15, 136, 166, 273n2
tokens, of godliness, 68–71, 82
Tom Jones (Fielding), 152
Tomasini, Wallace, 270n11–12
Tomlinson, T. B. 232n53
Tractarians and Tractarianism. *See* Oxford Movement
Transfiguration (Raphael), 133
Traveller, The (Goldsmith), 146, 151, 157
tree of the knowledge of good and evil, 30
Trilling, Lionel, 242n36
Trinity, 121, 216, 268n87; love among the persons of the, 29. *See also* God; Holy Spirit; Jesus Christ
true enthusiasm. *See* under enthusiasm
Trussler, Simon, 241n25
Tumbleson, Raymond, 23
Turner, James, 255n50

Uehlein, Friedrich, 260n36, 262n47
Ulmer, William A., 283n9
uncertainty, 234n86. *See also* indeterminacy
Underwood, David, 246n63
Underwood, T. L., 242n33
Unitarianism, 238n18
Universal Visiter, The, 145, 157, 158
utilitarianism, 96, 260n29

Van Sant, Ann Jessie, 17
Vanity Fair, 9, 83–84, 255n50
Vaughan, Henry, 235n1
Vertue, George, 271n25

Vicar of Wakefield (Goldsmith), 7, 11, 12, 137–39, 146, 147–57, 183; Advertisement, 148, 151, 154; Mr. Burchell/Sir William Thornhill, 151, 155–56; consumerism and print market, 152–54; evangelistic designs, 152; piety as "giving sensibility," 150, 152; piety as sentimentalized, 154; private prayer, 154; reading of sermons, Scripture, and Book of Common Prayer, 149–50, 154; reformist dimension, 147–48; secularizing values, 152; Vicar as ghost of Smart, 172–73; women in, 152; Whistonean controversy, 153

View of the Face Unmasked, 50

Vindication of Free and Unprescribed Prayer (Phelps), 47

violation of God, 10; *see also* under Shaftesbury, 3rd Earl (Anthony Ashley Cooper)

violence, 23, 32, 71–78, 94, 96, 115, 121, 122, 147, 151, 177, 182, 192, 194, 195, 197, 198, 199–200, 203, 207–9, 222–23, 224

Virgil, 193

Virgin Mary. *See* Mary, Virgin

Virgin's Nosegay, The, 280n103

Voitle, Robert, 97, 127, 133, 257n6, 258n14, 260n36, 261n41, 264n62, 269n88, 270n18

Waggoner, The (Wordsworth), 181

Walker, Jeanne Murray, 279n90

Wall, John, 235n1, 238n15

Wallington, Nehemiah, 97, 256n60

Wallis, Roy, 228n9

Warburton, William (Bp.), 269n91

Ward, Graham, 12, 24, 25, 29, 31, 32–33, 59, 139, 154, 212, 213, 221, 228n13, 232n52, 236n2, 247n68, 247n3, 252n36

Wardle, Ralph, 275n33, 276nn41–43, 277nn44–48

Ware, Timothy (Bp. Kallistos), 280nn99–100

Warner, William, 136–137

wars of religion (seventeenth-century), 23

Watson, Nicola, 288n60

Watt, Ian, 136

Watts, Isaac, 45–47, 51, 56, 171, 245n58

Watts, Michael, 238n17

Weber, Max, 26, 27, 59, 233n66, 246n63

Weinbrot, Howard D., 278n63

Welsh, Charles, 273n12, 273n14, 274nn17–20, 274nn22–24, 275nn27–28, 276nn42–43, 277n45, 277n49

Wesley, John, 137

Westbrook, Deanne, 288n53

Western Christianity, 60, 213, 214, 231n45; rationalization and secularization of, 25, 233n64

Westminster Assembly, 52, 245n53

Westphal, Merold, 213, 214, 289n13

Wheelock, John, 127

Whichcote, Benjamin, 119. *See also* Preface, Select Sermons of Dr. Whichcote (Shaftesbury)

Whistonean controversy, 153

White, Allon, 255n49

White, Eugene, 236n5, 242n37, 249n23

White, Ronald C., 277n55

White Doe of Rylstone, The (Wordsworth), 176–177, 190, 208, 284n36
Whitsuntide Gift: or, The Way to Be Happy, 142, 161
Wilkinson, Samuel, 206
Williams, Raymond, 173
Williamson, George, 239n20, 250n29
Williamson, Karina, 279n90, 279n93, 280nn96–97, 281n104
Wilson, Barbara, 220
Wilson, John, 181
Wind, Edgar, 123, 131, 269n3, 270n11, 271n25
Winquist, Charles, 221–22
Wolfe, Alan, 217
Wolfe, Richard B., 268n87
words, as money/tokens, 49
Wordsworth, Dorothy, 202, 204, 205
Wordsworth, Mary, 205
Wordsworth, William, 12–14, 175–209; agency connected to repetition, 189; free prayer in *Lyrical Ballads*, 176; effect of French Revolution on, 177, 178, 182, 187, 196, 201; belief and faith, 178, 182, 184–85, 207; connection of early, middle and late works, 195–96; criticism of market and industrialization, 183; criticism of sentimentality, 183; cultivation of love, 185–90, 208–9; evasion of history/politics, 207–9; freedom, 190–97; God of, 207; guilt, 196; hope, 208–9; interest in Oxford Movement/Tractarianism, 7; liturgy in, 176; moral weight of spontaneity, 176; connection between free prayer/spontaneity and liturgy, 177–78; liturgy linked to freedom, 206; loving, non–violent self, 208; moral uncertainty in *Lyrical Ballads*, 182; pacifism and just war, 286n43; paralysis and violence as danger of powerful feelings, 177; prayer, 189, 192; quest for moral certainty, 178–82; religious views, 206, 288n53; repetition, 187–89; reviews of poetry, 179–81; ritual as site of agency, 177–78; self-transformation, 206; spiritual liberty, 191; spontaneity, 182–90; "spontaneous overflow of powerful feelings," 1, 13, 60, 160, 175–76; sympathy with power, 190–97; violence and force, 192, 207

Wordsworth, William, works of: "Advertisement" to *Lyrical Ballads* of 1798, 179–80; *The Borderers*, 182; *Ecclesiastical Sketches* (republished as *Ecclesiastical Sonnets*), 176, 181, 191; *Ecclesiastical Sonnets*, 13, 177, 190–209; *The Excursion*, 180, 190, 287n50; "Expostulation and Reply," 179, 182; "Lines left upon a Seat in a Yew-Tree," 182, 197; "Lines Written a Few Miles above Tintern Abbey," 187–89, 192, 204, 208; "Lines Written at a Small Distance from My House," 176; "Lines Written in Early Spring," 184–85, 186, 187; *Lyrical Ballads*, 175–77, 178–82, 182–90, 195, 205; *Memorials of a Tour*, 181; "Musings Near Aquapedente, April, 1837," 176; Notes to

Ecclesiastical Sonnets, 286n40; Note to "The Thorn," 187; *Peter Bell*, 181; *Poems in Two Volumes*, 180; Prefaces to *Lyrical Ballads*, 3, 175, 178–79, 183, 186, 189; *The Prelude*, 177, 190, 192, 193, 195–96, 198, 201–2, 206–7; *The Recluse*, 190, 205; *The River Duddon*, 181, 191, 197; "The Tables Turned," 175, 179; "Thanksgiving Ode," 13; *The Waggoner*, 181; *The White Doe of Rylstone*, 176–77, 190, 208, 284n36
Works of Horace (Smart), 145, 172
Wotton, Samuel, 50

Wren, Sir Christopher, 92

Xenophon, 125, 130

Yack, Bernard, 288n58
Yates, Frances A., 245n60
Young, Edward, 1–2, 4, 160

Zaret, David, 26–27, 41, 59, 65–66, 93, 234n69, 240n23, 249n22
Žižek, Slavoj, 6, 29–30, 109, 118–19, 212, 214, 223–24, 251n32, 252n33, 252n37, 255n51, 255n53, 256n58, 264n66, 265n67, 265n71, 269n89